Joel
Chandler
HARRIS

a reference guide

A
Reference
Publication
in
Literature

Jack Salzman
Editor

Joel
Chandler
HARRIS

a reference guide

R. Bruce Bickley, Jr.

in collaboration with
Karen L. Bickley
and
Thomas H. English

G.K. HALL &CO.

70 LINCOLN STREET, BOSTON, MASS.

Copyright © 1978 by R. Bruce Bickley, Jr.

Library of Congress Cataloging in Publication Data
Bickley, Robert Bruce, 1942-
  Joel Chandler Harris: a reference guide.

  (Reference publications in literature)
  Includes index.
  1. Harris, Joel Chandler, 1848–1908 — Bibliography.
I. Bickley, Karen L., joint author.   II. English,
Thomas Hopkins, 1895–   joint author.   III. Series.
Z8387.7.B53   [PS1813]   016.818'4'09   77-15937
ISBN 0-8161-7873-9

This publication is printed on permanent/durable acid-free paper
MANUFACTURED IN THE UNITED STATES OF AMERICA

For
David *and* John

Contents

Preface

This Reference Guide brings together, in a chronological, annotated survey, all English-language commentaries on Joel Chandler
Harris that I have been able to locate in books (including major anthologies), dissertations, periodicals, and representative English
and American newspapers. It covers more than a century of Harris
criticism, from Joseph Addison Turner's prophetic open letter to his
thirteen-year-old printer's apprentice in 1862 through dissertations
and published scholarship appearing in 1976. All items listed in
the bibliography's 1442 entries were read and objectively abstracted,
usually by a combination of paraphrasing and quotation; throughout,
I have sought to reproduce the author's own emphases, judgments, and
tone. Although the nature of individual commentaries, particularly
biographical or informational items, often made this technique impossible, my essential method was to imagine what the authors would
have written had they been asked to compose their own abstracts.

The entries are generous, rather than overly compressed, in order
to make the bibliography as serviceable as possible to scholars.
Even passing references to Harris, so long as they are of critical or
biographical significance, have been included. Also documented are
Harris's appearances in bibliographies of literature, folklore, and
children's writings or recommended readings, for his inclusion in
such listings implies selective critical judgment on the part of the
compiler. To make the information in this Reference Guide as acces-
sible as possible, a forty-two item subject index is combined with an
index of authors, works, characters, and people; the subject categories are listed separately on page 307. Thus, in addition to finding
what has been said about the standard topics--biography, bibliography,
and literary technique--the reader can also review commentaries on
Harris's relationship to his editors, on his conversion to Catholicism, on his humor, and on a variety of folkloristic, critical, sociological, and psychological issues, to name but a few of the
categories indexed. The subject index, in short, keys the reader to
the major trends and themes in Harris scholarship.

In compiling this study I first developed a core bibliography of
known Harris items, pooling secondary materials identified by Julia
Collier Harris and R. L. Wiggins (1918.A1 and A2) and by Stella

Brookes and Paul Cousins (1950.A1 and 1968.A2) in their books on
Harris, and adding reviews and other items catalogued by Clayton
Eichelberger in his two bibliographies (1971.B3 and 1974.B5) and by
Arlin Turner and Charles Ray in their checklists (1968.B13 and
1969.B8). Dissertations on Harris revealed other materials, but the
secondary holdings in Emory University's Harris Collection doubled my
working bibliography. Especially valuable were several scrapbooks
and envelopes full of newspaper reviews cut from English and American
papers by clipping services that the Harrises subscribed to. There
are approximately 4000 hand-dated reviews in the Collection; because
the clippings are unpaginated, however, and the dating occasionally
suspect, the researcher must examine the original papers on microfilm
in order to obtain complete bibliographical data. Using the Emory
clippings as finding-list, I read 250 or so microfilm reviews from
twenty British and American papers, choosing papers from American
cities representing the Northeast (Boston and New York), Southeast
(Atlanta and New Orleans), Midwest (Chicago), and West (San Francisco). I am convinced that the papers I read fairly represent the
daily press's response to Harris's works.

With my bibliography standing at some 750 or 800 items, I searched
approximately 2000 additional books and periodical volumes for Harris
commentaries and reviews, turning up 600 or 700 more entries. While
this Reference Guide cannot be called a definitive bibliography, it
is as exhaustive a study of Harris scholarship as I could assemble.
Another scholar with the time and travel money should make a thorough
search of foreign commentary on Harris; so far only a scattering of
foreign items has been cited in my sources, and two-thirds of these
works were authored by English or American scholars who have also
written about Harris in their native language. Most of the important
folkloristic work on Harris has been published in the Journal of
American Folklore and other folklore journals printed in English.

This study of Harris's popular and scholarly acceptance has con-
firmed some widely held but previously undocumented notions about the
tremendous appeal the painfully shy "cornfield journalist" had both
at home and abroad as author and folklorist. But this survey also
discloses the trends that have developed in Harris scholarship. It
is now apparent, for example, that his short fiction, while it would
never have the following that the Uncle Remus tales have enjoyed, was
nevertheless broadly appreciated and regularly anthologized. As the
index suggests, it is also surprising how frequently, from the early
1880's on, Harris was compared favorably to Twain and seen as superior to Page, Richard Malcolm Johnston, Cable, Murfree, and other
popular local colorists. I have separately indexed references to
Harris's foreign reception and have also catalogued his general popularity (his ranking in popularity polls and other commentaries), but
it is both delightful and instructive to observe how many respected
authors, critics, and political and industrial leaders have commented
on or been influenced by Harris: from Twain, Garland, Page, Allen

Tate, Ellen Glasgow, and Ralph Ellison, to Teddy Roosevelt, Samuel
Gompers, and Andrew Carnegie.

Perhaps the most gratifying thing that the bibliography has revealed is that Harris has been so consistently praised by thoughtful
critics for the artistic and cultural richness of his work, as well
as for its sheer charm and entertainment value; Harris was recognized
from the beginning as a master storyteller. Although critics are
finding Harris's writings to be more complex than had been expected,
their seeming artlessness and effortlessness of expression continue
to make Harris an author for the masses. Perhaps the secret to
Harris's sustained popularity (formal or informal criticism of his
work has been published every year from 1880 to the present, and the
Uncle Remus books, at least, have been translated into most foreign
languages) is that his literary and folk heroes--Uncle Remus, Brer
Rabbit, and the poor white--appeal instinctively to readers from any
cultural framework. Harris took the common man, or in the case of
Brer Rabbit, a representative of the common man, and vested him with
canniness, humor, and either power or compassion. Harris's ability
to observe the universals of human experience through a narrative eye
that missed no important detail of behavior or setting makes him an
author for all times and all peoples.

Let me now briefly summarize the major emphases in scholarly and
popular commentary on Harris, keying my overview only to representative books and essays. Critics and historians, as well as the general
reader, will find that this volume can serve a multitude of purposes,
but a few generalities about its content may be helpful. The biographies of Harris, Julia Collier's (1918.A1), Wiggins's (1918.A2),
and Cousins's (1968.A2), while they tend toward the appreciative,
amass the central facts about his life and times and give useful
primary and secondary bibliographies. Julia's Joel Chandler Harris:
Editor and Essayist (1931.A1) is also a valuable source book. The
reader should not overlook the Harris essays in the standard literary
histories, The Cambridge History of American Literature (1918.B9),
The Literary History of the United States (1948.B17), and The Literature of the American People (1951.B8); Baskervill's early assessment
(1896.A1), Hubbell's classic The South in American Literature
(1954.B8), and headnotes in several anthologies of American writing
(see especially Brooks, et al., 1973.B2) also provide excellent sum-
maries of Harris's achievement. But the most exciting analyses of
Harris's problematic personality and his artistry, which are inextricably bound together, are scattered among several articles and
chapters in books on American literature; I shall cite some of these
works in a moment. The reader should also consult the dissertations
that treat Harris, particularly recent studies that offer revisionist
perspectives on the man and his work (Flusche, 1973.B8; Lea, 1973.A1;
MacKethan, 1974.B7), and those that compile bibliographical data that
earlier scholars only partially rendered (Griska, 1976.A1, and Strickland, 1976.A2). Some of Flusche's and Strickland's findings have
been published in articles.

Harris would have won enduring fame had he published no book
after Uncle Remus: His Songs and His Sayings. The three things that
readers have remained most enamored of over the years--Harris's portraits of the antebellum plantation, of wise old Uncle Remus, and of
Brer Rabbit, the trickster par excellence--are fully developed in his
first book. Uncle Remus was an instant classic, and the Remus tales,
published eventually in several volumes over four decades, have com-
manded greater critical attention than any other type of writing in
Harris's canon. Three schools of criticism have evolved in response
to the Remus stories. The student of Harris will find traditional
literary and historical commentaries in the three biographies, as
well as in Baskervill, Gaines (1925.B3), English (see especially
1940.B4), Hubbell, and for a study of the stories from a more classical perspective, Leyburn (1956.B11), to name just a few works. The
folklorists and linguists, the second group of specialists, have
written countless discussions of Harris's pioneering work in American
Negro folklore and Southern dialect. T. F. Crane (1881.B14) was one
of the first authoritative reviewers of Harris's folktales, and Jacobs
(1888.B16 and following), Espinosa, in articles across three decades,
and dozens of other folklorists, including Dundes (1965.B4 and later
works), Walton (1966.B9 and B10), and Piersen (1971.B12), have de-
bated for nearly a century such questions as the origin of the tar-
baby tale and the American Negro's modification of folktales brought
from Africa; Brookes has catalogued Harris's use of folk traditions
in her full-length study (1950.A1). Brer Rabbit's role as trickster
has also been a widely discussed subject among the ethnologists.
Krapp (1924.B7 and 1925.B7) and Ives, in several studies done in the
1950's, have verified Harris's dialectical accuracy.

    The third school of criticism has combined analysis of folk tra-
ditions with more modern sociological concerns. Starting with an
insightful reviewer in Spectator (1881.B9), and followed in time by
a number of black critics, including Benjamin Brawley, W. S. Braithwaite, Alain Locke, James Weldon Johnson, Saunders Redding, Sterling
Brown, Hugh Gloster, and Darwin Turner, the question of Harris's
authenticity as the black man's amanuensis and his awareness of the
racial implications of the folktales he retold has been vigorously
argued. The allegorical meaning of the Uncle Remus tales is still a
controversial subject, and the Harris enthusiast should make sure to
read at least Bernard Wolfe's and Jesse Bier's provocative discussions
(1949.B15 and 1968.B2), Robert Bone's analysis (1975.B2), Louis
Rubin's articles (1970.B19 and 1974.B11), and Lyle Glazier's and
Kathleen Light's essays (1969.B5 and 1975.B12), which explore the
question suggestively.

    The second major focus of Harris scholarship has been on his local
color short fiction. The Mingo and Free Joe collections of short
stories were very well received, as Derby's and Coleman's essays suggest (1884.B19 and 1887.B5), and soon Baskervill, Fiske (1903.B6),
Gaines, and other critics were pointing out how sensitively Harris
could portray "low life" characters: the poor white, the mountaineer,

and Uncle Remus's cousins, Aunt Minervy Ann, Mingo, and Free Joe.
Harris believed "Free Joe and the Rest of the World" to be his best
story, and many critics have agreed with him. Harris also impressed
critics and popular readers as well with his Civil War stories in On
the Wing of Occasions and Tales of the Home Folks. McIlwaine and
Skaggs have written thorough studies of Harris's poor whites, and
Wade Hall (1962.B4 and 1965.B7) and others have treated his war tales.
Several social historians have commented upon the reconciliation
theme in Harris's war stories as having in fact helped temper postwar
resentment and social and political conflict between North and South
during Reconstruction. Harris is now being given a larger place in
histories of the American short story; for example, see Voss's survey
(1973.B14). Also, John Tumlin has written a thoughtful introduction
to a long-overdue collection of Harris's local color tales (1975.B23).

Harris's novels, chiefly Gabriel Tolliver and Sister Jane, met
mixed reviews when they were published and, with a few exceptions,
have received only passing attention over the years. Nevertheless,
several critics (see especially Godbold, 1974.B6), have identified
Tolliver as the most sensitive Reconstruction novel that America produced—a more balanced study of the era than those authored by Cable,
Page, or Thomas Dixon. And Michael Flusche has found Sister Jane,
Tolliver, and other works to be surprisingly revealing self-portraits
of the insecure and only superficially optimistic Joel Chandler Harris
(1975.B8). It appears that Harris's novels are in the process of
being rediscovered.

Harris's "official" career was in journalism, and works indexed
under this heading like Julia Collier's Editor and Essayist and
Virginius Dabney's, Allen Tate's, and John Donald Wade's essays
(1932.B5; 1932.B18; 1932.B19 and 1933.B10) acknowledge Harris's role
in defining and shaping social and political values in the New South.
Cousins's biography is an important study of Harris's journalism, as
is Jerry Herndon's dissertation on Harris as a social critic
(1966.A2). Another aspect of Harris's career that needs further ex-
amination is his writing for children. Although some reviewers saw
the Uncle Remus tales as stories for children, most critics quickly
put them into the class of "serious" fiction. Yet throughout his
career Harris had one eye on the younger reader and would eventually
do six volumes of stories aimed directly at that audience. The child
psychologists need to take a long look at this phase of his work.

The latest trend in Harris scholarship, almost predictably, is
psychoanalytic criticism. Bernard Wolfe's essay and Jay Martin's
Harvests of Change (1967.B14) raise provocative ideas about Harris's
ambivalent feelings towards the black man and his schizoid personality
that have been echoed by other critics, each of whom has pursued his
own particular psychological bent. Harris was a stammerer and a terribly insecure and self-conscious person all his life; it is interesting that Twain was one of Harris's first contemporaries to comment

publicly on his diffident personality (1883.B8). Born out of wedlock and, with his mother, reliant on the generosity and forgiveness of the people of Eatonton for a start in life, Harris identified strongly with the plight of the slave--and the freedman--as well as with that of the poor white. He always called himself a Georgia cracker, and there was only a little false modesty in this comment. Like most Southerners of his day, however, when pressed on the issue he would admit that the Negro should probably have a separate place in society, although he should have the right to elevate himself according to his abilities. Hubbell, Martin, Rubin, and Flusche, among other critics, have pondered the effect of Harris's humble origins, psychological insecurity, and split vocation between journalist and creative writer upon the life and work of the mature man. It seems to me that Harris's well-cultivated sense of humor, which is another subject that deserves more investigation, was partly therapeutic, or at least periodically cathartic; his sense of humor may have given his anxiety-filled and contradictory life the only coherency and wholeness that he could ever know.

Acknowledgments

I am grateful to several people for helping me bring this book to fruition. My colleague Joseph R. McElrath, Jr., suggested the feasibility of a Harris secondary bibliography and imparted invaluable advice about its methodology. Without the generous assistance of Thomas H. English, who oversees the Harris Collection at Emory University's Woodruff Library, the project would not have gotten off the ground; Professor English, and Lucien Harris, Jr., manager of the Harris Estate, gave me complete access to the Collection's Harris notebooks and other secondary materials, putting me in touch with hundreds of items that otherwise would have been either unidentifiable or unobtainable. Linda Matthews of Special Collections at Emory also patiently followed up my questions and requests.

A summer grant from Duke University made it possible for me to research extensively the Perkins Library periodical holdings and Southern materials. And I owe special thanks to Sarah Connor, Kathleen Cooper, Anne Page Mosby, Patricia Simonds, and Carol Woolverton of Florida State University's Inter-library Loan services; they processed hundreds of book and periodical requests, often writing to a dozen or more libraries to chase down a single item. Louise Clay of Strozier Library's Humanities Section also persistently kept secondary items flowing in my direction.

My wife Karen is more than first collaborator on this volume. She searched out materials, wrote entries, helped me edit and index, and then typed the manuscript. The book is ours.

List of Periodical Abbreviations

AH	American Heritage	MLN	Modern Language Notes
AL	American Literature	MR	Massachusetts Review
ALR	American Literary Realism	MTJ	Mark Twain Journal
AN&Q	American Notes and Queries	NALF	Negro American Literature Forum
AQ	American Quarterly	N&Q	Notes and Queries
BB	Bulletin of Bibliography	NEQ	New England Quarterly
CathW	Catholic World	PBSA	Papers of the Bibliographical Society of America
CE	College English		
EJ	English Journal	PR	Partisan Review
GaR	Georgia Review	SAQ	South Atlantic Quarterly
HC	Hollins Critic	SCB	South Central Bulletin
JAF	Journal of American Folklore	SFQ	Southern Folklore Quarterly
JAmS	Journal of American Studies	SLJ	Southern Literary Journal
JFI	Journal of the Folklore Institute	SLM	Southern Literary Messenger (twentieth century)
JGE	Journal of General Education	SoR	Southern Review (Louisiana State University)
JHE	Journal of Higher Education		
JQ	Journalism Quarterly	SR	Sewanee Review
KFQ	Keystone Folklore Quarterly	SWR	Southwest Review
		VQR	Virginia Quarterly Review
LJ	Library Journal	WF	Western Folklore
MissQ	Mississippi Quarterly		

List of Short-Titles

Grady	Joel Chandler Harris' Life of Henry W. Grady (1890)
Home Folks	Tales of the Home Folks in Peace and War (1898)
Life and Letters	The Life and Letters of Joel Chandler Harris, by Julia Collier Harris (1918)
Little Boy	Uncle Remus and the Little Boy (1910)
Minervy Ann	The Chronicles of Aunt Minervy Ann (1899)
Mingo	Mingo and Other Sketches in Black and White (1884)
Mr. Rabbit at Home	Mr. Rabbit at Home: A Sequel to Little Mr. Thimblefinger and His Queer Country (1895)
Mr. Thimblefinger	Little Mr. Thimblefinger and His Queer Country: What the Children Saw and Heard There (1894)
Nights	Nights with Uncle Remus: Myths and Legends of the Old Plantation (1883)
Occasions	On the Wing of Occasions: Being the Authorised Version of Certain Curious Episodes of the Late Civil War... (1900)
Pageants	Plantation Pageants (1899)
Plantation	On the Plantation: A Story of a Georgia Boy's Adventures During the War (1892)
Qua	Qua: A Romance of the Revolution (1946)
Returns	Uncle Remus Returns (1918)
Rhymes	The Tar-Baby and Other Rhymes of Uncle Remus (1904)
Rockville	The Romance of Rockville (1878)
Shadow	The Shadow Between His Shoulder-Blades (1909)
Sister Jane	Sister Jane: Her Friends and Acquaintances. A Narrative of Certain Events and Episodes... (1896)
Songs of the South	Songs of the South, with an introduction by Harris (1896)

List of Short-Titles

Statesman	The Making of a Statesman and Other Stories (1902)
Stories of Georgia	Stories of Georgia (1896)
"The Tar-Baby Story"	"The Wonderful Tar-Baby Story"
Told	Told by Uncle Remus: New Stories of the Old Plantation (1905)
Tolliver	Gabriel Tolliver: A Story of Reconstruction (1902)
Uncle Remus	Uncle Remus: His Songs and His Sayings (1880)
Union Scout	A Little Union Scout (1904)
Wally Wanderoon	Wally Wanderoon and His Story-Telling Machine (1903)
Wiggins's Harris	The Life of Joel Chandler Harris: From Obscurity in Boyhood to Fame in Early Manhood (1918), by Robert Lemuel Wiggins
Wildwoods	Aaron in the Wildwoods (1897)

Writings about Joel Chandler Harris, 1862–1976

1862 A BOOKS - NONE

1862 B SHORTER WRITINGS

1   [TURNER, JOSEPH ADDISON]. "To a Young Correspondent." The
     Countryman, 3 (27 October), 40.
          An open letter by the editor of The Countryman declining
     an article [of Harris's] as too wordy and counseling him to
     "study simplicity, and artlesness [sic] of style.... You
     have a talent for writing, and I advise you to cultivate
     it. There is a glorious field just ahead of you for South-
     ern writers."

1864 A BOOKS - NONE

1864 B SHORTER WRITINGS

1   [TURNER, JOSEPH ADDISON]. "Why Is It?" The Countryman, 19
     (30 August), 468.
          Note protesting that a writer of an essay on Southern
     literature in the Raleigh Mercury "uses pretty freely" an
     article on Henry Lynden Flash done by Harris, "our young
     correspondent." Yet Harris is not given credit for his
     essay.

1866 A BOOKS - NONE

1866 B SHORTER WRITINGS

1   [NEVILLE, HARRY]. "The Question Partially Solved." Macon
     Daily Telegraph (5 August), p. 3.
          "An enthusiastic young friend, from Putnam [Harris]...
     was induced the other night to swallow four or five glasses
     of lager in rapid succession. Noticing that he looked a
     little swivel-eyed we asked him if he thought the Germanic
     liquid was of an intoxicating nature. Throwing his head

1866

back, and blinking considerably, he replied: 'C-a-n-'-t
s-a-y z-a-c-t-l-y t-i-s t-o-s-s-i-c-a-t-i-n, b-u-t m-a-k-e-s
a f-e-l-l-a-r-'-s t-o-n-g-u-u-e a-w-'-u-l t-h-i-c-k.' If
the young man wishes to speak German fluently, in a very
short time, we would advise him to drink lager daily...."
[See 1866.B2 for sequel.]

2   ____. "We Retract." Macon Daily Telegraph (9 August), p. 3.
The young gentleman from Putnam "begs us to correct the
statement made the other day [see 1866.B1], as to his at-
tempting to learn German by imbibing lager. For some fear
of [sic] the fair Turnwoldians should consider him 'de-
moralized,' we make the correction with pleasure. Although
our young friend had been taking a social glass of beer, we
assure the demoiselles of Turnwold that it had nothing to
do with the impediment in his speech. He stammers naturally
when the least excited."

1869 A BOOKS - NONE

1869 B SHORTER WRITINGS

1   DAVIDSON, JAMES WOOD. The Living Writers of the South.
New York: Carleton Pub., pp. 236-39.
Contends that few young writers rank higher than Harris.
Harris [mistakenly identified as a Forsyth lawyer] has
written essays, sketches, and lyrics for the past five
years for periodicals and plans an anthology of Southern
verse, "Gems of Southern Poetry." As a poet, he "recog-
nizes the twaddle about inspiration as twaddle," and looks
to "legitimate art." Praises "The Old and the New," which
he anthologizes, for its terse theme and musical expression.
Finds "Agnes," also printed here, to have the "playful
tenderness of Timrod" and a graceful antithesis.

1873 A BOOKS - NONE

1873 B SHORTER WRITINGS

1   ANON. "Jinks Conundrum Harris: An Illustrated Biographical
Sketch of One of Georgia's Funny Men." Atlanta
Constitution (23 April), p. 3.
Harris's humor made the Savannah News "noted for the
sparkle of its Georgia column." Comic biography follows,
in which Harris's progenitors are identified as Rabelais,
John Falstaff, and Twain. "Harris exudes, drools, eats,

breathes, looks, imagines, and gesticulates jokes. He, indeed, murmurs jokes, even in his tender hours of love....
But we must stop. The very suggestion of Harris sets our
paper to capering with laughter...."

1876 A BOOKS - NONE

1876 B SHORTER WRITINGS

1   ANON. Announcement about Harris's employment. Atlanta
    Constitution (21 November), p. 2.
      Many contemporaries have noticed that J. C. Harris,
    formerly of the Savannah News, has been temporarily engaged
    by the Constitution. Today the publishers gladly announce
    that Harris will be a permanent fixture on the editorial
    staff of the paper.

1879 A BOOKS - NONE

1879 B SHORTER WRITINGS

1   [LUKENS, H. CLAY]. "Uncle Remus in Brief. A Sketch of the
    Greatest Humorist in the South." Atlanta Constitution
    (20 April), p. 5.
      Reprints an article from an undated number of the New
    Haven Register, which that paper acquired from H. Clay
    Lukens of the New York News; Lukens plans to include this
    piece in a forthcoming compendium of American newspaper
    humor to be entitled "Don't Give It Away." Lukens mentions
    Henry Grady's and William Tappan Thompson's admiration for
    Harris and explains that Samuel W. Small of the Atlanta
    Constitution had at his request written a memoir on Harris.
    Small's sketch, here printed, stresses Harris's versatility,
    hard work, and sense of humor: Harris "'has placed negro
    dialect poetry as a distinctive feature in the literature
    of the country.'" "Uncle Remus" has no peer, and his poems
    are based on Harris's knowledge of plantation life. The
    "Revival Hymn" is familiar in nearly every house in America,
    and the "Camp-Meeting Song" and "Corn Shucking Song" also
    reveal Harris's ability to create dialect. Small briefly
    summarizes Harris's plantation experiences and earlier news-
    paper work.

2   S.[MALL], S.[AMUEL W.]. "The Constitutional Staff." Atlanta
    Constitution (22 March), p. 2.

1880

Item from undated number of the Philadelphia <u>Evening Telegraph</u>. What Harris, "Uncle Remus," lacks in length he makes up for in rotundity. "'He possesses the raw material for a handsome man, but by some accident he was spoiled in making up. If justice is meted out to him, he will never be hanged on account of his beauty. He is inordinately proud of his hair, which he dies [sic] red.'"

1880 A BOOKS - NONE

1880 B SHORTER WRITINGS

1   ANON. "New Publications. Negro Folk-Lore." <u>New York Times</u> (1 December), p. 3.
    Full-column review of <u>Uncle Remus</u> praises the all-round excellence of the volume but particularly stresses the book's folkloristic value and Harris's ear for dialect. Perhaps the rabbit's very abundance accounts for his popularity in myth and legend around the world; Harris stresses his cleverness and mischievousness. Harris's is the "first real book of American folk lore."

2   ANON. Review of <u>Uncle Remus</u>. <u>Nation</u>, 31 (2 December), 398.
    Several collections of Negro spirituals and stories have been published since the Civil War. Unlike his predecessors, however, Harris is an artist--a master representer of Negro dialect, of humor, and of episodical narrative. Praises the plantation proverbs as capital, but wishes that Harris had included more explanatory notes and the musical score for the Negro songs. His book is, nevertheless, "a serious aid to the study of primitive folk-lore."

3   ANON. Review of <u>Uncle Remus</u>. New Orleans <u>Daily Picayune</u> (19 December), [p. 4].
    A well-known writer for the Atlanta <u>Constitution</u> preserves the "genuine flavor of the old plantation" in this attractive collection. His phonetic transcription of slave dialect is more natural and truthful than that of other writers, and the African legends often have a "singular grotesqueness" that heightens their interest.

4   [LANIER, SIDNEY]. "The New South." <u>Scribner's Monthly</u>, 20 (October), 847.
    A sketch cut from the Atlanta <u>Constitution</u> [undated] reveals some of the South's more skeptical tendencies; it records the practical views of Uncle Remus, "a famous colored philosopher of Atlanta, who is a fiction so founded

upon fact and so like it as to have passed into true citi-
zenship and authority, along with Bottom and Autolycus."
Although Remus's dialect is real Negro-talk, Lanier wishes
that his tone of voice and gestures could also be wit-
nessed. Reprints characteristic dialogue between Brer
Remus and Brer Abner. Reprinted 1899.B24, 1945.B10.

1881 A BOOKS - NONE

1881 B SHORTER WRITINGS

1   ALLEN, W. F. "Southern Negro Folk-Lore." Dial, 1 (January),
    183-85.
        Uncle Remus is a contribution from a new and unworked
    field. The introduction is well-written, and, although the
    volume could have been better structured, the folkloric con-
    tent, the dialect, the Reconstruction portrait of the Negro,
    and the rare humor of the book are of great interest and
    value.

2   ANON. "Books of the Month...Folklore [review of Uncle Remus]."
    Atlantic Monthly, 47 (February), 304.
        Uncle Remus is not the first attempt to preserve South-
    ern plantation stories, "but all that have preceded it have
    been fragmentary and episodical." This contribution to
    folklore is well worth attention.

3   ANON. Review of Uncle Remus. Appleton's Journal, NS 10
    (February), 188-89.
        Finds it surprising that Harris was the first to provide
    an authentic and adequate collection of folklore and plan-
    tation songs and sayings, considering the recent attention
    given to the Negro and the familiarity Southerners have
    with these stories. Perhaps these were simply thought of
    as children's tales. Praises Harris's skill. The legends
    are arranged in almost "epical consecutiveness," with local
    color interludes and a realistic picture of Remus. Feels
    Remus will take a permanent place among the great "race-
    types."

4   ANON. Review of Uncle Remus. Godey's, 102 (February), 183.
        Uncle Remus is a treasure of information for anyone de-
    siring to know about true Negro life before the War. The
    dialect is perfect.

5   ANON. Review of Uncle Remus. Harper's, 62 (February), 479.
        The poems of "Uncle Remus" are "among the best, if not
    the best, that the South has contributed to our 'cullud'

1881

literature since the war." The hymns especially breathe
the "genuine air of devotion."

6   ANON. Review of Uncle Remus. Boston Literary World, 12
      (26 March), 118.
          Description of the format and contents of Uncle Remus.
      The book is a "really valuable contribution to the litera-
      ture of the negro character"; the "lifelikeness" of the
      sketches is perfect, and their humor irresistible.

7   ANON. Review of Uncle Remus. Public Opinion, 39 (26 March),
      391.
          Uncle Remus is a "genuine" book, written in "the real
      language of the negroes" and contributing scientifically
      valuable folk and philological material. These tales re-
      flect "the copious imagery of the African races, and the
      comic stories evoke a hearty laugh."

8   ANON. "Harris's 'Uncle Remus: His Songs and Sayings.'"
      Scribner's Monthly, 21 (April), 961–62.
          The daily press has produced America's greatest humor-
      ists, such as John Phoenix, Mark Twain, and Max Adeler.
      Now Harris adds his name to the list with Uncle Remus.
      This book contains "the best sustained and most elaborate
      study which our literature possesses, or, in all probabil-
      ity, ever will possess, of a type familiar to us all--the
      old plantation negro." Although the volume is among the
      most valuable contributions to folklore since Grimm, Harris
      "seems modestly incapable of realizing the importance of
      his work." Finds much worldly wisdom in Remus's sayings;
      the etymologist will learn from studying the old man's vo-
      cabulary. Review includes a glossary for some of Remus's
      more difficult dialecticisms.

9   ANON. Review of Uncle Remus. Spectator, 54 (2 April),
      445–46.
          Extended review of the English edition of Uncle Remus
      compares Harris's sympathetic view of the domestic slave
      and his apology for the old plantation system, as espoused
      in his introduction, with the "reality" of this "fascin-
      ating" volume: "cunning, deceit, and dishonesty, and the
      delight in them" are depicted in these tales of Negro ima-
      gination. Harris should have written in his introduction
      that, "'It is not virtue that triumphs, but cunning,'" for
      these tales admirably illustrate the wily ways in which
      physically inferior races can triumph over stronger ones.
      Yet perhaps it is not so much the curiously simple trickery
      of the rabbit or the terrapin that triumphs, but rather the

"infinite and immeasurable gullibility" of the fox, wolf, or bear. Evidently the Negro delighted in grotesquely exaggerating the gullibility of the stronger races. The reviewer quotes in full the episodes of the rabbit's riding the fox like a horse and the terrapin's gulling of the fox at the spring house, and analyzes Uncle Remus's way of verbally reducing the young boy into submission before he will begin a tale.

10 ANON. "Negro Humour and Imagination." London Literary World, NS[23?] (22 April), 250-52.
    Uncle Remus is a "valuable addition to our humorous and imaginative literature" and an important contribution to folklore. Extensive quotations from Harris's introduction stress the folkloristic content of these tales. Uncle Remus is a sly, inventive, and skillful storyteller. Reproduces "Tar-Baby" and two other tales.

11 ANON. "Some New and Light Reading [review of Uncle Remus]." Punch, 81 (16 July), 21.
    Better than any "one or Twain" of them is Harris's Uncle Remus. Difficult reading at first because of the spelling but worth mastering, as others in his style can't hold a candle to him.

12 ANON. "Southern Literature." Scribner's Monthly, 22 (September), 785-86.
    Defends Scribner's recent inclusion of Southern literature as a new literary era with New England no longer the king. Attributes the rise in Southern literature to the loss of provincialism after the War and to the abolition of slavery. Harris has recorded Ethiopian folklore in a style so true to character and tradition that no one can improve upon his work: "as artistic in its execution as it is characteristic in its humor."

13 AVERY, I.[SAAC] W. The History of the State of Georgia From 1850 to 1881. New York: Brown & Derby, pp. 614, 623-24.
    Constitution writers J. C. Harris and F. H. Richardson are two of the best writers of the Georgia press. Famous for his Remus sketches, Harris "can compass anything in newspaperdom from a strong editorial to a pungent paragraph. Everything he writes is both strong and dainty. His book reviews are scholarly and charming, with a vein of delicious humor and quaint reflection, and often a subtle and aromatic irony most exquisite." Harris "leads the quintette" of nationally known Georgia humorists (Harris, A. B. Longstreet, William T. Thompson, Richard M. Johnston and

1881

Charles H. Smith) with his masterful portrayals of the
plantation Negro; he has also captured the interest of
European critics. A pathetic, yet valuable personality,
Uncle Remus "is not less an inimitable and sustained piece
of character drawing, imbued with a matchless humor, than
a priceless contribution to ethnological science." Harris's
Rockville "betokens the power of the novelist."

14   CRANE, T. F. "Plantation Folk-Lore." Popular Science Monthly,
     18 (April), 824-33.
         Although Negro animal tales have been published else-
     where, Uncle Remus is the first attempt at a full collection
     of such tales and a "valuable contribution to comparative
     folk-lore." Harris's tales are superior in terms of dialect
     and literary character. Crane examines parallels between
     several of the Remus tales and stories from the Roman de
     Renart [sic], Hottentot fables, Basque legends, Venetian
     lore, Amazonian folklore, and other sources. He believes
     that the stories came initially from Africa, however.
     Crane trusts that the scientific side of Harris's "charming"
     book will not be overlooked and that an interest in Negro
     folklore will now be awakened.

15   W., E. T. "Paul H. Hayne. A Visit to the Home of the
     Southern Poet." Atlanta Constitution (29 September), p. 5.
         When asked what he thought about "Uncle Remus," Hayne
     termed Uncle Remus "'a grand success in every respect.'"
     Those who had not visited the plantations might, erroneous-
     ly, believe Harris's sketches overdrawn. Hayne had heard
     that Harris was writing a novel for Scribner's and was look-
     ing forward to seeing it.

1882 A BOOKS - NONE

1882 B SHORTER WRITINGS

1   ANON. News item. New Orleans Times-Democrat (1 May),
     p. 3.
         J. C. Harris, "'Uncle Remus,'" whose "pleasant plantation
     sketches are so familiar to the American people," is regis-
     tered at the St. Charles Hotel.

2   ANON. "Celebrities in Church." New Orleans Times-Democrat
     (1 May), p. 3.
         Yesterday morning [Sunday], Clemens, Harris, and Cable
     attended services at the Second Presbyterian Church. "In
     the evening they attended one of our leading colored
     churches."

1883

3   ANON. News item. New Orleans <u>Times-Democrat</u> (1 May), p. 4.
    Yesterday morning [Sunday] "Mr. Joseph [sic] Chandler
    Harris" arrived in the city, to visit Mark Twain. "This
    is the first time Mr. Clemmens [sic] and Mr. Harris ever
    met."

4   ANON. News item. New Orleans <u>Times-Democrat</u> (5 May), p. 4.
    Mr. Clemens and Mr. James Osgood will leave the city
    tomorrow afternoon. "Mr. Joe [sic] Chandler Harris (Uncle
    Remus) left for home on Tuesday morning last [2 May]."

1883 A BOOKS - NONE

1883 B SHORTER WRITINGS

1   ANON. Review of <u>Nights</u>. <u>Nation</u>, 37 (15 November), 422.
    Harris's reputation was made at a single stroke with
    <u>Uncle Remus</u>. Finds Harris an exquisite humorist whose
    "mastery of the negro dialect and skill as a story-teller
    placed him in the front rank of American writers." <u>Nights</u>
    is an extraordinary tour-de-force, although probably
    nothing in this volume can excel the tar-baby tale.
    Harris's ease and confidence as a writer, his development
    of Daddy Jack and the women house servants, with their own
    peculiarities of speech, and his subtlety in revealing the
    rabbit's deceptiveness are remarkable. Also praises
    Harris's capacity for "higher and more sustained efforts,"
    as evidenced in "At Teague Poteet's" [published in <u>Century</u>
    for May 1883]. Harris's powers of observation, sympathy,
    and dramatic presentation may help him make a name in fic-
    tion as well as in folklore. Notes that <u>Mingo</u> is in
    preparation.

2   ANON. "New Publications. Negro Folk-Lore." <u>New York Times</u>
    (20 November), p. 2.
    <u>Nights</u>, like its predecessor <u>Uncle Remus</u>, is a delight-
    ful work. It collects more interesting folk stories, and
    demonstrates that the American Indian borrowed folk tales
    from the Negro, rather than vice-versa. Harris's ear for
    dialect is absolutely truthful, and his portrait of Daddy
    Jack is an excellent new addition. Harris has the double
    talent of being an admirable <u>raconteur</u> and a philogist of
    no small merit. The Negro may have learned some of his ex-
    pressions from the circus and the "patter and gags" of the
    clown. For example, "How is your corporosity?" is reminis-
    cent of Mr. Merryman's address to the ringmaster in child-
    hood days. The fact that "Miss Meadows and Miss Mott,"

1883

those mythical individuals of the white race, control the
other animals suggests the "dominating power of the white."

3   ANON. Review of Nights. CathW, 38 (December), 427-28.
    Harris's latest collection is a treasure of Southern
    folklore and dialect. American Negroes have "a nature and
    a humor that are fascinating to all who have ever been
    brought in contact with them."

4   ANON. Review of Nights. Dial, 4 (December), 195.
    Everyone will welcome Nights, an even larger collection
    of folklore than Harris's first book. The skill with which
    the tales are introduced, the descriptions of the old man's
    demeanor, and the byplay between the man and the boy "show
    a high degree of dramatic power." A different dialect is
    introduced when the sea-islander, Daddy Jack, appears.

5   ANON. Review of Nights. Independent, 35 (6 December), 1547.
    Uncle Remus was but a sketch compared to the "full per-
    formance" in Nights. These tales are told with more command
    and accuracy; hopefully, Harris will not lay down his work
    until he "has gleaned the whole field."

6   ANON. Review of Nights. New Orleans Daily Picayune
    (16 December), [p. 14].
    Harris's Uncle Remus tales have worldwide fame. He
    transcribes the dialect, simplicity, and lightheartedness
    of the Negro as only a genius can. Nights is a book to re-
    turn to again and again and to read to one's friends. The
    tales are more than amusing; they are the "black's unwritten
    literature."

7   BRAINERD, E.[RASTUS]. "To the Editors of The Critic."
    Critic, 3 (29 December), 534.
    Explains in a letter that he disagrees with Harris's
    statements [in a 15 December 1883 essay on "Plantation
    Music" published in The Critic] that the plantation Negro
    does not play the banjo. Associated with Harris for a year
    on the Atlanta Constitution and admires him, but Negroes
    often played banjos outside the Constitution office. Also,
    other Negroes Brainerd knew said that the banjo was played
    on plantations. [For related letters, see also 1883.B9 and
    1883.B10.]

8   [CLEMENS, SAMUEL LANGHORNE]. "Uncle Remus and Mr. Cable," in
    his Life on the Mississippi. Boston: James R. Osgood and
    Co., pp. 471-72.

Recounts Twain's meeting with Harris in New Orleans in May 1882, stressing Harris's shyness. "There is a fine and beautiful nature ... and a fine genius" hidden behind his shyness, "as all know who have read the Uncle Remus book." Children who had gathered at George Washington Cable's house were "deeply disappointed" to learn that Harris was white; his "immortal shyness" also kept him from reading the tar-baby story aloud to the children, so Twain and Cable did the reading instead.

9   HARRISON, J. A. "To the Editors of The Critic." *Critic*, 3 (29 December), 534–35.
Recites instances of cornfield Negroes who played banjos, in New Orleans and in Lexington, Virginia, and criticizes Harris's December 15 statement in The Critic that plantation Negroes did not play the instrument. [For related letters, see also 1883.B7 and 1883.B10.]

10   STREET, HANNAH. "To the Editors of The Critic." *Critic*, 3 (22 December), 523.
Letter from a Negro woman, born and raised in Georgia, noting that despite what "Uncle Remus" said in The Critic she often heard Negro men play the banjo on plantations in Wayne County. [For related letters, see also 1883.B7 and 1883.B9.]

11   WATTERSON, HENRY. Oddities in Southern Life and Character. Boston: Houghton, Mifflin, pp. viii, 304–305.
Watterson, editor of the Louisville Courier-Journal, gathers an anthology of "characteristic pictures, taken from the most graphic chroniclers of the nether side of Southern life." Five of the "delicious" Remus tales and five Negro songs illustrate Harris's "genius for subtle observation" and his sensitivity to Negro character; Harris's is "the best picture of negro life and character which has yet appeared in any language." [A new illustration by F. S. Church faces p. 310.]

1884 A BOOKS - NONE

1884 B SHORTER WRITINGS

1   ANON. Review of Nights. *Spectator*, 57 (12 January), 53–54.
The stories in Nights are "fully as good" as those in Uncle Remus. Harris's skill at portraying Negro character is even better than the stories themselves. Aristocratic, shrewd, and imaginative, Uncle Remus is the chief portrait. Reviewer quotes several illustrative passages.

1884

2   ANON. Review of <u>Nights</u>. <u>Continent</u>, 5 (30 January), 158.
        Finds Harris always charming, but sees little fresh ma-
    terial in <u>Nights</u>. "There is a subtle undercurrent in the
    tales, and many times an unconscious parallel between the
    old slave life and its limited conditions and the sly eva-
    sions of force and authority." The Negro folklore will
    mean more to the student a century from now than it does
    today; Harris has "caught the vanishing spirit of the past."

3   ANON. Review of <u>Nights</u>. <u>Manhattan</u>, 3 (February), 188.
        The creator of Uncle Remus has brought something fresh
    and original to American literature. The tender pathos of
    <u>Nights</u> is delightful, and its folkloric contributions un-
    surpassed. As "editor" of the tales, Harris has shown
    judgment and careful appreciation.

4   ANON. "<u>Nights with Uncle Remus</u>." <u>Critic</u>, NS 1 (9 February),
    64.
        <u>Nights</u> is replete with shrewd wit and amusing episodes,
    and Daddy Jack, Aunt Tempy, and 'Tildy are actual figures.
    Harris pretends to be only an editor of tales, but his
    writings are "marvellously like the work of originality and
    genius." Someone should make a collection of Uncle Remus's
    sententious sayings.

5   ANON. "Our 'Forty Immortals.'" <u>Critic</u>, NS 1 (12 April), 169.
        Harris is not listed among the forty most popular Ameri-
    can writers, as determined by a poll of readers; he ranked
    in sixty-second position. [For updated poll, <u>see</u> 1890.B3.]

6   ANON. "Southern Sketches. <u>Mingo and Other Sketches in Black
    and White</u>." <u>New York Times</u> (16 June), p. 3.
        <u>Uncle Remus</u> was a remarkable book with inimitable by-
    play between the old Negro and the little boy. In his
    latest book, Harris displays the peculiarities of some
    Southern people as well as Mr. Cable. "Mingo" has dramatic
    force and Mrs. Bivins, an exact portrait of what some call
    "white trash," has something of Celtic passion in her char-
    acter. "At Teague Poteet's," the most ambitious of the
    stories, is masterfully told. Like Mr. Cable, Harris occu-
    pies ground distinctly his own; there is "nothing namby-
    pamby" about his dramatic writing.

7   ANON. Review of <u>Mingo</u>. Atlanta <u>Constitution</u> (22 June), p. 6.
        Harris has sustained himself "splendidly" in a compara-
    tively new field. The stories in <u>Mingo</u> are both Southern
    and national, with perfect dialect and character portrayals.
    The plots are striking and the descriptions vivid and

picturesque. The Georgia moonshiner and his daughter in "At Teague Poteet's" are highly individual figures.

8 ANON. "Talk about Books [review of <u>Uncle Remus</u>]." <u>Chautauquan</u>, 4 (July), 612.
Glad that so much of Uncle Remus's humor, shrewd sense, and peculiar dialect has been preserved. More than merely a humorous volume, <u>Uncle Remus</u> represents a perishing type of American life.

9 ANON. Review of <u>Mingo</u>. New York <u>Daily Tribune</u> (6 July), p. 8.
<u>Mingo</u> illustrates the life, character, and manners of the "poor whites" of Georgia, a class never before adequately represented in literature. To Harris's predecessors, the poor whites were ignorant and squalid, but he sees more deeply, accurately, and sympathetically than they. One "need not wonder that Mr. Harris has suddenly become one of the conspicuous figures of our time." "Mingo" is "exquisite," and "Blue Dave" and "At Teague Poteet's" are also striking. Reprint: 1884.B10.

10 ANON. "Mr. Harris's 'Mingo,' Etc." Atlanta <u>Constitution</u> (9 July), p. 4.
Reprint of 1884.B9.

11 ANON. Review of <u>Mingo</u>. Boston <u>Literary World</u>, 15 (26 July), 242.
<u>Mingo</u> is in the same class of fiction as C. E. Craddock's [Mary Noailles Murfree's], but the Georgian mountaineers in "At Teague Poteet's" are represented as more advanced than the Tennesseans in Craddock's work. "Mingo" and "Blue Dave" are "capital" studies of the faithful Negro.

12 ANON. Review of <u>Mingo</u>. <u>Critic</u>, NS 2 (2 August), 51.
Those who were troubled with the dialect in the Brer Rabbit tales will especially appreciate <u>Mingo</u>. All the endearing qualities of Harris are here, and there is just enough dialectical piquancy. Harris makes effective use of black and white contrasts, and these stories show that he can write a picturesque tale without writing dialect stories.

13 ANON. Review of <u>Mingo</u>. <u>Nation</u>, 39 (7 August), 115–16.
<u>Mingo</u> does not discredit the fame of "Uncle Remus." Harris succeeds as a storyteller in Negro and poor-white lingo because he "is very close to the untutored spirit of humanity." He discriminates nicely between natural emotions and those inherited by a class, and he never offends by

1884

incongruity between idea and form. Harris's perceptions
are thus more subtle and truthful, and his insights deeper
than those of Bret Harte. Mrs. Feratia Bivins is a perfect
example of "fitness between sense and sound," and Mingo's
narration effectively conveys the pathos and unconscious
humor in the story. Characters are also displayed effectively in "At Teague Poteet's" and "Blue Dave."

14 ANON. Review of Mingo. Independent, 36 (21 August), 1067.
The title story in Mingo is in some respects superior to
its companions; "At Teague Poteet's" is also admirable.
While Harris has no rivals in the depiction of dialect and
the Southern plantation Negro, his works suffer a little
besides the remarkable presentations of C. E. Craddock
[Mary Noailles Murfree].

15 ANON. "Editor's Literary Record [review of Mingo]." Harper's,
69 (September), 640-41.
Hard to find four more thrilling or perfect stories than
those in Mingo. Harris writes of the Georgia mountains
with the same "bracing vigor and dramatic force" that C. E.
Craddock [Mary Noailles Murfree] uses in In the Tennessee
Mountains; his delineations of plantation and village life
that is dissolving in the face of new social and industrial
conditions are both delightful and an important record of
a vanishing phase of Georgia society.

16 ANON. "Belles Lettres [review of Mingo]." Westminster
Review, 122 (October), 617.
The Georgian stories about Negroes in Mingo "have an in-
describable air of reality," despite their "bizarrerie."
The dialect bears all the marks of having been studied from
nature.

17 ANON. "American Books [review of Mingo]." The Academy, 26
(4 October), 215.
Although lovers of Negro dialect will like this book,
the reviewer's attempt was in vain.

18 ANON. "Southern Sketches [review of Mingo]." London
Saturday Review, 58 (4 October), 445.
Harris is a born storyteller, whose tales delight "the
student of dialects, the collector of folk-lore, and the
lover of humour." Mingo shows his insight into character,
his imagination, and his dramatic sense. Mingo and Blue
Dave are memorable Negro characters, and Teague Poteet and
Feratia Bivins, the poor white, are also admirable pictures. Harris could make a worthy American novelist, if
he "has wind for a long flight."

19 DERBY, JAMES CEPHAS. "Joel Chandler Harris," in his <u>Fifty</u>
    <u>Years Among Authors, Books and Publishers</u>. New York:
    G. W. Carleton and Co., pp. 433-40.
         Harris is "the very best delineator of Southern negro
    character which the country has developed." Charles A.
    Dana observed to Derby that <u>Uncle Remus</u> "will not only have
    a large sale, but an enduring sale," and John Bigelow be-
    lieved the book "will live as long as 'Aesop's Fables.'"
    But Harris "pictures equally well the life and characteris-
    tics of the poor white in the South"; "At Teague Poteet's,"
    for example, is the "very best description" of "moonshiners"
    and other kindred characters that has been written. Harris
    himself, Derby recalls from an interview, is "a very agree-
    able and intelligent gentleman, although diffident in the
    extreme."

<u>1885 A BOOKS - NONE</u>

<u>1885 B SHORTER WRITINGS</u>

1 BRAINERD, ERASTUS. "Authors at Home. XI. Joel Chandler
   Harris (Uncle Remus) at Atlanta." <u>Critic</u>, NS 3 (16 May),
   229-30.
        First half of two-part article [<u>see</u> 1885.B2 for conclu-
   sion]. Describes Harris's neat Southern cottage in West
   Point [End], Atlanta, and reconstructs his early years on
   Turner's plantation and up through his first days on the
   Atlanta <u>Constitution</u>. His editorials for the Forsyth <u>Ad-</u>
   <u>vertiser</u> on state abuses were widely copied for their "pun-
   gent criticism" and "bubbling humor." Reprinted: 1888.B14.

2 _____. "Authors at Home. XI. Joel Chandler Harris (Uncle
   Remus) at Atlanta." <u>Critic</u>, NS 3 (23 May), 241.
        [Concluding part of 1885.B1.] Harris's Uncle Remus
   sketches brought the North "a revelation of an unknown
   life." Praises the framework, fresh humor, and novelty of
   the folk tales; however, "Mingo" revealed Harris could also
   succeed in elaborate character-drawing and dramatic development. "At Teague Poteet's" evolved from a news item to a
   story which is praised for accurately representing a new
   phase of American life. Describes Harris's two lives,
   journalistic and literary, and feels Harris is approaching
   pure literary fame. His journalism has a broad and fair
   representation of national topics. Harris liked Shakespeare, Job, St. Paul, and Ecclesiastes. His diffidence
   comes from his excessive sympathy and tenderness. Reprinted: 1888.B14.

1885

3   SIMS, J. MARION. <u>The Story of My Life</u>. Edited by H. Marion-
     Sims. New York: D. Appleton, pp. 69-70.
         Harris has made a great hit with his Uncle Remus tales.
     When the author was seven or eight, in 1820 or 1821, a
     Negro named Cudjo used to tell African animal stories like
     Harris's. Sims is satisfied that the stories were of Afri-
     can derivation, although this source has been questioned
     by some.

4   SMITH, CHARLES FORSTER. "Southern Dialect in Life and
     Literature." <u>Southern Bivouac</u>, NS 1 (November), 346-47.
         The dialect of the Southern common people is much in de-
     mand in popular literature. Of the three great dialect
     writers of the South (Cable, Harris and Craddock [Mary
     Noailles Murfree]), Harris is the most accurate writer of
     Negro and cracker dialect, both in phonetic reproduction
     and spirit; his Negro dialect seems almost faultless. "At
     Teague Poteet's" is a good mountaineer story, and it is
     more realistic than Miss Murfree's sketches. But in "Mingo"
     and "Free Joe" Harris is most at home.

5   STEDMAN, EDMUND CLARENCE. <u>Poets of America</u>. Boston and
     New York: Houghton, Mifflin, p. 455.
         Praises American dialect writing and mentions Harris as
     one writer who "diligently cultivated the art of writing
     plantation-verse."

1886 A BOOKS - NONE

1886 B SHORTER WRITINGS

1   ANON. "The Lounger." <u>Critic</u>, NS 5 (20 March), 145.
         A statement claiming that Harris was born on the African
     coast has gained much currency of late, and the London
     <u>Literary World</u> says that his birth accounts for his success
     in delineating Negro character. Although Harris might have
     been born by accident in the Dark Continent, he was not.

2   ANON. "Constitutionals [humorous story on Harris]." Atlanta
     <u>Constitution</u> (1 April), p. 4.
         Recounts Harris's and Eugene Field's humorous exchanges
     in response to Field's burlesquing of Harris in the Chicago
     <u>Daily News</u> [dates unspecified]. Field had written in his
     column "Sharps and Flats" that Harris was born in Joel,
     Africa, of missionary parents and that his hair had turned
     white when, after the War, he had returned home to find his
     sweetheart dead. Harris's humorous protests about the

story elicited further bogus biographical material from
Field. Harris published "An Accidental Author" in Lippin-
cott's for April 1886 to clarify facts about his life.
[For sequel, see 1886.B4.]

3 ANON. "The Lounger." Critic, NS 5 (1 May), 219.
A good joke on "Uncle Remus" would be to circulate a
paragraph attributed to the Southern Industrial Record that
claims that Harris paid over all $20,000 of his royalties
to buy a celebrated peachblow vase. The notice claimed
further that Harris's West End cottage is valued at
$100,000, and that all of the Harrises are wealthy.

4 ANON. "Constitutionals [humorous story on Harris]." Atlanta
Constitution (28 August), p. 4.
[For earlier article, see 1886.B2.] Harris announced
yesterday that he was going to Chicago. When asked what
for, he said, "'To kill Eugene Field.'" Harris and Field
have continued to exchange humorous broadsides since Field
first circulated a bogus biographical sketch on Harris.
One of Field's "Sharps and Flats" paragraphs stated that
Harris was worth $1,000,000, owned 4000 acres of prime
timberland, and liberally spent his money to help the
needy. For the past four days Harris has received thirty
letters a day asking him for money; excerpts from letters
are reprinted.

5 BASKERVILL, W.[ILLIAM] M.[ALONE]. "Joel Chandler Harris."
Nashville Union (31 January), [p. 2].
After his early newspaper work in Macon, New Orleans,
Forsyth, and Savannah, Harris worked for the Atlanta Constitution, introducing Uncle Remus to the public when S. W.
Small, who had been writing dialect sketches as "Old Si,"
left for another position. Harris "is one of the brightest,
serenest lights of the new literary era in the south." The
first sentence in his first book "showed that he understood
and appreciated the peculiar relationship which existed between the white children of the south and the old 'daddie'
or 'mammie' of the plantations." "Mingo," "Blue Dave," and
"Free Joe" are "gems" that catch the spirit of Southern
life.

6 CABLE, GEORGE W. "The Dance in Place Congo." Century, 31
(February), 519-20.
The banjo is not the favorite instrument of the Negroes;
as "Uncle Remus" has pointed out, it is the fiddle.

1887

1887 A BOOKS - NONE

1887 B SHORTER WRITINGS

1   ANON. "Joel Chandler Harris." Book Buyer, 3 (January), 540.
     Biographical sketch. "A Southerner by birth and resi-
     dence, [Harris] shares none of the prejudices commonly at-
     tributed to Southern men." Engraved portrait of Harris
     that serves as a frontispiece for this issue "is, we be-
     lieve, the first ever given to the public of this very
     popular story-teller."

2   ANON. "The Author of 'Uncle Remus.'" Book Buyer, 4
     (February), 8.
          Harris blazes out "the main track" of his story mentally;
     he keeps no scrapbooks and "never blocks out his work on
     paper." He writes deliberately, preferring a goose-quill
     to steel or gold pens, which cause numbness in his wrist
     and arm. Most of his literary work is done at night, when
     he is free from the exigencies of journalism. "He has been
     a worker all his life, and he is as likely to die at his
     desk as anywhere else."

3   ANON. Review of Free Joe. New Orleans Daily Picayune
     (25 December), p. 9.
          No writer of Southern stories has contributed anything
     more artistic, charming, and tender than the stories in
     Free Joe. It is a welcome volume of "exquisite" Georgian
     sketches.

4   BEERS, HENRY A. An Outline Sketch of American Literature.
     New York: Chautauqua Press, p. 268.
          Harris's At Teague Poteet's [sic] and Murfree's books
     (In the Tennessee Mountains, and others) have made the
     Northern public familiar with the "moonshiners" of Georgia,
     North Carolina, and Tennessee. "These tales are not only
     exciting in incident, but strong and fresh in their de-
     lineations of character. Their descriptions of mountain
     scenery are also impressive, though, in the case of the
     last named writer, frequently too prolonged." Harris's
     Uncle Remus stories are transcripts, in Negro dialect, from
     the folklore of the plantation. Revision: 1891.B14,
     1895.B14.

5   COLEMAN, CHARLES W., JR. "The Recent Movement in Southern
     Literature." Harper's, 74 (May), 844–48.
          Biographical sketch and critical appraisal. Harris's
     reputation rests chiefly upon his skillful reproduction of

1888

Negro dialect, and the sayings and doings of that "delightful reprobate," Brer Rabbit, in the Uncle Remus stories.
Uncle Remus was an "immediate" success on both sides of the
Atlantic, and Nights gathered some of the best animal
stories. Mingo is a successful book about Middle Georgia
folk. "Then there is the pitiful figure of Free Joe, contrasting so forcibly with the careless happiness and self-
importance of Uncle Remus. Mr. Harris has done nothing
better than this. 'Free Joe and the Rest of the World'--
the very title is a sermon." Harris modestly denies his
abilities and thinks of himself as a journalist.

6   RICHARDSON, CHARLES F. American Literature: 1607–1885.
    Vol. 1: The Development of American Thought. New York:
    G. P. Putnam's Sons, p. 521.
       Refers to Harris as one of the reigning favorites of the
    day, but, unless he achieves higher literary achievement
    than the Remus stories, he will not be remembered. Humor
    alone does not give one a place in literature.

1888 A BOOKS - NONE

1888 B SHORTER WRITINGS

1   ANON. "The Newest Books [review of Free Joe]." Book Buyer,
    4 (January), 506.
       Harris displays dramatic instinct, firmness of touch,
    pathos, and humor in these flawless tales.

2   ANON. Review of Free Joe. Critic, NS 9 (14 January), 17.
       The Free Joe collection contains pleasing stories of
    higher life, strong feeling, and depth despite seeming
    simplicity. "Free Joe" is especially good.

3   ANON. Review of Mingo. Critic, NS 9 (14 January), 17.
       Four admirable and picturesque tales make up Mingo.
    Mingo, the faithful Negro, will be remembered.

4   ANON. Review of Free Joe. New York Times (15 January), p. 14.
       Knows of no story that equals "Free Joe" for simple
    pathos. Harris is especially admirable for never truckling
    to the opinions of the past or being subservient to those
    of today. The other stories in Free Joe feature likable
    characters of various sorts; the several stories are
    briefly summarized.

1888

5   ANON. Review of Free Joe. Boston Literary World, 19
    (21 January), 26.
    Magazine readers will notice the "fine quality and artis-
    tic finish" of Harris's Southern dialect stories: praises
    their individuality, proportion, and dignity. "Free Joe"
    is a little masterpiece, a pathetic picture skillfully
    drawn on a small canvas. "Trouble on Lost Mountain" intro-
    duces the now-familiar mountaineer, and of the remaining
    stories "Little Compton" shows North-South character con-
    trasts with fine effect.

6   ANON. "The Bookshelf [review of Mingo]." Cottage Hearth, 14
    (February), 58.
    "At Teague Poteet's" is the most interesting story in
    the Mingo collection. The character of the rough mountain-
    eers is strongly developed and the plot of the tale well
    sustained.

7   ANON. "Talk about Books [review of Free Joe]." Chautauquan,
    8 (February), 327.
    Free Joe presents the pathetic history of various charac-
    ters from Southern life at the time of the War.

8   ANON. "The Lounger." Critic, NS 9 (4 February), 57.
    Claims about Mark Twain's wealth may be close to the
    truth, but imagine what Harris must think when he reads as-
    sertions that he is worth a million dollars. He is very
    far from being one of the "'bloated bondholders.'"

9   ANON. "A Chat about New Books [review of Free Joe]." CathW,
    46 (March), 836-37.
    One of the most charming young women in modern fiction
    is Helen Eustis in "Azalia." The other tales in Free Joe
    possess "that unaffectedness and spontaneity characteristic
    of Mr. Harris' method."

10 ANON. "Recent Fiction [review of Free Joe]." Nation, 46
    (1 March), 183.
    In Free Joe Harris gives enduring life to the Georgia
    Negro, bond and free, as well as to the poor white and the
    mountaineer. His portraits of Southern aristocrats seem no
    less real. Harris prefers to describe the relation between
    master and slave as one of loving protection and devotion,
    rather than as one of brutality and fear. "Fortunately for
    those who like a pleasant tale, the author stands apart
    from the crusade to divorce the true and the beautiful."

1888

11 ANON. Review of Free Joe and Mingo. The Overland Monthly,
    Second Series 11 (April), 435-36.
       Harris is best known of the Southerners dealing with
    local color materials; he "caught the trick of the modern
    short tale." In Free Joe he has good method, but only
    "Free Joe" will last because of its human truth or pathos.
    Thinks Mingo is stronger than the Free Joe volume.

12 ANON. "The Best Novel. Various Opinions As to the Best Novel
    Ever Written." Atlanta Constitution (21 April), p. 4.
       Various literary figures of Atlanta were asked which
    novel they found to be the greatest of the genre. Harris,
    who "ought certainly to be a competent judge of novels"
    and whose opinion "carries influence with it among literary
    people," noted The Count of Monte Cristo the most entertain-
    ing and adventurous novel, and Henry Esmond, Adam Bede, My
    Novel, and A Tale of Two Cities the best works in terms of
    treating ethical and moral issues and the problems of life
    and character.

13 ANON. "Fiction for Idle Summer Days [review of Free Joe]."
    Book Buyer, 5 (June), 188.
       Harris's reputation as a short story writer is second
    to none. The sketches in Free Joe are drawn on a small can-
    vas, but they are perfect in composition, color, and feel-
    ing. Harris is a master.

14 BRAINERD, ERASTUS. "Joel Chandler Harris (Uncle Remus)," in
    his Authors at Home: Personal and Biographical Sketches of
    Well-Known American Writers. New York: Cassell and Co.,
    pp. 111-23.
       Reprinting of 1885.B1 and 1885.B2, combined.

15 [CLEMENS, SAMUEL LANGHORNE]. Mark Twain's Library of Humor.
    Edited by William Dean Howells and Charles Hopkins Clark.
    New York: Charles L. Webster & Co., p. 131.
       Provides a short biographical sketch and anthologizes
    "The Tar-Baby" and "Mr. Rabbit Grossly Deceives Mr. Fox."

16 JACOBS, JOSEPH, ed. The Earliest English Version of the
    Fables of Bidpai. London: David Nutt, pp. xliv-xlvi.
       The fables of Uncle Remus may seem remote from tales of
    ancient India, but the tar-baby story is connected to one
    of the Játakas, or Buddhist Birth-stories. The tale of the
    Demon with the Matted Hair involves an attacker being
    caught by both arms and both legs, and then by his head.
    The story must have been passed by slave-traders or mer-
    chants from India to Africa, and then to America. "No

1888

wonder Brer Rabbit was so 'cute, since he is thus shown to
be an incarnation of the Buddha himself."

17 JAMES, HENRY. Partial Portraits. London and New York:
    Macmillan, pp. 180-81.
    Feels Constance Woolson's careful philological study of
    the Negro dialect, as seen in Rodman the Keeper and East
    Angels, may be the first such study, if hers preceded Uncle
    Remus by a "considerable interval."

18 JONES, CHARLES C[OLCOCK], JR., ed. "Prefatory Note," in his
    Negro Myths from the Georgia Coast. Boston and New York:
    Houghton, Mifflin, pp. v-vi.
    Harris perpetuated the dialect and folklore of Middle
    Georgia Negroes with fidelity and cleverness. Folk stories
    of the swamp-region of Georgia and the Carolinas materially
    differ from those of Middle Georgia and deserve to be more
    widely known; sixty-one tales are published here. Reprint:
    1925.B6.

19 MOONEY, JAMES. "Myths of the Cherokees." JAF, 1 (July-
    September), 106.
    Cherokee stories featuring a rabbit as hero resemble the
    Uncle Remus tales, which the author someday hopes to prove
    are of American Indian origin.

20 REED, WALLACE PUTNAM. "Joel Chandler Harris." Literature:
    A Weekly Magazine (27 October), pp. 425-44.
    A bibliography of Harris's books through Free Joe and a
    brief biographical and character sketch preface five selec-
    tions from the Remus volumes and "Free Joe," published in
    its entirety. Harris was always surprised at the praise
    his works were generating, stating that he was only a re-
    porter. He enjoys his work and maintains a sense of humor
    continuously. His heroes are Lincoln, Lee, and Stonewall
    Jackson. What he seeks in literature is "a touch of na-
    ture," and he does not find any charm in the schools of
    Howells, James, and Tolstoi. Harris wrote an editorial
    lamenting the bullish market that publishers have created
    for "the dialect business," pointing out that Shakespeare,
    Thackeray, Scott, Dickens, Lowell, and Hardy are dialect
    writers who use it not as "jargon" but as the natural lan-
    guage of their characters. A Boston clergyman, G. L.
    Chaney, notes Reed, read a critique of Harris at the Atlanta
    literary circle recently. Chaney felt that the first two
    Remus volumes, despite their art, might have a "damaging"
    effect on young children, who would identify with the "cun-
    ning, duplicity, deceit, ingenuity, the absence of

conscience or conviction in which Brer Rabbit excels," although the Rabbit's antagonists are even more reprehensible. Chaney felt that in <u>Mingo</u> and <u>Free Joe</u> Harris shows his real mastery of storytelling.

21 TOURGÉE, ALBION W. "The South as a Field for Fiction." <u>Forum</u>, 7 (December), 408.
        Discusses the popularity after the War of Southern fiction and explores some of the reasons it appeals to many Northern readers. The Negro and the poor white are now the more interesting elements in Southern life and in the literature of the Southern renaissance. Harris's writings have "quaintness."

22 VANCE, L. J. "Plantation Folk-Lore." <u>Open Court</u>, 42 (14 June), 1029-32.
        Review of Jones's <u>Negro Myths of the Georgia Coast</u> [see 1888.B18] traces rise of international interest in Negro folklore, including collections by Harris. Jones's and Harris's stories differ in "lingo" but are similar in motifs. The sources and transmission of Negro folklore are open questions. [See 1888.B23 and B24 for continuation.]

23 _____. "Plantation Folk-Lore." <u>Open Court</u>, 42 (5 July), 1074, 1075, 1076.
        [Continuation of 1888.B22.] Passing references to Harris's folklore. [Concluded in 1888.B24.]

24 _____. "Plantation Folk-Lore." <u>Open Court</u>, 42 (12 July), 1094.
        [Continuation of 1888.B22, B23.] Passing references to Harris's folklore.

25 WILSON, JAMES GRANT and JOHN FISKE, eds. "Harris," in <u>Appleton's Cyclopaedia of American Biography</u>. Vol. 3. New York: D. Appleton, p. 92.
        Ten-line biographical sketch. Mentions that Harris was born on 8 December 1848, and practiced law in Forsyth, Georgia; lists <u>Uncle Remus</u>, <u>Nights</u>, and <u>Mingo</u> as works. Reprinted: 1900.B31.

1889 A BOOKS - NONE

1889 B SHORTER WRITINGS

1 ANON. Untitled notice concerning <u>Daddy Jake</u>. Atlanta <u>Constitution</u> (13 October), p. 18.

1889

"Eight editions of Joel Chandler Harris's new book,
'Daddy Jake,' were ordered before the publishers had
printed the first edition."

2   ANON. Review of Daddy Jake. New Orleans Daily Picayune
    (20 October), p. 8.
    The stories in Daddy Jake are fresh, charming, and in
    Uncle Remus's best vein. It is a book for all ages.

3   ANON. Review of Daddy Jake. Critic, NS 12 (2 November), 212.
    Refers to Putnam County, Georgia, as the Grecian classic
    soil of the South. Cites Richard Malcolm Johnston's
    stories but especially praises Harris's wonderful myths and
    prehistoric tales, which originally sprang from Africa. In
    this collection the "little boy" of the Remus volumes is
    divided into a girl and a boy, and Remus becomes Daddy Jake.
    The philologist, comparative mythologist, and the "juvenile"
    reader will delight to see Harris's powers undiminished.

4   ANON. Review of Daddy Jake. Boston Literary World, 20
    (23 November), 423.
    It would be "superfluous" to recommend Daddy Jake, al-
    though E. W. Kemble's illustrations are not up to the level
    of the text.

5   ANON. Review of Daddy Jake. Independent, 41 (28 November),
    1577.
    In matter, form, and illustration, this book of tales
    attains the high-water mark.

6   ANON. Review of Daddy Jake. Chautauquan, 10 (December),
    379-80.
    Daddy Jake holds both the young and the older reader
    spellbound with irresistible humor.

7   ANON. Review of Daddy Jake. Epoch, 6 (6 December), 709.
    The title story in Daddy Jake is told for children "in
    Uncle Remus's best manner." The other stories treat animals
    as human beings and "are utilized to point a moral."

8   [HOWELLS, WILLIAM DEAN]. "Editor's Study." Harper's, 78
    (February), 492.
    In our humorists "the American spirit is most truly re-
    flected." If "they are grotesque and extravagant, it is
    because most Americans are mostly so." Looking over Mark
    Twain's Library of American Humor [see 1888.B15] we find
    "such unassailable renowns" as Hosea Biglow, John Phoenix,
    Artemus Ward, Mark Twain, Josh Billings, Uncle Remus, and
    others [lists seven additional American humorists].

9   JACOBS, JOSEPH, ed. The Fables of Aesop as first printed by
    William Caxton.... Vol. 1. History of the Aesopic Fable.
    London: David Nutt, pp. 113, 136-37.
        Buddhistic Játakas seem to have been transmitted from
    India to Africa and Europe, and thence to America. The
    Uncle Remus tale about the rabbit's image being placed on
    the moon is similar to the Susa Játaka, and the tar-baby
    story resembles the Demon with the Matted Hair Játaka.
    Additionally, worship of Buddha's foot in later Buddhism
    parallels the mystical and magical virtues of the rabbit's
    foot as emphasized in a tale in Nights. In fact, the rab-
    bit, hero of Harris's collection, may be identifiable with
    Buddha himself. Reprinted: 1970.B13.

10 REED, WALLACE P., ed. History of Atlanta, Georgia, with
    Illustrations and Biographical Sketches of Some of its
    Prominent Men and Pioneers. Syracuse, N.Y.: D. Mason &
    Co., pp. 413-19.
        The Atlanta author recently receiving the most attention
    here and abroad is Harris. Mentions the successful recep-
    tion of his books in England. Describes his career in some
    detail, especially his early reading at Turner's. A hard-
    working journalist, Harris has not let success spoil his
    modesty, and readers appreciate his deft manner and subtle
    humor in the Remus tales. Aaron, his present "novel,"
    promises to be his most ambitious effort. Also gives a
    character sketch of Harris, quotes him on dialect, and
    finds much of his work to be unique and brilliant.

1890 A BOOKS - NONE

1890 B SHORTER WRITINGS

1   ANON. "New Books [review of Daddy Jake]." New York Times
    (5 January), p. 11.
        Daddy Jake reveals again that no one knows the Negro and
    little boys as well as Harris. The language and action of
    the book make for fun. Prints a characteristic quotation
    from "The Foolish Woman."

2   ANON. "The Problematic South [review of Grady]." Nation, 50
    (15 May), 398-99.
        Harris's Life of Henry W. Grady should be retitled as
    Speeches of Henry W. Grady, with a sketch of his life by
    Joel Chandler Harris, and Various Tributes to his Memory.
    The volume was hastily put together, as Harris admits:
    Harris and another contributor even give differing dates

1890

for Grady's birth. The tributes are overly effusive and
extravag ut, and the poems to Grady are "wretched doggerel."
Grady was more of a sentimentalist than Harris suggests,
but he was a talented man of warmth and contagious
enthusiasm.

3 ANON. "Nine New 'Immortals.'" Critic, NS 14 (19 July), 33.
     Since 12 April 1884, when the Critic published its first
list of the literary immortals [see 1884.B5], six have
passed away. A second balloting now puts Harris in eighth
position.

4 GRISWOLD, W. M. A Descriptive List of Romantic Novels.
     Cambridge, MA: W. M. Griswold, Publishers, p. 209.
     Critique is extracted from the Nation and the American,
numbers unidentified. The Georgian Negro, bond and free,
the poor white, and the mountaineer are "given enduring
life" by Harris in Free Joe. "It may be heresy to suggest
it, but one feels that his portraits of the southern aris-
tocrat, as he was before the war, are no less truthful."
Harris describes the relation between master and slave as
one of devotion and protection. Harris writes with pic-
turesqueness and pathos of the old days and traditions in
"Free Joe" and "Little Compton."

5 PENDLETON, LOUIS. "Negro Folk-Lore and Witchcraft in the
     South." JAF, 3 (July-September), 201-202.
     Some of the Middle Georgia Uncle Remus tales were
familiar to this author as nursery tales before they were
published by Harris. Others were undoubtedly part of the
same myth, but even in neighboring southern Georgia they
showed significant differences. For example, a southern
Georgia version of the tar-baby story was not humorous like
Harris's story but featured a vicious, live monster baby
made of tar, which it was impossible to pass without striking, "so provoking was its grin and so insulting its behavior generally--and when you had once struck it, you were
lost."

6 WARREN, F. M. "'Uncle Remus' and 'The Roman de Renard.'"
     MLN, 5 (May), 257-70.
     Harris's Uncle Remus tales have surpassed all other col-
lections of folktales made in the old world in terms of
widespread interest. Yet Harris's stories have "a striking
resemblance" to European animal tales, especially the "Roman
de Renard" compilation of Middle Ages lore, where the wolf
is usually the victim and the fox plays the jokes. The
style and language of the tales differ widely, and Harris's
stories--keen in observation, vigorous, concise, and

picturesque--demand a place "among the foremost works of
American literature." Warren compares episodes in sixteen
Renard and sixteen Remus tales, and also notes comparisons
between five Remus stories and their counterparts in other
Flemish lore.

1891 A BOOKS - NONE

1891 B SHORTER WRITINGS

1 ANON. Review of Balaam. New Orleans Daily Picayune (31 May),
   p. 12.
      Any one of the six fascinating Negro dialect tales could
   have been the title of this delightful volume. Harris is
   without an equal "in the cotton patch."

2 ANON. "New Books [review of Balaam]." New York Times
   (7 June), p. 19.
      When compared to his contemporary dialect writers,
   Harris alone can treat with minute shadings the Negro, his
   language, and his Georgia surroundings. The accurately
   drawn and occasionally powerful stories in Balaam will be
   read one hundred years from now for both fact and pathos.
   His stories preserve the "best idea of white and colored
   existence" about the time of the Civil War.

3 ANON. Review of Balaam. The Period (17 June), p. 6.
      Praises the beauty and romance of the sketches by the
   "Georgia Scheherazade." "Mom Bi" in Balaam presents a
   "pathetic, tender, loving" picture of the old mammy.

4 ANON. Review of Balaam. Book Buyer, 8 (July), 261.
      Balaam's loyalty to his master in the title story "em-
   phasizes an admirable trait of the race," and the master's
   portrait is sketched with dramatic force. A vein of tender
   pathos runs through "The Old Bascom Place."

5 ANON. Review of Balaam. Chautauquan, 13 (July), 552.
      The Balaam collection presents natural, entertaining,
   and original characters from the Southern plantation.

6 ANON. Review of Balaam. Critic, NS 16 (18 July), 29.
      The two disreputable characters in "Balaam and His
   Master" are neither clever nor interesting.

7 ANON. Review of Balaam. London Saturday Review, 72
   (25 July), 114.

1891

Balaam has nothing in it of the tar-baby and the other
creatures, but it does contain some excellent reading.
"Where's Duncan?" is short and powerful, and "The Old Bascom Place" pathetic; however, "A Conscript's Christmas" is
not likely to interest the English reader. "Ananias" is
"the pick of the basket."

8   ANON. "Belles Lettres [review of Balaam]." Westminster
     Review, 136 (August), 230-31.
        The stories in Balaam are made up of mingled pathos and
     humor. They "vividly recall the touching relations which
     often subsisted between old Virginia families and their
     household slaves before the war destroyed the old order of
     things, and brought about a state of chaos from which no
     new order has as yet been evolved."

9   ANON. Review of Balaam. The Academy, 40 (1 August), 92.
        Inimitable in stories of Negro life, Harris portrays the
     Negro's grim humor, and his devotion to his masters. He
     makes slavery seem not without its higher uses and compen-
     sations. Finds Balaam, Mom Bi and Ananias unique, es-
     pecially in the faculty of ready invention.

10   ANON. Review of Balaam. Nation, 53 (6 August), 107.
        Harris's Negroes in Balaam are "next in vitality to
     Nature's," and their dialect is precise. These Reconstruc-
     tion stories are "penetrated with the spirit of those ter-
     rible days as few Southern stories are, the more because of
     the humor that plays around the horrors like a child among
     graves."

11   ANON. Review of Balaam. Independent, 43 (27 August), 1283.
        These excellent Southern short stories are as good in
     their way as the Uncle Remus sketches were in theirs.
     Harris has more than one string to the bow of his genius.

12   ANON. Review of Balaam. Atlantic Monthly, 68 (November),
     711.
        Harris's "staying power" is anchored in the depth of his
     portraiture; his characters in Balaam are firmly drawn and
     evince real human nature, however grotesque they may be on
     the surface.

13   ANON. "The Lounger." Critic, NS 16 (29 November), 308.
        A reader accused Harris of plagiarizing a poem on the
     advisability of compressing one's prose; the poem was pub-
     lished in the Atlanta Constitution and reprinted in The
     Critic on 24 October 1891. The "Lounger" says Harris was
     not the plagiarist of "Boil It Down."

1891

14 BEERS, HENRY A. <u>Initial Studies in American Letters</u>.
    Meadville, PA: Flood and Vincent, The Chautauqua-Century
    Press, p. 212.
        Revised edition of 1887.B4. Harris commentary essential-
    ly unchanged. [<u>See</u> 1895.B14 for another edition.]

15 BROWN, CALVIN S., JR. "Joel Chandler Harris." <u>Christian
    Advocate</u> (17 October), p. 11.
        Little is known about Harris because of his modesty and
    aversion to notoriety. His stories are not new, but his
    genius shows in the way he puts them together. The Remus
    tales are of scientific interest, and <u>Mingo</u> and <u>Free Joe</u>
    are readable and interesting. Harris's dialectical usage
    is different from Page's, "but it is certainly as near an
    approach to the true negro speech as any I have read";
    hopes Harris's dialect will not be detrimental to his fame.
    His best series of stories is possibly <u>Balaam</u>.

16 CHAMBERLAIN, A. F. "African and American: The Contact of
    Negro and Indian." <u>Science</u>, 17 (13 February), 89-90.
        Refers reader to T. F. Crane's review of Harris [<u>see</u>
    1881.B14] and to Harris's preface to <u>Uncle Remus</u> and sug-
    gests that a few folk stories may have been borrowed by the
    blacks from southeastern Indians.

17 CLARK, KATE UPSON. Review of <u>Balaam</u>. <u>Epoch</u>, 9 (17 July),
    382.
        All of the stories in <u>Balaam</u> "have become favorites"
    through their magazine publication in the last year or two.
    If Harris fails somewhat in plot and love-making, the power,
    dialect, and "'seasoning'" of his stories are admirable.
    His "simple character-sketches are his best work."

18 HAWTHORNE, JULIAN and LEONARD LEMMON, eds. <u>American
    Literature: A Text-Book for the Use of Schools and
    Colleges</u>. Boston: D. C. Heath, pp. 293-95.
        Stresses Harris's progressive editorial views and the
    fame of his Uncle Remus sketches. "Free Joe," "Little
    Compton," "Azalia," "At Teague Poteet's," and "Trouble on
    Lost Mountain" treat other phases of Southern life truth-
    fully. "One is tempted to say that it is in Harris's op-
    tion to make himself the foremost American novelist; and
    since he is still a young man, it is worth his while to
    try."

19 MATTHEWS, BRANDER. "On Certain Recent Short Stories [review
    of <u>Balaam</u>]." <u>Cosmopolitan</u>, 11 (September), 639.

1891

The "Indian summer of the past" broods over <u>Balaam</u> even
more than it does over <u>A New England Nun</u>. Whoever wishes
to understand the Old and New South, and master and slave,
must read these studies in black and white. Balaam,
Ananias, and, to a lesser degree, Mom Bi are beautiful and
truthful. Harris's emphasis on the loyalty and other virtues of the slave is similar to Scott's portrait of the
clansman's loyalty to his chief. Harris shows extraordinary
insight into the Negro, but carves admirably in white ivory
as well.

20 PAGE, THOMAS NELSON. "Literature in the South since the War."
    <u>Lippincott's</u>, 48 (December), 748-49.
        Harris's inimitable <u>Uncle Remus</u> is not prized for its
    ethnological value or its dialect; rather, the power of
    the book "lies in the artistic and masterly setting and
    narration." Harris's dialect is difficult, but his picture
    of Southern life is "absolutely true." The fidelity of
    Harris's various books to the folklore of the South and his
    reproduction of Southern civilization make his work "perhaps
    the most valuable contribution to Southern literature that
    has yet appeared."

21 PAYNE, WILLIAM MORTON. "Recent Books of Fiction [review of
    <u>Balaam</u>]." <u>Dial</u>, 12 (June), 50-51.
        Harris is almost as welcome a storyteller as Richard
    Malcolm Johnston. <u>Balaam</u> primarily pictures the War and
    Reconstruction, and the devotion of the Negro to his former
    master is the predominant note.

1892 A BOOKS - NONE

1892 B SHORTER WRITINGS

1 ANON. "The Short Story [review of <u>Balaam</u>]." <u>Atlantic</u>
   <u>Monthly</u>, 69 (February), 261, 262, 263-65.
       Harris and Page both treat the South, before and after
   the War, and the master-slave relationship. Page is the
   more brilliant and versatile writer, yet no other writer
   approaches Harris in his knowledge of the Negro. The "real"
   Negro appears in Mingo, Free Joe, and Balaam, and in the
   variety of other characters, Ananias, Mom Bi, and Duncan,
   in the remarkable <u>Balaam</u> collection. The latter story may
   be theatrical, but the illustration of mulatto character is
   bold, free, and true to the race. Harris's favorite Negro
   type is the patient, long-suffering, loyal, and melancholic
   character; his white characters are less successful. No

1892

one has pointed out the way the author of Uncle Remus at-
tractively but unconsciously introduces folk and fairy tale
elements into stories such as "A Conscript's Christmas" and
"Where's Duncan?"

2   ANON. "At the Circulating Library. Diary of a Reader [review
     note on A Plantation Printer]." London Bookman, 2 (April),
     28-29.
          Reviews English edition of Plantation. Uncle Remus
     makes a casual reappearance in A Plantation Printer; he is
     good company and ought to make the book a favorite. The
     young plantation printer himself is enough of an attraction,
     however.

3   ANON. "New Books and Reprints [review of A Plantation
     Printer]." London Saturday Review, 73 (2 April), 403.
          Reviews English edition of Plantation. Those, like this
     reader, who never tire of Uncle Remus and his stories will
     enjoy the account of Joe Maxwell's experiences during the
     War of Secession. Although Uncle Remus does not appear in
     person, his influence is present in the hunting stories,
     folk superstitions, and animal adventures.

4   ANON. "New Novels [review of A Plantation Printer]." The
     Academy, 41 (23 April), 394.
          Reviews English edition of Plantation. The book is not
     a romance. Contains a great deal of "tiresome Transatlantic
     slang and negro talk," but some of the incidents are inter-
     esting, such as the hunting and war episodes.

5   ANON. Review of Plantation. San Francisco Chronicle
     (24 April), p. 9.
          This autobiographical story includes animal fables, but
     it is also a tale of pathos. Such incidents as that of the
     slave's hunger when hiding in the swamp and the misery of
     the family of the poor white soldier "make slavery and the
     war real, yet at the same time bring no bitterness with the
     recollection."

6   ANON. "Bret Harte's and Other Tales [review of Plantation]."
     New York Times (1 May), p. 19.
          Informal plot summary of Plantation, which "must be a
     leaf taken from Mr. Chandler Harris's own early life." We
     do not meet Uncle Remus and Sis Tempy, but we do enjoy Har-
     bert, Aunt Crissy, and others. Harris's sympathy for the
     white and colored man comes from within, and "a truer
     friend of the negro does not exist."

1892

7   ANON. "Literature [review of Plantation]." Independent, 44
     (12 May), 664.
          Glad that Plantation is not fiction. The glimpse of
     slave life is like an instantaneous photograph, and the
     "side view" of Turner's plantation is worth the price of
     the volume.

8   ANON. Review of Plantation. Nashville Daily American
     (22 May), p. 4.
          The charm of this book lies in its "graphic and wonder-
     fully life-like sketches of the distant past" and in its
     Negro portraits.

9   ANON. "Novels and Short Stories [review of Plantation]."
     Book Buyer, 9 (June), 212.
          Plantation describes Joe Maxwell's experiences with
     humor and spirit; the most entertaining pages recount the
     "Uncle Remus" type of episodical legends, "to which the
     author's fine literary instinct and exquisite sense of
     humor give much value."

10   ANON. "Talk about Books [review of Plantation]." Chautauquan,
     15 (June), 387.
          The Negro's dialect and disposition add to the bright-
     ness, freshness, and radiance of Plantation.

11   ANON. "Books and Authors. Recent Books [review of
     Plantation]." Boston Daily Advertiser (5 July), p. 5.
          Nights has become a classic. Plantation is fascinating
     semi-autobiography that will add to Harris's reputation.

12   ANON. Review of Plantation. Critic, NS 18 (6 August), 65.
          Harris knows Georgia like a book, and Plantation is full
     of verisimilitude, tragedy, humor, and "rural human nature."
     Harris makes the old plantation, its atmosphere and local
     color, live again.

13   ANON. "Uncle Remus and His Friends." San Francisco Chronicle
     (11 December), p. 9.
          With the exception of Richard Malcolm Johnston, no one
     can paint Southern life like Harris. Friends is of "per-
     manent value," and Harris has been the only successful
     worker in this type of writing. Its humor will keep it
     fresh for many years.

14   ANON. "Mr. Harris's Uncle Remus Again. Uncle Remus and His
     Friends." New York Times (18 December), p. 19.

1892

Uncle Remus does not take on age; he only "ripens" in
Friends. Harris's dialect is always a delightful study in
the changes the Negro has brought to Anglo-Saxon. The
little boy is the steel that makes the fire fly from the
old man's flint.

15   ANON. "Children's Books [review of Friends]." Chicago
      Tribune (24 December), Part Two, p. 12.
          While none of the tales in Friends quite equals the best
      examples of the older collection, "the general average is
      good." Harris's pretense that his stories are not litera-
      ture is "wholly uncalled for."

16   ANON. "Minor Notices [review of Friends]." Boston Literary
      World, 23 (31 December), 498.
          The friends of Uncle Remus must number in the thousands;
      they will regret to hear that Friends will be Harris's
      last volume.

17   ANON. Review of Friends. Critic, NS 18 (31 December), 372.
          Friends is a vivid volume, full of "ruddy life." The
      first two-thirds of the book collects folklore, songs, and
      ballads, and the last delightfully realistic part sees
      Uncle Remus entangled in our newfangled civilization.

18   ATHERTON, GERTRUDE. "Geographical Fiction." Lippincott's,
      50 (July), 114.
          Local color fiction tells the world something it did not
      know before. Page, Harris, and Richard Malcolm Johnston
      have immortalized the Negro and "his complex method of
      working his brain and tongue." When the Negro has passed
      away and Page, Harris, and Johnston are "ornamenting ...
      the cabinet shelves of their proud descendants," the world
      will do these faithful chroniclers "the full measure of
      justice it denies them now."

19   C., J. N. Review of Friends. Atlanta Constitution
      (11 October), p. 9.
          Harris's new book, with illustrations by A. B. Frost,
      is the best of the series, and displays a greater variety
      of tales than previous books. The origin of his stories
      presents an interesting problem for the "student of mythol-
      ogy"; cites Asia, Europe, and Africa as possible sources.
      The Negroes must have interchanged stories with white
      children, the Negro adding details from his own setting.
      Lengthy quotation from Harris's introduction follows.

1892

20 CHRISTENSEN, [MRS.] A. M. H. "Preface," in her Afro-American
    Folk Lore: Told Round Cabin Fires on the Sea Islands of
    South Carolina. Boston: J. G. Cupples Company, pp. ix-xiv.
       Christensen had published a South Carolina version of
    the tar-baby story two or three years before the advent of
    Uncle Remus, "followed by several other similar tales"
    [dates unspecified] in the New York Independent. In her
    book she gathers "verbatim" other South Carolina Negro
    tales, some of which resemble the Georgia legends. "Br'er
    Rabbit," the major figure in Christensen's tales, "repre-
    sents the colored man" and by his cunning "he gains success.
    So the negro, without education or wealth, could only hope
    to succeed by stratagem." The tales are chiefly of interest
    to students of folklore. For, if we believe "that the tales
    of our nurseries are as important factors in forming the
    characters of our children as the theological dogmas of
    maturer years, we of the New South cannot wish our children
    to pore long over these pages, which certainly could not
    have been approved by Froebel." Reprint: 1969.B4.

21 HIGGINSON, THOMAS WENTWORTH. "The Local Short Story."
    Independent, 44 (3 November), 1545.
       Harris has made Uncle Remus immortal.

22 JACOBS, JOSEPH, ed. Indian Fairy Tales. New York: A. L.
    Burt Co., pp. 309-12.
       The Indian Játaka "The Demon with the Matted Hair" and
    the tar-baby story are so similar that they could not have
    been independently invented; the fact that the story has
    turned up in South Africa "clinches the matter," for this
    was the "landing place" for the tale as it was transmitted
    to the West, possibly by Buddhist missionaries. The five-
    fold attack by fists, feet, and head as a motif in both
    stories is the telling indicator. Other parallels between
    Buddhistic lore and Uncle Remus are the identification be-
    tween Buddha and the hare, the rabbit-in-the-moon motif,
    and the foot-worship associated with Buddha and the rabbit.

23 JOHNSTON, RICHARD MALCOLM. "Middle Georgia Rural Life."
    Century, 43 (March), 741.
       Harris did not foresee how much "the learned and thought-
    ful everywhere" would marvel at Uncle Remus. The old Negro
    storyteller was based on real relationships of tenderness
    and loyalty between the black slave and his master. Pathos
    is the chief excellence of Uncle Remus, and Harris's writ-
    ings show genius and art.

24 McCLURG, ALEXANDER C. "Old-Time Plantation Life." <u>Dial</u>, 13
(June), 46–49.
    Review-essay of <u>Plantation</u> stresses Harris's exact use
of dialect, direct and attractive style, faithful portraiture of the Negro (who "today" has lost the best traits
shown here), and use of realism and philosophy in telling
his largely autobiographical tale. Reconstructs the plot,
using frequent quotations. Observes that many worthless
books bewilder today's reader, while genuine and wholesome
books like this are neglected.

25 RILEY, JAMES WHITCOMB. "Dialect in Literature." <u>Forum</u>, 14
(December), 444, 470–71.
    Writes in support of dialect in literature. Praises
Harris's reverential touch in portraying the slave.
Through his stories we glorify the weak, revel in their
victories, and see that right and law reside in even the
"barbaric breasts." Harris is equally successful in de-
scribing the moonshiners in "At Teague Poteet's."

26 WELLS, DAVID DWIGHT. "Evolution in Folk Lore." <u>Popular
Science Monthly</u>, 41 (May), 45–54.
    Compares Harris's "The Little Boy and His Dogs," pub-
lished in 1886, with "The Story of the Hunter," a folktale
in circulation in British Guiana, South America, in 1810.
The source for both stories is an African tale, but the
Southeastern United States version contains elements ger-
mane to the slave society that differ from elements in the
Guiana version.

<u>1893 A BOOKS – NONE</u>

<u>1893 B SHORTER WRITINGS</u>

1 ANON. Review of <u>Friends</u>. <u>Book Buyer</u>, 9 (January), 680.
    The sketches in <u>Friends</u> are "uproariously amusing; and
they all have a fine and high literary quality." Mentions
that Harris plans to discontinue the Remus tales and hopes
he will relent. A. B. Frost's pictures illustrate the
spirit of the tales themselves.

2 ANON. Review of <u>Friends</u>. New Orleans <u>Daily Picayune</u>
(8 January), p. 10.
    Hopefully, Uncle Remus does not bid the reader a perman-
ent farewell in this delightful volume. Despite Harris's
apologies that his work is not "'literature,'" it is in
fact literature "of a very high grade" and will outlive
more "pretentious stuff."

1893

3   ANON. Review of Friends. Atlantic Monthly, 71 (February),
    277.
    Although Harris proposes to shuffle Uncle Remus off
    after Friends, the reviewer does not believe in the old
    darky's disappearance. The songs and ballads in this enter-
    taining volume "especially reproduce remarkably the musical
    childishness of the race."

4   ANON. Review of Friends. Dial, 14 (16 March), 186.
    One hopes that, counter to what the introduction states,
    Friends is not Harris's last volume of such sympathetic and
    intelligent tales.

5   ANON. Review of Friends. Athenaeum, no. 3421 (20 May),
    p. 634.
    The reviewer is sorry to see Uncle Remus bid the public
    adieu, as these tales are as delightful as those in the
    last book [Nights]. Harris is unduly modest in saying his
    stories are not "'literature'": they are more worthwhile
    than many called by that name.

6   ANON. "American Short Stories." Brooklyn Daily Eagle
    (16 July), p. 4.
    "Aunt Fountain's Prisoner" [in Scribner's Stories of the
    South (1893)] is a delightful mix of the "easy, lazy but
    proud and aristocratic hospitality" of the South with the
    "practical sense and business aptitude of the North."
    Harris can always be depended upon for "honest, straight-
    forward and skillful" storytelling.

7   ANON. Review of Stories of the South. New Orleans Daily
    Picayune (16 July), [p. 19].
    Review note of a Scribner's collection of tales contain-
    ing "Aunt Fountain's Prisoner" and stories by Page, R. H.
    Davis, and Harrison Robertson. All the stories are "good."

8   ANON. "Stories of the South." Richmond Dispatch (23 July),
    p. 4.
    Scribner's volume contains stories by Page, Harris,
    Harrison Robertson, and Rebecca Harding David. "Aunt
    Fountain's Prisoner" is excellent and is better than Page's
    "No Haid Pawn." "We quarrel only with the manifest catering
    to the northern public and publisher, though [Harris] is not
    alone in this sin."

9   ANON. Review of Evening Tales. Atlanta Constitution
    (16 November), p. 4.

Evening Tales is a "delightful" book. Quotes an undated review in the Boston *Advertiser* that praises the volume's charm; the book is "'done into English--not translated'" and it is thus "'vastly better than any mere translation could possibly be.'"

10   ANON. Review of *Evening Tales*. Brooklyn *Daily Eagle* (19 November), p. 4.
     These tales are almost as delightful to children as the Uncle Remus stories.

11   ANON. "Some Delightful Fairy Tales. *Evening Tales*." *New York Times* (26 November), p. 23.
     There is a great deal of the author of *Uncle Remus* in *Evening Tales*. Harris's translation of Ortoli's tales also reminds one of the simplicity, imaginative wealth, and seemingly unconscious humor of Hans Christian Andersen.

12   ANON. Review of *Evening Tales*. *Book Buyer*, 10 (December), 560-61.
     Readers of all ages will enjoy *Evening Tales*, Harris's translation of Frédéric Ortoli's charming stories.

13   ANON. Review of *Evening Tales*. Nashville *Daily American* (17 December), p. 11.
     An entertaining book for all ages, done in Uncle Remus's style although of a different origin this time.

14   ANON. Review of *Evening Tales*. Richmond *Dispatch* (17 December), p. 11.
     Evening Tales is "fascinating reading" and carries the double recommendation of Harris and Ortoli.

15   ANON. Review of *Evening Tales*. San Francisco *Chronicle* (17 December), p. 9.
     Ortoli's French tales bear a striking resemblance to Uncle Remus's and were known in France before Harris collected his stories. Harris's translation will again suggest to the folklorist the common origin of animal tales.

16   BASKERVILL, W.[ILLIAM] M.[ALONE]. "Joel Chandler Harris." Nashville *Daily American* (27 July), p. 3.
     Harris is the pride and delight of the Atlanta *Constitution*. He looks at life with the eye of the realist and the heart of a poet, but he is extremely modest and hard-working. He writes exactly two editorials a day, but his serious business is to advocate the bi-metal standard of coinage and the principles of Thomas Jefferson. He likes

1893

Dumas, Shakespeare, and the Bible, especially Job and
Ecclesiastes.

17 BERGEN, FANNY D. "Uncle Remus and Folk-Lore." Outlook, 48
    (2 September), 427-28.
        While perhaps less genuine and valuable than Uncle Remus
    and Nights, Friends is still an interesting contribution to
    folklore. The original Negro slaves helped to lighten
    their burden of bondage by telling stories, and a Louisiana
    Negro once told Bergen that the rabbit is the black man's
    folk hero because, unlike the fox, he does not try to over-
    reach himself. Parallels between Harris's stories and
    European, Gaelic, and African legends are cited.

18 CRAIG, NEWTON. Review of Evening Tales. Atlanta Constitution
    (26 November), p. 22.
        Harris has "faithfully endeavored to give the spirit and
    individuality of the original" in translating Ortoli's
    Evening Tales. Among the stories are tales reminiscent of
    Uncle Remus.

19 GERBER, A[DOLF]. "Uncle Remus Traced to the Old World." JAF,
    6 (October-December), 245-57.
        Operating under the premise that the more complex the
    parallels between folktales the more likely they were dis-
    seminated from a common source, Gerber systematically cata-
    logues the Old World origins of the stories in Uncle Remus
    and Nights. The vast majority of the Remus tales have
    close counterparts in African folklore, Modern European
    stories, and medieval animal epics and fables; American
    Negroes brought the African tales with them and learned the
    European and medieval stories from white children and
    mothers. Gerber found no parallels in the Old World for
    twelve tales from Nights and one from Uncle Remus.

20 HABBERTON, JOHN. "All the Books [review of Friends]."
    Godey's, 126 (February), 234.
        It is high time for a new book by "Unc' Remus"; in
    Friends the old man is the same as ever, and thousands of
    children will be made merry by his collection of funny
    tales. The little boy seems as important to Remus as Bos-
    well was to Johnson, and scores of writers will wish that
    they could have the honor which Harris will, hopefully, se-
    cure in the distant future, when some tourist will scrawl
    on his tombstone: "'Author of Uncle Remus.'"

21 MABIE, HAMILTON W. "The Most Popular Novels in America."
    Forum, 16 (December), 516.

1894

A survey of the fiction called for most frequently in
all the important American libraries reveals some contradictions. Some of the most popular names in native fiction
are omitted: Cable, James, Page, Harris, Garland, Jewett,
Murfree, Wilkins, and others.

22 REED, WALLACE PUTNAM. "'Uncle Remus' As He Is." Atlanta
    Constitution (9 April), p. 9.
        Following a semi-dramatized biographical sketch, Harris's
    fellow editor on the Constitution recounts some interviews
    with Harris about how he came to write the Remus tales.
    Remus was a "composite plantation darky." After his work
    day at the Constitution, Harris had time, at home in the
    evenings, to write 500 words or so, with a pencil and usual-
    ly with the family around him. His favorite books include
    the Bible, Shakespeare, The Vicar of Wakefield, which his
    mother had exposed him to, The Portrait of a Lady, Monte
    Cristo, and others. Harris is sociable among friends but,
    constitutionally, he is "painfully modest, retiring, shy
    to the last extreme."

1894 A BOOKS - NONE

1894 B SHORTER WRITINGS

1   ANON. "Translations [review of Evening Tales]." Athenaeum,
    no. 3465 (24 March), p. 376.
        The reviewer confesses an ignorance about Frédéric
    Ortoli's writings, and finds a lack of background data in
    Evening Tales. The translated stories vary in entertain-
    ment power, but on the whole the tales "are decidedly good
    and interesting." The majority are beast-fables and
    Arabian Nights types of tales. "We are afraid the profane
    Briton will chuckle over 'The Rooster, the Cat, and the
    Reap-hook,' in which the discreet word we have italicized
    recurs with a frequency altogether destructive of gravity.
    But America must, we suppose, be allowed to speak American."

2   ANON. "In the Library. Joel Chandler Harris." Christian
    Work, 57 (September), 508.
        Though a Southerner, Harris shares none of the common
    Southern prejudices and prefers to call himself an American.
    Probably no living man is more diffident, "but his diffi-
    dence is the result of excessive sympathy and tenderness."
    He is devoted to his family and lives quietly and content-
    edly in an unassuming house.

1894

3 ANON. "Children's Books [review of Mr. Thimblefinger]."
   Nation, 59 (13 December), 448.
      In Mr. Thimblefinger the little boy is replaced by
   Sweetest Susan, Buster John, and Drusilla, and, despite the
   loss of the dialect flavor, some of the tales are very
   droll. Harris's fairy stories do not suffer when compared
   with the author of Alice, and Oliver Herford's illustrations
   are among the best that Harris has yet inspired.

4 CRAIG, NEWTON. Review of Mr. Thimblefinger. Atlanta
   Constitution (16 December), p. 2.
      Harris introduces some English folktales, as well as a
   few of pure invention, in Mr. Thimblefinger. Had Harris
   lived before the dawn of history, he would have assisted
   the fathers of cosmogony. Yet he is happily not a comparative mythologist, preferring the good will of the nursery
   for the theories of philosophers.

5 EGGLESTON, EDWARD. "Folk-Speech in America." Scribner's
   Monthly, NS 26 (October), 875.
      Harris writes "Brer Rabbit," but he and other Georgians,
   white or black, would pronounce it "Bruh Rabbit." The Vir-
   ginian and the Georgian "regard a final r only as a modifier
   of the vowel."

6 GARLAND, HAMLIN. Crumbling Idols. Chicago and Cambridge:
   Stone and Kimball, pp. 33, 95, and 150-51.
      "[E]very novelist who has risen distinctly out of the
   mass of story-writers in America, represents some special
   social phase," and Harris represents the new study of the
   Negro. Includes Harris and R. M. Johnston as two of the
   leading magazine-writers for the last ten years. New York
   should not assume supremacy in the arts; "the writers and
   painters who make her [New York] illustrious are very
   largely products of the South and West." Also comments
   that Harris is writing a drama of the South.

7 MOORE, RUBY ANDREWS. "Superstitions from Georgia. II." JAF,
   7 (October-December), 306.
      When this author was a child she was told most of the
   Uncle Remus fables by her grandfather's slaves, many of
   whom had been brought to Georgia in 1858 from the Galla dis-
   trict in the African Congo. We should not be overly puzzled
   by the currency of African, Asian, Indian, and Ceylanese
   folklore in America; immigrants and refugees have only
   interchanged their legends.

1895

8   RUTHERFORD, MILDRED. American Authors: A Hand-Book of
    American Literature from Early Colonial to Living Writers.
    Atlanta, GA: The Franklin Printing and Publishing Co.,
    pp. 610-14.
        Describes Harris's early interest in literature and folk
    stories. His reputation rests on the delineation of Negro
    dialect in Uncle Remus; Mingo is true to life but not equal
    in merit. Remus represents a large class of Southern
    Negroes and Harris presents truthful memories of the South.
    Quotes comments by Dr. Chaney [see 1888.B20] on the possible
    bad effects of the Remus stories on children. Harris is
    frank, outspoken, and cheerful. Quotes him on the "dialect
    story" and also gives examples of Remus's philosophizing.
    Reprinted: 1907.B11.

9   WHITCOMB, SELDEN L. Chronological Outlines of American
    Literature. New York and London: Macmillan, pp. 200 ff.
        Lists seven Harris volumes in his chronology.

1895 A BOOKS - NONE

1895 B SHORTER WRITINGS

1   ANON. "Books for Younger Readers [review of Mr. Thimble-
    finger]." Book Buyer, 11 (January), 752.
        Oliver Herford's illustrations for Mr. Thimblefinger
    put him on a level with the best American artists in
    cleverness and imagination. The book is "altogether
    delightful."

2   ANON. Review of Mr. Thimblefinger. Athenaeum, no. 3512
    (16 February), p. 214.
        Mr. Thimblefinger is a disappointment. Harris loses the
    effects of illusion and mystery by portraying a rabbit as
    large as a man sitting in a chair and grumbling about sup-
    per. Also, the adventures of the children are mildly imi-
    tative of Lewis Carroll's books. The illustrations make
    it worth buying the book, however.

3   ANON. "The Lounger." Critic, NS 24 (7 September), 155.
        The forthcoming edition of Uncle Remus illustrated by
    A. B. Frost should be a happy combination for both artist
    and author. This writer reviewed Uncle Remus fifteen years
    ago for the Springfield Republican and "gushed" over it.
    "I wish that some one could spring upon us again such a
    surprise as these stories were. It would add much to the
    gaiety of nations, weighted down with the sex question in
    modern fiction."

1895

4 ANON. "Mr. Frost's Edition of 'Uncle Remus.'" New York Times
(16 October), p. 16.
The 1895 edition of Uncle Remus is even more valuable
than its predecessor, since more time separates the present
day from the dialect and character type Harris so accurately
and profoundly records. As Uncle Remus himself observed,
the "educated twig" of the old parent stalk is a different
breed of Negro. Harris perfectly renders that "fundamental
element" in the Negro character, vanity, and also marvel-
lously displays the other attributes of the race: "its
credulity, its active fancy, its imitative instinct, and...
pride of family, loyalty, and a cunning humor." Frost's
pictures "breathe the very spirit of the text."

5 ANON. Review of Mr. Rabbit at Home. Boston Evening
Transcript (26 October), p. 7.
Mr. Thimblefinger was one of last season's most popular
books; its sequel, Mr. Rabbit at Home, will delight juvenile
audiences.

6 ANON. "Talk about Books [review of Uncle Remus]."
Chautauquan, 22 (November), 256.
The inimitable humor and rollicking imagination of both
author Harris and illustrator Frost are too well-known to
need further comment; welcomes the 1895 edition of the
classic Uncle Remus.

7 ANON. "Frost's 'Uncle Remus' Drawings." New York Times
(13 November), p. 4.
A display of a hundred-odd pen-and-ink and wash drawings
that Arthur Frost made for the new edition of Uncle Remus
will be shown until 21 November at the Frederick Keppel
gallery. Harris's classic Negro folktale breathes "the
very essence and spirit of the Southern darky." Frost's
drawings infuse humanity into Harris's animals and perhaps
more excellently delineate Negro character than has been
done in any of Frost's previously celebrated work.

8 ANON. "Mr. Rabbit Again [review of Mr. Rabbit at Home]."
New York Times (16 November), p. 3.
Harris's perfect portrait of Drusilla may be worth "the
price of admission" to Mr. Thimblefinger's queer country,
but the stories have not the ease or the originality of the
earlier books; one is reminded of Hans Christian Andersen,
the brothers Grimm, and Jean Macé in many of the tales.
Part of the problem may be that we are not as convinced of
the reality of these tales as we were of the reality of the
Uncle Remus animal tales.

1895

9   ANON. "Mr. Harris's Masterpiece [review of Uncle Remus and
    Mr. Rabbit at Home]." Critic, NS 24 (23 November), 343.
    A. B. Frost's drawings for the 1895 Uncle Remus are
    among the cleverest things he has done. At some points
    they fall below those of Church in the first edition, but
    Frost harmonizes the animals well and no two figures are
    alike. The stories in Mr. Rabbit at Home have a totally
    distinct flavor from those of Uncle Remus, and the interest
    in the book centers on the listeners.

10 ANON. "Mr. Rabbit at Home." Chicago Evening Post
    (30 November), p. 9.
    Nobody approaches Harris in the field of children's
    books. Children were eager for a sequel to Mr. Thimble-
    finger and now they have it in Mr. Rabbit at Home.

11 ANON. "Uncle Remus." Overland Monthly, Second Series 26
    (December), 675-76.
    Mentions the popularity of the "quaint, delightful, dear"
    Uncle Remus volume and praises Frost's illustrations in the
    1895 edition as original, humorous, and sympathetic.

12 ANON. "The Holiday Books [review of Uncle Remus]." Outlook,
    52 (7 December), 959.
    No one has so accurately portrayed the pleasant days be-
    fore the War or the old plantation darky as has Harris in
    Uncle Remus. A. B. Frost's illustrations for the 1895 edi-
    tion are his best work.

13 ANON. Review of Uncle Remus. San Francisco Chronicle
    (14 December), p. 11.
    Review of 1895 edition stresses Frost's genial and at-
    tractive drawings in "this most popular collection of the
    folk tales of the Southern plantation negro."

14 BEERS, HENRY A. Studies in American Letters. Philadelphia:
    George W. Jacobs & Co., p. 212.
    Revised edition of 1887.B4 and 1891.B14. Harris com-
    mentary the same as 1891 edition.

15 BLAIR, ALICE. "The Tar Baby." Pacific Educational Journal,
    11 (December), 561-65.   ◊
    Suggests pedagogical and multi-media applications of
    Harris's writings. A Santa Rosa, California, teacher de-
    scribes how her primary school pupils are taught reading,
    language forms, and plot study by first reading and dis-
    cussing the tar-baby tale, and by later reproducing it in
    oral, written, and pictorial form.

1895

16 EGAN, LAVINIA H. "The Future of the Negro in Fiction." <u>Dial</u>,
    18 (1 February), 70.
        For fifty years the Negro has occupied a prominent place
    in American song (chiefly in Stephen Foster's works) and
    story (in the works of Stowe, but mainly in those of Page
    and Harris). "Uncle Remus" has become a household word,
    and Harris and Page have struck the keynote of the Negro's
    artistic value. The next decade must surely show the last
    of the revered old-time darky; the black "'dude'" with his
    cane and eyeglass will only furnish material for the carica-
    turist, and future storytellers will have a hard time keep-
    ing the Negro up to his present valuation among readers.

17 ELLIS, A. B. "Evolution in Folklore. Some West African
    Prototypes of the 'Uncle Remus' Stories." <u>Popular Science
    Monthly</u>, 48 (November), 93–104.
        Discusses the role of the spider in Gold Coast stories
    as an antecedent for Brer Rabbit and the Slave Coast tor-
    toise as a prototype for the Remus terrapin. Reprints Gold
    Coast variants of the tar-baby story and other tales.

18 GRISWOLD, W. M. <u>A Descriptive List of Novels and Tales
    Dealing with History of North America</u>. Cambridge, MA:
    W. M. Griswold, Publisher, p. 182.
        Critique is extracted from the <u>Examiner</u>, number unidenti-
    fied. <u>Plantation</u> is a valuable, though modest, contribution
    to the history of the Civil War on the eve of the catas-
    trophe. Like <u>Daddy Jake</u>, it is a good anti-slavery tract
    and does credit to Harris's humanity; Remus's humor is
    "robbed of its contagiousness," however, when Harris as
    narrator refuses to embellish his own funny experiences.

19 _____. <u>A Descriptiv [sic] List of Books for the Young</u>.
    Cambridge, MA: W. M. Griswold, Publisher, p. 114.
        Critique identical to that for 1895.B18.

20 LEACH, ANNA. "Literary Workers of the South." <u>Munsey's
    Magazine</u>, 13 (April), 64.
        Reviews the Southern writers following the War. Speaks
    of the universal popularity of the Remus stories, and men-
    tions Johnston and Harris as the best known humorists in
    the South today.

21 PAGE, THOMAS NELSON. "Immortal Uncle Remus." <u>Book Buyer</u>, 12
    (December), 642–45.
        Reviews the 1895 edition of <u>Uncle Remus</u>. Summarizes the
    characteristic reaction of Harris's reading public to the
    first Remus volume--the delight that so many Southerners felt

in recognizing stories they had once heard, the book's
folkloric value and authentic dialect, and the contribution
to Negro history that it represented. But the humor,
philosophy, and "unadulterated human nature" of his book
was Harris's most important contribution. Uncle Remus
possesses a "fidelity to life" and "simplicity of recital"
that marks it as a work of genius. Brer Fox, Brer Rabbit,
and Uncle Remus are now immortal characters who have already
been cited as illustrations in a House of Commons debate.
"No man who has ever written has known one-tenth part about
the negro that Mr. Harris knows."

22 SOUTHERN HISTORICAL ASSOCIATION. Memoirs of Georgia. Vol. 1.
Atlanta, GA: The Southern Historical Association,
pp. 808-809.
Provides a brief biographical sketch and identifies
Harris as a leading editorial writer for the Constitution.
Refers to his popularity here and in England. In his prime
and successful in his "modest ambitions," he takes an active
interest in politics though he is noted for his love of
family and friends. He easily turns routine editorial work
to literature.

23 STARNES, VAL. "Southern Dialect." Century, 50 (May), 154.
Comments in an open letter on the proliferation of short
stories featuring Southern rural and Negro dialect. The
dialect is often humorous, but writers mistakenly think
they have displayed it with "the dash and precision of a
Harris or a Cable."

24 WYLIE, LOLLIE BELLE. "Literary Atlanta." Midland Monthly, 3
(March), 231-32.
Atlanta's literary growth since the Civil War is as phe-
nomenal as her physical and commercial progress. Harris
was the first Atlanta writer to win substantial recognition
from the North. His Negro dialect stories have attracted
world-wide attention, but success has not affected his
modesty. "Many believe it remains with Joel Chandler Harris
to write the great American novel. He has material on hand
for a book of fiction, and if it fails to become the brightest, clearest star in the firmament of romance, it will at
least be thoroughly charming."

1896 A BOOKS

1 BASKERVILL, WILLIAM MALONE. Southern Writers. Biographical
and Critical Studies. Joel Chandler Harris. Nashville:
Barbee & Smith, 48pp.

45

1896

Of the several original humorists that Middle Georgia
has produced, Harris is the most important and endearing
figure. His "Ethiopian Aesop," Uncle Remus, and the in-
quisitive little boy constitute the most permanent contribution to American literature in the last twenty-five years,
and Harris will always be celebrated for his authentic delineation of dialect, folklore, pathos, and human sympathy.
Along with Remus in his various moods and settings, Blue
Dave, Mingo, Daddy Jake, Balaam, and Free Joe admirably
represent the several phases of Negro character that Harris
observed so carefully; Harris's universal power as an artist, and his desire to overcome mere sectionalism, are
also strongly in evidence in stories such as "At Teague
Poteet's" and "Trouble on Lost Mountain." Reprinted:
1897.B35.

1896 B SHORTER WRITINGS

1   ADAMSON, ROBERT. "Mr. Harris in New Fields: Ventures Out in
    a New Book. 'Sister Jane' Is a Strong Story of Georgia
    Life, in Which Delicate Problems Are Masterfully Handled."
    Atlanta Constitution (6 December), p. 27.
        Review article praises the beauty, simplicity, power,
    and moral truth of Sister Jane. In comparison to works by
    [unnamed] "superficial" or "unhealthy" authors, Harris is
    one of the few "earnest" writers of the period. The novel
    is unpretentious in treating simple Georgia life, yet, as
    a study of sin and repentance, it teaches universal lessons.
    William Wornum, Jane, Mandy, and Jincy Meadows are analyzed
    and the plot of the novel recounted. Harris's book is a
    "radical departure" from his old lines, but it will last;
    it is one of the best works of the decade.

2   ALLEN, JAMES LANE. "The Gentleman in American Fiction."
    New York Bookman, 4 (October), 120.
        Except for Holmes's Autocrat, American literature has
    yet to produce an enduring American gentleman character but
    prefers lower types of figures. It is ridiculous and morti-
    fying that the only two characters that have achieved uni-
    versal acceptance are the two Negroes, Uncle Tom and Uncle
    Remus.

3   ANON. Review of Sister Jane. New Orleans Daily Picayune
    (17 January), p. 11.
        Although Harris says he is not wholly satisfied with
    this book and had even tried to recall it, it is being well
    received by critics and the public. The novel gives a

46

1896

"realistic sketch of a typical southern phase of life,"
and the slavery question is happily absent. This book renders for the antebellum white the service Harris previously
rendered for the antebellum Negro.

4   ANON. "Notes of Some New Books for Younger Readers [review
    of Mr. Rabbit at Home]." Book Buyer, 13 (February), 31.
        Mr. Rabbit at Home, a continuation of Mr. Thimblefinger,
    is told with Harris's "inimitable spirit and ingenuity."
    Every child who does not read these books "misses two very
    delightful excursions into fairyland."

5   ANON. "Our Literary Table [review of Mr. Rabbit at Home]."
    Athenaeum, no. 3563 (8 February), p. 182.
        Mr. Rabbit at Home is full of lively nonsense and is
    free from allegory. It should be a good book for children.

6   ANON. "The Lounger." Critic, NS 25 (14 March), 186.
        We are glad to read in J. H. Garnsey's sketch of Harris
    in Book Buyer [see 1896.B46] that Harris's modesty prevents
    his accepting·"the greatest position on earth." This means
    both an easier time for him, and more of his "inimitable"
    stories for us.

7   ANON. Review of "A Baby in the Siege." San Francisco
    Chronicle (22 March), p. 4.
        Harris writes few stories for the magazines. This story
    in the April Scribner's [collected in Home Folks] will
    please all with its dramatic power.

8   ANON. "American Historical Fiction [review of Uncle Remus]."
    Boston Literary World, 27 (27 June), 203.
        The fun, dialect, and allegory of Uncle Remus (1880) are
    so well known that the reader will rejoice in the new 1895
    edition, with illustrations by Frost. It is interesting to
    note that the Negro songs depend for melody upon time meas-
    urement rather than upon accented or unaccented syllables.

9   ANON. "The Rambler." Book Buyer, 13 (July), 343-44.
        Harris has recently visited Chicago to see his eldest
    son, a member of the staff of the Times-Herald. He told a
    friend he has been busy since the first of April, writing
    three short stories and a longer one that is "a decided de-
    parture from tales of mountains, negroes, or war." Harris
    loves the quiet life and did not like Chicago because there
    were too many people there.

1896

10   ANON. Review of <u>Aaron</u> and <u>Sister Jane</u>. New York <u>Daily</u>
     <u>Tribune</u> (27 September), Part 3, p. 2.
          <u>Aaron</u> is a book of "pure Harris" in the pattern of <u>Mr.</u>
     <u>Thimblefinger</u> and <u>Mr. Rabbit at Home</u>. Criticism will ap-
     proach <u>Sister Jane</u> on tiptoe, however, because Harris has
     never been heard of as a novelist and one wonders if "the
     Uncle Remus" of his writing will "be there."

11   ANON. Review of <u>Daddy Jake</u>. New York <u>Sun</u> (3 October), p. 7.
          <u>Daddy Jake</u> will be welcomed by little people and every-
     one else who has a sense of humor. The whole volume is
     worthy of the author.

12   ANON. Review of <u>Sister Jane</u>. <u>New York Times Literary and Art</u>
     <u>Supplement</u> (17 October), p. 2.
          <u>Sister Jane</u>, which will be published this month, must be
     based on a close relation of Uncle Remus's. Harris should
     not only be remembered for his folklore but also for his
     great naturalness and constructive powers.

13   ANON. "Uncle Remus Abroad: His Dialect Amused and Deceived
     the English Professor." New York <u>Daily Tribune</u>
     (18 October), Part 3, p. 8.
          Reprinted from undated issue of the Chicago <u>Times-Herald</u>.
     Humorous sketch about how Harris and his friend Ed Hammond
     fooled a Canadian literature professor, in Ottawa, by
     responding to his questions in Negro and cracker dialect.
     "'Do the British and Canadian peculiarities of speech
     bother you?'" Harris was asked. "'Yas, suh,' replied
     Harris. 'Comin' as we uns do from a section whar even the
     po'rest speak pewah English the talk of these people sounds
     pow'ful funny, but I expose hit can't be helped.'" [<u>See</u>
     <u>also</u> 1896.B17.]

14   ANON. "'Uncle Remus' Again." Chicago <u>Evening Post</u>
     (24 October), p. 5.
          Harris's stories never grow stale. The new edition of
     <u>Daddy Jake</u> is as interesting as it was the first time.
     <u>Aaron</u> is a different tale from the type Uncle Remus spins
     but is no less enjoyable.

15   ANON. "Uncle Remus and Mr. Kipling." <u>New York Times Saturday</u>
     <u>Review of Books and Art</u> (24 October), p. 4.
          <u>Daddy Jake</u> is published as a companion-piece to the
     Jungle Books, but a comparison reveals more differences than
     similarities in Harris's and Kipling's portraits of animals.
     Both see animals anthropomorphically, but Kipling dwells on
     the nobility of beasts whereas Harris reveals their crafty

wiles. Harris's title story may be considered a classic
when that "simple, curious people shall either have devel-
oped or died out." The folklorists should be no more grateful to Harris than the rest of us. Kipling has strong
talent, but Harris "has behind him the genius of an entire
race"; by "that much is his book richer than that of any
single writer."

16 ANON. Review of Stories of Georgia. Atlanta Constitution
    (1 November), p. 5.
    Stories of Georgia is a "coherent and absorbing story"
    of Georgia's history; its color and vitality make it more
    than a conventional history. Among other strong character-
    izations, Harris gives fresh insight into James Oglethorpe.

17 ANON. "Uncle Remus Abroad." Atlanta Constitution (1 November),
    p. 5.
    Reprints undated humorous account from the Chicago Times-
    Herald of Harris's practical joking with a British professor
    in Canada. [See also 1896.B13.]

18 ANON. Review of Daddy Jake and Aaron. Nation, 63 (5 November),
    353.
    A new edition of Daddy Jake appears coincidentally with
    the first edition of Aaron; one hopes for more editions of
    Aaron in the future. The art of Daddy Jake was admirable,
    but its mechanism all terrestrial. Aaron is neither as
    dramatic nor as pathetic as Daddy Jake, though its skill
    and supernatural element may make it the more attractive
    book. Harris displays several aspects of slavery inciden-
    tally: the slave coffle, the auction, the oppression of
    small proprietors by large slave-owners, and lynch law,
    "along with the passion of the Southern temperament and its
    instinctive resort to the shot gun whether for good or evil
    purposes."

19 ANON. Review of Aaron. New Orleans Daily Picayune
    (16 November), p. 6.
    Uncle Remus is probably the only character in American
    fiction to meet with worldwide recognition; Uncle Tom is
    his only rival. Harris departs from his usual round and
    gives us something different yet of "singular interest" in
    the story of Aaron.

20 ANON. Review of Aaron. Critic, NS 26 (21 November), 326-27.
    Brief plot summary. Oliver Herford's drawings are
    skillful and humorous.

1896

21 ANON. Review of Daddy Jake. Critic, NS 26 (28 November), 343.
    Harris's book has been issued by the Century Company as
    a companion volume to Kipling's Jungle Books. It will be
    interesting to watch the effect this experiment has on
    young readers.

22 ANON. Review of Daddy Jake. Chicago Tribune (29 November),
    p. 43.
    "Daddy Jake, The Runaway" is one of Harris's best
    s.tories; the book of the same title is out in a new edition.
    Uncle Remus knows the "master words" of the beasts in his
    domain, and it is appropriate that the volume is issued as
    a companion to Kipling's Jungle Books.

23 ANON. "Chronicle and Comment." New York Bookman, 4
    (December), 289-90.
    James Lane Allen recently observed [see 1896.B2] that
    Uncle Remus and Uncle Tom were the only two names in Ameri-
    can fiction that have attained near-universality of accep-
    tance. The enviable Harris lives a life of simplicity,
    serenity, and peace and has declined numerous offers of
    eminent positions. Like the author of Lorna Doone, Harris's
    greatest passion is not the literary passion but rather
    tending what is said to be the finest rose garden in At-
    lanta. His stories have endeared him to thousands of
    readers all over the world.

24 ANON. Review of Aaron. Chautauquan, 24 (December), 379.
    Harris again takes us into the pleasant land of Middle
    Georgia in Aaron and treats us to wonderful people and ani-
    mals. The superstition of the Negro and the devotion of
    the slave are skillfully brought out in this typographically
    artful edition.

25 ANON. Review of Daddy Jake. Chautauquan, 24 (December), 383.
    A new edition of Daddy Jake has appeared. "These re-
    markable collections of folk-lore cannot appear too often
    for those who enjoy and appreciate the new southern litera-
    ture."

26 ANON. "Short Stories by Uncle Remus." Overland Monthly,
    Second Series 28 (December), 718.
    Finds the new edition of Daddy Jake appropriately paired
    with Jungle Books, although there are differences as well
    as similarities between the two authors. Uncle Remus knows
    the "master words of the beasts in his domain." Praises
    Kemble's illustrations.

27 ANON. "Among the New Books. Brander Matthews on Phases of Modern Authorship." Chicago Tribune (2 December), p. 3. Review of Matthews's Aspects of Fiction (New York: Harper's, 1896) mentions that Harris's Sister Jane would have been an impossible book to write before the War, when slavery was held sacred. Now Page and Harris, Southern storytellers of "the first rank," are speaking the truth about the South.

28 ANON. Review of Aaron. London Saturday Review, 82 (5 December), 598.
Aaron has little in common with Uncle Remus; for the most part there is more serious business at hand. The tale is stirring and some of the effects remind one of Kipling's Jungle Book.

29 ANON. "Uncle Remus's White Sister." Chicago Tribune (5 December), Part 2, [p. 10].
Sister Jane is a quiet, homely, delightful book about Southern life. All the characters are commendable in this "sparkling" novel. It will raise Harris's reputation even higher.

30 ANON. "The Century Company's List [notice of Daddy Jake]." New York Times Saturday Review of Books and Art (12 December), p. 14.
Guide to publishers' offerings. Daddy Jake has already established itself as a favorite.

31 ANON. "Current Fiction [review of Daddy Jake]." Boston Literary World, 27 (12 December), 456.
Daddy Jake reintroduces some delightful old animal friends and adds a few new acquaintances. Hopefully "The Foolish Woman" is an invention of Harris's; she has no parallel in nature. The volume also contains nuggets of humorous wisdom.

32 ANON. "Houghton, Mifflin Co.'s Choice Books [notice of Aaron]." New York Times Saturday Review of Books and Art (12 December), p. 11.
Guide to publishers' offerings. Briefly summarizes Aaron, mentioning the "wonderful" tales it includes.

33 ANON. "Joel Chandler Harris." Chicago Tribune (12 December), p. 14.
The graceful picture of Southern life in Sister Jane but accentuates the fame of "Uncle Remus." Cites James Lane Allen's statement [see 1896.B2] that Uncle Remus and Uncle

1896

Tom are the only two names in American fiction that have
gained anything like universal acceptance. Also prints a
passage from the December Bookman [see 1896.B23] praising
Harris.

34   ANON. Review of Sister Jane. San Francisco Chronicle
     (13 December), p. 4.
     Harris's "close and loving study" of certain types of
     Southern character reminds one of Stowe's New England
     sketches and is as good as his Uncle Remus tales. Sister
     Jane is as fine a character as is found in recent fiction,
     and the climax of the novel comes "naturally and effective-
     ly."

35   ANON. Review of Daddy Jake. Brooklyn Daily Eagle
     (14 December), p. 11.
     The most touching part of the story of Daddy Jake is the
     account of Crazy Sue; the greatest charm of the whole
     volume is when Uncle Remus resumes his storytelling.

36   ANON. Review of Daddy Jake and Aaron. New York Daily Tribune
     (16 December), p. 8.
     Harris is "every inch himself" in Daddy Jake, but the
     speech of the animals and the "forced" nature of the book
     make one less sure about the merit of Aaron.

37   ANON. Review of Sister Jane. New York Daily Tribune
     (20 December), Part 3, p. 2.
     Sister Jane "is a dull book, and it is a pity that Mr.
     Harris should have published it." Sister Jane's aphorisms
     seem manufactured, William Wornum is too maudlin, and other
     "pale, soulless, bodiless personages" ramble through the
     novel. Harris, the author of "some of the most excellent
     pages of discursive narrative in recent American fiction,"
     is not necessarily qualified to write a novel.

38   ANON. Review of Sister Jane. Critic, NS 26 (26 December),
     417-18.
     Harris is one of the true masters of dialect, and he is
     a "'naturalist'" in the best sense: he holds the mirror up
     to the common people and to nature. In Sister Jane Harris
     brings a poor, commonplace, backwoods Georgia town to life
     and to art. Sister Jane is a commanding figure, and even
     the weak and foolish narrator is interesting.

39   ANON. "Joel Chandler Harris Again." New York Times Saturday
     Review of Books and Art (26 December), p. 2.

1896

Harris is famous for making his animal creatures human, but in the disappointing Sister Jane his human beings are, more or less, "lay figures," the dialogue heavy, and the plot creaking, if not improbable. In his own sphere, Harris is "perfect, incomparable," but the domestic novel is of another world than his. Evidently, Harris's friends talked him into writing a novel, and like so many brilliant writers he did not understand his own limitations.

40   BASKERVILL, W.[ILLIAM] M.[ALONE]. "Joel Chandler Harris." Chautauquan, 24 (October), 62–67.
Harris's heroes were Lee, Jackson, and Lincoln, and he loved Job, Ecclesiastes, and Paul. From his reading he imbibed simplicity and naturalness, but his sympathy for man was his greatest gift. The Remus tales are enduring because of their realistic representation of a past civilization and their humor, philosophy, wit, and human nature. The autobiographical Plantation is one of Harris's most interesting books, but he reveals "consummate literary art" in "Mingo," in the characters of the black man and Mrs. Bivins. "Free Joe" is powerful and "At Teague Poteet's" a sustained piece that captures the spirit of the people. "Trouble on Lost Mountain" has "tragic power," but "Azalia" is insipid.

41   BRIDGES, ROBERT. "Mr. Harris's Tales of the Domestic Jungle." Book Buyer, 13 (December), 734–36.
Each of Harris's books has an unselfconscious spontaneity and joy of expression. Aaron is in a way more original and artistically complete than anything he has previously written. The animal characters have real dispositions and the Arab, Aaron, is a mysterious and dramatic figure. The concluding Civil War scene is sensitive.

42   BROOKS, NOAH. "Holiday Books for Young People [review of Daddy Jake]." Book Buyer, 13 (December), 803.
The new edition of Harris's classic, Daddy Jake, is out. The stories are genuine folklore and are akin to Kipling's Jungle Stories.

43   CARPENTER, FRANK G. "Frank Carpenter Visits Uncle Remus." Atlanta Constitution (20 December), p. 27.
Harris is "painfully modest" and self-deprecating and feels most secure at his West-End home; there, he proudly displays sixty-nine varieties of roses in his garden. Harris is puzzled that grown-ups also like the Uncle Remus tales; Remus exists as an individual in Harris's mind, although he was a composite portrait. Harris admits he does

1896

not know why the Negro would choose the rabbit, a creature
of low intelligence, for a hero in folktales. While Carpenter sat with him, Harris wrote out a seventeen-line tale
about Brer Buzzard's taking Brer Tarrypin on his back for a
flying lesson and dropping him off, but failing to explain
how to land afterwards. "Before you begin to fly, be sure
and learn how to light" was the moral. Harris writes 2000
words of editorials at the Constitution office and, on a
good night, 1000 words of stories. His basic religious
principle is to "believe in all good men and all good
women."

44 CLARKE, JENNIE THORNLEY, ed. Songs of the South: Choice
Selections from Southern Poets from Colonial Times to the
Present Day. Introduction by Joel Chandler Harris.
Philadelphia: J. B. Lippincott, p. 323.
Notes that any of Harris's half-dozen books of stories
in Negro dialect would have made him famous. Prints his
poem "Juliette."

45 FRUIT, J. P. "Uncle Remus in Phonetic Spelling." Dialect
Notes, 1 (1896), 196-98.
Headnote by C. H. Grandgent to a phonetic transcription
of part of "How Brother Fox Was Too Smart," from Nights,
explains that the language Fruit spoke as a child was "essentially the dialect of Uncle Remus." Fruit also observed
that the Negro dialect was "a great factor in our spoken
language."

46 GARNSEY, JOHN HENDERSON. "Joel Chandler Harris: A Character
Sketch." Book Buyer, 13 (January), 65-68.
The Uncle Remus stories, "Trouble on Lost Mountain,"
"Mingo," "Blue Dave," and "Free Joe," one of the most pathetic tales in the English language, will always live;
Harris's one great defect is his inability to draw a woman
of the upper social classes. He has simple wants and walks
with a swinging stride that "tells of the freedom of his
boyhood days, when he roamed at will over all the plantations in Putnam County." When he is relaxed with a friend,
the slight hesitation in his speech disappears and he tells
thrilling stories of the South. But before the person who
"gushes" at him or seems visibly impressed, he is "more re-
served than the proverbial oyster." He despises interview-
ers and autograph-fiends. His roses, at West End, are his
one passion. He once said, "'If the greatest position on
the round earth were to be offered to me, I wouldn't take
it. The responsibility would kill me in two weeks.'"
Reprinted: 1896.B47.

54

1897

47   _____. "A Character Sketch of Joel Chandler Harris."
Atlanta Constitution (8 March), p. 27.
Reprint of 1896.B46.

48   MARDEN, C. L. "Some Mexican Versions of the 'Brer Rabbit'
Stories." MLN, 11 (January), 43-46.
Four stories collected from Indians of mixed blood in
Mexico City parallel the Remus stories. In some versions
the fox is substituted for the rabbit, but in these the
rabbit himself tricks the coyote.

49   STODDARD, RICHARD HENRY. "The World of Letters." New York
Mail and Express (19 December), p. 18.
Sister Jane reveals another manifestation of Harris's
genius. Harris's idiomatic language and portraits of Jane,
Jincy Meadows, and other characters are fine indeed; the
book, which is more a dramatized series of episodes than a
novel, suffers only mildly from improbabilities and other
weaknesses.

1897 A BOOKS - NONE

1897 B SHORTER WRITINGS

1   ANON. "Books for Young People [review of Aaron]." Boston
Literary World, 28 (9 January), 13.
Aaron is full of Harris's unexplainable charm. If you
want your children to have their "imaginations quickened,
their love of animals strengthened and deepened, [and] their
sympathies broadened," there is no better medium than this
fascinating volume of Southern child life.

2   ANON. "The Lounger." Critic, NS 27 (9 January), 26.
Reproduces a pen drawing by John Henderson Garnsey of
Harris at work, which was printed earlier in The Alkahest.
Comments that Harris seems to be motioning Brer Rabbit out
of the way while he works on Sister Jane.

3   ANON. "The Story of Aaron." Athenaeum, no. 3611 (9 January),
p. 46.
Brief plot summary of Aaron. Children may find the book
tedious, but in places it is good, as are the illustrations.

4   ANON. Review of Daddy Jake. Independent, 49 (14 January), 56.
Daddy Jake is irresistible for young and old. Uncle
Remus is just a little, if any, ahead of Daddy Jake for
pleasing young white children.

1897

5   ANON. Review of Sister Jane. Nation, 64 (28 January), 71-72.
Sister Jane is an old-fashioned, romantic, and improbable
narrative told in an appropriately grave and somewhat re-
pressed manner by a reflective, middle-aged bachelor who is
under his sister's thumb. Harris uses dialect with discre-
tion, not pushing it to incomprehensibility as does Richard
Malcolm Johnston. The portraits of Grandsir Johnny Roach,
Uncle Jimmy Crosby, and other figures are memorable, and
Harris's quiet portrait of the old-time Southern community
seems true to fact. But in the bewildering and tiresome
last chapters there is too much repenting, forgiving, and
straining for joy; Harris was trying to please his characters instead of his readers.

6   ANON. "The Rambler." Book Buyer, 14 (February), 22.
Facing page 22 is a sketch of Harris working at his desk
drawn by J. H. Garnsey. The sketch "gives a more intimate
idea of the creator of 'Uncle Remus' than is to be gained
from any of his photographic portraits."

7   ANON. "The Quiet Life." Chap-Book, 8 (1 February), 264.
Sister Jane "is no vertebrate novel, but a limp, formless
thing which falls apart wherever you grasp it." But "call
it Annals of a Quiet Neighborhood, name the chapters as if
each were a short story, and criticism is disarmed." The
book is discursiveness at its best.

8   ANON. Review of Sister Jane. Independent, 49 (4 February),
153-54.
Sister Jane is pervaded with human sympathy, quiet humor,
and imagination. Where Richard Malcolm Johnston gives us
caricature, Harris gives us genre; his characters are not
overdrawn. Harris handles what might have been an objec-
tionable subject with delicacy, cleverness, and taste. He
truthfully presents the lower middle class instead of the
old affluent class of plantation days.

9   ANON. Review of Sister Jane. Boston Literary World, 28
(6 February), 43.
It is difficult to avoid comparing a writer's later work
to his earlier productions; Harris created the "universally
appreciated" Uncle Remus tales, but Sister Jane fails to
keep the reader's interest. Sister Jane, William Wornum,
Grandsir Roach, and Uncle Jimmy Crosby are memorable,
however.

10 ANON. Review of Sister Jane. The Academy, NS 51
(13 February), 205.

1897

<u>Sister Jane</u> is the "best" recent story, containing a kind, comfortable humor. Praises the plot and points out the more effective character sketches.

11   ANON. "Brer Rabbit's Successor." London <u>Literary World</u>, [NS 57?] (26 February), 191-92.
      <u>Sister Jane</u>, an apparently autobiographical story, is entertaining and carefully put together; the wit and shrewdness of Uncle Remus are not lacking in this new work. Sister Jane is a distinct creation of wholesomeness and health; few heroines in fiction are as attractive. Includes three columns of quotations from the text.

12   ANON. Review of <u>Aaron</u>. <u>Atlantic Monthly</u>, 79 (March), 424.
      The charm of <u>Aaron</u> "lies much in the crossing and re-crossing of the belt which stretches between the natural and the supernatural." Harris, however, is always "at home" with unsophisticated children, darkies, and the animals, "which stupid people call dumb."

13   ANON. Review of <u>Sister Jane</u>. London <u>Saturday Review</u>, 83 (20 March), 301.
      <u>Sister Jane</u> is a sad fall after Harris's animal stories; although the people are interesting and it would be welcomed from a new author for its promise, it is not what we have been taught to expect from "Uncle Remus."

14   ANON. Review of <u>Sister Jane</u>. <u>Home Magazine</u>, 9 (April), 398-99.
      The hero of Harris's book is graying Sister Jane, and "woe unto the fourteen-year old, wasp-waisted, fainting, sentimental heroines of the earlier novelists." The homely wisdom of Jane and her friends makes up for the absence of fine speeches in the novel, and Harris's belief that "'Wimmen is mighty quare'" probably justifies his overly imaginative treatment of Mandy Satterlee.

15   ANON. "Mr. Joel C. Harris and Buddha." <u>New York Times Saturday Review of Books and Art</u> (10 April), p. 4.
      The folklorists have long been studying the origins of the tar-baby story. It appears to have no European origins, and its "rudimental stickiness" seems African. Professor Joseph Jacobs [<u>see</u> 1889.B9] insists rightly that the "adhesive element" in the tale originated in a folk story from India, and that the tale eventually was carried to Africa.

1897

16   ANON. "The Lounger." <u>Critic</u>, NS 27 (22 May), 359.
     A reader thought the Lounger had credited Harris's <u>Daddy</u>
     <u>Jake</u> to Harry Stillwell Edwards. He had not, but Edwards's
     story about two runaways is similar to Harris's in some
     ways.

17   ANON. Review of <u>Wildwoods</u>. <u>New York Times Saturday Review of</u>
     <u>Books and Art</u> (16 October), p. 6.
     Oliver Herford has made some "delightfully absurd" pic-
     tures for <u>Wildwoods</u>. The book precedes <u>Aaron</u> in chronology
     but its supernatural machinery is much better handled.
     Giving the swamp a personal being is familiar to readers of
     African and South American aboriginal stories but is novel
     in juvenile fiction.

18   ANON. "With Books and Those Who Make Them: Joel Chandler
     Harris and His New Work, Aaron in the Wildwood [sic]."
     Atlanta <u>Constitution</u> (17 October), p. 16.
     This book is "the acme of the artistic efforts of the
     author." Although especially "shaped" for children, it is
     more than a child's book. Aaron as the slave ideal is simi-
     lar to several slaves notable in Middle Georgia.

19   ANON. "<u>Aaron in the Wildwoods</u>." San Francisco <u>Chronicle</u>
     (24 October), p. 4.
     The youngest reader will understand <u>Wildwoods</u>, yet the
     oldest can appreciate its humor and pathos. The Arab's
     kindness to the little boy and the boy's popularity among
     the plantation slaves will please the young reader.

20   ANON. Review of <u>Wildwoods</u>. <u>Nation</u>, 65 (28 October), 340.
     <u>Wildwoods</u> is less a sequel to <u>Aaron</u> than it is a picking-
     up of dropped threads; the volume as a whole is less artis-
     tic than its predecessors. Harris's attention to Southern
     youth who hunted slaves as a kind of frolic adventure sheds
     light on one of the causes for the perpetuity of lynching.
     "On the other hand, children will be perplexed by the re-
     vival of the old plea in extenuation of slavery that God
     was using its tender mercies for the civilization of the
     victims of the African slave trade." This book also reveals
     the beginning of a Southern Lincoln legend--"'the greatest
     American of our time.'" Harris's personification of the
     swamp invites positive comparison with Kipling and the
     jungle.

21   ANON. Review of <u>Wildwoods</u>. <u>Public Opinion</u>, 23 (28 October),
     566.

1897

Wildwoods continues more poetically, and with more literary skill, the adventures of Aaron as originally displayed
in Aaron. Aaron as a type has not been overworked, and
perhaps one will hear of him soon as a freeman.

22   ANON. Review of Wildwoods. New York Times Saturday Review of
      Books and Art (30 October), p. 4.
          Some children may cry over the plaintiveness of Wild-
      woods. Harris gives a perfect, and poetical, depiction of
      the antebellum South in his "beautiful" story. The plot is
      summarized.

23   ANON. Review of Wildwoods. New Orleans Daily Picayune
      (31 October), p. 11.
          Sequel to Aaron, the stories in this volume are told
      with inimitable humor. "Little Crotchet" is exquisitely
      and sensitively portrayed.

24   ANON. "Books for Young People [review of Wildwoods]." Boston
      Daily Advertiser (2 November), p. 8.
          Wildwoods is stirring and pathetic. Harris shows liter-
      ary power in his description of the swamp, which is repre-
      sented "as being alert and alive, mindful of its own, and
      carefully guarding its secrets."

25   ANON. Review of Wildwoods. Critic, NS 28 (20 November), 310.
          Little folks will not be the only readers of Wildwoods,
      a story which contains just enough of the natural and the
      supernatural.

26   ANON. "Books for Boys and Girls [review of Wildwoods]."
      New York Bookman, 6 (December), 380.
          Wildwoods will delight young readers, and its illustra-
      tions are fascinating.

27   ANON. "For Young People [review of Wildwoods]." Home
      Magazine, 10 (December), 556-57.
          Little Crotchet in Wildwoods is one of the most sweet
      and pathetic of child characters, and Harris's book is in-
      tellectual enough to hold the attention of old as well as
      young.

28   ANON. "Some Books for the Smaller Children [review of
      Wildwoods]." Review of Reviews, 16 (December), 765.
          Brief plot summary of Wildwoods, "perhaps the very best
      children's book of the year."

1897

29 ANON. "Books for the Young [review of Wildwoods]." Dial, 23
    (1 December), 344.
    Harris's stories for children are always eagerly listened
    to. As Wildwoods reveals, his sympathy and understanding
    for every living thing is intuitive, and his books are both
    too simple and too subtle to be reserved entirely for
    children.

30 ANON. Review of Wildwoods. Academy, NS 52 (4 December), 480.
    Aaron is a treasure in this "Jungle Book" for Americans.
    The story is good, but the Abolitionist tutor is tiresome,
    the Negro talk unfunny, and the illustrations unsatisfactory;
    furthermore, the "tantalizing" references to Brer Rabbit and
    Brer Coon are not followed up.

31 ANON. Review of Wildwoods. Independent, 49 (9 December),
    1624.
    Wildwoods is illustrated with spirit. The reader can
    guess the author's vein; he will find new leads off the old
    lines.

32 ANON. "Juveniles [review of Wildwoods]." Nashville American
    (12 December), p. 18.
    Wildwoods needs no introduction other than to say it is
    the sequel to Aaron. The story of the crippled boy's death
    saddens the book yet gives it a surer hold on its young
    readers.

33 ANON. Review of Wildwoods. New York Daily Tribune
    (15 December), Part 1, p. 8.
    Harris's ingenuity in weaving droll tales, such as these
    in Wildwoods, seems endless. The book is "sure to delight
    juvenile readers."

34 ANON. Review of Wildwoods. Brooklyn Daily Eagle
    (18 December), p. 4.
    Plot summary. Aaron is such an interesting personnage
    that young readers will be sorry to part with him. The book
    is another proof of Harris's ability to write for the young.

35 BASKERVILL, WILLIAM MALONE. "Joel Chandler Harris," in his
    Southern Writers. Biographical and Critical Studies.
    Vol. 1. Nashville: Barbee & Smith, pp. 41-88.
    Bound series of essays that includes 1896.A1.

36 BATES, KATHARINE LEE. American Literature. Chautauqua, NY:
    The Chautauqua Press, p. 131.

1897

Unfortunately, Negro folk-songs are becoming a lost art
since the War. The Uncle Remus stories "have crystallized
a part of [the Negro's] unconscious literature."

37 BEERS, HENRY A. Brief History of English and American
    Literature. New York: Eaton & Mains; Cincinnati:
    Jennings & Graham, p. 582.
        While Uncle Remus provides transcripts of plantation
    folklore, the Mingo collection brings the "moonshiners" to
    Northern attention. The Mingo tales are exciting, strongly
    delineate fresh characters, and contain impressive mountain
    scenery.

38 _____. Review of Sister Jane. Book Buyer, 14 (April), 307.
        Old-fashioned Georgia society lives again in Sister Jane.
    Readers who liked Harris's short stories or folktales will
    not find tales as intense as "Blue Dave" or "At Teague
    Poteet's," or characters as fresh as Brer Rabbit, but Har-
    ris's old women characters are particularly vigorous and
    plenty of adventure and excitement are present.

39 FOLEY, P.[ATRICK] K.[EVIN]. American Authors: 1795-1895.
    A Bibliography of First and Notable Editions Chronologically
    Arranged with Notes. Boston: [P. K. Foley], pp. 109-110.
        Lists twelve of Harris's books through 1895.

40 JENKS, TUDOR. "Holiday Books for Young People [review of
    Wildwoods]." Book Buyer, 15 (December), 524.
        Wildwoods, like the Jungle Stories, appeals to every age.
    It is a fine piece of "massive imagination" that "unites the
    white man's South with a touch of African mysticism."

41 LINK, S.[AMUEL] A.[LBERT]. "Sister Jane." Nashville Daily
    American (31 January), p. 13.
        Great literature has worldwide themes. So it is with
    Sister Jane, which is only in part a local color novel.
    Genuine Southern humor runs throughout, and William Wornum,
    Sister Jane, and Jincy Meadows are delightful.

42 REMNITZ, VIRGINIA YEAMAN. Review of Sister Jane. New York
    Bookman, 5 (March), 77-78.
        Sister Jane is a vital and delightful book, and Harris's
    complaint that his novel does not show the "'knack of nar-
    ration'" is precisely what makes it good. The construction
    of the plot is flimsy, however; "the whole story of the
    finding and return of the lost child is deplorably uncon-
    vincing." Harris is at his best in portraying characters;
    his appeal lies in "the quiet, unforced humour and simple

1897

human qualities that appear in the work which is done in
the ordinary daylight of action."

43   TRENT, W.[ILLIAM] P.[ETERFIELD]. "Tendencies of Higher Life
      in the South." Atlantic Monthly, 79 (June), 767.
         The creator of Uncle Remus is a benefactor of his kind.
      The writers of fiction grouped around him "have produced a
      body of work that will compare most favorably with whatever
      has been done in the last twenty years by their rivals of
      the East and West."

1898 A BOOKS - NONE

1898 B SHORTER WRITINGS

1   ANON. "Books for Young People [review of Wildwoods]." Boston
     Literary World, 29 (19 February), 62.
        Wildwoods is an attractively illustrated and bound col-
     lection of tales about that delightful land where animals
     and humans "mingle in happy intercourse."

2   ANON. "Tales by Joel Chandler Harris." New York Times
     Saturday Review of Books and Art (9 April), p. 236.
        The South has dominated the field of the Civil War novel
     and tale, while the North has remained strangely silent
     about the War after an initial scandalously partisan out-
     pouring of material. Southern writers have had the addi-
     tional challenge of being judicious and impartial, since
     Northern magazines have been their chief vehicles of expres-
     sion. Nobody in the North, and few in the South, can
     approach Harris's art in Home Folks. The several stories
     are interesting and are impartially and skillfully told; a
     little manipulation would make a good novel of the war
     stories. Long may Harris continue to display his ability.

3   ANON. Review of Home Folks. Boston Daily Advertiser
     (12 April), p. 8.
        Some of the stories in Home Folks have already achieved
     widespread prominence by their magazine appearance; the
     tales have the mingled wit and pathos that make up Harris's
     "charming humor." The best of the stories are "How Whale-
     bone Caused a Wedding," "A Baby in the Siege," and "The
     Baby's Fortune." "The Colonel's 'Nigger Dog'" and "A Run
     of Luck" are distinctly "Southern," and other stories depict
     warm friendships between former opponents in war.

1898

4   ANON. Review of Home Folks. Chicago Evening Post (16 April),
    p. 5.
    The Home Folks collection is a model for what short
    stories ought to be. Harris never fails in variety and
    delight.

5   ANON. "More Stories from Joel Chandler Harris." Public
    Opinion, 24 (28 April), 537.
    Harris writes to entertain and in the process educates
    the reader about folklore and Georgians. The Canadian
    sketch in Home Folks also shows that he can write well about
    non-Georgians. His American soldier characters are as suc-
    cessful as Kipling's.

6   ANON. Review of Home Folks. Outlook, 58 (30 April), 1078.
    Harris is "quite at his best" in Home Folks; the stories
    are "satisfying in their reality and their cheerfulness."

7   ANON. "Latest from Uncle Remus." Chicago Tribune (7 May),
    Part 2, [p. 10].
    "A Belle of St. Valerien" is out of place in Home Folks,
    but it is one of the most interesting in the book. The
    other stories are not likely to add to the author's fame;
    their humor is too quiet and little ingenuity is shown in
    their plots, although the war stories are somewhat more ex-
    citing. These tales are "distinctly inferior" to Harris's
    animal stories.

8   ANON. "Tales of the South." Brooklyn Daily Eagle (14 May),
    p. 8.
    Each story in Home Folks involves some pleasing incident
    or odd circumstance, and the stories contain just enough
    dialect to make them picturesque. Harris's tales "are full
    of the genial spirit of an author who is beloved of old and
    young wherever the English language is spoken."

9   ANON. Review of Home Folks. Nation, 66 (26 May), 407.
    Harris has had the discretion not to overwrite about
    Georgia and the Civil War. The author's kind, genial, and
    humorous personality lives in every episode of Home Folks.
    "The Late Mr. Watkins of Georgia" is an excellent humorous
    account of the troubles brought upon Harris by the Uncle
    Remus tales.

10 ANON. Review of Home Folks. New York Bookman, 7 (June), 353.
    Harris's stories about white folks are not the classics
    that the Uncle Remus tales are. Thus Home Folks is met with
    satisfaction rather than enthusiasm. Most of the stories

1898

are typical of the kind that Harris likes: "simple happen-
ings in Southern country life, mingling sadness and mirth."
Harris never delineates the evil in mankind, and the hunch-
back in "A Baby in the Siege" is more afflicted than wicked.
"A Belle of St. Valerien" is a perfect piece and a real sur-
prise, for its Gallic qualities are unexpected in Harris.

11   ANON. Review of Home Folks. Independent, 50 (2 June), 729.
     Home Folks is a wholesome book for all ages and exhibits
     Harris's humor and pathos to good advantage. The "charac-
     teristic humors of black and white are presented with fine
     vigor and faithfulness."

12   ANON. "'Befo' the Wah' Stories [review of Home Folks]." Home
     Magazine, 12 (August), 170.
     Harris lived through the Civil War, and tales such as
     his "are doing so much to bring about the better understand-
     ing between the North and South."

13   ANON. Review of Wildwoods and Sister Jane. Athenaeum,
     no. 3695 (20 August), p. 252.
     ·Harris's reputation still rests upon his Uncle Remus
     books. The best part of Wildwoods is the introductory chap-
     ter; personal taste will determine whether one likes the
     rest of the volume. The defects of Sister Jane are obvious;
     Mr. Harris cannot tell a story. Also he "cannot keep clear
     of the inevitable negro. The great black and white question
     exerts a dreadful influence upon American fiction."

14   ANON. "Tales of the Home Folks." Critic, NS 30 (September),
     204.
     The instinct of resurrection of the Old South is strong
     in Home Folks. The volume is vital, and Harris's artless-
     ness is one of his excellences. He is not so deeply pathe-
     tic as Mrs. [Ruth McEnery] Stuart in his treatment of Negro
     life, but he is "unattainable" in his grasp of dialect and
     folklore. "The Colonel's 'Nigger Dog'" is original; how-
     ever, the "Creole" tale, "Belle of St. Valerien," is less
     successful than Cable's and Grace King's stories. Harris
     is the "genial historiographer" of the pulse and temper of
     central Georgia.

15   ANON. Review of Minervy Ann. New York Bookman, 8 (November),
     208.
     Harris's idea in the Minervy Ann volume is evidently to
     make Aunt Minervy take Uncle Remus's place, "for the sake
     of novelty and a fresh point of view."

16 CHAMBERLAIN, DANIEL H. "Civil War Histories Again." New York
    Times Saturday Review of Books and Art (19 February),
    [p. 113].
      Letter by the former governor of South Carolina refuting
    Harris's contention in a letter to the New York Times for
    12 February 1898 that the hour has come for writing good,
    impartial Civil War histories. Chamberlain contends that
    no history can be written that does not openly face what
    most Northerners believe to have been the real cause of the
    war, slavery, yet Harris suggests that Constitutional dif-
    ferences precipitated the struggle. No history written
    from that point of view would satisfy the North.

17 DRAKE, B. M. The Negro in Southern Literature Since the War.
    Nashville, TN: Cumberland Presbyterian Publishing House,
    pp. 6-7, 14, et passim.
      Harris enters into Negro character through humor, and
    there is a kinship of temperament between Harris and the
    black race. Harris surpasses all other American writers in
    his rendering of Negro character, dialect, and song; he uses
    various types, such as the black mammy, the body servant,
    the runaway, and the free Negro.

18 FITCH, GEORGE HAMILTON. "Noteworthy New Books and New
    Editions [review of Home Folks]." San Francisco Chronicle
    (12 June), p. 4.
      Lead review treats two Civil War books, Home Folks and
    Katharine Prescott Wormeley's The Cruel Side of War. There
    is no better picture of the South during the War than Har-
    ris's, and nowhere, other than in Uncle Remus, has Harris
    done better work than in these stories. Harris has a highly
    developed, but unhurried, storytelling faculty, and he
    thankfully does not have "the selfconsciousness of the new
    realist anxious to produce an impression on the reader."
    Singles out "The Comedy of War," "A Bold Deserter," and
    "The Colonel's 'Nigger Dog'" for special praise. In these
    days of literary straining after effect, Harris's writings
    are wholesome and genuine. The same page prints a boxed
    portrait of Harris with a caption stressing his skill in
    characterization, folklore, and dialect.

19 H., M. Review of Home Folks. Book Buyer, 17 (August), 62.
      In Home Folks the War appears as a "background for
    strange personal adventures, ending, perhaps too persistent-
    ly, in matrimony." The French Canadian story seems out of
    place, but all the tales are faithfully and agreeably drawn.
    Heartiness of good feeling and humor prevail.

1898

20 HOWELLS, W.[ILLIAM] D.[EAN]. "American Letter. The Southern
    States in Recent American Literature. First Paper."
    Independent, 3 (10 September), 231.
        George W. Cable and Harris are the best known of recent
    Southern writers. Harris "is not fully recognized as a
    student of white character (low life, to be sure) in the
    celebrity which his Uncle Remus stories have won for him...."

21 REED, WALLACE P. "Thirty Years of Southern Journalism Held
    Up for Review." Atlanta Constitution (16 June), pp. 11, 12.
        A history of the Atlanta Constitution. Passing referen-
    ces to Harris, who had joined the paper's staff after making
    a "brilliant reputation" as an editorial writer for the
    Savannah Morning News. The Constitution did not try to
    "monopolize" Harris's genius once he started making use of
    his "rare gifts" for writing.

22 SMITH, C. ALPHONSO. "The Possibilities of the South in
    Literature." SR, 6 (July), 302.
        In 1876 Harris annexed Irwin Russell's province and
    "Remus" filled a place in world humor and folklore. Dis-
    cusses the dearth of Southern literature before the War and
    the rise of the New South writers in postbellum times.

23 SPOFFORD, AINSWORTH R., et al., eds. "Harris," in National
    Cyclopaedia of American Biography. Vol. 1. New York:
    James T. White & Co., p. 410.
        Biographical sketch. When Joseph Addison Turner fled
    before Sherman's army in 1864, Harris was left in charge of
    The Countryman. Harris's Remus books are known the world
    over; his short stories illustrate the trusting, patriarchal
    relation between slave and master. His books have given
    him a "comfortable income," and he might be rich "but for
    his generous heart."

1899 A BOOKS - NONE

1899 B SHORTER WRITINGS

1   ADAIR, FORREST. "Joel Chandler Harris." American Illustrated
    Methodist Magazine, 2 (October), 124-32.
        Joe Harris is a family man, living quietly at "The Sign
    of the Wren's Nest" in West End Atlanta. An authority on
    Southern birds, as well as children, he is a good talker
    when he is in the mood for talk. He enjoys a good joke,
    once placing a glass doll's eye in position over his own
    and startling the men at the Constitution office, and three

1899

school girls and an old lady on the trolley home. A generous man and a perceptive judge of human nature, he obtained
a postmaster's job for a paralytic by quietly enlisting the
support of a senator and a postmaster who had been paralyzed themselves. Harris's dream is to write a novel accurately portraying the South in antebellum days.

2   ANON. "The Lounger." Critic, NS 34 (January), 7.
    The bust of Harris by Okerberg, here illustrated, is
striking and the best likeness the Lounger has seen. There
is no doubt that the original of the bust was the creator
of Uncle Remus and of "some of the best plantation songs
that have ever been written."

3   ANON. Review of Home Folks. Athenaeum, no. 3722
    (25 February), p. 239.
    Harris does well to drop Uncle Remus occasionally. The
war stories in Home Folks are the most acceptable of the
dozen tales. "It is pleasant to see Mr. Harris working a
vein that he has not exhausted, and working it successfully."

4   ANON. Review of Minervy Ann. Washington Post (9 October),
    p. 7.
    Minervy Ann is a portrait of an old-fashioned Negro mammy
now dying out in the South; she is as original and charming
as Uncle Remus.

5   ANON. Review of Minervy Ann. New York Times Saturday Review
    of Books and Art (14 October), p. 701.
    Uncle Remus's simple philosophy was dear to the memory
of Dr. Houghton of "The Little Church Around the Corner."
The chronicles of Minervy Ann, fit companion to Uncle Remus,
are things of joy and wisdom. Her artless narrative is full
of the pathos of the Reconstruction period, and such
chronicles are of greater value to the historian than the
so-called Northern and Southern partisan "histories." Aunt
Minervy gives an accurate picture of the defeated but un-
broken South; the wonderful humor of the book saves it from
tragedy, except in the pathetic story "The Case of Mary
Ellen." Minervy and Hamp are accurate portraits, and Harris's pictures of the whites, a little "too quick on the
trigger" at times, are fine companion-pieces to Page's sympathetic pictures. "When Jess Went a-Fiddlin'" is coincidentally similar to Margaretta Sutton Briscoe's "The Sixth
Sense"; the best of the stories is probably "How She Joined
the Georgia Legislature."

1899

6   ANON. Review of Pageants. New Orleans Daily Picayune
     (15 October), Part 2, p. 9.
     Harris's new book was extensively circulated through the
     South as a newspaper serial, and everyone already knows all
     about it. It is a handsomely prepared text of adventures
     and Southern folklore.

7   ANON. "Aunt Minervy Ann." Chicago Evening Post (21 October),
     p. 6.
     Minervy is "deliciously funny," and her adventures throw
     light on the Reconstruction era. Harris is the "matchless
     historian of the colored race."

8   ANON. Review of Minervy Ann. Independent, 51 (2 November),
     2964.
     Aunt Minervy is unforgettable and absolute. Notable also
     are the sketches, done in "broad wash," of certain Georgia
     whites of the Reconstruction period. Some of Harris's
     touches are a trifle too grotesque, perhaps, but as a whole
     the book is charming and the A. B. Frost illustrations true.

9   ANON. Review of Minervy Ann. New Orleans Daily Picayune
     (12 November), Part 2, p. 3.
     Nothing outside of Harris's Remus stories is better than
     Minervy Ann. His Negroes are living persons, and the Recon-
     struction vignettes are memorable. The book is one of
     "great strength, power and true genius."

10   ANON. Review of Minervy Ann. Independent, 51 (23 November),
     3171.
     Minervy Ann cannot be overlooked in reviewing the year's
     notable fiction. It is one of Harris's very best works.

11   ANON. "Literature in the South." Outlook, 63 (2 December),
     769–70.
     Harris is "one of the first writers of the day by virtue
     of the freshness of his materials and of his art."

12   ANON. Review of Minervy Ann. Outlook, 63 (2 December),
     771–72.
     Harris is one of the few living American writers likely
     to be known in the somewhat remote future; Uncle Remus will
     be present in the imagination of other generations. Har-
     ris's gift of humor is irresistibly displayed in Minervy
     Ann; Aunt Minervy "belongs with the elect."

13   ANON. Review of Pageants. Independent, 51 (7 December),
     3299.

1899

Pageants is a treat for readers young and old, rich and
poor, black and white. The illustrations catch Harris's
spirit.

14   ANON. "By Joel Chandler Harris." New York Times Saturday
Review of Books and Art (9 December), pp. 852-53.
"Mr. Harris can suffer from no comparison save with the
precedent he has set for himself." Pageants is only less
charming than Uncle Remus and Minervy Ann. Nothing could
be better than the opening chapter, "After the War," the
fox hunt, the Negro characterizations, and the animal tales,
although Harris makes a mistake in mixing the "perfect realism" of his plantation tales with "a sort of Alice-in-
Wonderland business," such as Mr. Bobs's magic bubble.
Young folks of all ages will enjoy the tales. Like all of
his stories, Pageants is more than a delightful tale; it
contains some of the material from which the true history
of the great Civil War and the dark days of Reconstruction
will be written.

15   ANON. Review of Minervy Ann. Richmond Dispatch (9 December),
p. 2.
Minervy Ann is one of the best things Harris has done.
Aunt Minervy is a "delightful creation," and all the characters are individual and alive. Harris is a humorist, not a
buffoon.

16   ANON. Review of Pageants and Minervy Ann. Nation, 69
(14 December), 451.
Pageants is a rambling collection and a "'patchwork,'"
to use Harris's own term for his book; yet it is not wholly
devoid of charm. Harris appears at his best in Minervy Ann,
a stirring narrative of rich dialogue, "executive ability,"
in the case of Aunt Minervy, and delicious humor. She gives
excellent vigorous descriptions of Reconstruction scenes:
the despoiled plantation, the moneyless proprietor and his
makeshifts, and the "general social demoralization attendant
upon the reversed relations of white and black."

17   ANON. "Chronicles of Aunt Minervy Ann." San Francisco
Chronicle (17 December), p. 4.
These stories are full of humor and delightfully illustrated by A. B. Frost. Aunt Minervy is an original, attractive, and shrewd character.

18   ANON. Review of Pageants and Minervy Ann. Athenaeum,
no. 3765 (23 December), p. 862.

1899

It is one of the mysteries of life that American readers
never get tired of stories in Negro dialect; the writer of
this review is out of sympathy with Harris, although Harris's faith in the reading public must be admired.
Pageants takes up Brer Rabbit yet again, and Harris likes
Aunt Minervy Ann so much, a character reminiscent of Uncle
Remus, that he gives her Minervy Ann all to herself. At
least Brer Rabbit is not mentioned in the latter volume.

19   BARDEEN, CHARLES WILLIAM. "December 9--Joel Chandler Harris,"
     in his Authors' Birthdays: Second Series. Syracuse, NY:
     C. W. Bardeen, pp. 425-59.
           Intermixing biographical commentary with selections from
     his writings, Bardeen points out Harris's effectiveness in
     characterization, description, social differentiation, and
     humor.

20   CURRELL, W. S. "Joel Chandler Harris. I." North Carolina
     Journal of Education, 3 (November), 15-18.
           Biographical sketch drawing upon Baskervill [see
     1896.A1] and Plantation. Harris wanted to learn how to
     write even as a boy, and as a man he is modest and unassum-
     ing although among America's most popular writers. His
     writings show common sense and individuality, a democratic
     spirit, and quick and broad sympathies. The success of
     Uncle Remus continues unabated. [Sequel: 1900.B19.]

21   DAVIS, VARINA JEFFERSON. "Mr. Harris and His Atmosphere."
     Book Buyer, 19 (November), 290-92.
           Minervy Ann is a "masterly genre-painting of several
     classes in the South." The study of the Negro's point of
     view is thorough, and Hamp and Minervy Ann are sensitive
     portraits. Harris, a "genius," is especially strong in
     his depiction of the pathos of Reconstruction.

22   HARTE, BRET. "The Rise of the 'Short Story.'" Cornhill
     Magazine, NS 7 (July), 8.
           Harris's charm lies in his individual flavor and style.
     The secret of the American short story is its faithful ren-
     dering of characteristic life and dialogue (even slang) and
     its freedom from set moral determinations and conventional-
     isms. Reprint: 1960.B4.

23   KNIGHT, LUCIAN L. Review of Minervy Ann. Atlanta
     Constitution Magazine Supplement (22 October), p. 4.
           In the opinion of "many competent critics on both sides
     of the line," Harris has produced nothing superior to the
     excellent Minervy. Quotes New York Times review of the
     book [see 1899.B5].

1900

24   LANIER, SIDNEY. "The New South," in his <u>Retrospects and
     Prospects: Descriptive and Historical Essays</u>. New York:
     Charles Scribner's Sons, pp. 121-24.
     Reprint of 1880.B4.

25   REPPLIER, AGNES. "<u>Chronicles of Aunt Minervy Ann</u>." <u>Saturday
     Evening Post</u>, 172 (30 September), 236.
         Harris tells all that is best and worst in Negro charac-
     ter, and all that the South knows and the North does not,
     in <u>Minervy Ann</u>. Bad-tempered but warm-hearted, Minervy Ann
     is well matched by her "'no account'" husband, Hamp. Har-
     ris's is a "vivacious narrative" told with humor, pathos,
     and "unfailing sympathy."

26   V., A. T. "Two Volumes by 'Uncle Remus.'" <u>Home Magazine</u>, 14
     (December), 561.
         Aunt Minervy Ann is almost as much of a character as
     Uncle Remus. "An Evening With the Ku-Klux" is one of the
     best chapters in <u>Minervy Ann</u>. <u>Pageants</u> contains adventures
     for younger readers.

27   WERNER, A. "The Tar-Baby Story." <u>Folk-Lore</u>, 10 (September),
     282.
         Further study of African folklore makes stronger the
     theory that Harris's tar-baby story is African in origin.
     Now three distinct African tar-baby tales have been found.

1900 A BOOKS - NONE

1900 B SHORTER WRITINGS

1   ANON. "At Monteagle. Dr. Currell Entertains an Audience with
     a Lecture on Joel Chandler Harris." Nashville <u>American</u>
     (20 July), p. 2.
         Datelined Monteagle, Tennessee, 19 July. Last evening
     Dr. [W. S.] Currell gave a lecture to the Ladies Association
     on Harris, sketching his life and stressing his knowledge of
     Negro character, his sense of humor, and his retiring per-
     sonality. He said, "'Mrs. Stowe's characters are silhou-
     ettes, are galvanized. [Harris's] are true. They live.'"

2   ANON. Review of <u>Minervy Ann</u>. New York <u>Tribune</u>, Supplement
     (22 July), p. 11.
         Harris gives Aunt Minervy Ann life, and her doings never
     fail to amuse. "At this time, when so much insincere and
     worthless writing receives encouragement," it is satisfying
     to see Harris keep working unflinchingly in his own way.

1900

3   ANON. Review of <u>Occasions</u>. <u>New York Times Saturday Review of
    Books and Art</u> (4 August), [p. 513].
    <u>Occasions</u>, now in press, is said to include a strikingly
    lifelike picture of the late President in a novelette en-
    titled "The Kidnapping of President Lincoln." Other stories
    treat the unwritten history of the Civil War and the secret
    service.

4   ANON. "A Loss to Journalism." Atlanta <u>Journal</u> (6 September),
    p. 4.
    Harris's resignation as chief editorial writer of the
    Atlanta <u>Constitution</u> is a loss to the profession and the
    public. He used humor, satire, and ridicule with great
    skill, but never unkindly. Harris leaves journalism to de-
    vote his entire time to purely literary work.

5   ANON. "Joel Chandler Harris." Atlanta <u>Constitution</u>
    (7 September), p. 4.
    Announcement of Harris's retirement from daily editorial
    work on the <u>Constitution</u>. He will, however, continue to
    contribute to the paper whenever a subject strikes his
    fancy. The "accumulation of his literary orders, which he
    has found it impossible to fill," necessitates his retire-
    ment; yet the world will be richer for the literary crea-
    tions he will produce during his leisure.

6   ANON. Review of <u>Occasions</u>. <u>Outlook</u>, 66 (20 October), 471.
    Harris successfully enters the field of the detective
    story with <u>Occasions</u>. The story about the plot to kidnap
    Lincoln is a "beautiful appreciation" of the former Presi-
    dent, and "Why the Confederacy Failed" is admirable narra-
    tive. Harris is here in the guise of "a successful claimant
    for the laurels which Dr. Conan Doyle has worn for a number
    of years."

7   ANON. "Uncle Remus's War Stories." Chicago <u>Tribune</u>
    (20 October), Part 2, [p. 10].
    These well-managed and action-filled stories deal with
    more or less imaginary episodes during the Civil War, but
    Harris's unwritten history is more interesting than history
    itself. The flower of the collection, and "the high water
    mark of the author's art," is "The Kidnapping of President
    Lincoln." Billy Sanders is "one of Mr. Harris' most de-
    lightfully successful creations," and the episode with
    Lincoln is told with "captivating humor."

8   ANON. Review of <u>Occasions</u>. Washington <u>Post</u> (5 November),
    p. 4.

1900

"The Kidnapping of President Lincoln" is humorous and a
lifelike portrait of the great President. Billy Sanders is
an appropriate character for displaying Harris's genius in
the homespun tale.

9   ANON. "Joel Chandler Harris's Short Stories." Brooklyn Daily
     Eagle (10 November), p. 13.
         Harris's magazine editor supposedly said that "The Kid-
     napping of President Lincoln," in Occasions, was the best
     story that had ever been sent to his periodical. The por-
     trait of Lincoln is a fine likeness, and the other stories
     about the Confederate secret service are well-written, in-
     teresting, and full of good humor. One can understand how
     Harris would desire to escape in some measure from the
     "trammels of his fame" as creator of Brer Rabbit. He tried
     it once with a novel [Sister Jane], but the book did not
     have the "go" about it that the Uncle Remus tales did. Not
     many writers, however, can write short stories as good as
     Harris's. "He is everywhere recognized as the dean of the
     new school of brilliant Southerners."

10   ANON. Review of Occasions. Independent, 52 (29 November),
     2874.
         The freshness and dramatic vigor of Occasions mark a new
     advance in Harris's versatile work. "Mystery is used with
     excellent effect, good detectives are baffled, plots and
     counter-plots abound."

11   ANON. Review of Occasions. Nation, 71 (29 November), 430.
         The narration in Occasions drags over unimportant matters
     and leaps over others; Harris apparently forgot "the really
     critical moves in the game of political conspiracy" in these
     spy stories. Captain McCarthy is an interesting and re-
     sourceful person, but his "gloomy confidence that Providence
     had decided against the South [disqualified him] for work
     requiring for success a hearty belief that God was with
     him." "The Kidnapping of President Lincoln" is an excellent
     portrait of Lincoln's remarkable personality, although the
     tale is improbable.

12   ANON. "General Gossip of Authors and Writers." Current
     Literature, 29 (December), 708–709.
         Relates how Harris came to write the Remus stories for
     the Constitution and his original apprehension over the
     stories. A success from the start, Remus was genuine as an
     antebellum Negro. Lately many praise Aunt Minervy as su-
     perior to Remus. Now retired, Harris is in "the meridian
     of physical and intellectual powers."

1900

13 ANON. Review of <u>Occasions</u>. <u>Chautauquan</u>, 32 (December),
    330-31.
        <u>Occasions</u> is a vivid collection of Civil War secret ser-
    vice tales that will only add to Harris's reputation. The
    best of the stories is "The Kidnapping of President Lin-
    coln," which provides a charming study of that great
    President's character.

14 ANON. Review of <u>Occasions</u>. New York <u>Bookman</u>, 12 (December),
    402.
        Aside from the Uncle Remus tales, Harris has not written
    anything much better than <u>Occasions</u>.

15 ANON. Review of <u>Occasions</u>. <u>Review of Reviews</u>, 22 (December),
    766-67.
        <u>Occasions</u> includes a novelette, "The Kidnapping of
    President Lincoln," which itself is sufficiently striking
    to give the whole volume significance. No biography of the
    great "War President" has afforded "a more lifelike picture
    of his giant figure, or a more vivid impression of his
    ready, homely wit and large simplicity."

16 ANON. Review of <u>Occasions</u>. <u>Academy</u>, 59 (1 December), 518.
        Harris is a great favorite and holds a warm place in
    our hearts. This volume contains five "stirring" stories.

17 ANON. Review of <u>Occasions</u>. Boston <u>Evening Transcript</u>
    (5 December), p. 21.
        "A quintette of good Civil War stories of scouting and
    spying, told with a cool earnestness that would deceive the
    very elect."

18 CLARK, KATE UPSON. "Realism and Romanticism." <u>Independent</u>,
    52 (26 July), 1793.
        Mentions Harris among fifteen or twenty writers belonging
    to the "realistic school" founded by Jane Austen.

19 CURRELL, W. S. "Joel Chandler Harris. II." <u>North Carolina</u>
    <u>Journal of Education</u>, 3 (March), 23-26.
        [An evaluation of Harris's literary art, sequel to
    1899.B20.] Harris's output has been great, perhaps too
    great; among the best tales are "Free Joe," "Mingo," "Blue
    Dave," and "At Teague Poteet's," and <u>Uncle Remus</u> marked an
    epoch in American literary history. Uncle Remus is Harris's
    most vital and original character; compared to his, Mrs.
    Stowe's Negroes are mere silhouettes. Harris shows both the
    good and the evil in slavery, although his tales of Blue and
    Gray reconciliation only make at times a paler Blue. Mrs.

1900

Bivins and Sister Jane are strong female portraits. Includes a checklist of Harris's books through 1899.

20 HALE, WILL T. "Joel Chandler Harris," in his Great Southerners.
    Vol. 1. Nashville and Dallas: Publishing House of the
    M. E. Church, South, pp. [245]-48.
    Shortly after the Civil War Harris was listed mainly as
    a writer of verse in a volume of Southern authors. Hale
    met Harris in 1898 in the Constitution offices and recalled
    that he worked with his hat on and observed with modesty,
    "'Yes ... I have published sixteen volumes of--trash.'"
    Harris's portraits of the Negro are true, unlike those of
    Mrs. Stowe; he appreciates the Negro's philosophy, "so
    pathetic because born of helplessness," and his humor. Sis
    Tempy, 'Tildy, and Uncle Remus "seem flesh and blood."

21 HOWELLS, W.[ILLIAM] D.[EAN]. Literary Friends and
    Acquaintance: A Personal Retrospect of American
    Authorship. New York and London: Harper & Brothers,
    p. 115.
    Howells came to Boston in 1866 and found it still the
    chief literary center. The Western writers, Riley, Thanet,
    Stoddard, and Garland, were as unknown as the Southern ones,
    Cable, Murfree, Page, and Harris. New England ideals and
    examples still prevail and, even today, the South and West
    do not match up.

22 KNIGHT, LUCIAN LAMAR. "Uncle Remus at Large." Boston Daily
    Evening Transcript (13 September), p. 8.
    Harris resigned from the Atlanta Constitution on 6 Sep-
    tember 1900 to turn his hand more completely to literary
    writing. His resignation was accepted reluctantly. In re-
    cent years, Harris's habit was to go to the office at nine
    in the morning and pick up his assignments and do them at
    home, returning his editorials in the afternoon. Includes
    biographical and character sketch.

23 MOONEY, JAMES. Myths of the Cherokee. Washington, D.C.:
    Government Printing Office, pp. 233-34, 448, 450, 452.
    Discusses Cherokee influences on Negro folktales. The
    Great White Rabbit and Brer Rabbit have similar characteris-
    tics; other parallels between Indian and Uncle Remus lore
    are also noted. Reprint: 1970.B16.

24 O., S. J. "An Interesting Display of Uncle Remus's Work."
    Atlanta Constitution (9 October), p. 6.
    Occasions is a wide departure from Harris's previous
    work and is being discussed with unusual interest by the

1900

critics. The [Saturday Evening Post] editor called "Why
the Confederacy Failed" the best short story his journal
had ever printed. A display of Harris's manuscript for the
book and of four illustrations may be seen at the American
Baptist Publication Society; the publishers of the book in-
tend to put the display on tour in various northern cities.
Harris wrote neatly with a fountain pen on large newspaper
copy sheets; he generally composed rapidly without making
many changes. At his West End home he did his newspaper
work in one room with one fountain pen, and his literary
work in another room with a different fountain pen. He says
his writing is done by two persons: one a newspaper man
and one an author. Recently Harris fell in with the "modern
spirit" and bought a typewriter.

25   REED, WALLACE PUTNAM. "The Real 'Uncle Remus.'" Chicago
      Times-Herald (2 June), p. 6.
          Harris is not only a Southern writer; he is as American
      an author as it is possible to be. Harris is modest and
      hates to talk, but he is "thoroughly companionable." It is
      not surprising that Harris so admired Lincoln; both have a
      similar sense of humor, parallel sentiments, and conscien-
      tiousness. Harris is planning to retire soon from the
      treadmill of journalism, to spend more time with his family.

26   SHIPMAN, CAROLYN. Review of Occasions. Book Buyer, 21
      (November), 300-301.
          Harris's stories of the secret service in Occasions are
      distinct and entertaining works of historical fiction.
      Billy Sanders is an unforgettable character, and "The Kid-
      napping of President Lincoln" is one of the best pieces of
      rapid narrative and "clear-cut character sketching" in many
      a day.

27   STEDMAN, EDMUND CLARENCE, ed. An American Anthology: 1787-
      1900. Selections Illustrating the Editor's Critical Review
      of American Poetry in the Nineteenth Century. Boston and
      New York: Houghton Mifflin, p. 796.
          Provides a brief biographical summary and lists ten of
      Harris's books. Refers to Uncle Remus as a "classic," and
      anthologizes "The Plough-Hands' Song" and "My Honey, My
      Love" on pp. 513-14.

28   THERRELL, MARIE CLOWE. "Southern Authors. Joel Chandler
      Harris." Georgia Education, 2 (March), 20-22.
          Harris is the "most original and ingenious dialect
      story-writer in America." Some critics think Aaron his
      finest work.

1901

29 TRENT, WILLIAM P. "American Literature." Dial, 28 (1 May),
    335.
        During its twenty years of existence, the Dial must have
    reviewed nearly forty thousand books, a large proportion of
    which were by American authors. Summing up the achievement
    of these authors is difficult. One does realize that the
    literature of today is very different from that of its
    predecessors. For example, 1891 saw the death of "Hermann
    [sic] Melville, famous for his sea tales," and the publica-
    tion of Stockton's Squirrel Inn and Harris's Balaam.

30 WELLS, BENJAMIN W. "Southern Literature of the Year." Forum,
    29 (June), 508–509, et passim.
        Minervy Ann, which is somewhere between the novel and
    the short story, is "on the whole the most delightfully
    humorous of the Southern books of the year." No Negro in
    fiction since Uncle Remus seems quite so real as Aunt
    Minervy; she is a "rare and genuine" creation. Aunt
    Minervy reappears in Pageants, which, however, is only a
    patchwork, as Harris himself terms it; it is too inconse-
    quent to be enjoyed by grown folks and not likely to be
    intelligible to children.

31 WILSON, JAMES GRANT and JOHN FISKE, eds. "Harris," in
    Appleton's Cyclopaedia of American Biography. Vol. 3.
    New York: D. Appleton, p. 92.
        Virtually identical to 1888.B25.

1901 A BOOKS - NONE

1901 B SHORTER WRITINGS

1   ADAMS, OSCAR FAY, ed. "Harris," in A Dictionary of American
    Authors. Boston, MA: H. O. Houghton and Co., pp. 171–72.
        Uncle Remus is a "unique character study of the Southern
    negro" as well as a "notable contribution" to the literature
    of folklore.

2   ANON. Review of Occasions. Athenaeum, no. 3820 (12 January),
    p. 48.
        Harris wisely avoids all reference to Uncle Remus in the
    five uncommonly well-told stories of the Civil War in Occa-
    sions, although a character in "The Kidnapping of President
    Lincoln" comes "perilously near" to Uncle Remus. The
    stories are exciting, spirited, and show Harris's gift of
    humor.

1901

3   ANON. Review of <u>Occasions</u>. London <u>Saturday Review</u>, 91
     (2 February), 149.
     American writers seem to delight in leaving comfortable
     fields where their reputation is safe: Twain preaches
     telepathy, Mr. Leland translates Heine, and the creator of
     "Uncle Remus" publishes Civil War sketches. Something of
     the romance of a lost cause surrounds these loosely threaded
     tales, but the plots are inconceivable.

4   ANON. "Uncle Remus in a Rage." <u>Saturday Evening Post</u>, 173
     (18 May), 14-15.
     Humorous sketch recounting how Harris, typically one of
     the "kindest-hearted" persons in the world, got upset with
     two furniture company agents who were attempting to remove
     some items from the cottage of Aunt Mandy, his cook. They
     said she had not paid her final installment, but when
     Harris identified himself and threatened to "'show up'"
     their firm in a newspaper article, the men agreed to cancel
     the debt. Harris felt that they were trying to take advan-
     tage of Aunt Mandy's ignorance and hard luck.

5   ANON. "Three Literary Lions Who Refused to Roar." Atlanta
     <u>Constitution</u> (24 August), p. 7.
     James Whitcomb Riley, Harris, and Frank L. Stanton--
     three "world-famous" literary lions--were guests yesterday
     at the Fulton Club, on the occasion of Riley's joining the
     Club. Riley said his desire to live increased as he grew
     older and that he hoped by saving breath to reach age
     seventy; he believed that Harris, his "'talkative friend,'"
     would, judging by past performances, see the dawn of the
     next century; Harris blushed at this juncture. All three
     men remained generally silent at the Club, although Harris
     mentioned his fondness for "'fine cut'" chewing tobacco
     while Riley praised "'Star plug.'"

6   ANON. "The Best Books for Children.... From Frank R.
     Stockton." <u>Outlook</u>, 69 (7 December), 880.
     <u>Uncle Remus</u> belongs among the ten best books for children.

7   ANON. "The Best Books for Children.... From Mary Mapes
     Dodge." <u>Outlook</u>, 69 (7 December), 869.
     Kipling's Jungle Books, or Seton-Thompson's <u>Wild Animals</u>
     <u>I Have Known</u>, or Harris's <u>Uncle Remus</u>, would be among
     Dodge's ten books best suited for children.

8   ANON. "Reading for Children." <u>Outlook</u>, 69 (7 December), 867.
     The best books in the world are written for children and
     their seniors. Scott's <u>Ivanhoe</u>, Cooper's <u>Leatherstocking</u>

1901

Tales, the poems of Scott, Lowell, Whittier, and Longfellow,
Aesop's Fables, Guy Mannering, Rob Roy, Uncle Remus, and
Pilgrim's Progress belong to all ages.

9   ANON. "Some Notable Holiday Books [review of Uncle Remus]."
    Independent, 53 (12 December), 2945.
        A. B. Frost's drawings add quaint charm to the 1895
    edition of Uncle Remus.

10 BRONSON, WALTER C. A Short History of American Literature:
    Designed Primarily for Use in Schools and Colleges.
    Boston: D. C. Heath, p. 288.
        Harris made a permanent contribution to folklore in the
    charming Remus stories. Revised edition: 1919.B3.

11 CHESNUTT, CHARLES W.[ADDELL]. "Superstitions and Folk-Lore
    of the South." Modern Culture, 13 (March), 232.
        In his Uncle Remus stories Harris has put into pleasing
    and enduring form the Negro plantation animal stories, but
    little attention has been paid to the tales of conjuration.

12 FORD, JAMES L. "A Century of American Humor." Munsey's
    Magazine, 25 (July), 489.
        Talks of newspaper humorists and mentions Harris, now
    known as a literary man.

13 [HALSEY, FRANCIS WHITING]. "Joel Chandler Harris." New York
    Times Saturday Review (28 December), p. 1016.
        Informal essay on Harris's home, his life there, and his
    work. Harris left journalism last year, finding that kind
    of work to be "'a good deal like pourin' water in a sieve.'"
    Perhaps Harris's peculiar kind of humor is the result of
    his bashfulness, "very much as an awkward boy falls into
    witticisms and practical jokes to hide his confusion." He
    now composes at the typewriter, writing 1500 to 2000 words
    a day, for six or seven hours, and seldom rewriting; he en-
    joys his family's interruptions. Always critical of him-
    self, Harris observed that his bound volumes were "'powerful
    pore' stuff." He regrets the passing of the Uncle Remus
    types from real life. "'The "Uncles" have larnt a heap o'
    blarney since the war,'" he sighs. Reprinted: 1902.B23.

14 HARKINS, E.[DWARD] F.[RANCIS]. "Harris," in his Famous
    Authors (Men). Boston: L. C. Page & Co., pp. 123-37.
        Mentions Harris's dislike for theater (even though he
    was a drama critic at one time), his happy days with Turner,
    his current literary tastes (Thackeray, Stevenson, Scott,
    Kipling, and Riley) and his various newspaper experiences.

1901

Harris's prodigious work, both literary and journalistic,
is owing to his inexhaustible good nature and simple life
style. He is shy but kind and hospitable to friends. He
is not interested in politics but kept writing editorials,
partly because he felt he owed his reputation to the Constitution. Remus, Minervy Ann, Brer Rabbit, and Brer Fox
are creations unsurpassed in originality. Reprinted:
1902.B24.

15 HOWELLS, W.[ILLIAM] D.[EAN]. "Professor Barrett Wendell's
    Notions of American Literature." North American Review,
    172 (April), 632.
        Faults Wendell's A Literary History of America (1900)
    for not including more comment on contemporary Southern
    writers. "The literary movement in the South since the war
    has been of the most interesting and promising character,"
    and several writers have distinguished themselves. Harris's
    "contributions to our imaginative literature are of absolute
    novelty, and Mr. G. W. Cable has written one of the few
    American fictions which may be called great." While these
    two men are not fully representative of the literary advance
    in the South, for Wendell not to consider their work "is to
    leave the vital word unsaid." Reprinted: 1959.B6.

16 NEWCOMER, ALPHONSO GERALD. American Literature. Chicago and
    New York: Scott, Foresman, pp. 304, 319.
        Harris's creation of Remus gave him a permanent place
    in fiction. Lists four Harris volumes in the Southern
    bibliography section.

17 ONDERDONK, JAMES L. History of American Verse (1610-1897).
    Chicago: A. C. McClurg & Co., p. 360.
        Irwin Russell and Harris were pioneers in presenting
    "the lighter and more humorous side of Southern life and
    character" in dialect tales and poems.

18 TRENT, W.[ILLIAM] P.[ETERFIELD]. "A Retrospect of American
    Humor." Century, 63 (November), 47.
        To the three classes of American humorists--the writers
    of humorous verse, the academic humorists, and the socio-
    political humorists--one might, if space permitted, add a
    group of writers of fiction such as Brackenridge, Stockton,
    Cable, and Harris, who "have either made their humor an ex-
    cuse for writing stories or have infused it into everything
    they have written."

19 WRIGHT, HENRIETTA CHRISTIAN. Children's Stories in American
    Literature 1861-1896. Vol. 2. New York: Charles
    Scribner's Sons, pp. 153-62.

1902

Informal biographical sketch of Harris's boyhood interest in animals, Negro lore, and writing. His Uncle Remus
tales are masterful and are valuable records of folklore.
"The skill with which [Harris] effaces himself, and makes
Uncle Remus the real narrator [,] is marvellous."

1902 A BOOKS - NONE

1902 B SHORTER WRITINGS

1   ANON. Review of Tolliver. Era, 9 (January), 53-54.
    The scenes of Harris's childhood contain poetic sentiment
    and his best vein of genuine humor. Though Southern and
    loyal to his own side, he is fair to the other as well. For
    the historian Harris pictures the manners, customs, and
    feelings of his time, and, of more value, includes motives
    and directing impulses.

2   ANON. "Joel Chandler Harris's New Stories." New York Times
    Saturday Review of Books and Art (19 April), p. 266.
    The stories in Statesman "are, by no means, up to the
    level of Harris's best work, and will not add to his repu-
    tation." The title story is impossible, and, for once in
    her life, even Aunt Minervy Ann is tiresome. "Flingin'
    Jim and His Fool-Killer" is the most characteristic tale,
    but it is not in Harris's "delightfully spontaneous vein."
    If only authors could "harden their hearts against publish-
    ers, and ... refuse to write unless the spirit moves!"

3   ANON. Review of Statesman. Dial, 32 (1 June), 389.
    Brief plot summary of title story in Statesman. The
    other tales in the book also treat well-drawn Southern
    characters and events filled with human interest.

4   ANON. "Emory College Honors Joel Chandler Harris." Atlanta
    Constitution (8 June), p. 9.
    For the first time in its history, Emory College will
    award the doctor of literature degree next Wednesday at
    Commencement. By unanimous choice of the faculty, Harris
    will be the recipient. It is hoped Mr. Harris will be
    present for the ceremonies. [Sequel: 1902.B5.]

5   ANON. "Farewell Said to Alma Mater." Atlanta Constitution
    (12 June), p. 4.
    At Commencement activities yesterday, President Dowman
    of Emory College conferred the Doctor of Letters degree upon
    Harris, saying he was proud that such an illustrious son of
    Georgia had been honored. [See also 1902.B4.]

1902

6   ANON. Review of Statesman. Nation, 74 (12 June), 471.
    The title piece in Statesman describes an era "preceding
    that of definite recognition of politics as business."
    Billy Spence's voluntary self-sacrifice for Featherstone is
    not probable, but once it is allowed "all that follows is
    natural and pathetic." The remaining tales sustain Har-
    ris's reputation for revealing Negro character in Negro
    dialect, and Aunt Minervy Ann is the perfect specimen of
    the "'Mammy.'"

7   ANON. "The Making of a Statesman and Other Stories." Critic,
    NS 41 (September), 279.
    Harris's novelette is as good as his work ever was. His
    place as a "preserver of Southern types is as secure as
    Bret Harte's as an interpreter of California mining-life."

8   ANON. "By Author of 'Uncle Remus.'" Brooklyn Daily Eagle
    (7 October), p. 7.
    Tolliver is "one of the best" novels--"not a problem
    novel or a caricature novel or a society novel or a politi-
    cal novel, but just a novel in which one meets a heap of
    interesting people and interesting circumstances" and finds
    humor and pathos. The setting is one of those real, but
    "side tracked [sic] Georgian villages which figure so often
    in Southern fiction." Politically, Harris's novel "presents
    the same features" as [Thomas] Dixon's The Leopard's Spots,
    but "without the partisanship."

9   ANON. "Gabriel Tolliver." Atlanta Constitution (12 October),
    p. 6.
    Announcement that Tolliver will soon be serialized in
    The Sunny South magazine supplement to the Constitution.
    The novel is a book of "romance, humor, pathos and literary
    strength" and it will readily satisfy those readers looking
    for a "real, photographic and psychologic [sic] story of
    southern life." [See 1902.B10.]

10 ANON. "Gabriel Tolliver." Atlanta Constitution [magazine
    supplement] The Sunny South (12 October), p. 8.
    Three-column review-essay on the novel. Sister Jane and
    "The Making of a Statesman" showed Harris's capacity to
    write longer fiction. The South's "oldest and best-loved
    author" makes his first extensive excursion into longer
    fiction with Tolliver. The book is a great success--the
    first half full of "warm local color and uneventful human
    realism" but the second half dramatic and exciting. It is
    clearly autobiographical. Unlike The Leopard's Spots [by
    Thomas Dixon], Tolliver shows no prejudice, but rather

1902

reveals Harris's close observation of Negro character and
sensitivity to Reconstruction problems. The novel is discussed, with frequent quotations from the text, under the
headings "The Opening Chapter," "The Portrayal of Women,"
"Gabriel's Love for Nan," and "Romance of Neighbor Tomlin."
[See also 1902.B9.]

11 ANON. Review of Tolliver. Nashville American (20 October),
p. 3.
Harris writes effectively of the extremely difficult
times in the South after the War when Southerners were exhausted and discouraged. Harris creates an "old-fashioned"
but sensitive novel about the people in a sidetracked
Georgia town and records their response to the carpetbaggers
and other problems. "The leading interest in the story is
that of Love."

12 ANON. "Harris' Gabriel Tolliver." Chicago Tribune
(8 November), [p. 18].
Just because Harris has found fame with character
sketches and short stories does not mean that he will at-
tain equal distinction with the novel. Tolliver is not a
novel but a series of sketches "connected by a thread of
continuity." The book is delightful and interesting, however, and it is told with humor and charm. The plot is
summarized.

13 ANON. "In the Quiet Village of Shady Dale." New York Times
Saturday Review of Books and Art (22 November), p. 808.
Harris has accomplished quite a feat in Tolliver, for he
has written 448 pages about nothing. Tolliver's life, from
start to finish, is uninteresting, and although the book
abounds with Negroes there is no Uncle Remus. For a small
town, Shady Dale seems to be thickly populated, and "whether
he is of moment to the story or not each inhabitant of the
blessed village is dragged into the book."

14 ANON. "Joel Chandler Harris' Stories." San Francisco
Chronicle (25 November), p. 24.
All five stories in Occasions deal dramatically with the
unwritten history of the Confederacy. The best is "The Kidnapping of President Lincoln," and "Why the Confederacy
Failed" is also fine. Harris can still do excellent work
when he abandons the Negro dialect that gave him his reputation.

15 ANON. "Joel Chandler Harris Essays First Novel in 'Gabriel
Tolliver.'" Chicago Evening Post (29 November), p. 7.

83

1902

Tolliver lacks sustained interest, despite Harris's sure
yet delicate touch in description and character portrayal;
the novel is more like a number of short stories strung together. Harris will be thanked for his graphic though
temperate depiction of the bitter Reconstruction period.
Although it is difficult to maintain interest in the book,
Harris's portraits of Nan Dorrington and other women will
be "a refreshment to the jaded novel reader wandering
through that wilderness of monkeys, the modern society
novel." Billy Sanders is also a joy.

16   ANON. "Harris--Gabriel Tolliver." Critic, NS 41 (December),
      581.
      Few later works by "standard authors" live up to their
      earlier reputations, but Harris's latest work is an excep-
      tion. Tolliver is "one of the sanest books on the South
      that has appeared in a long time, and one of the most
      charming as well."

17   ANON. Review of Tolliver. Independent, 54 (4 December),
      2903.
      Tolliver is a Reconstruction novel that is not afflicted
      with the animus and sectional bitterness of [Thomas Dixon's]
      The Leopard's Spots. While it is in no sense a great book
      (Harris is better suited for short stories and folktales),
      it is a quiet and faithful account, in fact a "sweet-tem-
      pered romance which runs its course in spite of the desper-
      ate times." There are no imprecations against the North or
      against the Negro. Harris is sincerely Southern, but he
      has too much Irish wit not to appreciate "the (to him) ab-
      surd plan of Reconstruction." And the Northern carpetbagger
      who figures in the novel was really only a good man with
      fanatical ideals.

18   ANON. Review of Tolliver. Nation, 75 (11 December), 467.
      Regarded as a novel, Tolliver is very poor work--
      rambling, shuffling, without form or style. A passage in
      the book's prelude finds Harris apologizing for his unim-
      pressive work, as if he were proud to say it. "We do not
      understand such pride." The African legend of Dilly Bal is
      beautifully told, but Harris's disclaimer about the art of
      his book makes the reader afraid of hurting his feelings
      by complimenting him on his artistry.

19   ANON. Review of Tolliver. Outlook, 72 (13 December), 900.
      Like Page's Red Rock, Gabriel Tolliver is a tale of Re-
      construction that will be regarded as an important footnote
      to contemporary history. It is a story of the heart, "free

from morbid psychology"; uncontrived, unpretentious, and
genuine, it has old-fashioned charm. "Mr. Harris is one
of our real novelists."

20   BURTON, RICHARD. Forces in Fiction and Other Essays.
      Indianapolis: Bobbs-Merrill, p. 14.
      Finds the introduction of Southern and Western types,
      saliently depicted by such writers as Harris, a hopeful
      sign for current fiction and hardly to be paralleled in
      England. Reprinted: 1969.B3.

21   [DENT, CHARLES W.]. "The Most American Books.... Marks of
      Distinction by Charles W. Dent." Outlook, 72 (6 December),
      788.
      Dent lists Uncle Remus among ten most characteristically
      American works. [See also 1902.B22, B26.]

22   [GARLAND, HAMLIN]. "The Most American Books.... Culture or
      Creative Genius? by Hamlin Garland." Outlook, 72
      (6 December), 780.
      In response to a questionnaire from Outlook, Garland
      lists Uncle Remus among ten books that are characteristical-
      ly American. [See also 1902.B21, B26.]

23   HALSEY, FRANCIS WHITING. "Joel Chandler Harris in Atlanta,
      Ga.," in his Authors of Our Day in Their Homes. New York:
      James Post & Co., pp. 159-71.
      Reprint of 1901.B13.

24   HARKINS, E.[DWARD] F.[RANCIS]. "Joel Chandler Harris," in his
      Little Pilgrimages Among the Men Who Have Written Famous
      Books. Boston: L. C. Page & Co., pp. 123-37.
      Reprint of 1901.B14.

25   HOWELLS, W.[ILLIAM] D.[EAN]. Literature and Life: Studies.
      New York and London: Harper & Brothers, pp. 176, 183, 295.
      After the Civil War America began to have a national
      literature representative of all the different sections of
      the country. Harris's Remus stories exploited the "local
      parlances" of the South. Rather than going to literary
      centers, some authors wisely stayed at home: Harris is the
      first such author cited. Harris writes political articles
      for a leading Southern journal.

26   [KING, GRACE]. "The Most American Books.... A Southern View
      by Grace King." Outlook, 72 (6 December), 787.
      Perhaps Mark Twain and Harris should head the list of
      the ten most characteristic American writers. "Not only

1902

have they contributed to the literature of the world new,
original, and characteristic elements of American genius,
but we may say absolutely that what they wrote could not
have been produced on any but American soil; and that they
are Americans in every sense of the word." [See also
1902.B21, B22.]

27 KIRK, JOHN FOSTER. A Supplement to Allibone's Critical
    Dictionary of English Literature and British and American
    Authors. Vol. 2. Philadelphia: J. B. Lippincott, p. 771.
        Quotes from contemporary reviews on Uncle Remus, Nights,
    and Mingo.

28 MARTIN, THOMAS H. Atlanta and Its Builders: A Comprehensive
    History of the Gate City of the South. Vol. 2. [Atlanta,
    GA.]: Century Memorial Publishing Co., pp. 121, 372.
        Harris's stories are read in every English-speaking
    country. He is also a famous editor for the Constitution.

29 SEARS, LORENZO. American Literature in the Colonial and
    National Periods. Boston: Little, Brown, p. 412.
        Praising the Uncle Remus tales in their portrayal of the
    "brighter side" of plantation life, Sears recognizes the
    common heritage between the beasts and Negroes: their aims
    and sympathies are not far apart. Here, dialect has "its
    lion's share of importance." There is too much second-rate
    imitation of dialect-writing now: "This is the penalty of
    originality ... the dialect story is manifolded by every
    writer who mistakes distortion of good English for the
    patois of the district." Harris is a true artist, however.
    Reprinted: 1970:B20.

30 SNYDER, HENRY N. "The Reconstruction of Southern Literary
    Thought." SAQ, 1 (April), 150, 151.
        In his works Harris sympathetically and with gracious
    humor interprets the essential human qualities of the Negro,
    the Georgia cracker, and the aristocratic planter. The in-
    troductions to his dialect stories also show him as a stu-
    dent of Southern affairs.

31 STOVALL, GENIE O. "When Joel Went Away." Children's Visitor,
    36 (23 November), 6.
        Dramatized sketch of Harris's departure from Eatonton,
    including a short narrative by Harris on his home town.
    Harris "has not outlived the purity and beauty of childhood."

32 WARNER, CHARLES DUDLEY, et al., eds. Library of the World's
    Best Literature: Ancient and Modern. New York: J. A.
    Hill & Co., pp. 6961-63.

1903

Anthologizes two Uncle Remus tales and "Uncle Remus at
the Telephone." Headnote mentions that Harris portrayed
Uncle Remus not to illustrate a principle, as had Stowe in
Uncle Tom's Cabin and Dred, but to create living character
in all its variations of emotions and perspective. Sepa-
rated from white society, the Negro invested his animal
acquaintances with characteristics that express his "revolt
from his own condition, and the not unnatural desire to
circumvent the master who has so long controlled him."

1903 A BOOKS - NONE

1903 B SHORTER WRITINGS

1   ANON. Review of Tolliver. Harper's Weekly, 47 (31 January),
     194.
         Tolliver is a patient work of many years' reflection by
     that writer whose name is a household word, Harris. This
     leisurely story is absorbing if one gives himself up to the
     author's reminiscent mood. Harris's art is at its best in
     his display of character.

2   ANON. Review of Tolliver. Dial, 34 (1 April), 243.
         Of the several good novels of the Reconstruction period,
     Page's Red Rock is probably the best. Tolliver is the most
     extended work of fiction attempted by Harris, and its
     strength lies in its individual episodes and character
     sketches, not in the continuous narrative. Harris's only
     rival in rural black and white portraiture is Richard
     Malcolm Johnston.

3   ANON. "Books for the Young.... Harris--Wally Wanderoon."
     Critic, NS 43 (December), 573.
         American folklore owes a debt of gratitude to Harris.
     There is a finish to Harris's storytelling, and the tales
     in Wally Wanderoon are narrated in the spirit of the "'good
     old times,'" and begin and end in the "'good old way.'" A
     book for an afternoon curled up in an armchair, "unconscious
     of the flight of time."

4   BAKER, ERNEST A. A Descriptive Guide to the Best Fiction:
     British and American. London: Swan Sonnenschein and Co.;
     New York: Macmillan, pp. 294-95.
         Lists and briefly evaluates ten of Harris's books. Re-
     vised edition: 1932.B3.

1903

5   BURTON, RICHARD. <u>Literary Leaders of America</u>. New York,
    Chautauqua, Springfield, and Chicago: Chautauqua Press,
    p. 315.
        Gifted Southern writers have added vitality to current
    writing and a more romantic tone, perhaps because of the
    "picturesque conditions both human and physiographic [sic]
    of that part of the land."   Cites Harris as one deserving
    mention but states that Page, Stuart, Lane Allen, Murfree,
    and Fox are equally deserving.

6   FISKE, HORACE SPENCER. <u>Provincial Types in American Fiction</u>.
    Chautauqua, NY: Chautauqua Press, pp. 76–79, 106–17.
        The Uncle Remus tales have been so popular that, as
    Howells suggests, Harris's stories of "low life" whites
    have not been fully recognized.   "Free Joe" and "Mingo"
    have had a wide reading.   "At Teague Poteet's" reveals
    subtle humor, a dramatic sense, and strong individualization
    of Teague, Uncle Jake, and Sis.   The Remus tales contain
    "beautiful inconsistency," as well as Remus's "sublime
    credulity" and "unconscious drollery."   Uncle Remus repre-
    sents "some of the more unusual phases of the Negro charac-
    ter," such as the poetic imagination, and quaint humor and
    superstitions.   The sympathy for the weaker animals is an
    allegory of black-white relations.   Fiske prefers the 1895
    <u>Uncle Remus</u> because of Frost's perfect illustrations.
    Harris has a "quiet but telling art."

7   HAWTHORNE, JULIAN; JOHN RUSSELL YOUNG; JOHN PORTER LAMBERTON;
    and OLIVER H. G. LEIGH, eds. <u>The Masterpieces and the</u>
    <u>History of Literature: Analysis, Criticism, Character and</u>
    <u>Incident</u>. Vol. 10.   New York and Chicago: E. R. DuMont,
    p. 332.
        Uncle Remus represents the most attractive vein of Ameri-
    can folklore.   In preserving these African tales, Harris
    made them interesting through his storytelling techniques
    and Remus's engaging personality.   His realistic Georgia
    sketches also reveal unusual incidents and characters,
    handled with a genuine dramatic sense.   Reprinted: 1972.B6.

8   HENNEMAN, JOHN BELL. "The National Element in Southern
    Literature." <u>SR</u>, 11 (July), 355, 360, 362–63.
        The local color movement brought increased interest in
    Southern literature.   From 1876–1886 the new <u>Century</u>
    stressed American literature and included writers such as
    Harris.   He is an unwearying student of local color and
    elemental human nature; Uncle Remus made Southerners remem-
    ber their childhood.   Although Uncle Remus is a contribution
    to world folklore, such later stories as <u>Minervy Ann</u> repro-
    duce a whole phase of Southern and American life.

9   _____. "The Trend of Modern Literature." <u>SR</u>, 11 (April), 166–67.

There seems to have been a falling off in Southern literature in the last twenty years: too much repetition of dialect stories and types since Harris, Cable, and Page were first popular. Harris has gone beyond his Remus stories and is one of the first contemporaries to portray faithfully the essentials of humor and human nature. Harris deserves to succeed not as a Southerner but as a literary man.

10   HOYT, ELEANOR. "In Lighter Vein [review of <u>Tolliver</u>]." <u>Book Buyer</u>, 25 (January), 623–24.

<u>Tolliver</u> is a shrewd, sane, and calm historical record of the Reconstruction period. "Possibly the novel violates rules of construction and style." It is rambling and desultory, but one becomes interested in the agreeable folk along the way. <u>Tolliver</u> is not a great novel, but it is delightful reading that will only add to the author's literary laurels.

11   LINK, SAMUEL ALBERT. <u>Pioneers of Southern Literature</u>. Vol. 2. Nashville and Dallas: Publishing House, M. E. Church, South, p. 548.

Praises the postbellum Southern writers for their humor: "The most delicate touches of humor, as well as the fun of the 'laugh and grow fat' kind, abound" in Remus, Page, and others.

12   NORRIS, FRANK. "New York as a Literary Centre," in his <u>The Responsibilities of the Novelist</u>. New York: Doubleday, Page & Co., pp. 96–97.

Cites Harris as the representative Southern writer, an author of "larger caliber," who did not claim New York as a literary base. Reprinted: 1964.B14.

13   PAINTER, F.[RANKLIN] V.[ERZELIUS] N.[EWTON]. <u>Poets of the South</u>. New York, et al.: American Book Co., p. 27.

The South promises an Augustan age of literature and Harris is the first significant Southern prose writer. Praises Harris's Negro folklore but does not mention his poetry. Reprinted: 1968.B10.

1904

1904 B SHORTER WRITINGS

1   ANON. "A War Story." New York Times Saturday Review of
        Books (7 May), p. 307.
            Union Scout is a charming spy tale and love story that,
        while set during the Civil War, emphasizes kindness, un-
        selfishness, and chivalry instead of bitterness. "Nothing
        morbid, questionable, introspective, or preachy" is ever
        found in Harris's work, but just good tales about human,
        likable people. Harris easily stands among "the very best
        of the story-tellers."

2   ANON. Review of Union Scout. Nation, 78 (23 June), 500-501.
            According to the writers, much of the scouting in the
        Civil War was done by girls disguised as boys, and so it is
        with Union Scout. Told with Harris's accustomed ease, it
        reveals his familiarity with details of the War and feeling
        on both sides.

3   ANON. "Harris--A Little Union Scout." Critic, NS 45 (July),
        94.
            Union Scout is a lamely told story that treats a tradi-
        tional romantic theme in a superficial way and that "con-
        tinually threatens climaxes but never produces them."

4   ANON. Review of Union Scout. Independent, 57 (28 July), 216.
            There is nothing to recommend the conventional Union
        Scout except the "brilliant report" of General Forrest's
        skirmishing and the "excellent" Negro character likeness
        found in "Whistling Jim." If "there were as many female
        spies in the Civil War as has since been revealed in
        Southern fiction, the Confederates alone had enough of
        them to make a lady regiment."

5   ANON. Review of Union Scout. Boston Literary World, 35
        (August), 229.
            Union Scout is a rather pretty little love story, with
        much capturing and escaping and a little blood for variety.
        It remains, however, a confused and inconsequential tale
        that adds nothing to the literature of the War or to Har-
        ris's reputation. It "serves to pass an hour pleasantly
        enough, if one is not feeling strenuous."

6   ANON. "The Southern Darky and the South in Books of Verse."
        New York Times Saturday Review of Books (12 November),
        p. 766.

1904

Uncle Remus is a poet with "style and distinction and
humor and pathos and joy of heart," and in Rhymes he opens
up a luxuriantly imaginative world of both wisdom and folly.
As the note to "Baylor's Mail" indicates, this volume is
rich in "archeological value." Uncle Remus is the saga man
of a race that has been almost entirely obliterated.

7 BAKER, RAY STANNARD. "Joel Chandler Harris." Outlook, 78
(5 November), 594-603.
With Harris literary ability and style were inherent.
Claiming to be only a journalist, Harris nevertheless "succeeded because he did not try," and the publishers came to
him rather than vice-versa. He told old familiar stories
that were part of the oral tradition, but his artistry is
revealed in his handling of gesture, inflection, and setting.
Despite his natural abilities, Harris still worked hard at
his writing; he once showed Baker sixteen discarded introductions to a single story. His best literary portraits
are those of runaway slaves and other Negroes--Free Joe,
Aaron, Mingo, Blue Dave, Daddy Jake, and others. The
Thimblefinger stories, Pageants, and Daddy Jake are especially appreciated by children. Harris's fame as a poet
has been somewhat obscured by his success as a storyteller,
but one should not overlook poems like the "Revival Hymn."
Includes a description of Harris.

8 HEWINS, CAROLINE M., comp. Books for Boys and Girls: A
Selected List. Second edition, revised. A. L. A.
Annotated Lists, No. 9. Boston: American Library
Association Publishing Board, p. 19.
Lists Uncle Remus and Nights as enjoyable if read aloud
to children; the dialect is sometimes hard for them to read
themselves. Revised: 1915.B2.

9 ORMOND, JOHN RAPER. "Some Recent Products of the New School
of Southern Fiction." SAQ, 3 (July), 284.
A review-essay on novels by Glasgow, E. C. McCants, and
Baldwin Sears. Harris and Page represent one side of the
two-part school of post-Civil War Southern fiction; they
treated the life of the family slave. The other school em-
phasizes the planter class after the War, and James Lane
Allen, Glasgow, McCants, and Sears are its representatives.

1905

1905 A BOOKS - NONE

1905 B SHORTER WRITINGS

1   ANON. Review of Union Scout. Academy, 68 (18 February), 150.
    The book is readable but easily put down. Characters
    are not striking and the plot seems meaningless; much is
    left to the reader to deduce. The atmosphere of quietude
    reveals some literary quality.

2   ANON. Review of Union Scout. London Saturday Review, 99
    (25 March), 389.
    Union Scout will appeal primarily to Americans, although
    others who like a dash of history with their romance will
    also enjoy this fresh and graphic tale. "Whistling Jim,"
    the servant, is a memorable character.

3   ANON. "Last Speech was to Boys of the Tech." Atlanta
    Constitution (21 October), p. 4.
    News story. After giving a speech to students at the
    Georgia Institute of Technology yesterday, President Theo-
    dore Roosevelt told Clark Howell of the Constitution that
    the best feature of the day was "'getting Joel Chandler
    Harris into that luncheon [at the Piedmont Club]. By
    George, that was great. He is a wonderful man. I regard
    him as the greatest educator in the south along the lines
    he writes of.'" [See also 1905.B4-B6.]

4   ANON. "Lunch to President a Brilliant Affair." Atlanta
    Constitution (21 October), p. 4.
    News story. Among those presented to President Theodore
    Roosevelt at the luncheon [at the Piedmont Club] yesterday
    was Harris. Roosevelt told him what pleasure he had re-
    ceived from the Uncle Remus tales and insisted that Georgia's
    distinguished author stand with him to meet the guests.
    [See also 1905.B3, B5, B6.]

5   ANON. "President Roosevelt an Official Character." Atlanta
    Constitution (21 October), p. 8.
    News story containing text of President Theodore Roose-
    velt's speech at yesterday's luncheon at the Piedmont Club.
    "Georgia has done a great many things for the union, but
    she has never done more than when she gave Mr. Joel Chandler
    Harris to American literature." Praises Harris for uphold-
    ing in his writings the cause of decency and righteousness
    and for exalting the South without showing bitterness.
    People rise up better citizens, trying to solve American
    problems, for reading his stories--"'I am not speaking at

the moment of his wonderful folk tales.'" [See also 1905.B3, B4, B6.]

6   ANON. "Roosevelt's Tribute to Famous Georgian." Atlanta News (21 October), p. 1.
    News story. At his speech at the Piedmont Driving Club, Atlanta, yesterday, President Theodore Roosevelt said: "'Now, I am going to very ill repay the courtesy with which I have been greeted by causing for a minute or two acute discomfort to a man of whom I am very fond--Uncle Remus. Presidents may come and presidents may go, but Uncle Remus stays put. Georgia has done a great many things for the Union, but she has never done more than when she gave Mr. Joel Chandler Harris to American literature.... Where Mr. Harris seems to me to have done one of his greatest services is that he has written what exalts the South in the mind of every man who reads it, and yet what has not even a flavor of bitterness toward any other part of the Union.'" [See also 1905.B3-B5.]

7   ANON. Review of Told. New York Sun (11 November), pp. 8-9.
    One always calls for more of some books. Told has not had time to become a classic but it will do so; the stories are as good as the earlier Remus tales, although nothing can supplant the tar-baby story.

8   ANON. Review of Told. Chicago Evening Post (14 November), p. 7.
    Told is full of the same "sly, quaint humor" that marks all the Remus volumes. The new little boy, even though he is shy and sensitive, cannot long resist Uncle Remus.

9   ANON. "Children's Books.--I [review of Told]." Nation, 81 (16 November), 407.
    A full generation has been delighted by the Uncle Remus tales, and now the second generation may properly listen to the old man talk to the little boy's son. The new little boy is cleverly differentiated from his father and is a delicately worked out psychological study. The "consummate art" of Harris the folklorist is nowhere better manifested than in "Brother Fox Follows the Fashion."

10 ANON. "Harris--Told by Uncle Remus. New Stories of the Old Plantation." Critic, NS 47 (December), 576.
    Told is a welcome addition to the Christmas stocking. Harris "has lost none of his delight for old or young."

1905

11 ANON. Review of <u>Told</u>. <u>Review of Reviews</u>, 32 (December), 753.
    The new book <u>Told</u> is the "same old Uncle Remus, and the
    same old marvelous tales of animal lore, full of gentle
    humor and kindly negro wisdom."

12 ANON. "Uncle Remus Again." <u>New York Times Holiday Book
    Number</u> (1 December), p. 836.
    Uncle Remus's fund of stories and humor has not run out;
    <u>Told</u> is as full of charm as ever, even though Uncle Remus
    is older and a new little boy is his listener. Many of the
    stories are identical with those told in the West Indies
    and Africa. The cunning spider Annancy is the West Indian
    Brer Rabbit.

13 ANON. Review of <u>Told</u>. <u>Dial</u>, 39 (16 December), 444–45.
    "In response to an urgent demand for more Uncle Remus
    stories," Harris has published <u>Told</u>. The same sly humor
    permeates the tales, and, although Uncle Remus is portrayed
    as having aged somewhat, his storytelling faculty is unim-
    paired.

14 ARMES, ETHEL. "Leaves from a Reporter's Notebook. III. A
    New Version of Brer Rabbit and the Tar Baby: Being the
    Only Interview Ever Granted to the Press by Uncle Remus."
    <u>National Magazine</u>, 21 (February), [515]–17.
    Harris was at first reluctant to give an interview and
    like the tar-baby sat there on his front porch without say-
    ing anything. He finally commented that he was only a
    "'Georgia cracker'" and did not know anything. He claimed
    that he burned any letters that came from autograph-seekers,
    unless they were written by young children. He was de-
    lighted to show off his vegetable garden, and then the
    interview was abruptly over.

15 BRUCE, PHILIP ALEXANDER. <u>The Rise of the New South</u>. Vol. 17
    of <u>The History of North America</u>, edited by Guy Carleton Lee.
    Philadelphia: George Barrie & Sons, pp. 415, 417.
    Includes Harris in a group of new Southern authors su-
    perior to any of the prewar writers in realism, originality,
    purity of sentiment, characterization, and style. In <u>Nights</u>
    Harris described the Negro with "unequalled fidelity" and
    preserved the African lore with its humor and pathos better
    than any other American author. Praises the realism of the
    postwar Southern local colorists and finds this new trend
    encouraging.

16 CHAPPELL, J. HARRIS. <u>Georgia History Stories</u>. New York, et
    al.: Silver Burdett, pp. 202, 215, 338.

1905

Stories of Georgia is a "charming little book." Chappell
recommends Harris's graphic tales of the Oconee War and his
interesting story of the cotton gin. Also quotes Harris on
Nancy Hart.

17   LEVERETTE, FANNIE LEE. "Uncle Remus Inspires a Library."
New York Teacher's Magazine, 27 (June), 591–92.
In 1900 an Eatonton public school teacher told her pupils
of Harris's youth and early love for reading, and the
children decided to raise money to establish a library for
the school. Named "Joel Chandler Harris Library," by 1905
it contained over 300 volumes, making it one of the largest
in Georgia. Harris wrote the children a letter of appreciation in 1900.

18   M.[IMS], E.[DWIN]. Review of The Clansman by Thomas Dixon,
Jr., and The Lion's Skin by John S. Wise. SAQ, 4 (April),
194.
Thomas Dixon is not a successful novelist. His book
The Clansman is didactic as compared to the artistic power
of Harris's and Page's Reconstruction novels [Gabriel
Tolliver and Red Rock].

19   MOSES, MONTROSE J. "Juvenile Books of the Season [review of
Told]." Independent, 59 (14 December), 1385.
No series of tales will be more welcome than Told; here
Harris reveals that the advance of years only makes his
tone surer.

20   PANCOAST, HENRY S. An Introduction to American Literature.
New York: Henry Holt, pp. 261, 262, 365.
Refers to Harris's restful fun and shrewd wisdom; his
inclusion of the Negro is an element previously unknown in
literature. Cites Songs of the South, Uncle Remus, and Free
Joe in his lists of literature.

21   PATTEN, WILLIAM, ed. Short Story Classics (American). Vol. 4.
New York: P. F. Collier & Son, p. 1359.
Harris's name is inextricably bound with his dear crea-
tion, Remus. A few biographical facts are included.
"Brother Rabbit's Cradle" is printed on pp. 1361–71.

22   TRENT, W.[ILLIAM] P.[ETERFIELD], ed. Southern Writers:
Selections in Prose and Verse. New York: Macmillan,
pp. 377, 423.
Harris carried on Longstreet's tradition as a "depictor
of the humors of Georgia life." Uncle Remus secured for
him an instant national reputation. Provides a brief

1906

biographical sketch and cites Baskervill on Harris [see
1896.A1]. "Mr. Benjamin Ram and His Wonderful Fiddle" and
"Brother Billy Goat Eats His Dinner" are anthologized on
pp. 423–31.

1906 A BOOKS - NONE

1906 B SHORTER WRITINGS

1   ANON. "Andy and Uncle Remus Meet, Talk and Laugh." Atlanta
    Journal (7 April), p. 5.
        News story. Since Harris will not seek out notables,
    they go to him. Andrew Carnegie and Harris met warmly at
    Harris's West End home yesterday and talked for awhile.
    Harris later said he was pleased with the democracy of one
    of America's richest men but protested to Carnegie that if
    Carnegie's spelling reform project went through everyone
    would be writing dialect, and Harris would be put out of
    business. Carnegie observed that one of his main objects
    in going South was to meet Harris.

2   ANON. "Folk Tales." Times Literary Supplement (12 October),
    p. 346.
        The Told collection shows that, sadly, Uncle Remus is
    aging. Uncle Remus has to toil to interest the skeptical
    and modern little boy now sitting at his knee, and the re-
    sult is that "joyousness and rollick" are alike missing from
    the pages. "Perhaps mechanical is the word for the whole
    book."

3   ANON. "Magazine by Uncle Remus." Editor and Publisher
    (3 November), p. 3.
        Some $250,000 has been raised to finance Uncle Remus's
    Magazine, which is due to appear in March 1907, bearing an
    April imprint. With Julian Harris as general manager, the
    journal will appeal to a national constituency and publish
    fiction by the best known writers.

4   CANDLER, ALLEN D. and CLEMENT A. EVANS, eds. "Harris," in
    Cyclopedia of Georgia. Vol. 2: F-N. Atlanta, GA.: State
    Historical Association, pp. 217–18.
        Provides a brief biographical sketch and lists Nights,
    Mingo, Free Joe, Daddy Jake, and Balaam. Reprinted:
    1972.B3.

5   DIBBLE, S. W. "Uncle Remus's Magazine by Joel Chandler
    Harris." Atlanta Constitution (28 October), B, p. 5.

1906

Four-column article announcing the forthcoming Uncle
Remus's Magazine; it will be edited by Harris, "the south's
premier litterateur," whose works are best known wherever
English is spoken. Praises the effects of Harris's wholesome and optimistic personality on the magazine's character
and discusses the financing, staffing, printing equipment,
and editorial scope of the magazine.

6   HARRIS, MRS. LUNDY H. (CORA HARRIS). "Joel Chandler Harris."
    Christian Advocate, 67 (9 November), 7-8.
       Harris modestly insists upon "reserving his own life and
    the life of his home from the morbid public stare." His
    reticence is not timidity, however, but refinement and
    "moral delicacy of mind and feeling." His Georgian and
    Irish sense of humor is not racy, but rather philosophical
    and imaginative; readers have also not perceived the sub-
    tlety and perceptivity of his portraits of the Negroes and
    their folklore. The Negro is a poser, reluctant to reveal
    himself, but Harris gained his confidence. Tolliver was
    insufficiently appreciated in the North, where a "swashbuck-
    lering" image of the South is cultivated. It is interesting,
    finally, that the two American authors whose works have been
    most widely translated in foreign languages are both South-
    erners, Poe and Harris; but Poe's genius fell like a shadow
    over life, whereas Harris is "the very effulgence of philo-
    sophical cheerfulness." Reprinted: 1908.B24.

7   HOLLIDAY, CARL. A History of Southern Literature. New York
    and Washington: Neale Publishing Co., pp. 380-82, et
    passim.
       Folklore is the most permanent part of literature, and
    Harris's Remus tales will long outlive his novels and other
    sketches. They are "one of the most original contributions
    ...ever made to any literature." Mingo and Free Joe are
    "very readable" but not comparable to Remus. "He is a true
    type of the aged negro slave and in his mystery-loving way,
    he shows the inner life of the old South, its pride, its
    folly, its social distinctions, its mingling of strength and
    weakness." Harris sometimes catches the "spirit" and "move-
    ment" of the Negro songs. Free Joe also reveals Harris's
    understanding of the "negro nature": a "noble tribute" to
    the faithful slave and "bitter rebuke to the merciless
    slave-owner." Harris is an artist, yet retains the simpli-
    city, mystery, and charm of the ancient tales. Notable are
    his use of setting, his abrupt endings and sudden returns
    from the imaginative to the real world, and his "explicit,"
    "rugged" expression.

1906

8   [LEWIS, FRED]. "Joel Chandler Harris--Some Incidents and
     Characteristics." Atlanta <u>Constitution</u> (7 October),
     [Part 6], p. 5.
        A full page of anecdotes and sketches about Harris along
     with three of his poems, "A Remembrance," "Juliette," and
     "In Memoriam," and several Uncle Remus tales and sketches.
     One short commentary stresses Harris's ability as a poet,
     a side of his work which the reviewer believes has not been
     commented upon by critics; another quotes Harris's thoughts
     on the deleterious effects on Negro children of inadequate
     family life; another cites his views on the historical
     novel, which Harris says he knows less about than "pot li-
     quor" and dumplings. Forrest Adair's essay in <u>Methodist</u>
     <u>Magazine</u> is reprinted here [<u>see</u> 1899.B1].

1907 A BOOKS - NONE

1907 B SHORTER WRITINGS

1   ANON. "Dreams of Uncle Remus." Richmond <u>News Leader</u>
     (4 February), p. 4.
        Harris is correct in a recent New York <u>Evening Post</u>
     article in contending that the Negro has made considerable
     progress in the last forty years. Because of traditions in
     the South, however, the two races must advance separately,
     says Harris. Harris may be too optimistic about the future,
     for economic and political strife between the two races must
     surely come.

2   ANON. "Uncle Remus's Magazine." <u>Practical Advertising</u>, 1
     (March), pp. 1-3.
        <u>Uncle Remus's Magazine</u> will make its appearance in June
     1907; this review stresses the journal's promise as the best
     "high class literary monthly in the South." Harris's son
     Julian, business manager of the magazine, is encouraged by
     the $200,000 backing and a list of contributors to the first
     issues that includes Page, Riley, Ruth McEnery Stuart, as
     well as Joel Chandler Harris as general editor and Don
     Marquis as associate editor.

3   ANON. "'Uncle Remus' Breaks Bread with Roosevelt." Atlanta
     <u>Constitution</u> (19 November), pp. 1, 5.
        News story. On 18 November Harris, along with his son
     Julian and Don Marquis, were dinner guests at the White
     House. Topics discussed included <u>Uncle Remus's Magazine</u>
     and "nature faking." President Theodore Roosevelt said how
     much his children enjoyed the Uncle Remus tales, and Harris

1907

observed later to newsmen, "'I had the biggest time I ever
had in my life.'" Harris denied to reporters that he was
a "literary" gentleman, saying "'I am just a plain Georgia
collard eater.'" Then he "beat a hasty retreat to the seclusion of his room."

4   ANON. "Uncle Remus's Christmas Issue." Atlanta Constitution
    (22 November), p. 6.
        Previews the contents of the Christmas number of Uncle
    Remus's Magazine. In his editorial "Santa Claus and the
    Fairies" Harris upholds the illusions of youth in the face
    of the all-too-prevalent materialism at Christmastime.
    Billy Sanders uses homespun satire in discussing the ideal
    legislature. The magazine has made "a splendid record of
    improvement" from issue to issue.

5   HORTON, MRS. THADDEUS. "The Most Modest Author in America:
    At Home with 'Uncle Remus' on his Georgia Farm." Ladies'
    Home Journal, 24 (May), 17, 75.
        Modest Mr. Harris is no misanthrope; he loves friends,
    neighbors, family, and associates, but he prefers to live
    the quiet life. He refuses to be lionized. Recounts a
    visit made to Harris's house in the spring of 1906 by Andrew
    Carnegie. The two men exchanged humorisms and got along
    well; later Harris sent Carnegie four inscribed copies of
    his books. When President and Mrs. Roosevelt came to At-
    lanta in October 1905, Mrs. Roosevelt succeeded in "captur-
    ing" modest Uncle Remus, to make him stand beside her during
    the military parade. Reprinted: 1907.B6.

6   _____. "The Most Modest Author in America: At Home with
    'Uncle Remus' On His Georgia Farm." Atlanta Constitution
    (5 May) [Part 4], p. 3.
        Reprint of 1907.B5.

7   KNIGHT, LUCIAN LAMAR. Reminiscences of Famous Georgians.
    Vol. 1. Atlanta, GA.: Franklin-Turner Co., pp. 482-92,
    551.
        "Uncle Remus not only speaks the dialect but he embodies
    the humor and reproduces the folk-lore of the old-time
    negro." Harris "persistently disclaims any original crea-
    tive merit" in producing Uncle Remus and his tales. Harris,
    who has also written some poetry, cloisters himself from
    the public and finds authorship perennially refreshing.
    Brief biographical facts are included. [See also 1908.B28.]

8   MANLEY, LOUISE. Southern Literature From 1579-1895. Richmond,
    VA.: B. F. Johnson Publishing Co., pp. 401, 403.

1907

Harris's Uncle Remus stories are "faithful reproductions" of popular Negro tales of South Carolina, Georgia, and Alabama, told in the dialect of the different states. Because of his books the tales are now known in England. <u>Plantation</u> is "well and simply told." Prints "The Tar-Baby" on pp. 403-405.

9   MIMS, EDWIN. "The South's Intellectual Expression." <u>World's Work</u>, 14 (June), 8979, 8982.
    Discusses the popularity of new Southern literature from 1875 on. Includes Harris in a list of writers realistically portraying all aspects of Southern life and quotes Harris on being unpartisan.

10 MORROW, JAMES B. "Joel Chandler Harris Talks of Himself and Uncle Remus." <u>Boston Globe</u> (3 November), p. 5.
    In this interview, Harris calls Theodore Roosevelt America's greatest president since Lincoln and reminisces about his life at Turnwold Plantation and his later newspaper work. Not a politician, Harris says he is a "democrat" on election day only. On the Negro, Harris says they are "'all right,'" that there may be bloodshed along the way, and that the "'disfranchisement of the negro will do him good--at least he will be out of politics and will cease to be a football for the politicians, who have done him more injury than any one else.'" Harris observes that education is good for blacks and whites. Those who term the Negro idle and thriftless are misrepresenting him.

11 RUTHERFORD, MILDRED LEWIS. <u>The South in History and Literature: A Hand-Book of Southern Authors From the Settlement of Jamestown, 1607, to Living Writers</u>. Atlanta, GA.: Franklin-Turner Co., pp. 505-509.
    Reprint of 1894.B8 with additional commentary on <u>Uncle Remus's Magazine</u>.

12 SMITH, C. ALPHONSO. "'You All' as Used in the South." <u>Uncle Remus's Magazine</u>, 1 (July), 17.
    Cites testimony from Harris and Page that the expression "'you all'" when used in the South always has a plural referent.

13 SNYDER, HENRY N. "The Matter of 'Southern Literature.'" <u>SR</u>, 15 (April), 223.
    Harris has made a genuine contribution to American humor. His is an original humor, "racy of the soil" and faithfully recorded.

1908

14 WASHINGTON, BOOKER T. "The Economic Development of the Negro
    Race Since Its Emancipation," in The Negro in the South:
    His Economic Progress in Relation to His Moral and
    Religious Development, by Booker T. Washington and W. E.
    Burghardt DuBois. Philadelphia: George W. Jacobs & Co.,
    pp. 64-65.
        There are few higher authorites than Harris on the prog-
    ress of the Negro, which he has followed closely since the
    War. Quotes Harris that Negroes are a temperate race, sober
    and industrious. Reprint: 1970.B21.

15 WENDELL, BARRETT and CHESTER NOYES GREENOUGH. A History of
    Literature in America. New York: Charles Scribner's Sons,
    p. 411.
        The Southern fiction since the War has faithfully repro-
    duced Southern scenery and dialect, with a greater courtli-
    ness, pathos, and artistic skill than the other local color
    stories. Harris's Remus and Mingo are almost as familiar
    as Uncle Tom and vividly depict Georgia Negroes.

16 WOOT[T]EN, KATHARINE HINTON. "Bibliography of the Works of
    Joel Chandler Harris." Carnegie Library of Atlanta Monthly
    Bulletin, 4 (May-June), 1-6.
        Harris wrote on 17 September 1907 to thank Miss Wootten
    for this tentative compilation of secondary commentary and
    primary works, observing with characteristic modesty that
    he did not think a "'fifth-rate author'" deserved so much
    kindness. Wootten lists among the primary works Harris's
    books, major editorials, introductions, separately published
    short stories and poems, and published portraits. [The
    bibliography is reprinted in 1908.B7.]

1908 A BOOKS

1 [LEE, IVY LEDBETTER]. "Uncle Remus": Joel Chandler Harris as
   Seen and Remembered by a Few of His Friends. Privately
   printed, 120pp.
       Memorial volume presents essential facts of Harris's life
   and personal tributes by Charles A. Leonard, Ivy Ledbetter
   Lee, and James W. Lee and poems by Grantland Rice and Frank
   L. Stanton. [See also 1917.B6.]

1908 B SHORTER WRITINGS

1 ANON. "Uncle Remus is Slowly Sinking." Atlanta Journal
   (3 July), p. 1.

1908

Harris is dying; children are especially grief-stricken,
but hundreds of thousands of persons have an impersonal love
for him. No other man in the nation lies so close to
Georgians' hearts.

2   ANON. "Death Calls 'Uncle Remus' and Whole World Mourns."
     Atlanta Georgian and News (4 July), p. 1.
         Harris died at 7:58 p.m. on Friday, 3 July 1908. He had
     been critically ill for several days with cirrhosis of the
     liver, but the immediate cause of death was acute nephritis,
     or inflammation of the kidneys. Harris was baptised the
     previous week at St. Anthony's Catholic Church in West End
     Atlanta. The first letter of sorrow came from President
     Roosevelt.

3   ANON. Harris eulogies. Atlanta Constitution (4 July), p. 6.
         A page of unsigned eulogies and commemorative notes about
     Harris's passing. He was admired by Theodore Roosevelt and
     by West End neighbors, as well as by the world at large.
     His creed was mutual trust, optimism, and tolerance for all
     things living.

4   ANON. "'In the Matter of Belief,' Last Editorial of Mr.
     Harris." Atlanta Constitution (4 July), p. 3.
         It is a weird and powerful coincidence that the last edi-
     torial Harris wrote before his death for Uncle Remus's The
     Home Magazine was "In the Matter of Belief," in which he
     states his humble and forceful belief in Christianity. The
     editorial is reprinted.

5   ANON. "Joel Chandler Harris Summoned by Master of All Good
     Workmen." Atlanta Constitution (4 July), pp. 1, 6.
         News item. Harris died at eight p.m. on 3 July of cir-
     rhosis of the liver and uremic poisoning; his family was
     present. The children of the world will mourn his loss, as
     will the animals watching from the hedges. Includes sketch
     of his life, career, works, and character.

6   ANON. "Uncle Remus is Called to Rest." Atlanta Journal
     (4 July), p. 1.
         News item. Harris died at the Wren's Nest at eight p.m.
     on Friday, 3 July. Telegrams have been coming in steadily
     since last night, including one from President Roosevelt.

7   ANON. "Uncle Remus Wrote 41 Books." Atlanta Journal
     (4 July), p. 3.
         Prints Katharine Wootten's bibliography of Harris's works
     and a checklist of writings about him. [See 1907.B16.]

1908

8   ANON. "Grief is Told by Telegrams." Atlanta <u>Constitution</u>
     (5 July), D, p. 3.
         Prints seven telegrams expressing sorrow over Harris's
     death, including one sent by James Whitcomb Riley.

9   ANON. "'Uncle Remus' Will Be Buried This Afternoon." Atlanta
     <u>Constitution</u> (5 July), [D, p. 1].
         News story. Services for Harris will be held at St.
     Anthony's Chapel, West End, followed by the burial at West-
     view cemetery. During the past several years many famous
     persons, including Richard Malcolm Johnston, James Whitcomb
     Riley, Andrew Carnegie, and Theodore Roosevelt, have sought
     out "Uncle Remus" at his home in West End. Sorrow over his
     death is universal.

10   ANON. "Obituary [death of Harris]." London <u>Times</u> (6 July),
     p. 8.
         Three-sentence biographical sketch, followed by critical
     comments. Grown men, as well as children, find the Uncle
     Remus tales as amusing and apt as <u>Alice in Wonderland</u>. The
     Uncle Remus stories were taken down from the Negroes them-
     selves, and Harris has earned a well-deserved place in the
     world of folklore and ethnology. He was a lover of children
     and nature.

11   ANON. "Uncle Remus." <u>Nation</u>, 87 (9 July), 26–27.
         The field that Harris opened has since been plowed indus-
     triously by folklorists and short story writers, but it is
     doubtful that any writer has equalled Harris's balance be-
     tween truth and art. Sadly, Harris has fallen away from
     this balance in his later Uncle Remus volumes, deflecting
     too much towards the truth. One should not bind the South-
     ern Negro too close to his African ancestry. It will be
     years before anthropologists know how much of Southern Negro
     lore comes from the Congo and how much from the banks of the
     "Rappchannoch [sic]" and Chattahoochee. The elements of the
     Remus stories are common to all people, but it will take
     someone following in the steps of a Paul Laurence Dunbar to
     discover the real African soul behind the American Negro's
     and his white brethren's modifications of atavistic belief.

12   ANON. "The Death of Joel Chandler Harris." <u>Christian</u>
     <u>Advocate</u>, 69 (10 July), 5.
         Harris will be remembered not merely as a humorist, but
     as a "gentle and loving philosopher." Harris has also done
     incalculable good "in interpreting and humanizing the mind
     of the negro, [and] in softening the asperities born of
     racial antagonisms and of the vicious social order which
     the South inherited from a cruder age."

1908

13   ANON. "The Author of 'Uncle Remus.'" <u>Outlook</u> (11 July),
       p. 548.
       None of the Georgian writers "has brought out the local
       color, the dialect, the dry, drawling wit, and the shrewd
       wisdom of the Northern Georgian as did Joel Chandler Harris."
       Harris, with Henry Grady, also did much "to establish new
       ideals and an open-minded spirit toward the Nation, not
       only in Georgia but throughout the South."

14   ANON. "Uncle Remus." <u>Harper's Weekly</u>, 52 (11 July), 29.
       "Uncle Remus" became a household word in 1880, and the
       humor, vividness, and charm of his stories made them affec-
       tionately known to Southerner and Northerner alike. Harris
       died on 3 July 1908. Includes a brief sketch of his life
       and a list of his major books.

15   ANON. "The Author of 'Uncle Remus.'" <u>Review of Reviews</u>, 38
       (August), 214-15.
       Sketches Harris's life and character and comments on his
       shyness. Harris's reading habits at Turnwold Plantation,
       where he went straight to the classics of English literature,
       as well as to Hugo and Goethe, help explain his kindly
       philosophy and shrewd humor. Even without the Remus tales,
       which have now been translated into twenty-seven languages,
       Harris would have had a respectable reputation on the basis
       of his short stories, <u>Tolliver</u>, his history of Georgia
       [<u>Stories of Georgia</u>], and <u>Grady</u>.

16   ANON. "How Joel Chandler Harris Came to Write the 'Uncle
       Remus' Stories." <u>Current Literature</u>, 45 (August), 164-66.
       Many works of genius come about by accident, as did the
       Remus stories. Quotes extensively from Baker's article in
       <u>Outlook</u> [1904.B7] on Harris's art and shyness. The <u>Nation</u>
       found Harris more subtle and truthful than Harte. He was
       concerned, like Howells and James, with the inward value of
       things: "the depth of a child's sudden glance." Amazed at
       his own success, Harris never sought to "formulate" life.

17   ANON. "A Letter to President Roosevelt and His Response."
       <u>Uncle Remus' The Home Magazine</u>, 24 (September), 5-6.
       Roosevelt wrote Julian Harris on 6 July 1908 that he be-
       lieved Harris created "one of the undying characters of
       story," Uncle Remus, and that "the ethical quality" of his
       writings was as important as their literary value. Harris
       was not didactic, yet his readers learned from them to set
       a higher value upon courage, honesty, truth, and kindly
       generosity. The best way for the country to pay its debt
       to Harris would be to support the magazine he founded.

1908

18 BAKER, FRANKLIN T., ed. A Bibliography of Children's
    Reading. New York: Teachers College, pp. 11–12, 18,
    63–64, 72, 77.
        Various of Harris's books are recommended under the cate-
    gories "Old Fairy Tales," "Modern Fairy Tales," "Stories of
    Southern Life," "Histories," and "Stories of Animals."
    Entries are briefly annotated.

19 BENNETT, JOHN. "Gullah: A Negro Patois [Part 1]." SAQ, 7
    (October), 335n, 336.
        Harris tentatively tried Gullah dialect in the character
    of Daddy Jack [in Nights]; Charles Colcock Jones did a re-
    markable Gullah collection, that was unfortunately over-
    shadowed by Harris's "easier" Remus tales in 1888 [see
    1888.B18]; in general, the dialect has been little exploited.
    It is richer in color and philological interest than Har-
    ris's or Page's Virginia Negro patois.

20 BREVARD, CAROLINE MAYS. Literature of the South. New York:
    Broadway Publishing Co., pp. 136–37.
        Harris brought the Negro into literature for entertain-
    ment and delight. His Remus stories "charmed Southerners
    by their very familiarity as they charmed Northerners by
    their novelty."

21 DOOLY, ISMA. "A Great World Spirit Passed in 'Uncle Remus.'"
    Atlanta Constitution (4 July), p. 6.
        Universal grief was felt at the passing of Harris. The
    nation lost one of her noblest citizens, American journalism
    one of its ablest writers, English literature one of its
    greatest exponents, and the world one of its greatest
    writers of folklore. His books have been translated into
    twenty-seven languages.

22 _____. "Some Incidents in Life of Lamented 'Uncle Remus.'"
    Atlanta Constitution (5 July), D, p. 3.
        Character sketch relates typical anecdotes about Harris's
    shyness and abhorence of personal notoriety. He died in
    the fullness of his career, while editing Uncle Remus's
    Magazine, collaborating with his son Julian in a "dramatic
    novel," and helping Dr. E. A. Alderman of the University of
    Virginia prepare an edition of Southern literature.

23 HARRIS, JULIAN. "To Our Readers--A Statement." Uncle Remus's
    The Home Magazine, 24 (September), 6.
        Joel Chandler Harris had trained Julian to take over the
    magazine one day, and his extreme kindness and sympathy to-
    wards individuals even carried over into the type of

1908

advertising he permitted the magazine to carry. The magazine will continue to seek to mend sectional differences
and "to promote a spirit of commercial progress allied to
...high ideals and movements of a beneficent nature."

24   HARRIS, MRS. LUNDY H. (CORA HARRIS). "Joel Chandler Harris."
     Christian Advocate, 69 (10 July), 16–17.
     Reprint of 1906.B6.

25   ____. "The Passing of Uncle Remus." Independent, 65
     (23 July), 190–92.
     Although Harris wrote magazine stories and a novel about
     Reconstruction, he is known chiefly for the Uncle Remus
     stories. He was of a retiring disposition and can never
     be regarded as one of the foremost literary men of his
     times. Rather, he sought out the long-buried lore of old
     races and became the seer and guide, the philosopher and
     historian, of man and creature relationships. His creative
     genius evoked an almost prenatal part of human memory.

26   KENNY, MICHAEL, S.J. "Joel Chandler Harris (Uncle Remus)."
     Messenger, 50 (September), 225–42.
     Examines Harris's character in the light of his interest
     in Catholicism and his espousal of the faith in the last
     month of his life. Harris had long admired Newman, liked
     to lend his copy of the Apologia to his friends, and had
     read The Messenger for five years; yet his French-Canadian
     wife Esther LaRose was his strongest argument. She appears
     in his fiction as Mary Bullard in Sister Jane, Sophia in
     Tolliver, and Miss Sally in the Uncle Remus tales. Further-
     more, charity and Christian understanding were themes in
     Harris's life as well as in his fiction. Pictures of Our
     Lady adorned Harris's library, and a rosary hung by his
     bed. Perhaps Harris did not join the Church sooner because
     he disliked crowds, but he did help to found St. Anthony's
     parish in West End Atlanta and bought the lot for the
     chapel-site. Tolliver and Plantation present viable solu-
     tions to postwar problems. Harris's trust in Providence is
     reminiscent of St. Francis.

27   KNIGHT, LUCIAN LAMAR. "Lucian Knight Commends The Children's
     Monument." Atlanta Journal (6 July), p. 6.
     How appropriate it would be for the children of America
     to rear a monument to Uncle Remus.

28   ____. Reminiscences of Famous Georgians. Vol. 2. Atlanta:
     Franklin-Turner Co., pp. 447, 507, 509.

1908

Over a score of celebrated Georgians, including Harris,
have had a background in journalism. Along with other
Georgians, Harris has made important contributions to historical literature. [See also 1907.B7.]

29   MARQUIS, DON. "The Farmer of Snap-Bean Farm." Uncle Remus's
     The Home Magazine, 24 (September), 7.
     Harris had a philosophy about the basic kinship of na-
     ture; this is the quality "which makes his 'critters' half-
     human, sympathetic, understandable characters instead of
     merely caricatures of animals or stories about animals."
     He loved his flower garden and once referred to a beautiful
     wisteria vine in full bloom as "'a poem of mine'"; he was a
     mystic, in touch with things hidden from ordinary vision.

30   MIMS, EDWIN. "The Passing of Two Great Americans." SAQ, 7
     (October), 327-31.
     Grover Cleveland and Harris died within a week of each
     other. Both were Americans with a national spirit. Harris
     was provincial but opposed sectionalism, and he drew uni-
     versal portraits. In the Uncle Remus books and other
     Southern stories he interpreted his people to America and
     the world. He was more beloved in family circles than any
     of his contemporaries. The Uncle Remus books realistically
     portray the old-time Negro, and his short stories are full
     of realism and romance. But Tolliver and other later works
     show a decline in his imaginative powers.

31   ORGAIN, KATE ALMA. Southern Authors in Poetry and Prose.
     New York and Washington: Neale Publishing Co., pp. 110-18.
     Describes Harris's early life on the plantation and
     praises his representation of the Negro and Middle Georgia
     life as the best of the Southern writers. Lists his pub-
     lished work and gives an extract from "The Old Bascom
     Place" [Balaam].

32   ROBINSON, ROBY. "Publisher's Announcement." Uncle Remus's
     The Home Magazine, 23 (August), 5.
     Before he died Harris requested that no monuments be
     erected in his name. He wished only that his magazine suc-
     ceed and that this line be printed somewhere on it:
     "'Founded by Joel Chandler Harris.'" He also urged, "'Keep
     the magazine clean and wholesome and fresh.... Never let
     it become just a money-making machine.'" His son Julian
     has been named editor.

33   TICKNOR, CAROLINE. "Some Glimpses of the Author of 'Uncle
     Remus.'" New York Bookman, 27 (August), 551-57.

107

1908

It has been said [see Allen, 1896.B2] that the two
genuine creations in American fiction are Uncle Tom and
Uncle Remus; Remus, however, is dedicated to purposes of
peace, not revolution. Harris wrote other books, but his
humorous studies in the Uncle Remus series are his best
works. Reproduces some of Harris's correspondence with the
J. R. Osgood publishing house about his preparation of materials for Nights (1883) and Mingo (1884), to show that
he, like any author, had anxieties and headaches about
deadlines, story-length, and revisions.

34   [WATSON, THOMAS E.]. "Uncle Remus is Dead." Watson's
     Jeffersonian Magazine, 2 (August), 437–39.
         Watson recalls reading Harris's humorous paragraphs in
     the Savannah Morning News. He met Harris in Atlanta in
     1880; he was red-headed, freckle-faced, and ugly, and "he
     was plainly incapable of adjusting himself to human miscel-
     lany." Harris never did any better work than the poems and
     fugitive pieces that appeared long before Uncle Remus.

1909 A BOOKS - NONE

1909 B SHORTER WRITINGS

1   ANON. Review of Bishop. Nation, 88 (18 February), 171.
         Bishop is a "sunny book" working out in Harris's own
     fashion the "leading motive" in Silas Marner: a young girl
     with imaginary playmates humanizes a crabbed old uncle. The
     book shows the structural weaknesses of rapid improvisation
     but its Southern characters and imagination make it charming
     nevertheless.

2   ANON. "Mysterious Cally-Lou." New York Times Saturday Review
     of Books (20 February), p. 103.
         Our debt of gratitude to Harris is only increased with
     Bishop, one of his last works. The book is a charming and
     quaint piece of whimsicality, and Cally Lou comes to be as
     real as "Miss Meadows and de Gals" or the tar-baby. Grown-
     ups will enjoy it even more than the children.

3   ANON. Review of Bishop. Times Literary Supplement, no. 375
     (19 March), p. 105.
         The invisible girl Cally-Lou is treated with delicacy
     and freshness, "but there is a sad decline into racial poli-
     tics," and the homely sagacity in dialect has a tendency to
     irritate--"shrewd and human though Mr. Saunders [sic], the
     chief talker, undoubtedly is."

1909

4 ANON. Review of Bishop. ALA Booklist, 5 (April), [113]-14.
   Bishop is "[s]light, uneventful and disconnected, but
   full of the author's characteristic charm and humor."

5 ANON. Review of Bishop. Athenaeum, no. 4249 (3 April),
   p. 403.
   Plot summary, essentially. Harris writes about children
   with sympathy, and the atmosphere of the tale is delightful.

6 ANON. Review of Bishop. London Saturday Review, 107
   (17 April), 502.
   Brief sketch of major characters and plot in Bishop.
   The orphan Adelaide touches the heart of her miserly old
   uncle in "the usual approved fashion."

7 ANON. "Personality of 'Uncle Remus.'" Journal of Education,
   69 (20 May), 546.
   Restates ideas from Stanton's article in the Delineator
   [see 1909.B20].

8 ANON. "An Unmitigated Villain [review of Shadow]." New York
   Times Saturday Review of Books (6 November), p. 689.
   Shadow is a story of a villain, but one relieved by many
   touches of humor and forms of racy speech; sadly, it is the
   last story by "'Billy Sanders.'" It has the "inimitable
   flavor of all Mr. Harris has written" and will be welcomed
   by the English-speaking world which knows and loves the
   author as "'Uncle Remus.'"

9 ANON. Review of Shadow. Independent, 67 (23 December), 1455.
   Shadow is a slight story but one redeemed by the method
   of the telling--much as a homely face is immortalized by
   the brush of an artist. Uncle Billy Sanders resembles Harris, and the story is typical of Harris in that it does not
   provoke bitterness about the War. Harris had the wisdom of
   peace, and no better example of his peculiar intelligence
   and tolerant humor can be found than in this book.

10 ARNOLD, GERTRUDE WELD, ed. A Mother's List of Books for
   Children. Chicago: A. C. McClurg & Co., pp. 101, 125,
   194.
   Uncle Remus is among books recommended for the ten-year-
   old; the Negro dialect makes reading the tales aloud de-
   sirable. Nights is appropriate for the child of eleven and
   Plantation for the thirteen-year-old. Entries are briefly
   annotated. Reprinted: 1912.B1.

1909

11 BALL, SUMTER MAYS. "'Uncle Remus' in His Career as Joel
    Chandler Harris, Author and Editor." Book News Monthly, 27
    (January), 311-16.
        Harris was surprised to learn the year before he died
    that he had written or edited close to forty books. Reviews
    Harris's life and works and his responses to the praise that
    was showered upon him. "Free Joe" shows Harris's severe in-
    dictment of slavery, while Tolliver is one of America's best
    Reconstruction novels, surpassing The Clansman and The
    Traitor. Harris evidently admired James's Portrait of a
    Lady and found Hawthorne's The Scarlet Letter the great
    novel of America; he argued firmly against a narrow provin-
    cialism in literature. Includes a partial bibliography of
    Harris's works.

12 BRADLEY, HENRY STILES. "Joel Chandler Harris," in Library of
    Southern Literature. Vol. 5. Edited by Edwin Anderson
    Alderman, Joel Chandler Harris, and Charles William Kent.
    New Orleans, Atlanta, Dallas: Martin & Hoyt Co.,
    pp. 2111-20.
        If one counts the children, there is no better loved man
    in the country today than Harris; he is as familiar around
    the country as Emerson, Whittier, Longfellow, or Holmes. A
    man as shy as his animal friends, he has glorified the com-
    monplace and was being quoted all over the English-speaking
    world a few months after he began to print his Uncle Remus
    sketches in the Atlanta Constitution. Although stories in
    Free Joe and Mingo have touches of pathos as tender as any
    stories in English, his fame will rest on the "cheerful,
    hopeful, mirthful" Uncle Remus tales. With the possible
    exception of Page, Harris is the best dialect writer in
    America. Uncle Remus settled the question of the inherit-
    ance of character traits that Darwin, Spencer, and others
    have argued. He decided that acquired traits are trans-
    mitted to offspring; for when Brer Rabbit lost his tail
    fishing, all his progeny became tailless. Includes some
    biographical facts, a brief secondary bibliography, and a
    full primary bibliography of Harris's books.

13 ELLIS, LEONORA BECK. "'Uncle Remus' and the Children."
    Book News Monthly, 27 (January), 321-23.
        Harris loved and was beloved by the children, writes a
    former friend who lived near his house; neighborhood chil-
    dren were always playing at the Wren's Nest.

14 LEE, JAMES W. "Joel Chandler Harris." Century, 77 (April),
    891-97.

1909

Biographical sketch and appreciation of Harris. Illus-
trates Harris's sense of humor and shyness and stresses his
formative years on Turner's plantation. The Negro was Harris's "human text-book, which he studied and mastered."
His was a retiring and unpretentious personality, and he
liked the seclusion of his home. His editorials for the
Atlanta Constitution were always clearly written.

15   [MIMS, EDWARD; ARTHUR HOWARD NOLL; GEORGE F. MELLEN; H. I.
     BROCK; and NORMAL WALKER]. History of the Literary and
     Intellectual Life of the Southern States. Vol. 7 of The
     South in the Building of the Nation. Richmond, VA.:
     Southern Historical Publication Society, pp. 40, 65, 66,
     67, 71-72, 87, 284, 289, 429, 467-68, 533.
        Separate chapters authored by several hands briefly com-
     pare Harris's writings to those of Irwin Russell, and note
     his contributions to Southern humor and folklore, as well
     as his portrayal of the "childlike happiness of the negro
     under the slave system." Harris has written "better negro
     literature" for popular consumption than the black man has.

16   MIMS, EDWARD. "Introduction," in his History of Southern
     Fiction. Vol. 8 of The South in the Building of the Nation.
     Richmond, VA.: Southern Historical Publication Society,
     pp. xlviii, xlix, lii-liii, liv, lviii.
        Harris initially wrote to fill newspaper space or for
     fun, and his celebrated tales appeal to Negroes as well as
     to people the world over. Anthologizes "Brer Wolf Says
     Grace," "Brer Rabbit and the Little Girl," and "Free Joe."

17   [PAYNE, LEONIDAS WARREN, JR.]. "Joel Chandler Harris," in
     Biography. Vol. 11 of The South in the Building of the
     Nation. Richmond, VA.: Southern Historical Publication
     Society, pp. 451-52.
        Biographical and critical sketch and partial bibliography
     of primary works. The Uncle Remus books "form one of the
     most notable contributions to folklore and general litera-
     ture produced in this country," and Uncle Remus is "one of
     the greatest creations in American fiction."

18   ROGERS, JOSEPH M. "Joel Chandler Harris: A Personal
     Recollection." Book News Monthly, 27 (January), 324-27.
        There was probably more public grief over the death of
     Harris than over that of almost any other literary man of
     this generation. Rogers had heard many of the Uncle Remus
     tales from his Negro nurse, prior to reading them, and he
     would later meet Harris. Henry Grady must have drawn in-
     spiration from Harris's non-partisan approach to postwar

1909

life, but few people know of Harris's short stories of the
South--especially "Little Compton" [in Free Joe], which
stresses North-South reconciliation. It is a better view
of the Southern philosophy towards rapprochement than the
hundreds of volumes by statesmen and warriors. Harris
sought to reveal the mind and soul of the South to the
whole nation, and even to the South itself. His greatest
achievement, however, was that he appealed to children in
a way no other author has equaled.

19   SMITH, CHARLES FORSTER. Reminiscences and Sketches.
      Nashville and Dallas: Publishing House of the M. E. Church,
      South, pp. 52, 54-56, 174.
          William Malone Baskervill had recommended Harris and
      Cable to Smith, who feels these new writers gave the South
      artistic expression. Quotes from Baskervill [see 1896.A1]
      and finds "Free Joe" to be his best and most sympathetic
      story.

20   STANTON, FRANK L. "At Snap Bean Farm." Delineator, 73 (May),
      678-79, 715-17.
          Account based upon a personal interview. Lengthy de-
      scription of Harris's physical appearance, personality, and
      residence at West End Atlanta. He always wore a soft felt
      hat, indoors and out, except at dinner, and a slight im-
      pediment in his speech accentuated his "native modesty."
      A genial and compassionate man, Harris liked to help those
      in distress and loved children, his gardens, and home life.
      He was troubled that the new generation of Negroes was grow-
      ing up in the streets, without a home life. Local Atlanta
      blacks did not call him "'Colonel,'" or "'Cap'n,'" or even
      "'[G]uv'ner.'" He was just "'Mr. Harris.'"

21   STANTON, THEODORE, et al., eds. A Manual of American
      Literature. Tauchnitz Edition, Vol. 4000. Leipzig:
      Bernhard Tauchnitz, pp. 241-42, 393-94, 499.
          Provides a brief biographical summary. The Remus tales
      are African variants of the beast epic. Harris gives a
      faithful picture of Middle Georgia in his books. After
      listing seven of Harris's short story collections, comments
      that the short story was better suited to his ability than
      novels. Tolliver was not successful. Most readers saw the
      popular Remus stories in a humorous light and neglected
      their anthropological significance.

22   TICKNOR, CAROLINE. "The Man Harris: A Study in Personality."
      Book News Monthly, 27 (January), 317-20.

1910

Harris loved the simple life, focused around family and a few good friends. He would characteristically explain that he was only an "accidental author," and someone [Baker; see 1904.B7] noted that Harris "succeeded because he did not try." Born and bred in the "briar patch" in Middle Georgia, Harris wrote about that corner of the world.

23 TRENT, WILLIAM P.[ETERFIELD]. A Brief History of American Literature. New York: D. Appleton, pp. 224, 242-43.
    Harris wrote unique Negro folklore and depicted the humors of life in Georgia.

24 WASHINGTON, BOOKER T. The Story of the Negro. Vol. 1. New York: Doubleday, Page & Co., pp. 161-62.
    Southern writers "have not failed to do full justice" to the part the Negro played in antebellum Southern life. Harris's Brer Rabbit stories recreate the Negro storyteller and American Negro folktales and are a lasting element in American literature.

25 [WOOTTEN, KATHARINE HINTON]. "Joel Chandler Harris: Dec. 9, 1848-July 3, 1908." Monthly Bulletin Published by Carnegie Library of Atlanta, 6 (June), 82.
    A list of articles and reviews published about Harris since his death.

1910 A BOOKS - NONE

1910 B SHORTER WRITINGS

1 ANON. Review of Shadow. ALA Booklist, 6 (February), 218.
   Shadow is a "dramatic little dialect tale, inimitably told with picturesque humor."

2 ANON. Review of Little Boy. New York Times Saturday Review of Books (10 September), p. 498.
   Fathers who read the first Uncle Remus stories will not want to neglect this group. Uncle Remus is his "perfect self," and one of the little boy's accomplishments is to write a letter that wipes out the whole Civil War.

3 ANON. "Books for the Young [review of Little Boy]." Independent, 69 (29 September), 707.
   No "'blurb'" is necessary in the case of Harris's latest work, Little Boy. Uncle Remus "goes without saying."

1910

4   ANON. "Uncle Remus." New York Times Saturday Review of
    Books (8 October), p. 559.
        Little Boy is like a gift from the grave. The "'cree-
    turs'" are as engaging and original in their projects as
    ever and Uncle Remus, as would be expected, shows a little
    more garrulity in his old age.

5   AVARY, MYRTA LOCKETT. "'The Sign of the Wren's Nest.'"
    Christian Herald, 33 (2 March), 196.
        Plans by the Uncle Remus Memorial Association to raise
    money to purchase Harris's West-End Atlanta home, "The Sign
    of the Wren's Nest," are progressing. Relates some anec-
    dotes about Harris's shyness at a New York dinner with
    Henry Grady, and with President and Mrs. Theodore Roosevelt
    when they came to Atlanta. The house got its name when
    Harris refused to remove a wren family from his letterbox
    at the gate.

6   COLBRON, GRACE ISABEL. "As a Little Child [review of Little
    Boy]." New York Bookman, 32 (December), 408.
        Who cannot love Uncle Remus's wholesome view of life,
    which is now displayed in Little Boy. The "delicious" story
    of the Doodang, the humorous poem "Ole Joshua an' de Sun,"
    and the portrait of commonsensical "Miss Sally" are recom-
    mended to the reader.

7   MIMS, EDWIN and BRUCE R. PAYNE. Southern Prose and Poetry for
    Schools. New York, Chicago, and Boston: Charles Scribner's
    Sons, pp. 10, 139 n.1, 427.
        "Free Joe" [anthologized on pp. 139-55] reveals the uni-
    versal elemental nature of man; its significance lies in
    the different view of slavery than that found in Page or
    the Remus stories. Biographical sketch and list of twenty
    of Harris's books are included on p. 427.

8   MOSES, MONTROSE J. The Literature of the South. New York:
    Thomas Y. Crowell, pp. 234, 236, 383, 466, 468, 470-71.
        Harris's genius is shown in the Uncle Remus tales. "We
    doubt, in the sum total of Southern literary activity for
    the past forty years, whether any more permanent contribu-
    tion has been made to America than [his] record of the
    folk-lore which sprang up among the negroes of different
    types, peopling the rice plantations and cotton districts
    during slavery." Harris's art preserved "the real African
    flavor of the originals," while unobtrusively adding "the
    rich background of plantation life in Middle Georgia before
    the war." Though folklore is the most original element in
    Southern literature, it has yet to be treated in relation

1911

to the poor whites and not much has been added to Harris's
investigation of the Negro folklore and folk-song. "Free
Joe" reflects "technical and artistic excellences." Tolliver is a "strong," graphic story of Reconstruction: despite
the fact that the issues are now dead, it gives a firsthand
treatment of a worthy civilization.

1911 A BOOKS - NONE

1911 B SHORTER WRITINGS

1   BEALE, ROBERT CECIL. The Development of the Short Story in
    the South. Charlottesville, VA: Michie Co., Printers,
    pp. 55-56, 65-67, 80, et passim.
        Harris continued the portrayal of cracker life that
    Richard Malcolm Johnston had begun in Dukesborough Tales.
    Harris admirably portrays the "narrowness of view, the
    strength of prejudice, the homely wisdom and quaintness and
    vigor of expression belonging to this class." He was also
    the first writer to give the world a full and vivid picture
    of the Negro. "Mingo," "Blue Dave," and "Balaam and His
    Master" show some of the social effects of slavery.

2   ESPINOSA, AURELIO M. "New-Mexican Spanish Folk-Lore." JAF,
    24 (October-December), 422-23.
        Espinosa found Brer Rabbit stories in New Mexican folk-
    lore, but contrary to Marden [see 1896.B48] believed the
    tales to be of European origin.

3   HALLECK, REUBEN POST. History of American Literature.
    New York, Cincinnati, Chicago: American Book Co.,
    pp. 320-23, et passim.
        Harris's animal stories are told with skill, humor, and
    poetic spirit; they challenge comparison with Kipling's
    jungle tales. The witty and resourceful rabbit, and the
    patriarchal Uncle Remus, who is no burlesque or "sentimental
    impossibility," are original characters. Harris also writes
    vividly about Georgia crackers and poor free Negroes in
    Mingo and Free Joe. Includes brief biographical sketch and
    study questions.

4   HART, ALBERT BUSHNELL. The Southern South. New York:
    Association Press, D. Appleton, p. 305.
        Southern writing is too sectional; Harris, however, typi-
    fies one school of Southern writers who found broader themes
    and provided "the delightful flavor of a passing and roman-
    tic epoch." The principal current literary work of the
    South is in its newspapers.

1911

5 HEYDRICK, BENJAMIN A. "III. The Short Story." Chautauquan, 64 (November), 320-21, 333.
The contrast between the past and present status of Southern aristocracy is the theme of many short stories. In Home Folks, for example, Harris portrays a Southern mansion before and after the Civil War [two passages from "A Run of Luck" are printed that show how the house had deteriorated]. Free Joe and Home Folks are listed under "Georgia" in a checklist of "Short Stories Dealing with Recent American Life: Local Studies."

6 JOHNSTON, FRANCES BENJAMIN. "Photographing 'Uncle Remus.'" Uncle Remus's Home Magazine, 29 (June), 7-8.
As a child in Georgia, Johnston had heard tales of Brer Rabbit, Brer Fox, and the tar-baby from a Virginia "mammy" before she met Harris. Harris disliked being photographed, but Johnston obtained permission and took several pictures of him at his West End home. His shyness and self-consciousness gradually disappeared, and he later thanked Johnston for capturing the "twinkle" in his eye.

7 KNIGHT, LUCIAN LAMAR. "Contributions of the South to the Republic of Letters." Atlanta Constitution (10 March), B, p. 6.
Open letter to President Taft surveys Southern writers. Harris is unsurpassed among the delineators of character in modern American fiction, and his Uncle Remus tales share an immortality of fame with Defoe and Dickens; they have been translated into seventeen languages. Irwin Russell's dialect songs paved the way for Harris and Page. Reprinted: 1919.B6.

8 MABIE, HAMILTON W.[RIGHT]. The Blue Book of Fiction: A List of Novels Worth Reading Chosen from Many Literatures. Cincinnati: Globe-Wernicke Co., p. 29.
Under "American Fiction," Mabie recommends Bishop, Minervy Ann, Free Joe, Tolliver, Union Scout, and the Uncle Remus series of books.

9 McBRYDE, JOHN M., JR. "Brer Rabbit in the Folk-Tales of the Negro and Other Races." SR, 19 (April), 185-206.
Uncle Remus is one of the most valuable contributions made by America to world literature. He is portrayed vividly, warmly, and without foolish sentiment, and he sums up "the best characteristics of the negro race" at the time of slavery. The rabbit figures as hero in tales from India, Mongolia, Africa, Mexico, and Western America, and other regions. Originally, he was portrayed as a god, but he has

in recent folklore degenerated into a lazy, shiftless, greedy, selfish, and deceitful rogue. Yet it is his very roguery that makes him so popular.

10 McQUEEN, ANNE. "The Teller of Tales. A Memory of 'Uncle Remus.'" Lippincott's, 88 (October), 543.
    Four-stanza poem in honor of "the Teller of Tales" who walked with children hand in hand "over the border-land."

11 TOULMIN, HARRY AUBREY, JR. Social Historians. Introduction by Charles W. Kent. Boston: Gorham Press, pp. 30, 133-64, 170-71.
    Harris's popularity rests on his "unfailing humanity" and universality. His plantation melodies are charming and his stories "simple enough to point a telling moral to a child, humorous enough to demand genuine laughter from middle age, philosophical enough to please the jaded palate" of the aged. Through Uncle Remus, Harris was a social historian of the plantation life, although it is unusual that the "consummate duplicity" of Brer Rabbit would appeal to the Negro. The master-servant relationship in "A Story of the War" [Uncle Remus] helps to make it the "finest story in fiction." Harris was cynical about second-generation blacks. Includes twenty-three item bibliography of primary works. Reprinted: 1969.B9.

12 WAITE, ALICE VINTON and EDITH MENDALL TAYLOR, eds. Modern Masterpieces of Short Prose Fiction. New York and Chicago: D. Appleton, p. 36.
    The Uncle Remus stories uniquely blend the "modern negro dialect setting and the old beast-fable."

1912 A BOOKS - NONE

1912 B SHORTER WRITINGS

1 ARNOLD, GERTRUDE WELD. A Mother's List of Books for Children. Chicago: A. C. McClurg & Co., pp. 101, 125, 194.
    Reprint of 1909.B10.

2 BOAS, FRANZ. "Notes on Mexican Folk-Lore." JAF, 25 (July-September), 250, et passim.
    Similarities between Mexican and American Negro folktales give further credence to the view that the Negro's cycle of Rabbit stories and European folklore are historically related.

1912

3   CAIRNS, WILLIAM B. <u>A History of American Literature</u>.
     New York: Oxford University Press, pp. 475-76.
     Much of Harris's work is unimportant, and like many
     journalists he wrote too fast; but the early Uncle Remus
     sketches "are among the most interesting and valuable con-
     tributions of the South to national literature." The later
     Remus tales are inferior to their predecessors, perhaps be-
     cause Harris tried to make them more accurate pieces of
     folklore. Revised edition: 1930.B2.

4   JOHNSON, JAMES WELDON. <u>The Autobiography of an Ex-Colored</u>
     <u>Man</u>. Boston: Sherman, French & Co., p. 87.
     The four things that demonstrate the Negro's originality
     and artistic ability are the Uncle Remus stories, the Fisk
     singers, rag-time music, and the cake-walk. Reprinted:
     1937.B8.

5   LEE, VIRGINIA. "President Gomper's Mascot." <u>Life and Labor</u>
     (February), pp. 45-48.
     Some years ago Samuel Gompers, President of the American
     Federation of Labor, was given a small stuffed rabbit by a
     secretary of his from the South. Placed on the corner of
     his desk in his office, it served as his "mascot," good-luck
     charm, and symbol of the need for "canniness" in labor re-
     lations. On 18 May 1907 Gompers met Harris for the first
     time and spent an hour of "transcendent pleasure" with him
     at "The Wren's Nest."

6   LIEBERMAN, ELIAS. <u>The American Short Story: A Study of the</u>
     <u>Influence of Locality in its Development</u>. Ridgewood, NJ:
     Editor Co., pp. 73-80, 173.
     Harris's representation of Georgia and the Negro charac-
     ter are firsthand impressions, not the idealizations of
     Stowe or Foster. The animals are thinly disguised masks
     for Negro traits; <u>Daddy Jake</u> illustrates the white attitudes
     of brutality and kindness. The master-slave relationship in
     "The Colonel's 'Nigger Dog'" in <u>Home Folks</u> is sensitively
     portrayed but not equal to <u>Uncle Remus</u>.

7   PICKETT, LaSALLE CORBELL. "Uncle Remus." <u>Lippincott's</u>, 89
     (April), 572-78.
     Recalls an interview with Harris. He would not speak
     through the phone, remarking, "'I do not like to talk in a
     hole.'" A born storyteller, Harris was astonished by suc-
     cess. Though at ease with children, he avoided public ap-
     pearances. Recounts his boyhood years in Eatonton and on
     the Turner plantation, where he encountered the "primitive,
     child-mind community, with its ancient traditions that made

it one with the beginning of time." Harris found the poet
Tom Moore his "most cherished companion," whom he read for
consolation. Harris had a "country soul" and loved the
beauty of nature. Reprinted: 1912.B8.

8 _____. "'Uncle Remus': Joel Chandler Harris," in her
Literary Hearthstones of Dixie. Philadelphia: J. B.
Lippincott, pp. 151-72.
Reprinted from 1912.B7.

9 TRENT, W.[ILLIAM] P.[ETERFIELD] and JOHN ERSKINE. Great
American Writers. The Home University Library of Modern
Knowledge. New York: Henry Holt, p. 244 n.1.
Lately many writers have preserved vanishing phases of
Southern life; Harris is "not the least loved" of these and
his stories of Negro folklore are almost household classics.

1913 A BOOKS

1 AVARY, MYRTA LOCKETT. Joel Chandler Harris and His Home: A
Sketch. Atlanta: Appeal Publishing Co., 38pp.
This pamphlet, authorized by the Uncle Remus Memorial
Association and by Mrs. Harris, includes an extensive biographical sketch of Harris, as well as anecdotes related by
family members and by Harris himself. Also gathers photographs of Turnwold Plantation, Harris's West-End home, the
Wren's Nest, and a gallery of photographs of Harris across
the years, his family, and friends. Contains a bibliography
of Harris's books, a memorial poem by Charles W. Hubner,
and an account of the formation and activities of the Uncle
Remus Memorial Association; founded 10 July 1908, the Association raised enough money to purchase the home on 18 January 1913. Mrs. Harris recalls how fond Joel was of animals
(cites his preserving of a wren's nest), and believes that
"Free Joe" was her husband's favorite story. Includes anecdotes about Harris's love of children and his friendships
with Andrew Carnegie, Teddy Roosevelt, Henry Grady, and
James Whitcomb Riley, and accounts of his shyness.

1913 B SHORTER WRITINGS

1 ABERNETHY, JULIAN W. American Literature. New York:
Charles E. Merrill Co., pp. 341-43.
Harris's sympathy with animals and Negroes is his "finest
gift." The Remus material is delightful and Nights, Mingo,
Free Joe, Daddy Jake, and Balaam broadly represent Southern

1913

life. Harris shows that the Negro lives in an "unsuspected
world of poetry," and the Uncle Remus volumes perfectly
interpret the Negro to the world.

2   AVARY, MYRTA LOCKETT. "The Winning of 'The Wren's Nest.'"
     Book News Monthly, 31 (May), 665-68.
     Formal transfer of Harris's home "The Wren's Nest" to
     the Uncle Remus Memorial Association occurred on 18 January
     1913. Harris had once told his wife that he did not want a
     memorial left to him that would stand out in the rain, or
     in the sun and the heat and get dust-covered, and he pointed
     to a sapling beside the front door saying, "'This shall be
     my monument.'" Teddy Roosevelt had given a benefit lecture
     in Atlanta for the Association that raised $5000; Andrew
     Carnegie duplicated this sum, and the Harris family lowered
     the assessed value of the property by $5000.

3   BRAWLEY, BENJAMIN GRIFFITH. A Short History of the American
     Negro. New York: Macmillan, p. 192.
     The Uncle Remus tales represent the chief literary monu-
     ment so far to the extensive Negro tradition of customs,
     superstitions, and tales. Revised edition: 1931.B2.

4   BROOKS, ROBERT PRESTON. History of Georgia. Boston, New York,
     Chicago, Atlanta, Dallas: Atkinson, Mentzer & Co.,
     pp. 372-73.
     Of the Southern writers Harris and Lanier alone have won
     international recognition. Harris has a keen appreciation
     for the oddities of Negro character and has no equal in re-
     producing Negro dialect. Stories of Georgia and his biog-
     raphy of Grady are works of a more serious vein. Reprinted:
     1972.B2.

5   CURTIS, NATALIE. "The Negro's Contribution to the Music of
     America: The Larger Opportunity of the Colored Man of
     Today." Craftsman, 23 (March), 667.
     The music of the Negro composers Will Marion Cook and
     J. Rosamond Johnson "is indeed the Negro's own musical
     speech set to verses, some of which have the quaint mixture
     of crude poetry and humor characteristic of the tales of
     Uncle Remus."

6   LEACH, JOSEPHINE. "The 'Uncle Remus' Stories." Story
     Teller's Magazine, 1 (July), 94-97.
     Harris did not try to place the stories in the first
     Uncle Remus volume in any logical sequence. However, one
     can categorize the tales as: those that account for animal
     traits or characteristics; stories with Brer Rabbit as hero;

1913

stories told to the little boy for their ethical value; and
stories that attempt to account for natural phenomena.
These stories were first told when "the human race was very
young"; like his primitive ancestors, the child makes human
and holds conversation with everything in his back yard.

7   MABIE, HAMILTON WRIGHT. American Ideals, Character and Life.
    Chautauqua, NY: Chautauqua Press, p. 176.
        Uncle Remus is as famous in America as Rip Van Winkle,
    and "the stories of the inimitable humor, pathos and cunning
    of the slave" put into the mouth of the old Negro "form,
    perhaps, the most original American contribution not only
    to the literature of the last two decades, but to folklore
    as well."

8   MACY, JOHN. The Spirit of American Literature. New York:
    Boni and Liveright, Inc., p. 16.
        Cites Harris in a list of short story writers "whose
    short stories are perfect in their several kinds."

9   MERRIAM, (MRS.) M. F. "At Snap Bean Farm." Southern Ruralist,
    19 (15 October), 22.
        Describes Harris's home, "The Wren's Nest," and comments
    upon Harris's warmth and affection towards nature's crea-
    tures, especially the birds. He would not allow the hedge
    on his veranda to be trimmed, for he did not want to fright-
    en off the birds; the day of his funeral a brown wren hopped
    from arm to arm of Harris's empty porch rocker, chirping
    and fluttering in distress.

10 PAYNE, LEONIDAS WARREN, JR., ed. Southern Literary Readings.
    Chicago, New York, London: Rand McNally & Co., pp. 268-71.
        Biographical and critical sketch and study questions ac-
    company printing of "The Tale of the Crystal Bell," from
    Wally Wanderoon. Harris was "a careful worker in black and
    white," rather than a painter of mighty canvasses. His
    Uncle Remus tales are natural, true, and among the greatest
    contributions to Negro folklore. Harris saw and preserved
    "the poetic simplicity and romanticism attached to our
    Southland."

11 SWANTON, JOHN R. "Animal Stories from the Indians of the
    Muskhogean Stock." JAF, 26 (July-September), 193.
        Prints twenty-six tales from Southern Indians that are
    similar in type to the Uncle Remus stories. Whatever the
    origin of the separate Rabbit tales, the Rabbit was appar-
    ently one of the "tricksters" in pre-Columbian Southern
    Indian lore.

1914

1914 A BOOKS - NONE

1914 B SHORTER WRITINGS

1 ANON. "The Little Theatre." London Sunday Times (3 May),
   p. 8.
   Mrs. Dearmer's fantasia on the legend of "Brer Rabbit
   and Mr. Fox" will be back in town for a Christmas holiday
   showing. Youngsters very much enjoyed the company's
   earlier performance. Mr. C. Hayden Coffin's singing of
   the quaint old-world plantation ditties added greatly to
   the charm of the production. [See also 1914.B2.]

2 ANON. "Brer Rabbit and Mr. Fox as Footlight Favorites in
   London." Current Opinion, 57 (July), 30.
   Mrs. Percy Dearmer has been delighting the children of
   London, and the English critics, with a stage dramatization
   of the adventures of Brer Rabbit and Mr. Fox. "'Miss Meadows an' de gals'" were dressed in the bonnets and crinolines
   of Uncle Remus's time and sang genuine plantation tunes,
   "not the exploited folk-songs of the negroes which have
   been degraded to the uses of modern rag-time." Includes a
   quotation from the play's program. [See also 1914.B1.]

3 AVARY, MYRTA LOCKETT. "Introduction," in Uncle Remus and His
   Friends, by Joel Chandler Harris. The Visitors' Edition.
   Boston and New York: Houghton Mifflin, pp. ix-xxxiv.
   A shy boy, Harris was always fond of animals, especially
   horses and stray cats and dogs. He later allowed his
   children to keep any pet they wished: a pony, donkey,
   chickens, pigeons, rabbits, cows, and calves. He loved to
   work within sound of his wife Essie's voice, and he often
   read a story to his children for their reactions. Although
   a keen observer of nature himself, Harris criticized those
   naturalists who wanted explanations and denied or doubted
   everything. A generous host and friend, Harris entertained
   many at the Wren's Nest and quietly aided the destitute
   peddlers who knocked at his door: a genteel soap peddler,
   an Oriental woman selling shawls, struggling writers, a
   paralyzed friend who needed a job, a blind landscape garden-
   er. Essie relates that he disliked changes in the house,
   particularly new things. He liked old-fashioned things,
   and did not like new furniture and new carpets. A strong
   believer in Providence--and especially fond of the phrase
   "I am the Resurrection and the Life"--Harris accepted death
   "sweetly." When a man dies, he said, say "'He is forever!'"
   rather than "'He is no more.'" He died in "childlike
   faith, 'to see what is on the other side.'"

1915

4   BAKER, ERNEST A., ed. A Guide to Historical Fiction. London:
    George Routledge & Sons, pp. 226, 229, 232, 235.
    Briefly summarizes Free Joe under "[America:] From the
    War of 1812 to the Civil War," and Occasions, Union Scout,
    and Plantation under "[America:] Period of the Civil War
    (1861-5)."

5   CROSS, ETHAN ALLEN. The Short Story: A Technical and
    Literary Study. Chicago: A. C. McClurg & Co., pp. 9, 485.
    The Uncle Remus stories represent the beast fables of
    ancient fiction and contribute to the love for and technique
    of modern short stories. Includes Friends in a list of the
    "best" short stories.

6   DAVIS, HENRY C. "Negro Folk-Lore in South Carolina." JAF, 27
    (July-September), 244.
    A Columbia, South Carolina, Negro told Brer Rabbit
    stories before the days of Uncle Remus.

7   ESPINOSA, AURELIO M. "Comparative Notes on New-Mexican and
    Mexican Spanish Folk-Tales." JAF, 27 (April-June), 216-17.
    Notes that the tar-baby story was popular in New Mexico
    fifteen years or so before Harris published his stories
    and at a time when "there were not a dozen negroes in all
    of northern New Mexico." The story is doubtless a tradi-
    tional one of European origins.

8   LEVERETTE, FANNIE LEE. "Gems from the 'Gully Minstrels.'"
    Macon Telegraph (13 December), p. 8.
    Young Joe Harris organized his Eatonton friends into the
    Gully Minstrels, who charged ten pins for admission to their
    shows. The boys sang plantation songs and clowned about.

9   METCALF, JOHN CALVIN. American Literature. Atlanta,
    Richmond, Dallas: B. F. Johnson Publishing Co., pp. 326-29.
    Biographical sketch and commentary confined, for reasons
    of "unity," to the celebrated Uncle Remus sketches. The
    scene in the old darky's cabin is the real one, and Remus
    is an original character in the nation's literature. The
    stories seem to have allegorical significance.

1915 A BOOKS

*1 WIGGINS, ROBERT L.[EMUEL]. "Joel Chandler Harris: The
    Formative Years." Ph.D. dissertation, University of
    Virginia, [pp. unknown].
    Dissertation reported lost by the University. For
    published version, see 1918.A2.

1915

1915 B SHORTER WRITINGS

1 HAWTHORNE, HILDEGARDE. "Books and Reading: Joel Chandler
   Harris--'Uncle Remus.'" St. Nicholas, 42 (March), 453-55.
   Harris had a twinkle in his eye and shook with merriment
   when telling humorous stories. He tried to interpret
   clearly the wisdom and homely fun of the Negro and produced
   a matchless set of folk stories. Atlanta became synonymous
   with Harris; praises his help for the New South.

2 HEWINS, CAROLINE M., comp. Books for Boys and Girls: A
   Selected List. Third edition, revised. Chicago: American
   Library Association Publishing Board, pp. 36-37.
   Substantially equivalent to 1904.B8.

3 KELLNER, LEON. American Literature. Garden City, NY:
   Doubleday, Page & Co., pp. 245-46, 248-49.
   Harris vividly and with dialectical fidelity presents
   the soul of the Negro. In Puritan households, "the negroes
   represent the natural, or, as theologians term it, the
   'creature' element in the family," in whom the children
   sought refuge from parental chastisement. Harris portrays
   this loyal relationship between slaves and children. In
   the tales "the oppressed negro race takes its harmless re-
   venge by representing the strong and unscrupulous creature
   as a victim of the weaker one." The "seamy side" of Negro
   emancipation is brought out in "Free Joe."

4 PATTEE, FRED LEWIS. A History of American Literature Since
   1870. New York: Century Co., pp. 291, 301-308, 319, et
   passim.
   Harris accidentally fell into a literary career: "never
   once did he write a line with merely literary intent." His
   permanence depends on his Negro folklore and his realistic
   sketches of the cracker. Remus is one of America's few
   original characters, and here the storyteller is "more
   valuable than his story" as he reveals the soul of the
   Negro race at a transitional point in time. Brer Rabbit
   represents qualities of the Negro and his racial situation.
   Harris also admirably recorded Negro music and poetry. He
   is "essentially fragmentary" and left no long masterpiece,
   although his novels and Pageants do contain delightful
   fragments. Lists Harris's principal works from 1880 to
   1905. Reprinted: 1922.B11.

1916 A BOOKS - NONE

1916 B SHORTER WRITINGS

1   ALEXANDER, HARTLEY BURR. North American [Mythology].
    Vol. 10 of The Mythology of All Races. Edited by Louis
    Herbert Gray. Boston: Marshall Jones Co., pp. 67, 121,
    297 n.47.
        "The Brer Rabbit stories, made famous as negro tales by
    Joel Chandler Harris, appear as a veritable saga cycle
    among the Cherokee, from whom they are doubtless borrowed."
    Brer Rabbit is "a southern and humorous debasement of the
    [Algonquian] Great Hare," and the tar-baby is the Cherokee
    tar-wolf. Reprinted: 1964.B2.

2   ANON. "Letters and Art. Colleges Blamed for Our Lack of
    Authors." Literary Digest, 53 (5 August), 304.
        William G. Ellsworth, late president of the Century
    Company, is quoted as blaming the spread of higher education
    for reducing the number of good American authors. Whitman,
    Twain, Harris, Howells, and many others learned to write
    in the printing-office or in some other job, but not in
    college.

3   ANON. "'Uncle Remus.'" Christian Science Monitor
    (8 December), [p. 16].
        Beginning today, an "Uncle Remus Day" is being set aside
    annually in Georgia. Like so many American authors, Harris
    started his career setting type and proofreading galleys;
    he soon struck a new vein in Southern literature and at the
    same time became imbued with the atmosphere of the New
    South.

4   BRAWLEY, BENJAMIN [GRIFFITH]. "The Negro in American Fiction."
    Dial, 60 (11 May), 446, 447.
        For decades, charming old Uncle Remus has been held up
    to the children of the South as the "perfect expression of
    the beauty of life in the glorious times 'befo' de wah.'"
    The Negro of the new day needs to be painted, also; he may
    not be so poetic, but "the human element is greater."
    Reprinted: 1929.B2, 1934.B2, 1944.B3.

5   ROLLINS, HYDER E. "The Negro in the Southern Short Story."
    SR, 24 (January), 43, 46, 47-49, 50, 59, et passim.
        Harris's delicate, half sentimental affection toward the
    old slave is indicative of the Southern attitude at large.
    Uncle Remus is perhaps the greatest creation in American
    literature, although Minervy Ann is fully as lovable a

1916

character. Also commendable are Aunt Fountain, Ananias,
Free Joe (one of the most pathetic fictional characters),
and Balaam. Harris wrote of slavery with sympathy that is
"half regret." Page's "Ole 'Stracted" borrows an idea from
"Free Joe," and Ruth McEnery Stuart far excels Harris, Page,
and Dunbar in portraying realistic Negro characters.

6   TASSIN, ALGERNON. The Magazine in America. New York: Dodd,
     Mead, p. 296.
     Discusses the inclusion of Southern stories by the
     Northern magazines starting in the 1870's; in fact, Century
     readers complained of too many dialect stories. Harris is
     one of the authors coming to the front at this time.

1917 A BOOKS - NONE

1917 B SHORTER WRITINGS

1   FULTON, MAURICE GARLAND, ed. Southern Life in Southern
     Literature: Selections of Representative Prose and Poetry.
     Boston: Ginn and Co., pp. 324, 512.
     Uncle Remus gave Harris a national reputation which his
     later books on folklore and Georgians have sustained. Most
     distinctive in preserving American Negro folklore, Harris
     created the setting and provided "one of the best-sustained
     studies American literature has of the old plantation ne-
     gro." The Uncle Remus volumes are primarily appreciated
     for the delineation of Remus rather than the folklore.
     Uncle Remus and Nights are his most important works. An-
     thologizes "Brer Rabbit Grossly Deceives Brer Fox" and "The
     Cunning Fox is Again Victimized" on pp. 324-31.

2   GARLAND, HAMLIN. A Son of the Middle Border. New York:
     Macmillan, p. 387.
     [Early version of Garland's interview with Howells; pub-
     lished in revised form in 1929.B6.] Garland told Howells
     that Harris, Cable, Kirkland, Jewett, Harte, and Mary
     Wilkins "'are but varying phases of the same [local color]
     movement, a movement which is to give us at last a really
     vital and original literature!'"

3   KNIGHT, LUCIAN LAMAR. A Standard History of Georgia and
     Georgians. Vol. 2. Chicago, New York: Lewis Publishing
     Co., p. 811.
     In Uncle Remus, Harris "carried the glow of the cabin-
     fireside around the globe" and "made the southern cotton-
     patch as classic as the Roman arena." [See also 1917.B4,
     B5.]

1917

4 ____. A Standard History of Georgia and Georgians. Vol. 3.
Chicago, New York: Lewis Publishing Co., pp. 1421–22,
1753–54.
Harris caught the spirit of the old-time Southern Negro
and preserved the plantation dialect. Recounts how Harris
came to write the first Uncle Remus sketches. Includes
brief biographical sketch. [See also 1917.B3, B5.]

5 ____. A Standard History of Georgia and Georgians. Vol. 6.
Chicago, New York: Lewis Publishing Co., p. 3142.
Short biographical sketch. [See also 1917.B3, B4.]

6 LEE, JAMES W. "Joel Chandler Harris: An Intimate Record of
a Beautiful Life." Southern Woman's Magazine, 8 [?]
(December), 18, 33, 34.
Restatement of praise in 1908.A1.

7 LONG, WILLIAM J. Outlines of American Literature. Boston,
New York, et al.: Ginn and Co., pp. 521–22.
America's best writer of dialect stories, Harris con-
tributed to folklore as well as literature. Brer Rabbit is
an original symbol for the Negro race; in creating him and
Uncle Remus, both of whom are "as real as Poor Richard or
Natty Bumppo and far more fascinating," Harris has made
"one of the most notable achievements in American fiction."

8 PARSONS, ELSIE CLEWS. "The Provenience of Certain Negro
Folk-Tales. I. Playing Dead Twice in the Road."
Folk-Lore, 28 (December), 408.
This tale has been collected by Negroes from North Caro-
lina, Bahama, and the Cape Verde Islands. Harris gives two
variants of the story in Uncle Remus and Friends.

9 SMALL, SAM W. "Story of The Constitution's Half Century of
Service to the City, State and Country." Atlanta
Constitution (26 September), [pp. 21, 24].
Briefly recounts Harris's writing of dialect sketches
for the Constitution and how this led to the Uncle Remus
series. The sketches were hard to write at first, but he
continued to produce them out of loyalty to Evan Howell.

10 WOOT[T]EN, KATHARINE HINTON. "At the Sign of the Wren's Nest."
Southern Woman's Magazine, 8 [?] (December), 19, 33.
Describes the formation of the Uncle Remus Memorial Asso-
ciation in Atlanta and Harris's West End home and grounds.
The Harris family reduced the asking price of the home to
$20,000; a benefit lecture by former president Theodore
Roosevelt netted $4000; Andrew Carnegie donated $4000; and

1917

John D. Rockefeller sent $1000. The Association acquired
the house in January 1913.

11   WOOT[T]EN, KATHARINE HINTON. "A Tribute to 'Uncle Remus.'"
     St. Nicholas, 45 (December), 130-31.
     Describes the Uncle Remus mantelpiece in the children's
     room at the Carnegie Library of Atlanta. The tiles sur-
     rounding the opening are based on A. B. Frost's drawings.
     Every December 9 the library celebrates Harris's birthday
     with a program of his stories and songs; more than five
     hundred children came to one such party but not Harris, who
     sent a letter of regret.

1918 A BOOKS

1   HARRIS, JULIA COLLIER. The Life and Letters of Joel Chandler
    Harris. Boston and New York: Houghton Mifflin, 621pp.
    The wife of Harris's eldest son Julian includes a con-
    siderable number of previously unpublished letters and
    reminiscences of Harris's family and friends in her biog-
    raphy. The first third of the book covers Harris's boyhood,
    early professional career, and initial years in Atlanta.
    The remainder combines a running commentary on his books
    and editorial views with an account of his life from 1880
    to his death in 1908. Recalls her father-in-law as a shy
    and genuinely modest man who stammered when he was self-
    conscious and always disliked crowds. Those who knew him
    well found him to be warm, generous, and humane, and de-
    voted to his family. As an artist, he consistently under-
    rated his abilities. Full primary and secondary bibliog-
    raphies are included.

2   WIGGINS, ROBERT LEMUEL. The Life of Joel Chandler Harris:
    From Obscurity in Boyhood to Fame in Early Manhood.
    Nashville, Dallas, Richmond: Publishing House Methodist
    Episcopal Church, South, iv, 447pp.
    [Published version of 1915.A1.] Reconstructs Harris's
    life through the publication of the first Uncle Remus animal
    fables in 1879. Appraises Harris's personality and his re-
    lationships with boyhood friends, Joseph Addison Turner, and
    various Negroes in Putnam County. Also illustrates the
    growth of Harris's journalistic and literary talent by a
    substantial inclusion of previously uncollected boyhood
    essays, Countryman articles, poetry, and humorous newspaper
    paragraphs. The second half of the book gathers in a
    lengthy appendix additional essays, poems, and newspaper
    editorials, and reprints Rockville. Bibliography lists all

128

1918

of Harris's books; twenty-eight books and sixty articles
that refer to Harris; portraits of Harris; and the short
stories, verses, and editorials published by Harris in
periodicals.

1918 B SHORTER WRITINGS

1   ANON. Review of Life and Letters. New York Bookman, 48
    (September), 50-56.
        Even though she was his daughter-in-law, Julia Collier
    Harris tells Harris's life skillfully and discreetly. For
    example, she does not gloss over the facts of her father's
    unfortunate birth. Quotes extensively from the biography.

2   ANON. Review of Returns. Outlook, 120 (2 October), 189.
        As with the earlier Remus books, both younger and older
    readers will enjoy the humor and human nature of these
    tales.

3   ANON. "The 'Accidental' Genius of Joel Chandler Harris."
    Current Opinion, 65 (November), 324-26.
        Review of Life and Letters. Reading an article in
    Lippincott's in the 1870's led Harris to attempt some Negro
    folklore sketches. He always insisted he was only a "'corn-
    field journalist'" and downplayed his success. Quotes ex-
    tensively from Julia Collier Harris's biography.

4   ANON. "Children's Books [review of Returns]." ALA Booklist,
    15 (November), [73].
        An old man in Returns, Uncle Remus muses philosophically
    on the mumps, politics, and the mule, while the animals
    have some more adventures.

5   ANON. Review of Returns. Review of Reviews, 58 (November),
    557.
        Ten previously uncollected Uncle Remus tales and some
    sketches of the old man have been bound together as Returns.

6   E., E. F. "The Reappearance of Uncle Remus." Boston
    Evening Transcript (21 August), p. 6.
        Returns, the final Uncle Remus volume, features the son
    of the first little boy. Raised by a very matter-of-fact
    mother, he sometimes asked Uncle Remus disconcerting ques-
    tions about animal morality; Remus learned to be an excel-
    lent casuist. All of the Remus volumes are immortal and a
    "permanent chronicle of one phase of American life."

129

1918

7   HANNIGAN, FRANCIS J., comp. The Standard Index of Short
    Stories: 1900-1914. Boston: Small, Maynard & Co.,
    p. 123.
        Lists nineteen Harris short stories and their magazine
    publication data.

8   HARMAN, H.[ENRY] E. "Joel Chandler Harris: The Prose Poet of
    the South." SAQ, 17 (July), 243-48.
        A "golden thread of poetry" runs through Harris's writ-
    ings about the Negro, about animals, and about the South in
    general. James Whitcomb Riley, Harris, and the author spent
    a good deal of time together in Lithia Springs, Georgia, in
    1902 or 1903, and Harris and Riley loved to swap humorous
    stories. Later, Riley recalled Harris's poetic strain.
    When Harman met Harris, in his later years, at the old post
    office on Marietta Street, Atlanta, Harris would often use
    poetic expressions in his greetings.

9   TRENT, WILLIAM PETERFIELD; JOHN ERSKINE; STUART P. SHERMAN;
    and CARL VAN DOREN, eds. The Cambridge History of American
    Literature. Vol. 2. New York: G. P. Putnam's Sons;
    Cambridge, England: University Press, pp. 303, 347-60
    passim, 389, 408, 611-14, 617, 635.
        Harris's early poetry is markedly unlike his later writ-
    ings. Uncle Remus perpetuates a vanishing civilization,
    lays the foundation for the scientific study of Negro folk-
    lore, and has dialectical authenticity. Uncle Remus and
    Nights are the best of his books; they sum up the Negro's
    past and dimly hint at his future. Harris's humor is from
    the "world of the underman," and he harmonizes the universal
    with the individual in Uncle Remus. In Mingo Harris wrote
    with a surer hand than Craddock. Headnote to extensive
    primary and secondary bibliography states that Uncle Remus
    was in its fifty-second printing in January 1915 and that
    at least ten British publishers had printed Remus editions
    since 1881; Punch and The Westminster Gazette show a wide
    use of "the Uncle Remus idea" for political satire. Uncle
    Remus and Mingo are among a list of "notable" volumes in
    the history of the short story. Reprinted: 1933.B8.

1919 A BOOKS - NONE

1919 B SHORTER WRITINGS

1   BOWEN, EDWIN W. "Joel Chandler Harris, a Faithful Interpreter
    of the Negro." Reformed Church Review, Fourth Series, 23
    (July), 357-69.

1919

Summarizes Harris's life and briefly surveys his works. Harris and Page are the best portrayers of the antebellum Negro, but Harris puts the Negro into the foreground instead of the background of his stories and pays a great deal of attention to black folklore. The Uncle Remus stories were sufficient to make Harris immortal.

2   BOYNTON, PERCY H. <u>A History of American Literature</u>. Boston: Ginn and Co., pp. 425–26.
    Harris's material "goes back to the farthest sources of human tradition," but "new" Uncle Remus is a genius of a storyteller. The Remus stories "have the double charm of recording the lore of the negro and of revealing his humor, his transparent deceitfulness, his love of parade, his superstition, his basic religious feeling, and his pathos."

3   BRONSON, WALTER C. <u>A Short History of American Literature</u>. Revised and enlarged. Boston, New York, Chicago: D. C. Heath, p. 295.
    Revision of 1901.B10. Praises Harris's skillful rendering of the Negro's primitive, poetic imagination, his contributions to folklore, and his high literary merit. Cites <u>Uncle Remus</u>, <u>Nights</u>, and <u>Friends</u>.

4   ELLSWORTH, WILLIAM WEBSTER. <u>A Golden Age of Authors: A Publisher's Recollection</u>. Boston and New York: Houghton Mifflin, The Riverside Press, pp. 112, 196.
    Praises Harris's realistic observations as being touched "with the divine fire of literary art."

5   HARRIS, JULIA COLLIER. "'Uncle Remus' to His 'Gals.'" <u>Ladies' Home Journal</u>, 36 (April), 45, 126.
    Harris wrote charming letters to his two girls, Lillian and Mildred, while they were away at school. Article extracts characteristic passages from a dozen letters; dates are not provided.

6   KNIGHT, LUCIAN LAMAR. <u>Memorials of Dixie-land</u>. Atlanta: Byrd Printing Co., pp. 10, 487–88, 495–96.
    Translated into seventeen languages, the Uncle Remus stories and cabin songs are classics in the North and around the globe. Harris's interpretation of Negro character is unsurpassed in modern American fiction; Harris is the "most beloved" of Southern writers. [Includes reprint of 1911.B7.]

7   PARSONS, ELSIE CLEWS. "Joel Chandler Harris and Negro Folklore." <u>Dial</u>, 66 (17 May), 491–93.

131

1919

Returns features the son of the boy who listened to
Uncle Remus's earlier tales, a lad who is a priggish product
of his mother's quasi-scientific theories of education.
The stories in this volume seem to be variants of Portu-
guese, Jamaican, Angolan, and other tales. Harris characteristically embroidered the outlines of folktales that he
gathered, but both their embroidering and their folkloric
content are enjoyable.

8 ____. "The Provenience of Certain Negro Folk Tales. III.
Tar Baby." Folk-Lore, 30 (September), 227–34 passim.
Uncle Remus's tar-baby story is, ironically, the most
notable exception to the traditional tar-baby story plot:
the tar-baby trap is "almost always set to catch a thief."
The story appears to be part of the Master Thief cycle of
European-Indian folklore tales, and it appears in the Cape
Verde Islands. Jacobs [see 1888.B16; 1889.B9; 1892.B22]
suggests that the story may originally have been an Indian
one, which seems plausible.

9 PAYNE, LEONIDAS WARREN, JR. History of American Literature.
Chicago and New York: Rand, McNally & Co., pp. 251, 287–88,
297–301, et passim.
Harris is more prominent than his contemporary writers
of local color fiction and is one of America's most original
authors. Although he failed with the full-scope novel, his
Uncle Remus tales have become immortal. He created characters almost unconsciously. Includes a biographical sketch
and list of Harris's writings.

10 [ROOSEVELT, THEODORE]. Theodore Roosevelt: An Autobiography.
New York: Macmillan, pp. 15, 347.
Roosevelt's mother and Aunt Anna told him tales of the
Georgia plantations and slave quarters; he was brought up
on the "Br'er Rabbit Stories." One uncle, Robert Roosevelt,
recorded them from dictation and published them in Harper's,
where they failed. It took Harris's genius to make them
immortal. Mentions that he once lured Harris, that shy
recluse, to the White House: "a deed in which to triumph."

1920 A BOOKS - NONE

1920 B SHORTER WRITINGS

1 CURTIS, NATALIE. "Introduction," in her Songs and Tales from
the Dark Continent. New York, Boston: G. Schirmer, p. xix.

1920

The legendary gentleness and concern of the Negro for
white children are typified in the figure of Uncle Remus.
Brer Rabbit has an African ancestor in Shu'lo the Hare.

2   GANTT, T. LARRY. "Recollections of Joel Chandler Harris."
    Raleigh News and Observer (2 February), p. 10.
    Author became friends with Harris when both were working
    on the Savannah Morning News. Harris dressed in baggy and
    ill-fitting garments and was generally ungainly in appear-
    ance; but he had "rare genius" as a paragrapher and pro-
    duced copy that was always technically perfect. He was
    modest and appeared unsocial but would unlimber himself
    with friends. At his request, Gantt later sent Harris
    Negro folklore, gathered from a black nurse, which Harris
    rewrote and published.

3   HAWTHORNE, HILDEGARDE. Review of Uncle Remus. New York Times
    Book Review and Magazine (28 November), pp. 4-5.
    Review of 1920 Appleton edition. Illustrated by Frost
    and Kemble, Uncle Remus is a world to itself of mischief,
    fancy, humor, adventure, and philosophy. One never outgrows
    these tales or is ever too young to listen to them.

4   HOWELLS, WILLIAM DEAN, ed. "A Reminiscent Introduction," to
    his The Great Modern American Stories. New York: Boni and
    Liveright, pp. x, xi, xii.
    Comments on Clemens's reading of Remus stories in his
    native speech. "How Joel Chandler Harris might have inter-
    preted them I cannot venture to say. From an almost inar-
    ticulate meeting with him at Boston I have the impression
    of a transcendent bashfulness in which we made no way with
    him in any hospitable endeavor and he left us with the re-
    membrance of nothing more distinctive than a meeting at
    his publisher's, who was also mine; but I could imagine all
    delightful things in him if once I could get beyond that
    insuperable diffidence of his." Reprinted: 1957.B4.

5   KAYE, JAMES R. Historical Fiction Chronologically and
    Historically Related. Chicago: Snowdon Publishing Co.,
    p. 562.
    Union Scout relates to the battle of Chickamauga.

6   MENCKEN, H.[ENRY] L.[OUIS]. "The Sahara of the Bozart," in his
    Prejudices: Second Series. New York: Alfred A. Knopf,
    pp. 141-42.
    Georgia has not produced a single idea. Once a Georgian
    wrote a couple of books that attracted notice, "but immedi-
    ately it turned out that he was little more than an

1921

amanuensis for the local blacks." Writing afterwards as a
white man, "he swiftly subsided into the fifth rank." Yet
he is not only the glory of Georgian literature, he is almost the whole of the literature of Georgia. Reprinted:
1949.B8, 1965.B11.

1921 A BOOKS - NONE

1921 B SHORTER WRITINGS

1   BROWN, W. NORMAN. "Hindu Stories in American Negro Folk-Lore."
     Asia, 21 (August), 703-707, 730, 732.
        A "rapid survey of the delightful Uncle Remus books and
     other collections of American folk-lore reveals more than
     sixty tales that reproduce Hindu stories." Parallel plots
     and motifs are informally discussed.

2   FERGUSON, THOMAS E. "Joel Chandler Harris." Texas Review, 6
     (January), 214-21.
        Reinterprets Wiggins's findings on Harris [see 1918.A2]
     to show that Harris was not abnormally timid or sensitive,
     and stresses Harris's importance as an interpreter of the
     Negro and journalist opposed to mere sectionalism.

3   HARRISON, M. CLIFFORD. "Social Types in Southern Prose
     Fiction." Ann Arbor, Mich.: Edward Brothers, Inc.,
     pp. 58-65, 67, 69-71, 90, 91-92, 98, et passim.
        Mimeoed copy of Ph.D. dissertation, University of Vir-
     ginia, 1921. Harris knew the cotton plantation Negro well
     and was made immortal by the Negro he immortalized, Uncle
     Remus. Remus "is always at his best as a tale-teller when
     his animal hunger is satisfied." He believes in witches
     and haunts, loves music, is willing to tell an occasional
     white lie, and "retains much ante-bellum pride and preju-
     dice." Aunt Minervy Ann is another successful Negro charac-
     ter, and Harris portrayed the rice field Negro, poor whites,
     and mountain folk with sensitivity.

4   HUBBELL, JAY B. "On 'Southern Literature.'" Texas Review, 7
     (October), 13, 15.
        The stories of Harris, Page, and other writers belong to
     America rather than to "Southern" literature.

5   PERRY, BLISS. The American Spirit in Literature: A Chronicle
     of Great Interpreters. The Chronicles of America Series,
     Vol. 34, edited by Allen Johnson. New Haven: Yale
     University Press; Toronto: Glasgow, Brook & Co.; London:
     Humphrey Milford, Oxford University Press, pp. 246-47.

1922

Russell, Harris, and Page portrayed the humorous, pathetic, and unique traits of the Southern Negro, a type previously sketched either in caricature or by strangers.

6 RAMSEY, ROBERT L. <u>Short Stories of America: Edited with an
   Introductory Essay, Course Outline, and Reading Lists</u>.
   Boston, New York, Chicago, San Francisco: Houghton
   Mifflin, pp. 5, 12, 13, 14, 22, 341, 344.
       Quotes Pattee that Harris caught the romance of the Old
   South. Includes Harris with a list of good Appalachian
   local colorists and, as a Lower South writer, finds him unsurpassed in the Negro and cracker types. Groups Harris
   with the first local colorists who were primarily interested
   in people. Reading lists cite "At Teague Poteet's" ("Appa-
   lachia"), "Ananias" ("Lower South"), and "The Tar-Baby"
   ("Social Background").

7 TRENT, WILLIAM PETERFIELD; JOHN ERSKINE; STUART P. SHERMAN;
   and CARL VAN DOREN, eds. <u>The Cambridge History of American
   Literature</u>. Vol. 3. New York: G. P. Putnam's Sons,
   pp. 86, 89, 316.
       Harris wrote novels of merit but his talents were for
   the short story. He painted amiable antebellum plantation
   life and was a contributor to <u>McClure's</u>. Reprinted:
   1933.B9.

8 ____. <u>The Cambridge History of American Literature</u>. Vol. 4.
   New York: G. P. Putnam's Sons, p. 615.
       When he wrote them, Harris did not know that the Uncle
   Remus tales were of Cherokee origins; "their essential
   frolicsomeness is transmitted with surprisingly few African
   interpolations." Reprinted: 1933.B9.

1922 A BOOKS - NONE

1922 B SHORTER WRITINGS

1 ALLEN, HERVEY and DuBOSE HEYWARD. "Poetry South." <u>Poetry:
   A Magazine of Verse</u>, 20 (April), 37-38.
       Praises Harris and others for correctly recording the
   Negro dialect of their own localities.

2 BROWN, W. NORMAN. "The Tar-Baby at Home." <u>Scientific Monthly</u>,
   15 (September), 228-34.
       Brown disagrees with the theories of Jacobs [<u>see</u>
   1888.B16, 1889.B9, and 1892.B22], Parsons [<u>see</u> 1919.B7], and
   others that the tar-baby story originated in India and was

1922

transmitted to the West via Africa. To substantiate their
claims one would have to prove that the stick-fast motif
and the tar-baby story have a "settled place" in Hindu fiction, and that the course of these stories westward can be
geographically traced. Neither of these assumptions can be
proved. Africa is a far more likely source, and an African
narrator's observation of the qualities of pitchblend or
any sticky substance could readily have spawned the tale.
Three-fifths of the "genuine" versions of the story are the
Negro's, and with the popularity of the Uncle Remus volumes
the tale has now become broadly circulated in the East and
West.

3 DICKEY, MARCUS. The Maturity of James Whitcomb Riley.
   Indianapolis: Bobbs-Merrill, pp. 232, 304, 333.
   Harris wrote letters of advice to Riley.

4 GONZALES, AMBROSE E. The Black Border: Gullah Stories of the
   Carolina Coast (With a Glossary). Columbia, SC: The State
   Co., pp. 13-17.
   A "genius," Harris recorded Negro stories of the South
   and West Indies with little creative work. His artistry
   lies in his understanding and tender rendition of the relationship between the boy and Remus. Believes in the African
   origin of the myths, and mentions Jamaican parallels for the
   Remus tales. Harris touched the Gullah dialect "lightly and
   not with authority" in Nights. He lacked firsthand contact
   and missed speech construction subtleties; his comment that
   Gullah is easier to read than Remus's dialect has proven
   wrong. Col. Charles Colcock Jones [see 1888.B18] provides
   a much more accurate representation than Harris. Mrs.
   A. M. H. Christensen [see 1892.B20] primarily uses variants
   of stories by Harris and Jones. Cites Harris's and Jones's
   versions of "The Tar-Baby Story" on pp. 343-48.

5 HIND, C. LEWIS. "Joel Chandler Harris," in his More Authors
   and I. New York: Dodd, Mead, pp. 135-40.
   The author viewed a musical called "Brer Rabbit and Mr.
   Fox," by Mabel Dearmer, in Hyde Park, London; gives his impressions of Harris's genius with language and animal lore.

6 HORNADY, JOHN R. Atlanta: Yesterday, Today and Tomorrow.
   [Atlanta:] American Cities Book Co., pp. 193-98.
   Biographical sketch and description of the Wren's Nest.

7 JESSUP, ALEXANDER and HENRY SEIDEL CANBY, eds. The Book of
   the Short Story. New York and London: D. Appleton, p. 439.
   Cites Nights in a list of "Representative Tales and Short
   Stories." Revised edition: 1948.B3.

1922

8   JOHNSON, JAMES WELDON. "Preface," in his The Book of American
    Negro Poetry. New York: Harcourt, Brace, p. viii.
    The Negro has created the only distinctly American artis-
    tic products: the Uncle Remus stories collected by Harris,
    which "constitute the greatest body of folklore that America
    has produced," the Negro spirituals, the cakewalk, and rag-
    time. Revised edition: 1931.B10.

9   MABIE, HAMILTON W. Commemorative Tributes to Richard Watson
    Gilder, Joel Chandler Harris, Edward Everett Hale, Carl
    Schurz, Winslow Homer. New York: American Academy of Arts
    and Letters, pp. 3-6.
    Uncle Remus emerged from "the romanticism and tragedy"
    of the antebellum period and from "the cheap exaggeration"
    of the minstrel-shows that followed the War to attain sta-
    ture as one of the "real" figures in American literature.
    Unconsciously, Remus displays his humorous philosophy,
    shrewd observation of people, sense of the mystery of the
    animal kingdom, and cleverness and mischievous spirit of
    fun.

10 PARSONS, ELSIE CLEWS. "Tar Baby." JAF, 35 (July-September),
    330.
    Although it is still likely that the earliest version of
    the tar-baby or stick-fast tale appears in India, Parsons
    agrees with Brown [see 1922.B2] that the tar-baby stories
    in the Cape Verde Islands probably came from Africa rather
    than Asia.

11 PATTEE, FRED LEWIS. A History of American Literature Since
    1870. New York: Century Co., pp. 291, 301-308, 319, et
    passim.
    Reprint of 1915.B4.

12 RANKIN, THOMAS E. and WILFORD M. AIKIN. American Literature.
    New York: Harcourt, Brace, pp. 207, et passim.
    Harris gave American Negro folklore its best expression.
    While his Uncle Remus tales are not of the literary quality
    of Aesop's Fables or Reynard the Fox, they are "filled with
    the spirit of primitive man's experience with nature" and
    are among the world's richest treasures for the child and
    the adult who has sympathy with nature.

13 TALLEY, THOMAS W. Negro Folk Rhymes: Wise and Otherwise.
    With a Study by Talley. New York: Macmillan, pp. 240,
    242-43, 246, 247, 265-67, 303, 307, 308-310, 313, 316.
    Comments on Harris's extensive use of Negro folk-rhymes,
    citing several examples. Many of Remus's characteristic
    sayings are also from old folk-rhymes.

1922

14 THOMPSON, STITH. "The Transmission of Folk Tales."
    University of California Publications in Modern Philology,
    No. 11, p. 136.
    The history of a folktale among the various peoples who
    have preserved it must be carefully studied before any con-
    clusions about its transmission can be drawn. Even the
    Uncle Remus tales, which the Indians borrowed from the
    Negro, seem to be ultimately of Spanish origin.

15 TICKNOR, CAROLINE. "Letters from 'Uncle Remus,'" in her
    Glimpses of Authors. Boston and New York: Houghton
    Mifflin, pp. 152–68.
    Informal sketch of Harris's character that includes pre-
    viously unpublished letters of the 1880's to the publisher
    James Osgood and others. The letters reveal his diffidence
    and his concern about the merit of his writing.

16 VAN DOREN, CARL. Contemporary American Novelists, 1900–1920.
    New York: Macmillan, p. 6.
    The Uncle Remus stories may "outlast all that local
    color hit upon in the South." These stories are "contempor-
    ary and perennial," and, while grounded in the "universal
    traits of simple souls," also whimsically mirror a particu-
    lar race in a now extinct phase of its career. "They are
    at once as ancient and as fresh as folk-lore."

1923 A BOOKS - NONE

1923 B SHORTER WRITINGS

1 FIRKINS, INA TEN EYCK, comp. Index to Short Stories.
   Second and enlarged edition. New York: H. W. Wilson Co.;
   London: Grafton & Co., pp. 191–97.
   Lists periodical and book publications for over three
   hundred of Harris's short stories and folktales. Supple-
   ments: 1929.B5, 1936.B4.

2 HANEY, JOHN LOUIS. The Story of Our Literature: An
   Interpretation of the American Spirit. New York, Chicago,
   Boston: Charles Scribner's Sons, pp. 180–81, 354.
   Harris's writings often seem hasty, but the Remus
   stories are immortal. All his works were diversions from
   journalism.

3 HIBBARD, C. A.[DDISON]. Studies in Southern Literature.
   Revised edition. University of North Carolina Extension
   Bulletin. Chapel Hill, NC: University of North Carolina
   Press, p. 24.

1923

Includes Harris as one of the greatest names in Southern
literature. Provides study questions and brief bibliography
under Meeting Nine, "Story Writers of the South."

4   JESSUP, ALEXANDER, ed. Representative American Short Stories.
    Boston, New York, Chicago, Atlanta, San Francisco, Dallas:
    Allyn and Bacon, pp. xxxiii-xxxiv.
        Harris is a first rank humorist but only secondarily a
    short story writer. "His humor is not mere funniness and
    diversion; he is a humorist in the fundamental and large
    sense, as are Cervantes, Rabelais and Mark Twain." Reprints
    "Trouble on Lost Mountain" [pp. 500-517] because it is a
    better short story than other writing "considered more typi-
    cal of his genius"; the Remus stories are often just anec-
    dotes. Praises Harris's style in this story, although
    Harris "is not commonly thought of as a writer of felicitous
    prose."

5   JOHNSON, ROBERT UNDERWOOD. Remembered Yesterdays. Boston:
    Little, Brown, pp. 122, 377-83.
        Uncle Remus is "probably the most enduring contribution
    to Afro-American folklore that has been made." Harris was
    modest and needed encouragement in his work, as his letters
    to Johnson at Century indicate. Johnson met Harris in New
    York in 1882 and enjoyed his "racy" talk. But Harris was
    either too shy or grew homesick, for he left for Atlanta
    without following up Johnson's invitation to see him at his
    home. Johnson suggested revisions in "At Teague Poteet's"
    that Harris followed.

6   LONG, WILLIAM J.[OSEPH]. American Literature: A Study of the
    Men and the Books that in the Earlier and Later Times
    Reflect the American Spirit. Boston: Ginn and Co.,
    pp. 105, 468-70.
        Calls Uncle Remus, Leatherstocking, and Poor Richard
    "enduring creations of American fiction"; Remus is, in some
    respects, our "most natural and lovable character." Harris
    was a genius; and his thorough preparation makes the dialect
    tales seem natural. Describes the simple frame for the
    tales and sees them as a reflection of a race that could
    laugh in spite of slavery.

7   O'BRIEN, EDWARD J. The Advance of the American Short Story.
    New York: Dodd, Mead, pp. 160-61, 171, 174, 299.
        Harris's reputation lies in his Negro folklore and his
    sympathetic rendering of Tennessee mountain life. His Remus
    sketches gave impetus to dialect studies, and Remus is the
    embodiment of all the Negro has contributed to American

culture. Finds a strange traceable indebtedness to Kipling.
Harris was among the important early regionalists. Lists
eleven Harris books and Life and Letters. Revised edition:
1931.B13.

8 OVERTON, GRANT. American Nights Entertainment. New York:
D. Appleton; George H. Doran Co.; Doubleday, Page & Co.;
Charles Scribner's Sons, pp. 160, 167-68.
Humorous comparison of Uncle Remus and Alice in Wonder-
land. In a list for children Overton cites Uncle Remus and
praises Frost's illustrations.

9 PATTEE, FRED LEWIS, ed. Century Readings for a Course in
American Literature. Revised and annotated. New York:
Century Co., p. 905.
Harris is the most spontaneous and, in many ways, the
most original literary creator of the period. Stresses his
education at Turnwold and the accidental start for the Remus
tales. He can never have a successor in depicting the Negro
slave, as the old plantation life has disappeared. His
strength lies in his "artlessness, his perfect naturalness"
and truth to nature. Remus is both a type and an individual;
he evinces simplicity, pathos, duplicity, suavity, and
loyalty. Anthologizes "How a Witch Was Caught," "The Creature with No Claws," and "Uncle Remus's Wonder Story" on
pp. 905-911.

10 PATTEE, FRED LEWIS. The Development of the American Short
Story. New York and London: Harper & Brothers, pp. 277-83,
289.
Biographical summary prefaces comments that Harris,
though a journalist, wrote genuine folk stories and made
the Negro come alive. Uncle Remus "is one of the most vital
creations in modern literature," and his tales are subtle
but dramatic art. Brer Rabbit represents the Negro. Harris's novels were failures, because he dealt best with
shorter units. "At Teague Poteet's," "Free Joe," and
"Trouble on Lost Mountain" are softened and idealized though
"they are as near to realism as the South has ever got."
Harris's mountain tales surpassed those of Craddock [Mur-
free] in genuineness and human sensitivity. Includes a
primary bibliography of eleven works, with magazine publication data for the tales in Mingo, Free Joe, and Balaam.

1924 A BOOKS - NONE

1924 B SHORTER WRITINGS

1 ANON. "Friends of Children." NEA Journal, 13 (December), 349.
Portraits of twelve writers with brief captions about their literary materials for children. Harris is notable for his Uncle Remus tales.

2 BRAITHWAITE, WILLIAM STANLEY. "The Negro in Literature." Crisis, 28 (September), 205.
Of all Americans, Harris made the most permanent contribution of Negro folk materials. Yet he was only the amanuensis for the Race, which supplied his pen and was his artist; in its illiteracy it lacked the power to record its speech.

3 BYRD, MABEL. "Plantation Proverbs of 'Uncle Remus.'" Crisis, 27 (January), 118-19.
Harris, remembered as one of the five social historians of America, recorded in the plantation proverbs in Uncle Remus the wit and wisdom of the slave, who learned not from books but from the hard school of experience. Several proverbs are analyzed for psychological and philosophical content.

4 [CLEMENS, SAMUEL LANGHORNE]. Mark Twain's Autobiography. Vol. 1. Edited by Albert Bigelow Paine. New York: Harper & Brothers, p. 112.
Twain heard Uncle Dan'l tell the "immortal tales which Uncle Remus Harris was to gather into his book and charm the world with, by and by."

5 DuBOIS, W. E. BURGHARDT. The Gift of Black Folk: The Negroes in the Making of America. Boston: Stratford Co., pp. 295-96.
Harris deftly and successfully translated the Negroid Brer Rabbit tales for white America. Harris's version of tar-baby shows the white literary touch in comparison to an early nineteenth century version by C. C. Jones which records the primitive tale [see 1888.B18].

6 GONZALES, AMBROSE E., ed. "Foreword," in his With Aesop along the Black Border. Columbia, SC: State Co., p. xi.
"Apologists for the Negro have attempted to condone [the] apotheosizing of the mendacious heroes of his folk-lore by assuming that the Negro saw in the Rabbit and the weaker

1924

creatures the poor slave forced to resort to cunning and
lying to protect himself from the harshness of his cruel
master! But the slave brought these myths from Africa,
whence, also[,] he brought his race characteristics!"

7   KRAPP, GEORGE PHILIP. "The English of the Negro." American
    Mercury, 2 (June), 191–92, 195.
    Harris was painstaking in his use of Negro and Southern
    white dialect, but their speech is so similar that the
    speaker could be either white or black. The Remus stories
    are burdened with phonetic detail, which makes the language
    seem different from familiar English speech. The phonetic
    spelling emphasizes what would pass unnoticed in hearing.
    Thanks to literary artists like Page and Harris, everyone
    accepted Negro English as an American colloquial form, no
    longer a mutilation.

8   MILLER, DAISY. "Negro Dialect in American Literature." .
    Opportunity, 2 (November), 329.
    Deplorably little attention has been paid to Negro speech
    in America. An immeasurable debt is owed to Harris's pains-
    taking collection of lore in Uncle Remus, but this is the
    Negro's contribution; Harris just wrote down what he heard.

9   PETTUS, CLYDE. "Brer Rabbit's Brier Patch: A Sketch of
    'Uncle Remus.'" Southern Magazine, 1 (June), 22–28.
    Surveys Harris's life and passes on familiar anecdotes.
    Harris had a variety of nicknames when he worked for the
    Savannah Morning News, including "Pink-Top" and "Vermillion
    Pate"; his humorous paragraphs were sometimes called "Hot
    shots from Red Hair-is."

10 SAMPSON, J. MILTON. "The Negro in Anglo-Saxon Literature."
    Opportunity, 2 (June), 170.
    Uncle Remus was the outstanding antebellum slave charac-
    ter for the South, as Uncle Tom was in the North. A type
    of the true plantation Negro, Remus observes and interprets
    life in the animal stories. But the burlesque is apparent
    in the stories about Remus himself, such as the phonograph
    sketch.

11 WADE, JOHN DONALD. Augustus Baldwin Longstreet: A Study of
    the Development of Culture in the South. New York:
    Macmillan, pp. 62, 167.
    Comments on the generosity and democracy of Middle
    Georgians in their gracious treatment of Harris as a child
    despite his personal history. Harris had affectionate
    memories of the region. Indebted to Longstreet, Harris

1925

continued his tradition. He probably heard anecdotes of
Longstreet and Middle Georgia through W. T. Thompson.

12 WEATHERFORD, W. D. *Negro Life in the South: Present
    Conditions and Needs.* Revised edition. New York:
    Association Press, p. 126.
       Surmises that the Remus stories are direct descendants
    of African folktales.

1925 A BOOKS - NONE

1925 B SHORTER WRITINGS

1   ANON. "The Snap-Bean Sage." *Saturday Review of Literature*
    (2 May), p. 721.
       Harris should be set beside Mark Twain and Walt Whitman
    as one of America's greatest authors. His Negro dialect
    writings are "a national heritage," and his later children's
    works reassert his creative and imaginative abilities.

2   FOERSTER, NORMAN, ed. *American Poetry and Prose: A Book of
    Readings: 1607-1916.* With Robert Morss Lovett, general
    editor. Boston, et al.: Houghton Mifflin, The Riverside
    Press, p. 1047.
       Provides a brief biographical summary and cites two cri-
    tical studies. Harris's delightful work is not artifice but
    record, as he preserved the Old South Negro and plantation
    folklore. Prints "Mr. Benjamin Ram and His Wonderful Fiddle"
    on pp. 872-74.

3   GAINES, FRANCIS PENDLETON. *The Southern Plantation: A Study
    in the Development and the Accuracy of a Tradition.*
    New York: Columbia University Press, pp. 17, 74-78, 212,
    et passim.
       Harris's plantation Negro symbolizes "a spirit of adula-
    tion and self-effacement," and is a "sentimental perversion."
    Yet Harris's work is "the literary history of the planta-
    tion," and he ushered in the old regime as a field for fic-
    tion. He writes romantically of the old days but also treats
    more realistically the dominance of caste and hunger for
    land in *Mingo*, the problems of the fugitive in *Plantation*,
    of mixed blood in *Minervy Ann*, and of the cruel overseer and
    slave economies in *Bishop* and *Free Joe*. With the public,
    "Harris is most significant for the revelation of the planta-
    tion darkey."

143

1925

4   HARMAN, HENRY E. "Joel Chandler Harris." New York <u>Bookman</u>,
    61 (June), 433-36.
        Recalls the "royal fellowship" that existed between
    Harris and James Whitcomb Riley, when Harman saw them at
    Lithia Springs, Georgia, in 1902 or 1903. The two swapped
    stories enthusiastically. Harris said to Harman later that
    the two weeks with Riley would stand out as the happiest he
    had ever known. Riley felt that Harris's writings were the
    best Southern literature yet. Harris's stories mix the
    charms of nature with a faithful delineation of the old-time
    Negro.

5   HARRIS, JULIA COLLIER. "Joel Chandler Harris: Constructive
    Realist," in <u>Southern Pioneers in Social Interpretation</u>.
    Edited by Howard W. Odum. Chapel Hill, NC: University of
    North Carolina Press, pp. 143-64.
        Briefly describes Harris's life, personality, and humane
    values and stresses his realism and sympathetic portraiture
    in "Mingo" and "Blue Dave" (<u>Mingo</u>), and "The Case of Mary
    Ellen" (<u>Minervy Ann</u>). "Where's Duncan?" reveals poignantly
    a side of Harris that is nowhere else developed. In his
    editorials and through Billy Sanders Harris stressed jus-
    tice, kindness, compassion, and morality. Reprinted:
    1967.B9.

6   JONES, CHARLES C.[OLCOCK], JR. "Prefatory Note," in <u>Negro
    Myths from the Georgia Coast: Told in the Vernacular</u>.
    Columbia, SC: State Co., p. v.
        Reprint of 1888.B18.

7   KRAPP, GEORGE PHILIP. <u>The English Language in America</u>.
    Vol. 1. New York: Century Co., pp. 240-42, 248-51, et
    passim.
        "No more skilful literary transcriptions of Southern
    speech, both the speech of whites and of negroes, have been
    made than those of Joel Chandler Harris." Krapp analyzes
    dialect in "Mingo" and in Uncle Remus's speech, and affirms
    what Harris's writings reveal--that there are few differ-
    ences between Southern rustic Negro and rustic white speech.

8   QUINN, ARTHUR H.[OBSON]. "Passing of a Literary Era."
    <u>Saturday Review of Literature</u>, 1 (21 March), [609]-610.
        The recent deaths of Cable, James Lane Allen, Francis
    Hopkinson Smith, and Page close "one of the most significant
    chapters in our literary history." The early work of these
    five writers will surely endure; with Harris, this would be
    the Uncle Remus tales and <u>Free Joe</u>. But their later work
    has merit, too. Harris effectively contrasted Northern and

1926

Southern characters and "rivalled Page" in his portraits of
sectional conflicts. Occasions is not read often enough;
its picture of Lincoln from the Southern point of view is
striking and original. Harris had "profound significance"
as a writer and belongs to all English-speaking peoples.

9 SCARBOROUGH, DOROTHY. On the Trail of Negro Folk-Songs.
   Cambridge, MA: Harvard University Press, p. 173.
   The rabbit by nature is not as witty or resourceful as
   portrayed in the Uncle Remus stories and in folksongs. Perhaps his very defenselessness and mild ways make him attractive to the Negro.

10 WERNER, ALICE. African [Mythology]. Vol. 7 in The Mythology
   of All Races. Edited by John Arnott MacCulloch. Boston:
   Marshall Jones Co., pp. 283-84, 292, 307.
   The hare, hero of Uncle Remus's tar-baby story, appears
   in Angolan folklore, and Africa is the likely origin of many
   of the Brer Rabbit stories. Reprinted: 1964.B21.

1926 A BOOKS - NONE

1926 B SHORTER WRITINGS

1 ANON. "Notes on Rare Books." New York Times Book Review
   (19 September), p. 24.
   James Carleton Young of Minneapolis was an avid book-
   collector and persuaded many famous authors to inscribe
   books for him. Apparently Harris was in "a rollicking mood"
   when he wrote some of his inscriptions. He wrote in Nights
   that he was "'terribly in earnest'" when he penned the introduction but that he knew no more about comparative folklore "'than a blind horse knows about Sunday.'" A humorous
   inscription in Friends is also quoted. He inscribed in
   Sister Jane: "'Artistically this book is a rank failure.
   The author tried to withdraw it after a part of it was in
   type, but was prevailed on to let it go.'" When the collection was sold in 1916, Friends brought $20, Nights $60, and
   Sister Jane $18.50.

2 BEER, THOMAS. The Mauve Decade: American Life at the End of
   the Nineteenth Century. New York: Alfred A. Knopf,
   pp. 179-80.
   Oliver Herford's illustrations in some tales by the "de-
   clining" J. C. Harris made children of the 1890's think they
   enjoyed Wildwoods and Mr. Thimblefinger.

1926

3 BLOODWORTH, JENNIE AKERS. "Uncle Remus," in her Getting
   Acquainted with Georgia. Dallas: Southern Publishing Co.,
   pp. 126-42.
   A book for schoolchildren that briefly retells through
   dialogue Harris's life, manner, and achievement.

4 DOWD, JEROME. The Negro in American Life. New York: Century
   Co., pp. 283-84.
   Harris is the preeminent masterful interpreter of the
   Negro of the Georgia hinterland and the Carolinas. His at-
   tempts at the quainter coastal dialect in Nights are not as
   successful because he was not at home in handling their
   mode of speech and thought. He transformed the native African tales to suit the New World's animal life. Credits
   C. C. Jones with the most authentic record of Negro myth in
   correct Gullah dialect [see 1888.B18].

5 GAINES, FRANCIS P.[ENDLETON]. "The Racial Bar Sinister in
   American Romance." SAQ, 25 (October), 398.
   The consequences of love between members of different
   races are always portrayed tragically in American litera-
   ture. "Where's Duncan?" (Balaam) and "The Case of Mary
   Ellen" (Minervy Ann) are among several examples cited.

6 L.[ANIER], H.[ARRY] W. "'Million' Books and 'Best' Books."
   Golden Book Magazine, 4 (September), 382.
   Four hundred teachers of high school and college litera-
   ture listed Uncle Remus in fifth place among the ten works
   by American writers that should have a permanent place in
   the world's literature. Poe's tales, The Scarlet Letter,
   The Adventures of Huckleberry Finn, and The Last of the
   Mohicans were ranked ahead of Uncle Remus, and Moby-Dick,
   The Rise of Silas Lapham, Ethan Frome, Harte's tales, and
   Uncle Tom's Cabin followed it.

7 LAW, FREDERICK HOUK, ed. Modern Short Stories. New York:
   Century Co., p. 275.
   Anthology includes "The Adventures of Simon and Susanna"
   from Daddy Jake. Under "Critical Comment" at the end of the
   volume Law suggests that the story originated in man's primitive past and gradually became invested with the magic and
   exaggeration of the oral folktale. "Every story that Mr.
   Harris wrote has plot interest, but it also has pith and
   wisdom."

8 LOCKE, ALAIN. "American Literary Tradition and the Negro."
   Modern Quarterly, 3 (May-July), 220.

1926

Page and Cable began with good genre drawings of the
Negro, but ended in "mediocre chronographic romanticism."
False values promulgated in the North and South spoiled
Page's and Cable's writing; Harris was an exception,
however.

9   MIMS, EDWIN. The Advancing South: Stories of Progress and
    Reaction. Garden City, NY: Doubleday, Page & Co.,
    pp. 187-88, 202-203.
        A progressive editor, Julian Harris lived up to his
    father's ideal. Joel Chandler Harris was a "kindly, genial
    humorist" but characteristically frank. "Free Joe" reveals
    a critical attitude towards the "old regime."

10 NELSON, JOHN HERBERT. "Uncle Remus Arrives" and "The
    Contemporaries and Successors of Harris," in his The Negro
    Character in American Literature. Bulletin of the
    University of Kansas: Humanistic Studies. Vol. 4, no. 1.
    Lawrence, KS: Department of Journalism Press, pp. 107-37.
        Along with the Indian and the frontiersman, the American
    Negro is one of the world's most original literary types.
    Harris will be known as the "supreme interpreter" of the
    American Negro in his "most attractive period of develop-
    ment"--that of his picturesque transition from his "past
    benighted years" into the "fierce light of freedom." Har-
    ris's portrait of the Negro is "realistic" and his use of
    dialect precise. Free Joe is a carefully realized indi-
    vidual; Minervy Ann, Mingo, and Daddy Jake are also able
    characterizations. The greatest portrait is that of Remus,
    but the animals in the tales are also studies in Negro atti-
    tudes and behavior. No "real advance" in other literary
    portrayals of the Negro has occurred since Harris's first
    books.

11 [PALMER, HENRIETTA R., ed.]. "Introduction," to In Dixie
    Land: Stories of the Reconstruction Era by Southern
    Writers. New York: Purdy Press, pp. xix-xx.
        Prints selection from Tolliver; the novel presents a
    philosophical picture of Southern character and of postwar
    conditions in Georgia.

12 SHERLOCK, CHESLA C. "'The Sign of the Wren's Nest,' Home of
    Joel Chandler Harris," in her Homes of Famous Americans.
    Des Moines, IA: Meredith Publications, pp. 295-308.
        The description of Harris's "quaint and commodious" old
    house merges with the author's comments on his life.

1926

13   WILLIAMS, STANLEY THOMAS. The American Spirit in Letters.
     Vol. 2 of The Pageant of America. Edited by Ralph Henry
     Gabriel. New Haven: Yale University Press, pp. 254-55.
     Harris revealed the Negro's soul; Remus is genuine like
     Leatherstocking and a "vigorous type." In recreating Negro
     folklore, Harris combined the "half-unconscious symbolism"
     of the tragic history of the race and "natural art" to
     achieve reality. He wrote too much, however, and the qual-
     ity of his work suffered as he "became more conscious of a
     purpose." His work on the cracker "may be disregarded."
     Provides a brief biographical sketch.

1927 A BOOKS - NONE

1927 B SHORTER WRITINGS

1   BEARD, CHARLES A. and MARY R. BEARD. The Industrial Era.
    Vol. 2 of The Rise of American Civilization. New York:
    Macmillan, p. 443.
    In his books Harris made the Southern Negro "laugh and
    weep."

2   BLASSINGAME, LURTON. "Julian Harris and His Father."
    Commonweal, 6 (10 August), 334-36.
    Commends Julian Harris for his courageous journalism,
    which resulted in a Pulitzer Prize for his work in 1925.
    Julian said that he acquired his humane idealism from his
    father. Joel Chandler Harris's writings about the Old South
    are eternal; he understood "sorrow and beauty and love and
    truth" in those dark days after the War. A biographical
    sketch is included. Harris died a Catholic, his soul at
    last finding the refuge it had been seeking.

3   BRAITHWAITE, WILLIAM STANLEY. "The Negro in American
    Literature," in The New Negro: An Interpretation. Edited
    by Alain Locke. New York: Albert and Charles Boni, p. 32.
    For his time Harris made the most permanent contribution
    on the Negro. In Uncle Remus is "something approaching
    true portraiture," but in these stories the race was the
    artist and Harris only the means.

4   BRICKELL, HERSCHEL. "The Literary Awakening in the South."
    New York Bookman, 66 (October), 141.
    Such writers as Ambrose E. Gonzales of South Carolina are
    honorably upholding the Negro folk traditions in literature
    that were so firmly established by Harris.

1927

5   FAUSET, ARTHUR HUFF. "American Negro Folk Literature," in
     The New Negro: An Interpretation. Edited by Alain Locke.
     New York: Albert and Charles Boni, pp. 238-44.
          Harris's portraits of the black man were more successful
     than those by other Southern whites, yet his were still ro-
     mantic, literary adaptations of Negro folklore. Through
     Uncle Remus Harris interprets Negro character from a white
     perspective. The rabbit's meaning is based more upon primi-
     tive folk symbolism than, as Harris thought, upon the Ameri-
     can Negro's situation.

6   _____. "Negro Folk Tales from the South." JAF, 40 (July-
     September), 213-14.
          In his introduction to transcriptions of several dozen
     tales, songs, and riddles gathered from Negroes in Alabama,
     Mississippi, and Louisiana, Fauset notes that modern Negroes
     are less spontaneous in tale-telling than they once were;
     but, when moved to talk, Negroes will relate countless
     stories of Brer Rabbit, of Pat and Mike the Irishmen, and
     of other characters.

7   LEVERETTE, FANNIE LEE. "Did She Turn Into a Rabbit?" Atlanta
     Journal Magazine (23 October), p. 11.
          Betsey Cole was a celebrated white soothsayer who lived
     in Eatonton. When Harris was still a young boy, Betsey told
     his mother that "'Writings from your family are going to be
     read all over the world.'"

8   NASH, J. V. "Joel Chandler Harris, Interpreter of the Negro
     Soul." Open Court, 41 (February), 103-110.
          Recounts Harris's life and journalistic career. His
     Uncle Remus stories reflect the Negro's folk heritage and
     aspirations, as well as human nature in general, and are
     "perhaps the most vital literary productions springing out
     of American soil." Harris was an extremely shy man, and the
     "underlying pathos" in all of his writings is traceable to
     the circumstances of his birth, the loneliness of his child-
     hood, and the shock of the War.

9   SMITH, C.[HARLES] ALPHONSO. "Joel Chandler Harris: A
     Discussion of the Negro as Literary Material," in his
     Southern Literary Studies. Chapel Hill, NC: University
     of North Carolina Press, pp. 128-57.
          Summarizes Harris's life and stresses his characteriza-
     tion and use of dialect in the Remus tales, mentioning other
     works in passing. Irwin Russell, in "Christmas Night in the
     Quarters" (1878), discovered the literary potential of Negro
     character, and, earlier, Simms, Poe, Stowe, and Stephen

1928

Foster had made use of Negro types. Yet in Uncle Remus
Harris not only brought the folklore of the Negro into
literature and reproduced Negro dialect with great accuracy,
but he also caught the "quaint indirectness" of old-time
Negro speech and nuances of Negro character and philosophy.
Uncle Remus blends the universal with the particular. In
his animal tales, Remus reveals "the universal desire to
correlate the unknown with the known."

1928 A BOOKS - NONE

1928 B SHORTER WRITINGS

1   ANON. "Two Unpublished Letters of Joel Chandler Harris Given."
     Eatonton Messenger (14 December), [p. 1].
         Harris used to play with Charlie Leonard and Hut Adams
     of Eatonton; in 1879 and 1880 he wrote to a citizen of
     Eatonton, in response to a query, that Uncle George Terrell
     was the "original" of Uncle Remus. The newspaper columnist
     adds that Joseph Sidney Turner, son of Joseph Addison Turner
     of Turnwold, was the "little boy" in the Remus tales. The
     last time Harris came to Eatonton he would not give a
     speech.

2   BIKLÉ, LUCY LEFFINGWELL CABLE. George W. Cable: His Life
     and Letters. New York: Charles Scribner's Sons,
     pp. 127-28.
         Reviews the "Banjo Imbroglio" between Harris and Cable
     of 1883-1884, in which Harris claimed that the fiddle was
     the Negro's favorite plantation instrument and Cable ini-
     tially argued for the banjo. On 28 July 1884 Cable wrote
     his good friend Harris agreeing that the fiddle was the
     Negro's preferred instrument, after all [see 1886.B6 for
     his public statement].

3   ESSENWEIN, J. BERG. Writing the Short-Story. Revised edition.
     New York: Noble and Noble, Inc., p. 90.
         Alludes to the human guise of Brer Rabbit and Fox; ani-
     mals must have human aspects to be interesting.

4   GREEN, ELIZABETH LAY. The Negro in Contemporary American
     Literature. University of North Carolina Extension
     Bulletin, Vol. 7, no. 14. Chapel Hill, NC: University of
     North Carolina Press, p. 38.
         Study guide. The local colorists gave a romanticized
     haze to plantation days. Praises Harris for popularizing
     and preserving Negro folklore.

1928

5   HENDRICK, BURTON J. The Earlier Life and Letters of Walter H.
     Page: The Training of an American. London: William
     Heinemann, Ltd., pp. 147-54, 275-76, 329, 331-33.
        Page met Harris in 1881 and theirs was a lasting friend-
     ship. Harris earned two national reputations, as a news-
     paper paragrapher and as a folklorist. Newspaper editors
     did not realize that. they had been reprinting Harris edi-
     torials until the Uncle Remus popularity; Harris was
     responsible for making the Atlanta Constitution the most
     influential Southern paper. Harris is essentially a humor-
     ist, although he claims he tries not to be, and he was drawn
     unconsciously to Remus's underlying humor. Next to Uncle
     Remus, no Southern characters are as lifelike as Sister
     Jane and William Wornum [Sister Jane].

6   LEVERETTE, FANNIE LEE. "Mother of Joel Chandler Harris."
     Atlanta Journal Magazine (29 July), p. 4.
        Mary Harris and her son lived in a quaint Dutch cottage
     next door to the Leverette house. Mary, originally from an
     aristocratic Georgia family and attractive, dark-haired, and
     "of the Latin type" in appearance, used to entertain her
     son and neighborhood children with stories; her favorite
     was the tale of the Irish Banshee. A spinster, Jane Connor,
     helped Mary in her tailor shop and was the model for Sister
     Jane.

7   LOCKE, ALAIN. "The Negro's Contribution to American Art and
     Literature." Annals of the American Academy of Political
     and Social Science, 140 (November), 235, 236-37.
        Uncle Remus created himself, so to speak, and Harris be-
     came an "improvising amanuensis of the mid-Georgian Negro
     peasant whom he knew and liked so well." Harris and Cable
     helped to rescue Negro folklore, but "modern scholarship
     has yet to winnow out the sentimental additions which
     glossed over the real folksiness of the originals."

8   MARQUIS, DON. "Confessions of a Reformed Columnist."
     Saturday Evening Post, 201 (22 December), 6-7, 53.
        Marquis once worked as an assistant editor on the staff
     of Uncle Remus's Magazine; Marquis wrote a monthly column
     but wanted daily work instead. After Harris's death, the
     staff was reorganized; Marquis did not want the half-time
     position offered him and quit. Harris was "one of the
     world's great golden hearts."

9   SPINGARN, J.[OEL] E.[LIAS]. "Foreword" to The Conjure Woman,
     by Charles W. Chesnutt. Boston and New York: Houghton
     Mifflin, p. vi.

1928

Uncle Julius is a "character" and is thus more real than
Uncle Remus, who is but a mouthpiece for the Brer Rabbit
tales. Julius's tales tend toward self-portrayal; the old
Negro has "seldom been given more truthfully" than in The
Conjure Woman.

10   WHITE, NEWMAN I. American Negro Folk-Songs. Cambridge, MA:
Harvard University Press, p. 224.
The "Uncle Remus stories, with their interpolated songs,
correspond in form to the song-interpolated animal story of
Africa and Jamaica." The American Negro substituted local
animals for jungle beasts, however.

11   WORK, MONROE N., comp. A Bibliography of the Negro in Africa
and America. New York: H. W. Wilson Co., pp. 430, 437,
462, 468.
Under "Folklore of the Negro in the United States," lists
nine Harris volumes. In the category "Short Stories Relating to the Negro or Having Negro Characters," lists
eleven Harris volumes. Lists Tolliver in the section "Novels by White Authors treating the Reconstruction Period."
The section, "Discussions of Negro Folk Songs," mentions
Harris's 1883 article in Critic on plantation music and the
replies by Brainerd and Harrison [see 1883.B7, B9].

1929 A BOOKS

1   HALE, MRS. ARTHUR. My Souvenir of "The Wren's Nest."
Atlanta: Donaldson-Woods Co., 26pp.
Written as a souvenir to be sold at "The Sign of the
Wren's Nest," Harris's West-End Atlanta home, this booklet
briefly recounts Harris's life and takes a walking tour of
the house and grounds; the Uncle Remus Memorial Association
purchased the Wren's Nest in 1913. The pamphlet includes
a dialect poem of Harris's, "De Ol' Stan'by's," a poem in
the manner of Uncle Remus by Mrs. Hale, and four photographs, including one of George Terrell, a Negro from
Eatonton who was thought to have told young Joe folktales.

1929 B SHORTER WRITINGS

1   ANON. "Two Gates of Atlanta." NEA Journal, 18 (March), 81,
83.
Atlanta, the Gate City of the South, has two gates: the
downtown railroad gate, and a modest garden gate at 214
Gordon Street, where Harris's home, the Wren's Nest, is

1929

located. The span of Harris's life roughly corresponds
with the rise of Atlanta.

2   BRAWLEY, BENJAMIN [GRIFFITH]. "The Negro in American
    Fiction," in Anthology of American Negro Literature.
    Edited by V.[ictor] F.[rancis] Calverton. New York:
    Modern Library, pp. 238, 240, 247.
    Reprint of 1916.B4.

3   ENGLISH, THOMAS H. "Memorializing Pride in an Adopted Son."
    Emory Alumnus, 5 (March), 7-8.
        Emory University conferred her first honorary degree on
    Joel Chandler Harris in 1902, and, thanks to the generosity
    of his heirs, the University is now establishing a sub-
    stantial collection of his manuscripts. Invaluable manu-
    scripts of the unpublished Qua, as well as Rockville,
    portions of Nights, Mingo, Free Joe, and several other
    works are now among the University's holdings.

4   ESPINOSA, A.[URELIO] M. "European Versions of the Tar-Baby
    Story." Folk-Lore, 40 (September), 217-27.
        Jacobs [see 1888.B16; 1889.B9; 1892.B22] and Brown [see
    1922.B2] did not know of any European versions of the tar-
    baby story and argued for Indian or African origins of the
    tale. Espinosa found Mexican and Spanish versions of the
    stick-fast and five-fold attack story [see 1914.B7]; his
    evidence suggests that, while the tale may have originated
    in India, it acquired special features in Africa and in
    Europe. The version known among American Negroes is a com-
    bination of African and Hispanic-African versions.

5   FIRKINS, INA TEN EYCK. Index to Short Stories. Supplement.
    New York: H. W. Wilson Co., p. 129.
        [Supplement to 1923.B1.] Cites an anthology that in-
    cludes "Trouble on Lost Mountain." [See also 1936.B4.]

6   GARLAND, HAMLIN. "Roadside Meetings of a Literary Nomad. II.
    William Dean Howells and Other Memories of Boston."
    New York Bookman, 70 (November), 248.
        Reprint of 1917.B2. Garland told Howells that the
    stories of Harris, Cable, Jewett, and other local colorists
    are but varying phases of the vital national movement to
    give attention to the peculiar conditions of the country.
    Reprinted, with minor revisions: 1930.B9.

7   _____. "Roadside Meetings of a Literary Nomad. III. Early
    Stories--Meetings with Walt Whitman--Sidney Lanier."
    New York Bookman, 70 (December), 401.

153

1929

Garland told Whitman that Cable, Joseph Kirkland, Harris, Mary E. Wilkins, and others were forerunners of a "'powerful native literature.'" Reprinted, with minor revisions: 1930.B9.

8   HARRIS, JULIA COLLIER. "Joel Chandler Harris--Fearless Editor." Emory Alumnus, 5 (March), 9-10.
    Harris's fame as the creator of the Uncle Remus tales has eclipsed his other achievements, as a journalist and author of stories about Georgia life. Harris affirmed the need for humanity, justice, and charity in his editorials and stories like "Free Joe," "Blue Dave," Sister Jane, and "The Case of Mary Ellen." His mouthpiece Billy Sanders spoke out against lynching, mob rule, and dishonesty in politics. As early as 1876 Harris wrote that an editor must have a purpose and, work to mow down old prejudices, especially in the aftermath of the Civil War.

9   HART, BERTHA SHEPPARD. Introduction to Georgia Writers. Macon, GA: J. W. Burke Co., pp. 63, 137-39.
    "Nowhere in America has folk-lore reached such perfection" as in the Remus tales. Provides a brief biographical background. In "glorifying the typical negro man-servant of the Old South he set at rest the harsh criticism of the white man's attitude" towards the plantation servant and brought worldwide attention to Southern literature. Compares Harris to Kipling and Ernest Thompson-Seton in animal tales and to Page and Harry Stillwell Edwards in depicting Negro nature and dialect.

10 LEISY, ERNEST ERWIN. American Literature: An Interpretative Survey. New York: Thomas Y. Crowell, pp. 185-86.
    Although told for amusement, the Remus stories have sound ethnological and documentary value. Discusses Brer Rabbit as typifying the Negro and Remus as one of the few figures Americans added to world fiction.

11 MILLER, H. PRENTICE. "Bibliography of Joel Chandler Harris." Emory Alumnus, 5 (March), 13-14, 22.
    Annotated bibliography of Harris's books and volumes he wrote introductions for. [Some inaccuracies and omissions.]

12 NEWCOMER, ALPHONSO GERALD; ALICE E. ANDREWS; and HOWARD JUDSON HALL. Three Centuries of American Poetry and Prose. Revised and edited by Howard Judson Hall. Chicago, et al.: Scott, Foresman, p. 742.
    The Uncle Remus tales reflect the genuine folk imagination of the Negroes, possibly as modified by the American

experience. Pagan and naive, they show the kindliness,
humor, and inventiveness of the race. Harris's first tales
were almost verbatim from the Negro narratives; the extent
of his later inventions is not known. Anthologizes "How
Mr. Rabbit was Too Sharp for Mr. Fox" and "Why Mr. Possum
Loves Peace."

13 OVERTON, GRANT. An Hour of the American Novel. The One Hour
Series. Philadelphia: J. B. Lippincott, p. 53.
Lists Uncle Remus as among the best fiction of the 1870-
1880 period.

14 PAINE, ALBERT BIGELOW, ed. Mark Twain's Letters. Vol. 1.
New York and London: Harper & Brothers, pp. 395, 401-404,
417-18.
In a letter to Howells for 27 February 1881, Twain writes
that he had recently given a reading in Reverend Joseph
Twichell's church in Hartford, Connecticut, and that "the
thing that went best of all was Uncle Remus's Tar Baby."
Twain was planning to read that tale to members of a Hartford African Church, too. "They've all heard that tale
from childhood--at least the older members have." On
August 10 Twain sent a transcription of "The Golden Arm"
ghost story to Harris, which he had heard as a boy from old
Uncle Dan'l, a slave of his uncle's. He complimented Harris
on the technique of the Remus stories ("the stories are only
alligator pears--one merely eats them for the sake of the
salad dressing") and gave him advice about publishing his
stories by subscription. Later in 1881 Twain wrote Harris
that he was glad Harris had found a version of the Golden
Arm tale, and in a letter dated 2 April 1882 he arranged to
meet Harris in New Orleans and to talk with him about a
possible joint lecture tour.

15 QUINN, ARTHUR HOBSON; ALBERT CROSS BAUGH; and WILL DAVID HOWE,
eds. From the Civil War to the Present. Vol. 2 of The
Literature of America: An Anthology of Prose and Verse.
New York, Chicago, Boston: Charles Scribner's Sons,
pp. 894, N40 [in back pages].
Harris was the first great interpreter of folklore. In-
cludes biographical sketch and checklist of major works.
Also anthologizes "The Story of the Deluge," "Mr. Rabbit
Nibbles up the Butter," and "Free Joe."

16 [ROWLAND, J. M.]. "A Tribute to Uncle Remus." Richmond
Christian Advocate, 37 (25 April), 14.
The editor visited Harris's West Atlanta home after his
death. A Negro down the street said that Harris was the

1929

best friend that the Negroes and the whites had "'down
here.'" His writings were always wholesome.

17   THOMPSON, STITH. Tales of the North American Indians.
      Cambridge, MA: Harvard University Press, p. xxii.
      Animal tales (including those involving animal-trick-
      sters) and migration legends are prevalent among Southeast-
      ern Indians. "The animal cycle has become so greatly
      influenced by the 'Uncle Remus' tales as to be at least as
      much negro as Indian."

1930 A BOOKS - NONE

1930 B SHORTER WRITINGS

1   BECKER, MAY LAMBERTON, ed. Golden Tales of the Old South.
     New York: Dodd, Mead, pp. x, 165-67.
     Harris is unforgettable. Biographical sketch stresses
     the Turnwold experience and the beginnings of the Remus
     stories. The tales are interesting for their characteriza-
     tion of Remus. "The Fate of Mr. Jack Sparrow" is antholo-
     gized.

2   CAIRNS, WILLIAM B. A History of American Literature: Revised
     Edition. New York: Oxford University Press, pp. 493-94.
     Revision of 1912.B3. Whether or not it is true that the
     relationships between whites and blacks were more democratic
     in Georgia than in other Southern states, Harris did succeed
     in "giving the most sympathetic and at the same time unsen-
     timentalized view of the Negro as the Southerner saw him."
     The Remus stories are his best work, valuable for "their
     rendition of the child-like beliefs and imaginings of the
     Negro; for the external portrayal of Uncle Remus himself;
     and for the veiled representation of the Southern Negro in
     Brer Rabbit."

3   CHASE, GRACE F. A. and ELLEN PERRY. Southern Hero Stories.
     New York: Macmillan, pp. 196-204.
     A father gives his two children a brief [and only par-
     tially factual] account of Joel Harris's boyhood in Eaton-
     ton, his life in Atlanta, and authorship of the Remus tales.

4   CLINE, RUTH I. "The Tar-Baby Story." AL, 2 (March), 72-78.
     Details elements in Harris's story that seem directly
     derivative of versions of the story found in the lore of
     India and concludes that India, not Africa, is the original
     home of the story.

1930

5   COTTRELL, GEORGE W., JR. and HOXIE N. FAIRCHILD. <u>Critical</u>
    <u>Guide: Prepared for the Home Study Course in World</u>
    <u>Literature, Based on the Columbia University Course in</u>
    <u>Literature.</u> New York: Columbia University Press, p. 370.
    The Uncle Remus dialect is a delightful extreme. Refers
    to the human qualities of the animals and Harris's use of
    repetition. Harris gives a "thoroughly rounded" sketch of
    the prewar Negro.

6   COUSINS, PAUL M. "The Debt of Joel Chandler Harris to Joseph
    Addison Turner." <u>The Chimes</u> [Shorter College], 42 (March),
    3-10.
    Recounts the life of the owner of Turnwold Plantation,
    where Harris served as a printer's apprentice. Under
    Turner's tutelage, Harris not only acquired practical ex-
    perience in journalism, but also was exposed to English and
    American literary classics and heard at firsthand the slave
    folktales that he would later retell as the Uncle Remus
    stories. Also thanks to Turner, Harris was able to present
    the "fullest picture of plantation life ever given to the
    world."

7   ESPINOSA, AURELIO M. "Notes on the Origin and History of the
    Tar-Baby Story." <u>JAF</u>, 43 (April-June), 129-209 passim.
    Probably no single folktale or short story of any kind
    has been as popular and attracted as much scholarly atten-
    tion as Harris's tar-baby story. Folklorists have studied
    the tale because of their interest in its sources and for
    its intrinsic worth, especially as a "stick-fast" and
    multiple-attack story. Stick-fast or tar-baby tales have
    been found in folktales from old and modern India, Europe,
    Spanish America, and Africa, and in American Indian folk-
    lore. Article summarizes author's research into one hundred
    and fifty-two different tar-baby and stick-fast stories and
    reviews scholarship on the tale. The oldest version is a
    2000-year-old Indian story, and Espinosa believes the story
    was transmitted to other countries from India, not Africa,
    and differentiated in the process. An extensive bibliog-
    raphy of works consulted is included. [<u>See also</u> 1943.B9.]

8   GARLAND, HAMLIN. "Roadside Meetings of a Literary Nomad. VII.
    Editors of the Nineties—Southern Novelists—The Klondike."
    New York <u>Bookman</u>, 71 (April, May), 200-201.
    Garland met Harris once, at the offices of the Atlanta
    <u>Constitution</u>. He was "not prepossessing in appearance and
    plainly showed that he was aware of it." His office was
    cluttered, ugly, and noisy. Harris had few illusions about
    the South, seeing it as Garland saw it: "a place of mental

1930

emptiness as well as of physical unkemptness," but a place
that was, too slowly, changing for the better. He said he
was of mountain stock; his stories were similar to Garland's
in Main-Travelled Roads. Garland surprised Harris by praising his mountaineer stories over the Uncle Remus tales.
Harris "knew the Negro's soul better than any of his contemporaries, but he also knew the men and women of the mountains." He painted aristocrats from an entirely different
angle than Page's and was "bluntly critical" of "the old
régime." Harris probably avoided public appearances because
of his self-consciousness about his own appearance. Reprinted, with minor revisions: 1930.B9.

9 _____. Roadside Meetings. New York: Macmillan, pp. 59, 135,
351-54.
Reprinting, with some wording changes, of 1929.B6, B7;
1930.B8.

10 HART, NINA and EDNA M. PERRY, eds. Representative Short
Stories. Revised by H. Y. Moffett. [New York]:
Macmillan, p. xxvi.
Cites "The Late Mr. Watkins" in a list of stories inter-
esting primarily for their characters.

11 MARBLE, ANNIE RUSSELL. A Study of the Modern Novel: British
and American Since 1900. New York: D. Appleton,
pp. 405-406.
Harris, Twain, and Stockton are listed as humorists
leaving an "indelible" influence on American literature.
Harris produced "whimsical and wise tales." Remus is one
of the original creations of American literature; his humor
"was that of symbolism and philosophy, rather than of pe-
culiarities or situations of drollery. The humor is the
elemental, spontaneous type of childish minds and natural
expressions."

12 ODUM, HOWARD W. An American Epoch: Southern Portraiture in
the National Picture. New York: Henry Holt, pp. 15,
296-301.
Describes Harris's mixed heritage but states that Mary
Harris married Harris's day laborer father. Harris ranked
as a creative pioneer and prophet. He wrote more than
twenty-five books, but his realistic criticism of the South
in his articles and editorials is equally significant and,
in fact, more characteristic of Harris. A vigorous realist,
he wrote of the tragic side of the South while hoping to
develop a regional consciousness. "He picked out from a
mass of southern ruins what was considered inchoate

1930

materials and through clear delineation, new and effective
form, admirable proportion, rhythm and symmetry, he developed an art at once harmonious and beautiful."

13 PARRINGTON, VERNON LOUIS. The Beginnings of Critical Realism
in America: 1860–1920. Vol. 3 of Main Currents in
American Thought. New York: Harcourt, Brace, pp. vii, 400.
Completed only to 1900. Harris discovered Negro primitive folk-poetry and portrayed the romantic traditions of
the Southern plantation Negro and mountaineer.

14 PATTEE, FRED LEWIS. The New American Literature, 1890–1930.
New York: Century Co., pp. 8, 313–15.
Part of the "National Period" of literature, Harris's
Balaam is listed as one of twenty-one important books of
short stories published between 1891–1893. The 1870's
through 1890's also brought a revolt from romance; Harris
attempted real backgrounds and "apparently realistic
characters."

15 [RILEY, JAMES WHITCOMB]. The Letters of James Whitcomb Riley.
Edited by William Lyon Phelps. Indianapolis: Bobbs-
Merrill, pp. 14, 34, et passim.
Riley became a good friend of Harris's, frequently mentioning him in letters to others and writing to him in time,
signing his letters "'Jamesy.'" The two men visited in Atlanta for two weeks in the spring of 1900. Each highly
praised the other's work.

16 SULLIVAN, MARK. Pre-War America. Vol. 3 of Our Times: The
United States 1900–1925. New York: Charles Scribner's
Sons, p. 558.
Harris is one of the very few American authors of an in-
disputable classic, Uncle Remus. Told, Friends, and Uncle
Remus are his best-known works.

17 WILLIAMS, STANLEY T. and NELSON F. ADKINS, eds. Courses of
Reading in American Literature with Bibliographies.
New York: Harcourt, Brace, pp. 113–14.
Uncle Remus and Mingo are recommended readings by Harris
for the college student or individual reader. A nine-item
secondary bibliography is included.

18 WINTERICH, JOHN T. "Romantic Stories of Books: XVI: Uncle
Remus." Publisher's Weekly, 118 (15 November), 2279–83.
Recounts briefly Harris's literary development from a
young boy writing romantic compositions in his notebook to
the master storyteller whose first book, Uncle Remus, would

1931

go through four editions in its first year. Harris explained that he was only a transcriber of tales; he had a
finely tuned ear for dialect and, although most of the Remus
stories that he heard directly from Negroes were acquired
during the 1860's on Turnwold Plantation, he recalls an ex-
hilarating tale-swapping session as late as 1883 [1882], at
a Georgia train depot.

1931 A BOOKS

1 HARRIS, JULIA COLLIER, ed. Joel Chandler Harris: Editor and
   Essayist. Miscellaneous Literary, Political, and Social
   Writings. Chapel Hill, NC: University of North Carolina
   Press, 429pp.
   Harris's daughter-in-law here gathers uncollected essays,
   articles, and editorials from the early 1870's, when Harris
   worked for the Savannah Morning News, to July 1908, when his
   last editorial appeared in Uncle Remus's Magazine. The
   writings are grouped under four headings, which are roughly
   chronological: "The 'Cornfield Journalist'" (early newspaper writings), "Joel Chandler Harris and the Negro Question" (from the Constitution and the Saturday Evening Post),
   "The Philosopher of Shady Dale" (consisting chiefly of Billy
   Sanders essays), and "The Sage of Snap-Bean Farm" (later
   pieces). Harris's miscellaneous articles reveal him in the
   role of "a truthful, sympathetic interpreter of his section's problems and aspirations, and of a leader who sought
   a way out of a narrow, bitter sectionalism into an enlight-
   ened and a neighborly attitude toward Americans of every
   race and section."

1931 B SHORTER WRITINGS

1 ANON. "Harris Portrait Given Emory for Memorial." Emory
   Alumnus, 7 (January), 10.
   The Uncle Remus Memorial Association recently gave Emory
   University the only portrait of Harris that he sat for; it
   was executed in 1902. [The portrait is now in the Uncle
   Remus Museum at Eatonton, Georgia.]

2 BRAWLEY, BENJAMIN. A Short History of the American Negro.
   Third revised edition. New York: Macmillan, p. 237.
   Commentary identical to 1913.B3.

3 BRIGHT, M. ALINE. "Introduction," to her edition of Uncle
   Remus: His Songs and His Sayings. New York: D. Appleton-
   Century, pp. xi-xxiv.

1931

Accompanied by footnotes explaining Harris's dialectical
usage, this high school text reprints the first Remus volume. Introduction provides a brief biographical sketch of
Harris, an account of how "The Wren's Nest" became a
memorial, a survey of Harris's works, and an overview of
Southern literary traditions and the science of folklore.
The Remus stories are Harris's distinctive contribution to
world literature.

4   CHESNUTT, CHARLES W. "Post-Bellum--Pre-Harlem." Colophon, 2
    (February), [5].
         Uncle Julius, narrator in The Conjure Woman (1899), as
    well as the locale of the stories and the book's cover de-
    sign, "were suggestive of Mr. Harris's Uncle Remus, but the
    tales are entirely different." The stories are "the fruit
    of my own imagination," whereas the Uncle Remus stories are
    folktales. Reprinted: 1937.B6.

5   ENGLISH, THOMAS H. "Joel Chandler Harris as a Journalist."
    Emory Alumnus, 7 (November-December), 25.
         Julia Collier Harris's Editor and Essayist permits a
    fuller view of Harris's career as a journalist writing
    literary, political, and social essays for the Constitution,
    the Saturday Evening Post, Uncle Remus's Magazine, and other
    periodicals. Harris's "patriotic view of the relation of
    the South to the nation, reunited through bitter conflict,
    did much to neutralize the poison of sectionalism," North
    and South. His articles on the "Negro question," helpfully
    gathered in Editor and Essayist, reveal that "his ideal of
    human relations was that of neighborliness, and that ideal
    he held aloft as a torch to guide sections, races, and
    creeds to mutual understanding and toleration."

6   GARLAND, HAMLIN. Companions on the Trail: A Literary
    Chronicle. New York: Macmillan, pp. 207, 254.
         Comments on Balaam: "One of these tales, which dealt
    with the pathetic life of a faithful negro, put a big lump
    into my throat--and the fiction which does that for me,
    these days, must needs be vitally true. Harris is a
    genius."

7   HIBBARD, [C.] ADDISON, ed. Stories of the South: Old and
    New. Chapel Hill, NC: University of North Carolina Press,
    pp. xi, 508, 518-19.
         Anthologizes "Why the Confederacy Failed" as representa-
    tive of the North-South struggle. Provides a brief bio-
    graphical note, lists Harris's major works, and praises the
    charm of his Negro stories as well as his high position as

1931

a folklorist. Lists eight Harris books in a suggested
bibliography of short story volumes relating to the South.

8 HUTCHISON, PERCY. "Literary Strays from the Pen of Joel
Chandler Harris." New York Times Book Review (29 November),
p. 2.
Review of Editor and Essayist [see 1931.A1]. This important collection of Harris's essays and editorials reveals
his trenchant wit, his interest in promoting localism rather
than sectionalism, and his role as social and political
critic. He was a well-rounded man, and Dubose Heyward,
Paul Green, Roark Bradford, and others who write of the
Negro today do not know the plantation Negro as Harris did
so well. While less provocative of laughter than Twain,
Harris was nevertheless an effective social and political
satirist with a mission to rebuild Georgia; furthermore,
he was a humanitarian.

9 JENKINS, W. F. "Joel Chandler Harris." Eatonton Messenger
(8 January), [pp. 1, 4].
Reprints a paper read recently before the Ten Club of
Atlanta by a man whose father was a boyhood friend of Harris. Joel had organized an informal group called the "Gully
Minstrels" and would use Harvey Dennis's hounds to hunt
rabbits. William H. Seward had once lived in a room in the
Ward mansion nearby, and Joel and the Ward boys used to slip
in and "borrow" his violin. Seward, whose affections for a
belle in the neighborhood were unrequited, later departed,
leaving the violin behind. Harris had once talked of writing a novel about life in the South with the abandoned violin as a motif. After fame came to him, the author
remembers seeing Harris with Grady at a Putnam County Fair,
but only with a great deal of embarrassment did Harris
stand before the crowd. Jenkins's father had heard many
of the Remus tales himself as a youth in Eatonton, but
Harris gave them the mark of genius.

10 JOHNSON, JAMES WELDON. "Preface [to first edition]," in his
The Book of American Negro Poetry. Revised edition.
New York: Harcourt, Brace, p. 10.
Identical to 1922.B8.

11 LOGGINS, VERNON. The Negro Author: His Development in
America to 1900. New York: Columbia University Press,
pp. 255, 309-11, 312, 314-15, 349, 360.
Harris helped white America appreciate the beauty of
Negro tales and music. Later Negro writers, such as Charles
W. Chesnutt, "leaned heavily upon Harris and Page" in their

1931

exploration of the primitive Negro mind; in fact, Chesnutt's most artistic work was his imitation of Page and
Harris. The frame of The Conjure Woman is similar to Uncle
Remus, and Uncle Julius has Remus's "clever sense of self-
protection." The Remus tale gives the "impression of spontaneous reality." Paul Laurence Dunbar's Folks from Dixie
(1898) is also largely indebted to Harris. Dunbar's Negro
dialect verse surpassed Harris's because Harris was detached from the material, while Dunbar was part of it. The
Harris versions of Negro folktales were not always accurate
but gave Negro customs and language dignity: "Br'er Rabbit,
a portrait begun by the Negro folk in Africa and completed
on the Georgia plantations, emerged as a distinguished
character in American Fiction." Reprinted: 1964.B13.

12 MARBLE, ANNIE RUSSELL. Builders and Books: The Romance of
    American History and Literature. New York: D. Appleton,
    pp. 199-200, 314.
       Harris's grip on readers is still strong. Praises the
    illustrations in the new editions of Nights, Balaam, and
    Rhymes. Harris is ranked as a juvenile favorite inter-
    nationally.

13 O'BRIEN, EDWARD J. The Advance of the American Short Story.
    Revised edition. New York: Dodd, Mead, pp. 160-61, 171,
    174, 282.
       Harris commentary identical to 1923.B7.

14 PRESCOTT, FREDERICK C.[LARKE] and GERALD D. SANDERS, eds. An
    Introduction to American Prose. New York: F. S. Crofts &
    Co., pp. 670, 672 n.3, 756.
       Provides a brief biographical sketch and comments on the
    success of the Uncle Remus volumes. Some of Harris's short
    stories about blacks and poor whites have few American
    rivals for vividness and dramatic intensity. Remus, the
    most lasting creation, is one of the only indisputably
    American characters. Lists Uncle Remus, Nights, Mingo,
    Free Joe, and Plantation and four secondary references and
    anthologizes "Old Mr. Rabbit He's a Good Fisherman" and
    "Jacky-My-Lantern."

15 ROURKE, CONSTANCE. American Humor: A Study of the National
    Character. New York: Harcourt, Brace, p. 228.
       From the late 1860's and on into the 1880's American
    literature reveals "a distinct flow back to a native re-
    gional life." Along with the writings of John Hay, Cable,
    and Eggleston, in 1880 "the animal fables of Uncle Remus
    joined with remnants of that Negro minstrelsy which had
    taken shape fifty years earlier."

1931

16   WHICHER, GEORGE F.   "Poetry after the Civil War," in American
     Writers on American Literature: By Thirty-Seven
     Contemporary Writers.   Edited by John Macy.   New York:
     Horace Liveright, p. 380.
          The fresh rhythms of Negro folklore, echoed in the dia-
     lect poems of Russell, Harris, and Page, suggested the
     South's most important contribution to the resources of
     American poetry.

17   WHITE, WILLIAM ALLEN.   "Fiction of the Eighties and Nineties,"
     in American Writers on American Literature: By Thirty-
     Seven Contemporary Writers.   Edited by John Macy.
     New York: Horace Liveright, p. 395.
          Southern stories of the 1880's and 1890's contrasted
     the old and new South.   Page, Edwards, Smith, and, "some-
     what," Harris told of decayed, proud, kind agrarians treat-
     ing the problems of an industrial age.   The black man was
     seen in comic relief only; he was "pure basswood, all
     painted and strung on wire."

1932 A BOOKS - NONE

1932 B SHORTER WRITINGS

1   ANON.   Review of Editor and Essayist.   Nation, 134 (30 March),
     377.
          A volume of Harris's essays and editorials that gives a
     clearer understanding of Harris and his period but is other-
     wise unimportant [see 1931.A1].

2   AUSTIN, MARY.   "Regionalism in American Fiction."   EJ, 21
     (February), 104.
          A story-region to which every American child deserves
     access is the world of American Indian lore.   Three guides
     to this region recommended by the author are Harris, James
     Willard Schultz, and Arthur Parker.

3   BAKER, ERNEST A. and JAMES PACKMAN.   A Guide to the Best
     Fiction: English and American Including Translations from
     Foreign Languages.   New and enlarged edition.   New York:
     Macmillan, pp. 228-29.
          Revision of 1903.B4.   The only addition is Union Scout;
     the brief evaluations of the other ten books are reworded
     in some instances.

4   CALVERTON, V.[ICTOR] F.[RANCIS].   The Liberation of American
     Literature.   New York: Charles Scribner's Sons, pp. 146-47.

1932

Part of the romantic plantation tradition, Harris looked
to the Negroes for the "rich human possibilities" in their
"forthright, dynamic reaction to life." Later Southern
writers also turned to the Negro for artistic inspiration,
but, while Harris looked to the past, modern writers look
to the facts and fables carried into the present. Reprinted: 1973.B4.

5 DABNEY, VIRGINIUS. Liberalism in the South. Chapel Hill, NC:
   University of North Carolina Press, pp. 220, 222-23, 233-34,
   380, 384, 409.
       Harris, along with Lanier, Cable, and Murfree, were lead-
   ing protagonists for the new spirit in Southern letters.
   The Uncle Remus series is significant as a faithful rein-
   carnation of the antebellum slave and because a Negro is
   the central figure. His Reconstruction and Old South
   stories and novels are realistic and do not deserve their
   present oblivion. Harris's editorials for the Savannah
   News were recognized as among the ablest and most courageous
   of the South. A liberal, like Grady, Harris's Constitution
   and Uncle Remus's Magazine columns stressed education for
   the Negro and a departure from the Southern attitude of
   looking to the past.

6 DANCE, W. L. Review of Editor and Essayist. AL, 4 (March),
   82-85.
       It is regrettable that Julia Collier Harris did not in-
   clude all of Harris's uncollected writings in Editor and
   Essayist [see 1931.A1]. She omits too many passages, as
   well as important essays and editorials, and she is reluc-
   tant to criticize Harris's writing flaws. A few editorial
   errors by Mrs. Harris are noted.

7 DEVINE, ERIC. "The Sage of Snap-Bean Farm." Commonweal, 16
   (18 May), 79.
       Review of Editor and Essayist [see 1931.A1] stresses
   Harris as an American, even though his canvas was Georgia.
   This volume is an important contribution to Harris's full
   stature as a writer and thinker.

8 DICKINSON, THOMAS H. The Making of American Literature.
   New York: Century Co., pp. 561-62, 588, 703.
       "[T]he most important figure in Southern literature,"
   Harris had perfect command of Negro dialect; his scientific
   study established "for all time folklore as a strain in our
   literary tradition." Uncle Remus "is one of the most completely observed characters in American literature"; Harris
   helped other white writers understand the Negro.

1932

9   [ENGLISH, THOMAS H.]. "Harris Memorial Collection Gets Rich
    Addition." Emory Alumnus, 8 (January), 7.
    Among valuable items recently added to the Harris Collec-
    tion at Emory University are an early composition book
    dating from the 1862-1866 period, when Harris was an appren-
    tice-printer at Turnwold, two scrapbooks of clippings of
    Harris's contributions to the Savannah Morning News and the
    Constitution, and a third book of newspaper reviews of Har-
    ris's works, through 1896. Letters to Harris from Theodore
    Roosevelt, John Hay, Paul Hamilton Hayne, Richard Malcolm
    Johnston, Alexander H. Stephens, Constance Fenimore Woolson,
    and others, have recently been placed in the Collection.

10 GARLAND, HAMLIN. My Friendly Contemporaries: A Literary Log.
    New York: Macmillan, pp. 232, 303.
    Harris selected his characters for their picturesque
    qualities; he was at his best in "At Teague Poteet's" and
    "Trouble on Lost Mountain." Recalls that Howells praised
    Harris and other realistic local colorists.

11 [GENZMER, GEORGE H., ed.]. Dictionary of American Biography.
    Vol. 8. Edited by Dumas Malone. New York: Charles
    Scribner's Sons, pp. 312-14.
    Biographical and critical sketch. Harris's boyhood study
    of the English prose masters, while at Turnwold, enabled him
    to create Uncle Remus tales often from bare outlines. Al-
    though he wrote many books, he never surpassed Uncle Remus
    and Nights; his short stories of Georgia reveal a "tactful
    realism." A seven-item secondary bibliography is included.

12 HUBBELL, JAY B. "Sympathetic Interpretation." SAQ, 31
    (January), 126-27.
    As is revealed by Julia Collier Harris's Editor and Es-
    sayist [see 1931.A1], Harris's Remus books have too much
    overshadowed his interesting journalistic writings. His
    portraits of the poor whites and perceptive views on the
    importance of localism in literature should not be for-
    gotten.

13 JOHNSON, MERLE, ed. American First Editions. Revised
    edition. New York: R. R. Bowker Co., pp. 149-51.
    Lists, with occasional descriptions, twenty-nine first
    editions, adding Friends as an errata insert, three bio-
    graphical works on Harris, and fifteen books edited by or
    containing contributions by Harris. Revised: 1942.B1.

14 KNIGHT, GRANT C. American Literature and Culture. New York:
    Ray Long & Richard R. Smith, Inc., pp. 348-49.

1932

The best sequels to Uncle Remus are Nights, Friends, and
Told. These stories tell of a subject race--"imaginative,
kindly, superstitious, and pathetic"--with the rabbit sym-
bolizing helplessness. The dialect is "unusually accurate,"
and ethnologists think some plots are an "almost universal
part of folk-lore." Children like the animal characterizations and the way the weak protects himself, while the
adult finds the "wisps of satire upon human nature give an
added fillip to beast tales that rank with the best."

15 LEWISOHN, LUDWIG. Expression in America. New York and London:
    Harper & Brothers, p. 292.
        A handful of fables from Harris's "amiable semi-folk
    lore" along with a few pages from Woolson, Page, James Lane
    Allen, and others, will serve to illustrate the period of
    transition and sectionalism in American literary expression.

16 PATTEE, FRED LEWIS, ed. Century Readings in American
    Literature. New York and London: D. Appleton-Century, Inc.,
    pp. 806 et passim.
        Harris learned his art on Turner's plantation and caught
    a vision of the romance of the Old South. He portrayed
    "the non-tragic Negro seen through a softened romantic
    haze." He was the most original literary creator of the
    local color movement and wrote with perfect naturalness and
    artlessness. "No one has succeeded so well in depicting the
    childish simplicity, the pathos, the duplicity, the suavity,
    the elemental cunning, the loyalty and dog-like faithfulness
    of the Southern slave." Uncle Remus is one of the few ori-
    ginal characters in American literature; Harris can never
    have a successor. His best work was Uncle Remus.

17 SMITH, REBECCA WASHINGTON. "The Civil War and Its Aftermath
    in American Fiction, 1861-1899, with a Dictionary Catalogue
    and Indexes." Ph.D. dissertation, University of Chicago,
    pp. 37-39, 153-251 passim.
        Harris presents an unheroic image of the Civil War in
    some of his magazine stories, and in others he treats the
    Confederate secret service and other aspects of the
    struggle. No one "has written more variously" of the Civil
    War in fiction, but a few ideas appear consistently: the
    South was wrong, but not disgraced; whites and blacks can
    get along, each in their place; and common sense and an em-
    phasis upon reconciliation can bring both sides together
    after the struggle. Harris's war stories are indexed in a
    chronological table, with brief plot summaries, on pp. 153-
    251 passim. Reprint of introduction: 1937.B11.

1932

18   TATE, ALLEN. "The Cornfield Journalist." New Republic, 71
     (3 August), 320-21.
          Review-essay of Editor and Essayist [see 1931.A1]
     praises Harris's "fugitive writings" for disclosing a ma-
     ture and important phase of Harris's career. Julia Collier
     Harris's book, "a model of editing," reveals Harris's be-
     lief in the importance of localism in literature, but he
     "fiercely resented" the tyranny of politics over the South-
     ern writer. His essay on James's study of Hawthorne
     stresses the importance of a writer's having a provincial
     instinct, not a sectional bias; the good author will write
     about the things that he knows. Harris's point of view is
     of enduring critical value and of special merit in this
     time of industry's and Big Business's ascendancy over the
     arts. "Trotsky and Harris, on the fundamentals of litera-
     ture, are closer together than Trotsky and Dos Passos, or
     Trotsky and Max Eastman."

19   WADE, JOHN DONALD. "Joel Chandler Harris." VQR, 8 (January),
     124-27.
          Editor and Essayist [see 1931.A1] is admirably thorough
     and is especially valuable for revealing what intelligent
     people in the South were thinking between 1865 and 1914.
     Harris was suspicious of Southern politicians before the
     War and alien ones after, and he urged neighbor-knowledge,
     love, and forbearance. Yet he did see confusion and indif-
     ference ahead for the nation in the early twentieth century.

20   WYNN, WILLIAM T.[HOMAS], ed. Southern Literature: Selections
     and Biographies. New York: Prentice-Hall, Inc., pp. 466-67.
          Provides a brief biographical sketch and lists seven of
     Harris's major works. Describes Harris as reserved. Remus
     preserved Negro folklore, habits, and dialect. Anthologizes
     "Mr. Rabbit and Mr. Bear."

1933 A BOOKS - NONE

1933 B SHORTER WRITINGS

1   BROWN, STERLING. "Negro Character as Seen by White Authors."
     Journal of Negro Education, 2 (April), 180, 184, 185, 187,
     193, 197.
          Brown examines seven white literary stereotypes of the
     Negro: the Contented Slave, Wretched Freeman, Comic Negro,
     Brute Negro, Tragic Mulatto, Local Color Negro, and Exotic
     Primitive. In the character of Uncle Remus, Harris made a
     nostalgic and influential contribution to type one, and in

1933

Free Joe, type two, he suggested that the freeman is
"wretched" largely because of his incapacity for freedom.

2   COULTER, E. MERTON. <u>A Short History of Georgia</u>. Chapel Hill,
NC: University of North Carolina Press, pp. 338, 384, 390,
406.
Harris and Grady "first spied out the New South and began telling about it"; their liberal "preachments of progress" in the <u>Constitution</u> greatly aided the industrial
growth of Atlanta and the whole state. Exemplifying the
literary developments following Reconstruction, Harris felt
that controversial sectional writing could wither the soul
of the people and kill a true literature. He used Georgia
and the South as subjects for interpretative writing to
promote North-South understanding. The Northern politicians
created the Negro problem themselves by insisting "that the
property and the intelligence of the South should be placed
in charge of those who had no property and intelligence."

3   DeVOTO, BERNARD. <u>Mark Twain's America</u>. Chautauqua, NY:
Chautauqua Institution, pp. 97, 241, 293, et passim.
Harris was a distinguished writer of newspaper humor.
Cable and Harris, though "romancers," depicted slavery less
sentimentally than Page but were "ineffective--and, besides,
had received instruction from Mark Twain." Twain was the
South's first realist. Nigger Jim is the only Negro who
truly lives in nineteenth-century literature apart from
Harris's folktales, some of which are "dark."

4   ENGLISH, THOMAS H. "Joel Chandler Harris Collection Now One
of Best in Nation." <u>Emory Alumnus</u>, 9 (November-December),
9-10.
Thanks largely to the efforts of Harris's son Lucien and
wife Esther LaRose, Emory University's Harris Collection
has continued to grow. Recent acquisitions include the
typescript of <u>Bishop</u>, his boyhood copy of <u>The Vicar of Wake-
field</u> (Harris's favorite book), and letters from his daugh-
ters Lillian and Mildred, from Clemens, Page, Garland, J. W.
Riley, A. B. Frost, Kipling, Lanier, and from members of
Theodore Roosevelt's family.

5   HICKS, GRANVILLE. <u>The Great Tradition: An Interpretation of
American Literature Since the Civil War</u>. New York:
Macmillan, p. 57.
Harris preserved Negro folklore and, with the other re-
gionalists, brought about a new literature, self-expression,
and new understanding. Revised: 1935.B6, 1967.B10.

1933

6 JOHNSON, JAMES WELDON. Along This Way: The Autobiography of
   James Weldon Johnson. New York: Viking Press, pp. 199,
   327.
       In the early 1900's Johnson contemplated making a musi-
   cal American pantomime out of the Uncle Remus stories, but
   for some forgotten reason never went to Atlanta to talk
   with Harris about rights. Without doubt, Uncle Remus made
   into "an artistic music spectacle, would have been successful at that time. The idea still has possibilities." In
   a paper read in the summer of 1917, Johnson said that the
   folklore of the American Negro, as collected by Harris,
   and Negro dances and music, were the only artistic things
   to have sprung from American soil that were universally
   recognized as distinctly American.

7 STARKE, AUBREY. Sidney Lanier: A Biographical and Critical
   Study. Chapel Hill, NC: University of North Carolina
   Press, pp. 106, 115, 184, 185.
       In a letter written in April 1868, Harris praised Sidney
   Lanier's Tiger-Lilies and termed him a "man of genius" and
   "the most accomplished flute player in America." Lanier
   anticipated both Irwin Russell and Harris in a dialect poem
   published in Scribner's in 1875.

8 TRENT, WILLIAM PETERFIELD; JOHN ERSKINE; STUART P. SHERMAN;
   and CARL VAN DOREN, eds. The Cambridge History of American
   Literature. Vol. 2. New York: Macmillan; Cambridge,
   England: University Press, pp. 303, 347-60 passim, 389,
   408.
       Reprint of 1918.B9, without bibliography.

9 _____. The Cambridge History of American Literature. Vol. 3.
   New York: Macmillan; Cambridge, England: University Press,
   pp. 86, 89, 316, 615.
       Reprint of 1921.B7 and B8, combined.

10 WADE, JOHN DONALD. "Profits and Losses in the Life of Joel
   Chandler Harris." American Review, 1 (April), 17-35.
       Describes life in Eatonton when Harris was a boy, his
   instinctive belief in the binding power of love, and his
   life at Turnwold. Harris seemed like an "up-country bump-
   kin ... stunted and pale" while working for the Savannah
   Morning News. On the staff of the Constitution, Harris and
   Grady wrote with clarity and force against abuses of their
   times. After Grady's death, Harris was "king" in Georgia.
   He worked to make his Remus stories propagandist to reduce
   sectional rancour and seek people to sympathize with one
   another. As he grew older, Harris felt an increased sense

of futility; he seemed out of accord with the paternalistic government and monopolies. A romanticist, he "only wanted people to do right." The small town personal qualities seemed lost in the big cities. Reprinted: 1938.B10.

11   WANN, LOUIS, ed. The Rise of Realism: American Literature from 1860 to 1888. New York: Macmillan, pp. 14-15, 793-94.
        Provides brief biographical sketch. Praises Harris's work on the Constitution as a strong force for liberalism. His fiction earned him "a deservedly high place among the founders of American realism." The Uncle Remus stories are the most important "salvage" of native folklore in America, but Harris's more serious work has been "unduly neglected." His realistic portrayals of the Negro and mountaineer show "an understanding of human nature that is far beyond local color." Anthologizes "How Mr. Rabbit Was Too Sharp for Mr. Fox" and "Aunt Fountain's Prisoner." Revised: 1949.B14.

1934 A BOOKS - NONE

1934 B SHORTER WRITINGS

1   ANON. "Eatonton Welcomes Remus Highway as a Dream Come True." Eatonton Messenger (25 October), [p. 1].
        The opening of the link [of Route 441] from Eatonton to Madison, Georgia, marks the completion of the first major highway through Putnam County and Eatonton. An "Uncle Remus Motorcade" formed at Macon will drive north through Eatonton today and on to Washington subsequently. The high-way itself will be called the Uncle Remus Highway.

2   BRAWLEY, BENJAMIN. The Negro in Literature and Art in the United States. New York: Dodd, Mead, pp. 9, 187, 189, 198.
        Harris's Uncle Remus tales are the "chief literary monu-ment" so far to Negro folklore and folk-music. Reprints 1916.B4.

3   CANBY, HENRY SEIDEL. The Age of Confidence: Life in the Nineties. New York: Farrar & Rinehart, p. 187.
        Writes of his town, Wilmington, in the 1890's. His own library, typical for its period, contained Uncle Remus.

4   DAVIDSON, DONALD. "The Trend of Literature," in Culture in the South. Edited by W.[illiam] T. Couch. Chapel Hill, NC: University of North Carolina Press, p. 186.
        Harris was one of the Southern novelists with "more than passable and fleeting results."

1934

5   FOERSTER, NORMAN, ed. American Poetry and Prose. Revised
     and enlarged edition, with Robert Morss Lovett, General
     Editor. Boston: Houghton Mifflin, The Riverside Press,
     pp. 983, 1154.
     Local color was a joint product of realism and romanti-
     cism. Harris amused a million people with the Remus
     stories of vanishing plantations; his delightful work is
     not artifice but a record of Old South folklore and life.
     Provides a brief biographical summary, cites four Remus
     volumes and five major critical and biographical studies,
     and anthologizes "Mr. Benjamin Ram and His Fiddle." Re-
     printed: 1947.B7.

6   HUBBELL, JAY B. "Southern Magazines," in Culture in the South.
     Edited by W.[illiam] T. Couch. Chapel Hill, NC: University
     of North Carolina Press, p. 171.
     Uncle Remus's Magazine was the only noteworthy post-
     bellum attempt to establish a Southern magazine with na-
     tional scope. The magazine had little real literary merit,
     however; it too closely resembled the Curtis Publishing
     Company magazines.

7   KUNITZ, STANLEY J. and HOWARD HAYCRAFT, eds. The Junior Book
     of Authors: An Introduction to the Lives of Writers and
     Illustrators for Younger Readers from Lewis Carroll and
     Louisa Alcott to the Present Day. Assisted by Wilbur C.
     Hadden and Julia E. Johnsen. New York: H. W. Wilson Co.,
     pp. 174–75.
     Recounts major events in Harris's life. He was called
     the "Hans Christian Andersen of America." Once when a fire
     broke out, Harris calmly noted that he insured the house
     against such a contingency.

8   M.[ABBOTT], T.[HOMAS] O. "Joel Chandler Harris; A Debt to
     Poe." N & Q, 166 (3 March), 151–52.
     In "Grumblers," an early essay, Harris makes fictitious
     quotes from a volume entitled "Tell me now; Is it so or
     not." He takes the title from Poe's "1002nd Tale of
     Scheherazade."

9   McWILLIAMS, CAREY. "Localism in American Criticism: A Century
     and a Half of Controversy." Southwest Review, 19 (July),
     421–23.
     Unfortunately, few local colorists gave definite views
     of the relation of their work to their localities. Harris,
     however, "left a comprehensive and emphatic avowal of his
     creed," seeking to outlaw mere sectionalism while exalting
     localism in art.

10 MILLER, JAMES McDONALD. An Outline of American Literature.
    New York: Farrar & Rinehart, pp. 224-25, 333.
    Ten-line biographical sketch mentions Harris's best work
    as his Negro portraits. "His style is always journalistic
    and fragmentary." Lists Harris's books.

11 WADE, JOHN DONALD. "Southern Humor," in Culture in the South.
    Edited by W.[illiam] T. Couch. Chapel Hill, NC:
    University of North Carolina Press, pp. 619-20, 622.
    Harris, R. M. Johnston, Lanier, and others are similar.
    Initially modeling on Addison, they added dialect and mis-
    spelling and used unsophisticated country-folk as subjects.
    Cultivated readers were meant to enjoy the "hearts of gold"
    beneath the superficial crudities.

12 WILSON, LOUIS R. and R. B. DOWNS. "Special Collections for
    the Study of History and Literature in the Southeast."
    PBSA, 28 (November), 105.
    Briefly describes the Harris Collection at Emory
    University.

1935 A BOOKS - NONE

1935 B SHORTER WRITINGS

1   BECKER, MAY LAMBERTON, ed. Golden Tales of Our America:
    Stories of Our Background and Tradition. New York: Dodd,
    Mead, pp. ix, 153-54.
    Recounts some of Harris's boyhood experiences. Though
    Remus is antebellum, Brer Rabbit is "born anew" for each
    child. These legends are classics where helplessness and
    mischievousness, not malice, triumph. Anthologizes "Mr.
    Rabbit Grossly Deceives Mr. Fox."

2   BROOKS, CLEANTH, JR. The Relation of the Alabama-Georgia
    Dialect to the Provincial Dialects of Great Britain.
    Baton Rouge, LA: Louisiana State University Press, pp. 4,
    5, 63, et passim.
    The word-list for this study is "based largely on the
    negro dialect as it is transcribed by Joel Chandler Harris
    in his Uncle Remus stories [in Uncle Remus and Friends,
    primarily], and on L. W. Payne's 'A Word List from East Ala-
    bama' [Dialect Notes, 3 (1892), 278-328, 342-91]." The most
    important conclusion drawn is that "the speech of the negro
    and of the white is essentially the same, the characteris-
    tically negro forms turning out to be survivals of earlier
    native English forms."

1935

3   FERGUSON, J. DeLANCEY. "The Roots of American Humor."
    American Scholar, 4 (Winter), 49.
        Discusses the English origins of American humor. Twain
    and Harris have a rare genius in that they can think in folk
    language. It would have been more desirable had Americans
    written down prose exactly as it was told to them; the "im-
    proved versions" are deplorable.

4   HARRIS, JULIA COLLIER. "Introduction" to Harris's Tales From
    Uncle Remus. Boston and New York: Houghton Mifflin,
    pp. xi-[xvi].
        Introduction to selected tales from Nights provides in-
    formal biographical sketch, which stresses Harris's years
    at Turnwold Plantation. Boys and girls of today will hope-
    fully continue to enjoy the tales that children of Harris's
    time so greatly loved.

5   HERZBERG, MAX J. Classical Myths. Boston, New York, Chicago,
    Atlanta, San Francisco and Dallas: Allyn & Bacon, p. 11.
        Harris is an example of a modern writer interested in
    myths; he puts myths in Remus's mouth.

6   HICKS, GRANVILLE. The Great Tradition: An Interpretation of
    American Literature Since the Civil War. Revised edition.
    New York: Macmillan, p. 57.
        Harris and other local color writers were important as
    interpreters of the life in their respective sections. Re-
    vised edition of 1933.B5; reprinted: 1967.B10.

7   HUBER, MIRIAM BLANTON. "Preface," in her The Uncle Remus Book.
    New York: D. Appleton-Century, pp. v-vi.
        Uncle Remus, as a well-defined myth, deserves a place
    next to Robin Hood, Paul Bunyan, and Robinson Crusoe in the
    consciousness of boys and girls. This volume retells
    twenty-seven of the Remus stories in simplified dialect,
    choosing tales that illustrate both life on the old planta-
    tion and the lore of the animals. Includes a brief biog-
    raphy and a glossary of Remus's terms.

8   HURSTON, ZORA NEALE. Mules and Men. Philadelphia: J. B.
    Lippincott, p. 17.
        "From the earliest rocking of my cradle, I had known
    about the capers Brer Rabbit is apt to cut and what the
    Squinch Owl says from the house top. But it was fitting me
    like a tight chemise. I couldn't see for wearing it."
    Reprinted: 1969.B6.

1936

9   JOHNSON, GERALD W. "The Horrible South." VQR, 11 (April),
    203.
    "Dixie is full of spirited old women of both sexes who
    decline to recognize any merit in men and women who have
    scandalized them." Furthermore, if writers like Glasgow,
    Cabell, Page, and Harris had been restricted in their sales
    to the South, they would never have survived.

10 KENDRICK, BENJAMIN BURKS and ALEX MATHEWS ARNETT. The South
    Looks at Its Past. Chapel Hill, NC: University of North
    Carolina Press, p. 56.
    Uncle Remus was mythical only as a composite of his type
    and as being more gifted with folklore.

11 KNOX, ROSE B. "The South in Books for Children. A Survey:
    1852-1933." Wilson Bulletin, 9 (January), 247-48.
    Recommended under the heading "The In-Betweens--1880-
    1918" are Uncle Remus, Nights, Friends, Told, Returns, Mr.
    Thimblefinger, Mr. Rabbit at Home, and Stories of Georgia.
    Brief descriptive tags accompany entries. Headnote mentions
    the truth, delight, and profundity of Harris's tales.

12 VANCE, RUPERT B. Human Geography of the South: A Study in
    Regional Resources and Human Adequacy. Second edition.
    Chapel Hill, NC: University of North Carolina Press,
    p. 509.
    Harris, Murfree, Page, and Washington heralded the be-
    ginning of a genuine regional renaissance, a folk movement.

1936 A BOOKS - NONE

1936 B SHORTER WRITINGS

1   BOYNTON, PERCY H. Literature and American Life: For Students
    of American Literature. Boston, New York, Chicago, London,
    Atlanta, Dallas, Columbus, San Francisco: Ginn and Co.,
    pp. 578, 585-90, et passim.
    Of the new literature and criticism in the 1870's only a
    few works rose above the sectional and approached Harris's
    standard for a "millennial literature." Harris stands out
    after the Civil War for his balance, wisdom, and journalis-
    tic and storytelling achievements. Sister Jane, Tolliver,
    and Statesman are negligible, but the Remus stories, criti-
    cism, and editorials are praiseworthy. Harris's short fic-
    tion lacks consistency and singleness of conception; it is
    a confusing oscillation between "literary-sentimental local-
    colorism" and simple tale-telling. His common women who

1936

rose to high refinement--Sis Poteet, Pud Hon, Zepherine
Dion--are unconvincing. Transcription, not creation or interpretation, was Harris's gift. He was a political sec-
tionalist on the Negro question.

2   EASTMAN, MAX. Enjoyment of Laughter. New York: Simon and
Schuster, p. 133.
Harris claimed to be phonetically accurate in his dialect, but either Harris or Remus must have had some "conscious fun of word-distortion" when Brer Rabbit said, "'How
duz yo' sym'tums seem ter segashuate?'"

3   FAGIN, N.[ATHON] BRYLLION, ed. America Through the Short
Story. Boston: Little, Brown, pp. 12-13, 58, 210.
Includes Harris in a list of local colorists who "enlarged the substance of the American short story." These
writers generally overemphasized background and quaint dialect; only a few saw the total significance of their material against the larger background of human life. The
Remus stories contain the valuable qualities of tradition,
wisdom, and quaintness, yet are also a record of toil and
suffering. "Why the Confederacy Failed" [Home Folks] tells
of heroic self-sacrifice.

4   FIRKINS, INA TEN EYCK. Index to Short Stories. Second
Supplement. New York: H. W. Wilson Co., p. 111.
Cites anthology appearances of five Harris folk stories.
Supplement to 1923.B1 and 1929.B5.

5   FULLERTON, B. M. Selective Bibliography of American
Literature, 1775-1900. Introduction by Carl Van Doren.
New York: Dial Press, pp. 127-28.
"Few writers have succeeded more notably than Harris in
giving a unique touch to American literature." The Remus
stories are important contributions to American folklore
and are literary masterpieces; Harris's sketch of the
Georgia cracker, in Mingo, shows "almost equal understanding." Lists Uncle Remus, Mingo, and Friends as representative works.

6   HERNDON, MARY LUCY. "Joel Chandler Harris and His Magazine."
Atlanta Constitution (6 December), A, p. 19.
History of Uncle Remus's Magazine with commentary on
Harris's editorial policies and his mouthpiece, Billy
Sanders.

7   LEISY, ERNEST E. "The Novel in America: Notes for a Survey."
Southwest Review, 22 (October), 93.

1937

Cable, Jewett, Wilkins, Harris, and Page gave the dialect story its heyday in the 1880's.

8   PARKS, EDD WINFIELD, ed. Southern Poets: Representative
    Selections, with Introduction, Bibliography, and Notes.
    American Writers Series, with Harry Hayden Clark, General
    Editor. New York, et al.: American Book Co., pp. xliv,
    lxxvii, cxix, et passim.
        In later years Harris doubted the New South doctrine of
    progress and reconciliation; it "put business above poli-
    tics." He wrote about the intangible values of neighbor-
    liness and kindness, values inserted indirectly into the
    Remus stories. Compares Harris's "artless artistry" with
    Irwin Russell's. [No poems by Harris are anthologized.]

9   QUINN, ARTHUR HOBSON. "Joel Chandler Harris and the Fiction
    of Folklore," in his American Fiction: An Historical and
    Critical Survey. New York: Appleton-Century-Crofts,
    pp. 374-84, 759.
        Biographical sketch accompanies comments on Harris's
    artistic use of Uncle Remus as folktale narrator, his skill
    in his local color stories of low life and North-South con-
    trasts, and his work as a novelist. Harris, a master of
    dialect, had a democratic vision and was no apologist for
    slavery. A four-item secondary bibliography is appended.

10 TAYLOR, WALTER FULLER. A History of American Letters. With
    bibliographies by Harry Hartwick. Boston, Atlanta, Dallas,
    San Francisco, New York, Cincinnati, Chicago: American
    Book Co., pp. 633-34.
        Checklists books and articles on Harris and four of his
    books.

11 WOODSON, CARTER C. The African Background Outlined or
    Handbook for the Study of the Negro. Washington, D.C.:
    The Association for the Study of Negro Life and History,
    p. 400.
        With his "Brer Rabbit" stories Harris immortalized him-
    self by doing well what the Negro did not consider worth-
    while.

1937 A BOOKS - NONE

1937 B SHORTER WRITINGS

1   BLAIR, WALTER. Native American Humor. New York: American
    Book Co., pp. 137-38, 140, 143-46, 147, 157, et passim.

1937

A humorist and a local colorist, Harris shows his
knowledge of earlier Old Southwest humor in his essays and
editorials as well as in his literary characters. "Uncle
Remus reveals his character thoroughly in exactly the manner of the earlier humorous figures--by extensive monologues
and by tall tales within a framework, tall tales the very
fantasy of which is an excellent device for character depiction." Bill Arp [Charles Henry Smith] was possibly the
model for a cracker dialect sketch by "Obediah Skinflint"
that Harris published at Turnwold; Harris met Arp in 1878
and obviously reincarnated him in the Billy Sanders persona
later. The Remus stories deserve praise because they col-
lectively create Uncle Remus the man and so sensitively
record the philosophy, poetry, and anthropomorphic folklore
of the Negro. Also, Harris's use of sentimentality "made
for a fuller and more human portraiture."

2   BRAWLEY, BENJAMIN. The Negro Genius. New York: Dodd, Mead,
    pp. 3, et passim.
        Harris's Uncle Remus stories constitute the chief liter-
    ary monument to Negro customs, superstitions, and tales.

3   BROWN, STERLING. The Negro in American Fiction. Washington,
    D.C.: Associates in Negro Folk Education, pp. 53-58, 79.
        Harris was a true artist and thus more than just a re-
    teller of Negro tales: "he altered, adapted, polished and
    sharpened until the products differ from folk tales." Har-
    ris sacrificed authenticity in having Uncle Remus tell his
    stories to a white boy, instead of having them be "by the
    folk and for the folk," but he gained Uncle Remus--"one of
    the best characters in American literature." Brer Rabbit
    was perhaps a symbol for people "who needed craft in order
    to survive," but Aunt Fountain, Mingo, Balaam, Ananias, and
    even Uncle Remus represent orthodox Southern attitudes about
    the Negro's social position. "Where's Duncan?" and "Free
    Joe," however, show Harris's awareness of the uglier side
    of slavery. Harris was more acute in his portraits than
    Page, but falls short of Cable's and Twain's sensitivity.
    Despite his value as a realist, "Harris never came fully to
    grips with the reality of the South or of Negro experience."

4   BROWN, W. NORMAN. "The Stickfast Motif in the Tar-Baby Story,"
    in Twenty-fifth Anniversary Studies. Vol. 1. Publications
    of the Philadelphia Anthropological Society. Philadelphia:
    University of Pennsylvania Press, pp. 1-12.
        In order to identify the home of the tar-baby story, a
    distinction must be made between the tar-baby as a motif
    and the Stickfast motif. Jacobs [see 1888.B16], Parsons

[see 1919.B8], Espinosa [see 1930.B7], and Cline [see 1930.B4] failed to make this distinction and argued that the story as a whole originated in India and spread westward; later, after reading Brown's earlier essay [see 1922.B2], Parsons admitted the India theory was tenuous. Brown particularly takes Espinosa to task for misleading statistics and contradictions in his work. Brown points out that not every story with a Stickfast motif is a tar-baby story, but every tar-baby.tale contains the Stickfast motif. The Indian stories contain the more general Stickfast motif, but not the essential tar-baby pattern, which is apparently a creation from Africa or some other place. Indeed, the Stickfast motif itself could have arisen independently among two or more peoples.

5   BUCK, PAUL H. The Road to Reunion: 1865–1900. Boston: Little, Brown, pp. 173, 203–205, 211–12, 214–15, 217, 226–27, et passim.
        Harris revered the Old South and urged the New to emulate its virtues. He was the "greatest white interpreter of Negro character," and he, along with Cable, Page, and Murfree, brought sympathetic realism, perfect dialect, and technical excellence to the short story. Uncle Remus gave "unique insight into the Negro soul" and antebellum life; Harris's other black characters are types. Only Free Joe showed the sordid aspect of slavery, yet even he reveals white attitudes towards the free slave. Harris's answer to the free slave problem was to keep the friendship and respect of plantation days. Discusses themes in several other local color tales and in Tolliver and mentions the role of Scribner's and other journals in promoting reconciliation literature. Harris had a critical ability most Southerners lacked.

6   CHESNUTT, CHARLES WADDELL. "Post-Bellum--Pre-Harlem," in Breaking into Print. Edited by Elmer Adler. New York: Simon and Schuster, p. 50.
        Reprint of 1931.B4.

7   GAVIGAN, WALTER V. "Two Gentlemen of Georgia." CathW, 145 (August), 584–87, 589.
        Briefly reviews the lives and works of two converts to Catholicism, Harris and Richard Malcolm Johnston. Draws on Julia Collier Harris's books [1918.A1; 1931.A1] for biographical and literary materials that disclose Harris's interest in Catholicism and his conversion.

1937

8   JOHNSON, JAMES WELDON. The Autobiography of an Ex-Colored Man.
     New York and London: Alfred A. Knopf, p. 87.
     Reprint of 1912.B4.

9   LEACOCK, STEPHEN [BUTLER]. The Greatest Pages of American
     Humor. London: Methuen & Co. Ltd., pp. 159, 162.
     Harris's talking animals are as old as Aristophanes and
     his stories have folkloric origins, but he strung a Ulysses
     bow in telling them. Until Harris, the Negro had appeared
     in literature only as Sambo, the "'faithful black,'" or the
     martyred Uncle Tom; Harris revealed him as Uncle Remus.
     Prints "Uncle Remus Initiates the Little Boy."

10   LOGGINS, VERNON. I Hear America...Literature in the United
     States since 1900. New York: Thomas Y. Crowell, p. 217.
     Of all the whites who have tried to write about the
     Negro--and not excepting Joel Chandler Harris--Julia Peter-
     kin [Green Thursday, Black April, Scarlet Sister Mary] is
     the "truest and the finest."

11   SMITH, REBECCA WASHINGTON. The Civil War and Its Aftermath in
     American Fiction, 1861–1899. Chicago: University of
     Chicago Libraries, pp. 37–39.
     Reprint of 1932.B17, less chronological tables.

12   WARFEL, HARRY R.; RALPH H. GABRIEL; and STANLEY T. WILLIAMS,
     eds. The American Mind: Selections from the Literature of
     the United States. New York, et al.: American Book Co.,
     pp. 911–12.
     Harris's other books lack the distinction of his Remus
     tales; Remus is one of America's few immortal folk charac-
     ters. Discusses the Cherokee Indians' influence on the
     Negro legends, especially the rabbit stories. Cites five
     books on Harris and provides a biographical sketch. An-
     thologizes "The Tar-Baby" and "How Rabbit Was Too Sharp for
     Fox."

13   YOUNG, STARK, ed. Southern Treasury of Life and Literature.
     New York, Chicago, Boston, San Francisco, Dallas and
     Atlanta: Charles Scribner's Sons, p. 358.
     Brief biographical sketch. Anthologizes "Mr. Terrapin
     Shows His Strength" and "Old Mr. Rabbit He's a Good
     Fisherman."

1938

1938 A BOOKS - NONE

1938 B SHORTER WRITINGS

1 DEPEW, OLLIE. Children's Literature by Grades and Types.
   Boston: Ginn and Co., p. 441.
   Remus's childlike imagination, kindly humor, and native
   cheerfulness made him "typical of the idealized Negro of
   the romanticized South." Though the dialect is difficult
   for children, to adapt it ruins the charm of the tales.
   Anthologizes for sixth grade students "The Tar-Baby" and
   "How Mr. Rabbit Was Too Sharp for Mr. Fox."

2 [ENGLISH, THOMAS H.]. "Queries [about Uncle Remus]." South
   Atlantic Bulletin, 4 (April), 10.
   Uncle Remus was published in November 1880, but all
   copies of the book found thus far have 1881 on the title-
   page. Julia Collier Harris has a detached title-page bear-
   ing the date 1880. English asks whether anyone has found
   an intact copy of the book imprinted with the date 1880.

3 ESPINOSA, AURELIO M. "More Notes on the Origin and History of
   the Tar-Baby Story." Folk-Lore, 49 (June), 168-81.
   Challenges Brown's theory [see 1937.B4] that the stickfast and tar-baby motifs must be distinguished in any search
   for the origins of the tar-baby story. The multiple-point
   attack on a sticky object or person is the central motif in
   the tar-baby tale, not the fact that a tar-baby per se was
   fashioned to catch someone. "Stick-fast tales" may be a
   more accurate term than "tar-baby tales." Cites four old
   and medieval Indian tales that contain all the motifs necessary for identifying India as the home of the tale: the
   five-point attack, the dramatic dialogue between the attack-
   er and the object, and the sticky object itself.

4 HUBBELL, JAY B. "Two Letters of Uncle Remus." SWR, 23
   (January), 216-23.
   Two letters to William Malone Baskervill, then professor
   of English at Vanderbilt, have recently been obtained by
   the Duke University Library. Dated in March and April 1895,
   these letters were sent to Baskervill while he was preparing
   his Harris essay for his Southern Writers: Biographical and
   Critical Studies [see 1896.A1 and 1897.B35]. In response
   to a series of questions from Baskervill, Harris says that
   his books were written for pleasure, that he was "'not in
   any sense a literary man,'" and that truth is more important
   than sectionalism. Harris also explained that Uncle Remus
   was a "'composite'" character.

1938

5   JOHNSON, AMANDA. Georgia as Colony and State. Atlanta:
    Walter W. Brown Publishing Co., pp. 971-72.
    Provides brief biographical sketch. Praises the unique
    handling and subtle humor in Uncle Remus but cites criti-
    cism by Thomas Watson that Remus, an "ethereal slave,"
    never lived. Harris's dialect poems, such as "Revival
    Hymn" and "Uncle Remus Addresses Brother Wind," are excel-
    lent. His publication with Mrs. M. S. Young of Songs and
    Ballads of the Old Plantations was an attempt to preserve
    the original simplicity and droll philosophy of the old-time
    Negro lore. Reprint: 1967.B12.

6   KUNITZ, STANLEY J. and HOWARD HAYCRAFT, eds. "Harris," in
    American Authors: 1600-1900. New York: H. W. Wilson Co.,
    pp. 339-40.
    Biographical sketch emphasizes Harris's years at Turnwold
    and journalistic career. Harris was "almost pathologically
    shy" all his life, but he worked to overcome sectionalism
    and produced "an unmatched humor." Lists principal works
    and eight biographical or critical commentaries.

7   MOTT, FRANK LUTHER. A History of American Magazines: 1850-
    1865. Cambridge, MA: Harvard University Press, Belknap
    Press, p. 111.
    ° Harris served as printer's apprentice to the remarkable
    Joseph Addison Turner, whose Countryman reached 2000 sub-
    scribers. At Turnwold Harris gathered material he was to
    use later in the Uncle Remus tales.

8   _____. A History of American Magazines: 1865-1885.
    Cambridge, MA: Harvard University Press, Belknap Press,
    pp. 228, 347, 465, 548-49, 558.
    Harris, G. E. Craddock, and Thomas Nelson Page were the
    outstanding magazine writers of Southern short stories.
    Lists Harris as among contributors to The Nation, Scribner's
    and Century, where R. W. Gilder gave editorial assistance,
    Critic, where Harris first published, outside Atlanta, ma-
    terial from the "Nights with Uncle Remus" series, and The
    Continent.

9   PARKS, EDD WINFIELD. Segments of Southern Thought. Athens,
    GA: University of Georgia Press, pp. 40-41, 69, 110, 125,
    278.
    Harris, in his later years, doubted the value of progress,
    where business was put above politics, and "turned to writ-
    ing directly of neighbor-knowledge, and of personal kindness,
    and of all the intangible values which he had indirectly put
    into his stories of Uncle Remus." Irwin Russell's "artless

1939

artistry" in "Christmas-Night in the Quarters" is equalled
only by Harris's Remus. Harris recognized Russell as the
first Southern writer to "appreciate the literary possibilities of the negro character," and, had he lived, he might
have proven equal to Harris. After the Civil War Harris
and Thomas Nelson Page expressed loyalty to the Old South,
while Grady and Walter H. Page heralded the New South.
W. H. Page did admire Harris but looked instead to a literature of the present.

10   WADE, JOHN DONALD. "Profits and Losses in the Life of Joel
     Chandler Harris," in America Through the Essay. Edited by
     A. Theodore Johnson and Allen Tate. New York: Oxford
     University Press, pp. 407-20.
     Reprint of 1933.B10.

1939 A BOOKS - NONE

1939 B SHORTER WRITINGS

1   BEUST, NORA E., ed. 500 Books for Children. United States
    Department of the Interior, Office of Education, Bulletin
    1939, No. 11. Washington, D.C.: United States Government
    Printing Office, p. 26.
    Uncle Remus is recommended for grades three through
    eight.

2   BROWN, STERLING A. "The American Race Problem as Reflected
    in American Literature." Journal of Negro Education, 8
    (July), 283.
    Traces what American authors said of the Negro "problem"
    from antebellum to modern times. Though Remus was scornful
    of "nigger 'book-larnin,'" Harris had greater decency than
    Page. Uncle Remus was still a mouthpiece speaking the white
    Georgian social policy.

3   FLANDERS, B. H. "Two Forgotten Youthful Works of Joel Chandler
    Harris." SAQ, 38 (July), 278-83.
    Harris published "Charlie Howard; or, Who Is the Good
    Boy?" a moral tale about the good deeds of a young boy, in
    the Child's Index, a Macon, Georgia, religious periodical.
    Harris's review of poems by the young Southern writer Henry
    Lynden Flash was published in The Countryman on 14 June
    1864.

4   GARLAND, HAMLIN. "Let the Sunshine In." Rotarian, 55
    (October), 8-11.

1939

When he was teaching in Boston in 1888, Garland recalls giving lectures on local color writers; Joaquin Miller, Harte, Eggleston, Joseph Kirkland, Riley, Mary E. Wilkins, and Harris reflected regional life sincerely in their works. These authors wrote with vigor and honesty, to create a colorful and vital literature.

5   HERRON, IMA HOMAKER. The Small Town in American Literature. Durham, NC: Duke University Press, pp. 290, 292, 322, 329. The rapid growth of newspapers and periodicals after the 1830's encouraged the local humorist; Harris is an example. Harris, continuing in the Longstreet–Johnston school, "understandingly analyzed" prewar small town life in five Free Joe stories. Tolliver combines romance and realism in depicting an old Georgia town noted for its long-established, hospitable families.

6   LOCKE, ALAIN. "The Negro's Contribution to American Culture." Journal of Negro Education, 8 (July), 521, 524. Should work by white authors be included as Negro literature? James Weldon Johnson praises Remus as a Negro "contribution," with titular white authorship. What counts is the color of the art, not the color line of the author.

7   [MALONE, TED]. "Joel Chandler Harris: 'Wren's Nest,' 1050 Gordon Street Southwest, Atlanta, Georgia," in his NBC. A Listener's Aid to Pilgrimage of Poetry: Ted Malone's Album of Poetic Shrines. New York: Columbia University Press, unpaginated. A one-page description of Harris's home, accompanied by a photograph of the house.

8   McILWAINE, SHIELDS. The Southern Poor-White from Lubberland to Tobacco Road. Norman, OKL.: University of Oklahoma Press, pp. 110–24, 161, et passim. Proud to call himself a "'cracker,'" Harris came from humble origins and was the first in the 1880's to write sympathetically and realistically of the Southern poor whites. His love for the plain people remained an "abiding passion" in his life, although Harris often bogged down in sentimental portraiture. He was probably the best literary conciliator after the War, but propagandizing harmed his stories. His memorable portraits include Mrs. Bivins in "Mingo," the Staleys in "Free Joe," and Emma Jane and Bud Stucky in "Azalia." Mrs. Bivins is the "nearest approach before the twentieth century to the tragic poor-white." The "finest fictional representation of the aristocratic pre-war attitude toward the trash" is found in "Mom Bi."

9   MOTT, G. WILLIAM. "Irwin Russell, First Dialect Author."
      SLM, 1 (December), 809–14.
         Russell, author of "Christmas Night in the Quarters,"
      was "one of the very first to appreciate the true literary
      possibilities of Negro character and approach his subject
      with artistic fidelity." Page and Harris acknowledged
      their debt to Russell, and Harris wrote a highly compli-
      mentary introduction for Russell's collected poems (1888).

10   PATTEE, FRED LEWIS, ed. "Introduction," in his American Short
      Stories. New York: Dodd, Mead, pp. 18, 30, 31.
         Cites Balaam in a list of the significant short story
      collections of 1891. The Uncle Remus stories are "inimi-
      table"; Mingo deals with the Craddock region "with a surer
      hand" than In the Tennessee Mountains. By no means a
      "cracker," Harris spoke with the knowledge of a native, not
      as an outsider like Murfree. [Does not anthologize any of
      Harris's stories.]

11   REDDING, J. SAUNDERS. To Make a Poet Black. Chapel Hill,
      NC: University of North Carolina Press, pp. 52, 69.
         Two serious artists in the use of dialect preceded Paul
      Laurence Dunbar: James Edwin Campbell and Harris. Harris's
      dialect is "skillful and effective misrepresentation, a
      made language in every sense of the word, conveying the
      general type impression of untaught imagination, ignorance,
      and low cunning with which he believed the Negro endowed."
      Also, Harris may have seen the other side of the popular
      Negro buffoon figure, the face of "improvident generosity
      and loyalty," but to Harris the Negro was still a Negro:
      lazy, ignorant, and dependent.

12   REED, T. W. "An Early Member of The Constitution Staff
      Remembers." Atlanta Constitution Sunday Magazine and
      Feature Section (26 March), p. 2.
         Harris used to tell the Constitution staff a particular
      Uncle Remus story [title not specified].

13   REELY, MARY KATHERINE. "American Authors as Printers: Joel
      Chandler Harris." Demcourier, 9 (January–February), 3–7.
         Essay in a library products journal recalls Harris's ex-
      periences as a printer's devil for Joseph Addison Turner.
      Harris believed that Turner's The Countryman was the only
      real county newspaper in the history of American journalism,
      as it was not edited near a post-office or in a small vil-
      lage. Turner's library of 4000 [sic] volumes gave Harris
      a considerable start toward a liberal education.

1940

1940 A BOOKS - NONE

1940 B SHORTER WRITINGS

1 ANDERSON, CHARLES ROBERTS. "Charles Gayarré and Paul Hayne:
   The Last Literary Cavaliers," in American Studies in Honor
   of William Kenneth Boyd: by Members of the Americana Club
   of Duke University. Edited by David Kelly Jackson.
   Durham, NC: Duke University Press, pp. 221–22.
   Harris wrote sentimentally of an old regime that never
   existed outside his pages, all under the cover of the realistic local color technique.

2 CASH, W. J. "Literature and the South." Saturday Review of
   Literature, 23 (28 December), 3.
   While trying to render the Old South as an idyl, Harris
   succeeds with Uncle Remus in "catching almost without exaggeration and without false feeling a fact and a mood which
   actually existed."

3 CRUM, MASON. Gullah: Negro Life in the Carolina Sea Islands.
   Durham, NC: Duke University Press, pp. 55–56, 108–109.
   The Remus stories reflect the Negroes' intimate knowledge
   of nature and animals and "reveal how profoundly the Negro's
   personality has been influenced by the 'critters' of the
   woods." Harris's Gullah stories are popular largely because
   he uses a modified dialect; pure Gullah is often unintel-
   ligible to the general reader. The Remus stories over-
   shadowed all other Negro dialect stories, even though
   excellent ones had appeared previously.

4 ENGLISH, THOMAS H. "In Memory of Uncle Remus." SLM, 2
   (February), 77–83.
   Harris's career spanned two periods of shock to the
   South and the American nation: the Civil War and its dis-
   rupting aftermath, the industrial reorganization of the
   South, where the supporters of the New South joined forces
   with the North seemingly to "obliterate the last vestiges
   of the Old South." Harris welcomed in the new era, but his
   philosophy "was one of rural simplicity" and his virtues
   those of "honesty, industry, neighborliness." Reconstructs
   Harris's apprenticeship and journalistic and literary career. Although Harris always insisted upon himself as an
   "accidental author" and a "cornfield journalist," his manuscripts and letters reveal his self-discipline and careful-
   ness as a man of letters. His newspaper editorials, his
   collections of Georgia sketches and tales, and his children's
   stories are also important parts of his canon. Harris was a

1940

proponent of progress and of a "living culture," a blend
of past, present, and future. His "chief claim to fame
must be that he interpreted the Negro to a generation to
whom the Negro had almost ceased to be a person and had
become chiefly a problem."

5 HARRIS, JULIA COLLIER. "Uncle Remus at Home and Abroad."
   SLM, 2 (February), 84-86.
   Harris was one of the leading spirits in fighting for
   an international copyright law. Prior to the passage of
   the law, some pirated English and French editions of Uncle
   Remus appeared. A small Indian collection of the tales was
   also printed, although the translator offered to share
   royalties in this instance.

6 [HARRIS, LUCIEN and JULIA COLLIER HARRIS]. "Significant Dates
   in the Life of Joel Chandler Harris." SLM, 2 (February),
   76.
   Harris was born near Eatonton, Georgia, on 9 December
   1848, married to Esther LaRose on 21 April 1873, and died
   on 3 July 1908. He was buried in Atlanta's Westview Ceme-
   tery. The Harrises had nine children and twelve grandchildren, whose names are also given here.

7 HUBBELL, JAY B. "Literary Nationalism in the Old South," in
   American Studies in Honor of William Kenneth Boyd: By
   Members of the Americana Club of Duke University. Edited
   by David Kelly Jackson. Durham, NC: Duke University Press,
   p. 219.
   Simm's theory of sectionalism resembles Harris's on
   localism: both were interested in the creation of a national American literature.

8 JESSUP, ALEXANDER, ed. "Introduction," in his The Best
   American Humorous Short Stories. New York: Random House,
   The Modern Library, pp. v-vi.
   Excludes Harris because of copyright and his own opinion
   that Harris is primarily a humorist of the first rank and
   only secondarily a short story writer. His is a fundamen-
   talist humor in the large sense like Rabelais, Cervantes,
   and Twain.

9 JOHNSON, JEAN BASSETT. "Three Mexican Tar Baby Stories."
   JAF, 53 (April-September), 215-17.
   The three stories printed here are particularly interesting in the light of all the literature on the tar-baby,
   because they are among the shortest collected and yet they
   have the essential elements identified by Brown [see

1940

1937.B4], Cline [see 1930.B4], and Espinosa [see 1930.B7].
European and African influences are in evidence. Johnson
has also collected Rabbit-Coyote Mexican tales, in addition
to one printed here, that contain the Trickster motif. Perhaps the Trickster element promoted the story's wide diffu-
sion and its acculturation in America.

10   LENROW, ELBERT. Reader's Guide to Prose Fiction. New York
     and London: D. Appleton-Century, pp. 63, 69.
        Three Uncle Remus books are listed, with a brief headnote
     description, under "Beast Fables"; Uncle Remus is included
     under "Folk-Lore & Legend."

11   ORIANS, G. HARRISON. A Short History of American Literature:
     Analyzed by Decades. New York: F. S. Crofts & Co.,
     pp. 219, 255-56, 276.
        Harris wrote two kinds of literature: his Negro folk
     tales, his chief contribution, and his tales of Georgia
     crackers and moonshiners, which reveal his "attachment to
     the Georgia hills and his knowledge of agrarian conditions."
     Uncle Remus and Nights are his best volumes of fables; "At
     Teague Poteet's" is outstanding among his cracker stories.
     His stories of freed, runaway, or former slaves, such as
     "Blue Dave," "Mingo," and "Ananias," are also distinctive.
     In his stories about Georgia, Harris "frequently expressed
     dissatisfaction with planter-owners for their lack of busi-
     ness acumen," yet no propaganda mars his "clear analysis of
     contemporary social problems."

12   SMITH, LILLIAN H., ed. Books for Boys and Girls. Toronto:
     Ryerson Press, p. 38.
        Uncle Remus and Nights contain invaluable stories, al-
     though the dialect is difficult for children to read by
     themselves.

13   SMITH, REBECCA W. "Catalogue of the chief novels and short
     stories by American authors dealing with the Civil War and
     its effects, 1861-1899. Part III." BB, 17 (May-August),
     35.
        Lists one local color story and one volume of tales.
     [See 1940.B14 and 1941.B10 for continuation of bibliography.]

14   _____. "Catalogue of the chief novels and short stories by
     American authors dealing with the Civil War and its effects,
     1861-1899. Part IV." BB, 17 (September-December), 53, 54.
        Lists three local color stories and two volumes of tales.
     [See 1940.B13 and 1941.B10 for first and third installments
     of bibliography.]

1941

15   VAN DOREN, CARL. The American Novel 1789–1939. Revised and
     enlarged edition. New York: Macmillan, p. 205.
     Harris's Remus stories "promise to outlast all that lo-
     cal color hit upon in the South." They are as ancient and
     fresh as folklore and Remus is a "classic figure." [The
     first edition in 1921 simply lists Harris as a local color
     writer.]

1941 A BOOKS

1   HARLOW, ALVIN F. Joel Chandler Harris: Plantation Story-
    teller. Foreword by Thomas H. English. New York: Julian
    Messner, ix, 278pp.
    Biography for young readers illustrates, as English sug-
    gests in his foreword, that "The child is father of the
    man." Harlow dramatizes Harris's life freely through scene
    and dialogue but follows the major facts and events of his
    youthful and adult years.

1941 B SHORTER WRITINGS

1   ANON. The Negro: A Selected List for School Libraries of
    Books by or about the Negro in Africa and America.
    Nashville [TN]: State Department of Education, p. 15.
    Uncle Remus and Nights are recommended for reading in
    the elementary grades.

2   CASH, WILBUR F. The Mind of the South. New York: Alfred A.
    Knopf, p. 143.
    At times in Southern literature art breaks through a
    more propagandistic or polemical surface. "Plainly having
    in it the will to render the Old South as an idyl, Uncle
    Remus nevertheless succeeds in being an authentic creation,
    in catching almost without exaggeration and without false
    feeling a fact and a mood which actually existed."

3   EATON, CLEMENT. "The Humor of the Southern Yeoman." SR, 49
    (April–June), 175, 178, 182.
    Not until Harris did the Negro assume a prominent place
    in Southern humor. Unlike the cracker, the black slaves
    were considered property and thus a congruous part of the
    plantation; antebellum writers could not see them with the
    detachment that they did the poor white. The realistic
    Southern antebellum humorists proved to be a germinal fac-
    tor in the rise of the local color school following the

1941

War. Harris, Cable, and Murfree consciously interpreted
the South to the North and aided in the reconciliation of
the two sides.

4   HART, ALBERT BUSHNELL and HERBERT RONALD FERLEGER, eds.
Theodore Roosevelt Cyclopedia. New York: Roosevelt
Memorial Association, p. 222.
Quotes Roosevelt on Harris in his speech at the Piedmont
Club, Atlanta [see 1905.B5], and in a letter to Harris dated
12 October 1903. In the letter Roosevelt notes that he is
fond of Brer Rabbit, but prefers Harris's other stories.
"Free Joe" seems to be America's most genuinely pathetic
tale. Harris's art brings people closer together, is a
force for decency, and blots out sectional antagonism.

5   HASTINGS, WILLIAM T. Syllabus of American Literature.
Second edition. Chicago: University of Chicago Press,
p. 73.
Cites Harris in a listing of Southern local colorists.
He preserved valuable animal folklore and surpassed all
others in the depiction of Negro character. Lists Uncle
Remus, Nights, and Friends.

6   HERSKOVITS, MELVILLE J. The Myth of the Negro Past. New York
and London: Harper & Brothers, p. 75.
Just as prevalent in the slaving belt as the myths are
Harris's "historical" tales, stories for children, and other
types; however, the popularity of the Remus volumes has
caused these American Negro stories to be regarded as the
characteristic form of African folktales. In Africa many
elements of the Remus tales are found in the sacred myths
but are handled subtly, often with a double-entendre:
moralizing for children and obscene for adults. Also found
in Africa are proverbs, riddles, and rich poetic imagery.
Reprinted: 1958.B9; 1970.B12.

7   PARKS, EDD WINFIELD. Charles Egbert Craddock (Mary Noailles
Murfree). Chapel Hill, NC: University of North Carolina
Press, p. 92.
Refers to Harris's unpretentious but immortal Remus tales
and his less important mountaineer stories.

8   SCHLESINGER, ARTHUR MEIER. Political and Social Growth of the
American People 1865–1940. Third edition. New York:
Macmillan, p. 207.
Harris immortalized the whimsical tales of Negro folklore
through his Uncle Remus. [No mention of Harris in 1925 and
1933 editions.]

1941

9   SIMPSON, CLAUDE M. and ALLAN NEVINS, eds. The American Reader.
    Boston: D. C. Heath, p. 856.
        Brer Rabbit and Mr. Fox seem just as real as Remus and
    the boy because of the human traits they "half-grotesquely
    exemplify." Mentions Harris's surprise at finding South
    American and Indian analogues, but, by revealing the uni-
    versality of human nature found in folklore, he transcended
    localism. Harris goes beyond the Negro race to mirror the
    wisdom and guile of human nature. Anthologizes "The Tar-
    Baby" and "How Mr. Rabbit Was Too Sharp for Mr. Fox."

10 SMITH, REBECCA W. "Catalogue of the chief novels and short
    stories by American authors dealing with the Civil War and
    its effects, 1861-1899. Part V." BB, 17 (January-April),
    72, 73, 74, 75.
        Lists two local color stories and two volumes of tales.
    [See 1940.B13 and 1940.B14 for first two installments of
    bibliography.]

11 SPENCER, BENJAMIN T. "The New Realism and a National
    Literature." PMLA, 56 (December), 1123, 1125.
        Such authors as Cable, Harris, and Craddock were recog-
    nized abroad and in the North as "'soaked in Americanism,'"
    yet the South in the 1880's and 1890's did not feel the same
    pride in her authors as the West did in hers.

12 THORP, WILLARD; MERLE CURTI; and CARLOS BAKER. The Literary
    Record. Vol. 2 of American Issues. Chicago, Philadelphia,
    New York: J. B. Lippincott, pp. 665-66.
        Provides a brief biographical sketch. The first two
    Remus volumes are the "fullest and freshest," but the high
    quality is sustained in later volumes as well. Seldom
    marred by "sentimental nostalgia," the tales and Remus are
    strikingly genuine. The Remus volumes are Harris's best;
    he seemed uncomfortable with the novel form, and his fugi-
    tive essays are chiefly interesting for their opinions on
    the Negro question. Some sketches in Mingo and Free Joe
    deserve wider fame. Anthologizes "Death and the Negro Man"
    and "Brother Rabbit's Money Mint." Reprinted: 1954.B13,
    1961.B11.

13 WARFEL, HARRY R. and G. HARRISON ORIANS, eds. American
    Local-Color Stories. New York, et al.: American Book Co.,
    pp. xxii, 409.
        Praises Harris's scientific precision in his Negro and
    mountain dialect. He subtly and accurately characterized
    plantation Negro habits and lore. His seven collections of
    realistic short stories are localized as folklore rarely is

191

1941

and reveal Harris's deep love for the mountains and his
awareness of Georgia social conditions. Anthologizes
"Trouble on Lost Mountain" and "Ananias."

14 WHITE, E.[LWYN] B. and KATHARINE S. WHITE, eds. A Subtreasury
of American Humor. New York: Coward-McCann, p. xxi.
The masses cannot appreciate subtle humor; they want
"something to get a grip on," such as Brer Rabbit. Anthologizes "Miss Fox Falls a Victim to Mr. Rabbit."

1942 A BOOKS - NONE

1942 B SHORTER WRITINGS

1 BLANCK, JACOB. Merle Johnson's American First Editions.
Fourth edition. Revised and enlarged. New York: R. R.
Bowker Co., pp. 212-15.
Lists and occasionally describes thirty of Harris's
books; lists five books edited or translated by Harris and
thirteen books with introductions or contributions by him.
Also cites four biographical studies. Revision of 1932.B13.

2 COLLINS, CARVEL EMERSON. "Nineteenth Century Fiction of the
Southern Appalachians." BB, 17 (September-December), 188,
189, 190.
Lists three of Harris's local color stories with mountain
settings. [See 1943.B3 for continuation of bibliography.]

3 DABNEY, VIRGINIUS. Below the Potomac: A Book About the New
South. New York: D. Appleton-Century, p. 235.
Quotes Harris on education as the solution for the Negro
problem; otherwise there is nothing but "'political chaos
and demoralization.'" Finds this statement still true, although now there are some advances in the education of the
Negro.

4 DeVOTO, BERNARD. Mark Twain at Work. Cambridge, MA: Harvard
University Press, p. 97.
Contrasts Twain's depiction of Jim in Huckleberry Finn
with Uncle Remus who, "though he greatly tells the great
fables of his race, is himself false-face and crêpe hair."

5 EBEL, MSGR. JOHN B. "Wise 'Uncle Remus' is Joel Chandler
Harris." Register (20 August), p. 6.
Harris, whose humorous but sagacious works have been
translated into twenty-seven languages and made the basis
of a current nationally syndicated comic strip, showed

1943

supernatural faith in embracing Catholicism a few weeks be-
fore his death. His favorite reading included the Bible,
Cardinal Newman, Father Faber, Thomas à Kempis, and Bishop
Sheehan; his wife was a cultured Canadian Catholic.

6   ROURKE, CONSTANCE. The Roots of American Culture and Other
     Essays. Edited, with preface, by Van Wyck Brooks.
     New York: Harcourt, Brace, pp. 263, 273.
     The absorption of Negro art and character is not a new
     thing but a culmination of a long stream of expression where
     whites and Negroes have joined. The Remus stories belong
     to "the nearer foreground of time." The vogue of the Remus
     stories occurred with a renewed wave of absorption following
     the Civil War. Other Negro legends of the time reveal a
     more savage and grotesque central figure than Harris's.

7   TALLEY, THOMAS W. "The Origin of Negro Traditions." Phylon,
     3 (Fourth Quarter), 373–74.
     When Harris asked antebellum American Negroes for
     "'stories,'" he got "'stories'" rather than folk traditions,
     except in a very fragmentary way. The Brer Rabbit stories
     of Harris "were looked upon by Negroes with few exceptions
     as fiction pure and simple." The folk stories Talley has
     collected, however, combine fact and fiction. Harris did
     obtain some traditional Negro stories: "A Ghost Story,"
     "The Story of the Deluge," "A Plantation Witch," "Why the
     Negro is Black," and "The Cunning Snake." But he did not
     realize that Negroes placed these tales in a different
     category.

1943 A BOOKS - NONE

1943 B SHORTER WRITINGS

1   BEMENT, DOUGLAS and ROSS M. TAYLOR. The Fabric of Fiction.
     New York, Burlingame: Harcourt, Brace & World, pp. 146,
     615–16.
     Not many writers can do a literal dialect transcription
     successfully: Harris's "Uncle Remus" is one example. Also
     includes Harris's letter to his daughters on the "'other
     fellow.'"

2   BURKE, W. J. and W. D. HOWE. American Authors and Books:
     1640–1940. New York: Gramercy Publishing Co., p. 315.
     Checklists Harris's books.

1943

3   COLLINS, CARVEL EMERSON. "Nineteenth Century Fiction of the
    Southern Appalachians: Part II." BB, 17 (January–April),
    216, 217.
        Lists three more of Harris's local color stories with
    mountain settings. [See 1942.B2 for first part of bibliog-
    raphy.]

4   CURTI, MERLE. The Growth of American Thought. New York and
    London: Harper & Brothers, p. 432.
        The slaves used secrecy and humor to get along. Another
    "compensatory device" was their allegorical use of the weak-
    er animal as the victor. Remus's folklore shows "a fondness
    for getting even with the stronger by a kind of craft or
    trickery which does no real harm, and shows, withal, a cer-
    tain lack of sympathy with the white man's ways." Re-
    printed: 1951.B3.

5   DALY, CHARLES A. "National Unity through American Literature."
    EJ, 32 (October), 439.
        "The Awful Fate of Mr. Wolf" [Uncle Remus] is antholo-
    gized in a text recently adopted by the Detroit, Michigan,
    high schools. That a few Negro authors are now being in-
    cluded in textbooks is a sign of friendly black-white
    attitudes.

6   ENGLISH, THOMAS H. "Emory's Joel Chandler Harris Collection."
    South Atlantic Bulletin, 9 (April), 3–5.
        Begun in 1927, the Harris Collection is outstanding in
    terms of the unique value of individual items and the com-
    pleteness of the whole collection. In addition to hundreds
    of letters, the Collection gathers 5900 sheets of manu-
    script, from Harris's boyhood to his work for his last
    project, Uncle Remus's Magazine. Included among letters to
    Harris is Mark Twain's of 10 August 1881, which contains
    the germ of the sketch "How to Tell a Story" and the folk-
    tale "De Woman wid de Gold'n Arm."

7   _____, ed. "Introduction," to Autobiography of "The Country-
    man." 1866. By Joseph Addison Turner. Emory University
    Sources and Reprints Series I, no. 3. Atlanta, GA: Emory
    University, pp. 6, 7.
        Turner's ideal of a regional literature came to "trium-
    phant fruition" in Joel Chandler Harris's writings; Turner
    gave Harris "informal but careful and effective guidance"
    in developing Harris's literary tastes.

8   ENGLISH, THOMAS H. "The Treasure Room at Emory University."
    SWR, 29 (Autumn), 32–33.

1944

Among other holdings in the Harris Collection at Emory
is Harris's own copy of the first edition of Uncle Remus,
interlined with penciled revisions of the dialect; Harris
would later decide against making any changes in his render-
ing of dialect in subsequent editions.

9   ESPINOSA, AURELIO M. "A New Classification of the Fundamental
     Elements of the Tar-Baby Story on the Basis of Two Hundred
     and Sixty-Seven Versions." JAF, 56 (January-March), 31-37.
     Adds one hundred and fifteen additional versions of the
     tar-baby story to his earlier gathering [see 1930.B7] and
     reclassifies the tale's dominant motifs. He maintains that
     the origin of the tale is ancient India.

10   GLASGOW, ELLEN. A Certain Measure: An Interpretation of
     Prose Fiction. New York: Harcourt, Brace, p. 140.
         The folklore of Uncle Remus is "incomparable": "nothing
     better or truer than Uncle Remus has appeared in the whole
     field of American prose fiction." When the Southern writer
     escapes into the consciousness of a different race or class,
     he loses "his cloying sentiment and his pose of moral su-
     periority. Some literary magic worked as soon as the
     Southern novelist forgot that he had been born, by the
     grace of God, a Southern gentleman."

11   NIXON, RAYMOND B. Henry W. Grady: Spokesman of the New
     South. New York: Alfred A. Knopf, pp. 86-87, 128-29, 155,
     157, et passim.
         Grady had written Harris in the spring of 1871 of his
     admiration for the humorous paragraphing Harris was doing
     for the Savannah Morning News; the two men met in August in
     Rome, Georgia, where Grady was editor of the Commercial.
     Grady recommended that Evan Howell sign Harris on the At-
     lanta Constitution's staff as editorial paragrapher in 1876
     and two years later called "Jake" Harris "the most promis-
     ing" young writer in Georgia. Harris helped Grady edit the
     Atlanta Sunday Gazette in 1878-79, a weekly that featured
     human interest stories, dramatic and literary criticism,
     and editorials. Harris recalled Grady's phenomenal memory
     and fascinating conversational abilities.

1944 A BOOKS - NONE

1944 B SHORTER WRITINGS

1   ADAMS, JAMES DONALD. The Shape of Books to Come. New York:
     Viking Press, pp. 29, 168.

1944

At the turn of the century the South was "gripped in a
wistful nostalgia for the days of its vanished glory"; its
"closest approach to the bone and sinew of American life"
had been in the folk quality of the Uncle Remus tales.

2   BOTKIN, B.[ENJAMIN] A., ed. A Treasury of American Folklore:
     Stories, Ballads, and Traditions of the People. New York:
     Crown Publishers, p. 652.
        Animal tales originated in the primitive's kinship with
     animals and lend themselves to allegory and satire. That
     our best known tales, the Uncle Remus stories, survive at
     the nursery level reveals the "'downward process' of tradi-
     tion...by which children retain what was once the property
     of adults." Many plantation stereotypes linger in Harris's
     "nostalgic" versions of Negro stories. Harris's stories are
     more literature than folklore as compared to the scientific
     dialect stories of Gonzales or C. C. Jones [see 1888.B18].
     Prints four Remus tales.

3   BRAWLEY, BENJAMIN. "The Negro in American Fiction," in
     Anthology of American Negro Literature. Edited by
     Sylvestrie C. Watkins. New York: Modern Library, pp. 109,
     110-11, 116.
        Reprint of 1916.B4.

4   BURGUM, EDWIN BERRY. "The Lonesome Young Man on the Flying
     Trapeze." VQR, 20 (Summer), 396.
        William Saroyan's stories resurrect "a less boisterous,
     a paler, version of the 'good nigger' of Joel Harris and
     the old vaudeville stage in his easy-going, unskilled,
     white-faced workers, from the lower strata of our foreign
     born, Armenian, Greek, Italian." Reprinted: 1947.B4.

5   GLOSTER, HUGH M. "Charles W. Chesnutt: Pioneer in the Fiction
     of Negro Life," in Anthology of American Negro Literature.
     Edited by Sylvestrie C. Watkins. New York: Modern Library,
     pp. 295-96.
        Compares Chesnutt with Harris and quotes Chesnutt on how
     his stories differ from the Remus tales [see 1931.B4].

6   GOHDES, CLARENCE. American Literature in Nineteenth-Century
     England. New York, Morningside Heights: Columbia
     University Press, pp. 25, 28, 36, 58, 59, 76.
        Inexpensive English "libraries" of the 1880's list works
     by some of the newer American authors, including Harris.
     In books for children, The English Catalogue of the 1890's
     lists twenty-two issues or editions of Harris. The Remus
     stories were received enthusiastically, although the dialect

1945

was sometimes deleted and the setting changed. David Douglas produced authorized Harris volumes, and Harris also
"enjoyed a fair vogue" in English magazines. Punch praised
Harris [see 1881.B11], and in 1890 Punch attempted its own
Remus story, "The Hibernian Brer Fox; or Uncle Remus in Ire-
land." British and Americans alike saw the Negro as a
humorous character.

1945 A BOOKS - NONE

1945 B SHORTER WRITINGS

1   ANDERSON, CHARLES R., ed. Sidney Lanier: Poems and Poem
    Outlines. Vol. 1 of Centennial Edition of the Works of
    Sidney Lanier. Edited by Charles R. Anderson, et al.
    Baltimore: Johns Hopkins Press, pp. xlix, 385.
        Lanier's dialect poems "The Power of Prayer" (1875) and
    "Uncle Jim's Baptist Revival-Hymn" (1876) preceded the dia-
    lect writings of Irwin Russell, Harris, and Page.

2   _____ and AUBREY H. STARKE, eds. Sidney Lanier: Letters
    1857-1868. Vol. 7 of Centennial Edition of the Works of
    Sidney Lanier. Edited by Charles R. Anderson, et al.
    Baltimore: Johns Hopkins Press, pp. 360, 376, 381.
        Harris corresponded with Sidney Lanier in June 1868
    about James Wood Davidson's proposed biographical sketch of
    Lanier. Harris told Sidney in another letter that Davidson
    wanted to write up Clifford Lanier's life as well.

3   _____. Sidney Lanier: Letters 1869-1873. Vol. 8 of
    Centennial Edition of the Works of Sidney Lanier. Edited
    by Charles R. Anderson, et al. Baltimore: Johns Hopkins
    Press, p. 220.
        In December 1871 Sidney Lanier sent Harris some poems to
    be included in a proposed second edition of James Wood
    Davidson's Living Writers of the South; the second edition
    never appeared.

4   BLANKENSHIP, RUSSELL. American Literature as an Expression of
    the National Mind. New York: Henry Holt, pp. 443, 640.
        The Uncle Remus tales are immortal as long as there are
    children or adults with "the easy imagination of childhood."
    Harris, like the Grimm brothers, kept the folklore of a
    people from oblivion; he "wrote to give delight to those
    who cared to read, just as true literary artists always
    write." A "simple literature coming straight from the
    heart of a people," the Remus tales contain a "whimsical

1945

humor" and a "direct appeal to the reader's primitive imagination." Though Harris's stories were the climax of early
Negro literature, the "New Negro" gently dismisses Harris
as the "'kindly amanuensis of the illiterate Negro peasant.'"

5 BROWN, STERLING. "Georgia Sketches. I. I Visit the Wren's
   Nest." Phylon, 6 (Third Quarter), 225–26.
   Brown and Griff Davis, a Negro photographer, were denied
   admission to the Wren's Nest, Harris's home in Atlanta.
   The caretaker said the [Harris] Association would have his
   job if he let them in, even though Brown explained that he
   had a scholarly interest in Harris and had written research
   papers on him. The two men were permitted to take pictures
   outside, one of which included a shot of the front of the
   house and of the "capacious rear of the caretaker, scram-
   bling up the steps."

6 [CINCINNATUS]. "The 'Countryman': A Lone Chapter in
   Plantation Publishing [I]." AN&Q, 5 (November), 115,
   118–19.
   Historians and biographers have given so much attention
   to Harris's experiences on Joseph Addison Turner's plantation that the achievements of Turner himself have not been
   recognized. This article and its sequel [see 1945.B7] dis-
   cuss Turner's life and literary enterprises, mentioning
   Harris in passing.

7 _____. "The 'Countryman': A Lone Chapter in Plantation Publishing. II." AN&Q, 5 (December), 132.
   Harris mentioned in passing. [For Part I of article see
   1945.B6.]

8 COAN, OTIS W. and RICHARD G. LILLARD. America in Fiction: An
   Annotated List of Novels That Interpret Aspects of Life in
   the United States. Revised edition. Stanford University,
   CAL: Stanford University Press, pp. 40, 101, 130.
   Nights is listed under the heading "The Old South
   (Plantation and Slavery)" and described as humorous Negro
   folklore picturing a "pleasant relationship between white
   and black." Free Joe is listed under "The Civil War and
   Reconstruction," and Uncle Remus, Nights, and Free Joe are
   included under "The Negro." Revised: 1956.B6, 1966.B4.

9 GREEVER, GARLAND and CECIL ABERNETHY, eds. Sidney Lanier:
   Tiger-Lilies and Southern Prose. Vol. 5 of Centennial
   Edition of the Works of Sidney Lanier. Edited by Charles R.
   Anderson, et al. Baltimore: Johns Hopkins Press, pp. x,
   xxviii.

1946

Harris reviewed August J. Evans's Macaria in 1865 [for
the Countryman], a book that Sidney Lanier also read and
which probably influenced Tiger-Lilies. Harris later reviewed Tiger-Lilies and commended Lanier's originality and
his skill as a flutist. Lanier praised Uncle Remus in his
Scribner's essay, "The New South" [see 1880.B4].

10   LANIER, SIDNEY. "The New South," in Tiger-Lilies and Southern
     Prose. Edited by Garland Greever and Cecil Abernethy.
     Vol. 5 of Centennial Edition of the Works of Sidney Lanier.
     Edited by Charles R. Anderson, et al. Baltimore: Johns
     Hopkins Press, pp. 348-50.
          Reprinting of 1880.B4.

11   LEE, CHARLES, et al., eds. North, East, South, West: A
     Regional Anthology of American Writing. [New York:]
     Howell, Soskin, Publishers, pp. 267, 541.
          Anthologizes "Old Mr. Rabbit, He's a Good Fisherman,"
     from Uncle Remus. Headnote and biographical sketch at the
     back of the volume stress Harris's pioneering work in gath-
     ering native folklore; he was "one of America's greatest
     humorists."

12   MENCKEN, H.[ENRY] L.[OUIS]. The American Language:
     Supplement I. New York: Alfred A. Knopf, p. 667.
          Harris's "'not by a long sight'" in Sister Jane is a
     variation of "'not by a darned sight.'" [See also
     1948.B13.]

1946 A BOOKS

1   ANON. Song of the South: World Premiere. Printed 1946,
     60pp. [No place of publication or publisher given.]
          Souvenir program for the premiere of "Song of the South"
     distributed on 12 November 1946 includes an account of Walt
     Disney's decision to put Uncle Remus and his stories into
     movie form; Disney felt that Harris's work combined humor,
     fantasy, and human understanding in just the right propor-
     tions to give his writings universality. The partially
     animated movie could bring together effectively the dream-
     world of Remus's imagination and the real world of the ante-
     bellum plantation. In a brief essay, Harris's son, Joel
     Chandler Harris, Jr., explains that his family had hoped
     many years earlier that Disney would use the Remus tales in
     episode form, but that a full-length feature was even more
     promising. A granddaughter, Mary Harris Rowsey, shares
     some characteristic anecdotes about Harris's shyness [see
     also 1946.A2].

1946

2   ANON. Walt Disney's Song of the South. [No place of pub.]:
    Walt Disney Productions, [15pp.].
    Disney's movie "The Song of the South" (1946) was based
    on the Uncle Remus tales, rewritten by Dalton Reymond,
    Morton Grant, and Maurice Rapf. This official theater bro-
    chure reproduces cartoon drawings from the movie and gives
    a brief history of the film's production. The Disney staff
    researched the Putnam County, Georgia, area and talked with
    members of the Harris family in planning the movie. James
    Baskett played Remus, and Hattie McDaniel was cast in the
    role of Tempy, the cook. The movie was Disney's first full-
    length production that combined live-action with animation.
    [See also 1946.A1.]

3   BROOKES, STELLA BREWER. "Folklore in the Writings of Joel
    Chandler Harris." Ph.D. dissertation, Cornell University,
    269pp.
    The first two chapters briefly survey Harris's experi-
    ences at Turnwold and the newspaper work that led him to
    write the first Uncle Remus tales and discuss Harris's
    waning interest in folklore after Nights (1883). The re-
    maining eight chapters analyze the narrative pattern of the
    Remus tales and describe the personalities of Remus, the
    little boy, and the other human characters in the stories,
    before investigating the various kinds of Remus materials.
    Brookes catalogs 109 trickster tales involving Brer Rabbit
    or the other creatures, twenty-four myths, fifteen super-
    natural tales, several types of proverbs and folk-say, some
    examples of dialectical usage, and six major kinds of folk
    songs. Brer Rabbit's tricks are listed in an appendix;
    full primary and secondary bibliographies are included.
    [For published version of this dissertation, see 1950.A1.]

1946 B SHORTER WRITINGS

1   ANON. "Harrises Give Emory Priceless Collection." Emory
    Alumnus, 22 (November), 11.
    Emory University had been temporary custodian of original
    manuscripts, correspondence, and first editions of Harris
    since 1927, but the Harris family made the arrangement
    permanent this year. Signing the agreement for the family
    were Harris's sons Joel C., Jr., Evelyn, Lucien, and Julian,
    and his daughters Mildred Harris Camp and Lillian Harris
    Wagener.

2   BORING, BILL. "Famed Joel Chandler Harris Failed to Achieve
    Life's Literary Desire." Atlanta Constitution (10 March),
    B, p. 6.

1946

Harris died without writing the novel he always wanted
to do. He told Miss Frances Lee Leverette, a school teacher
friend from his own Putnam County, that he wanted to write
a novel based on the tragic life of William H. Seward,
Lincoln's Secretary of State. As a young boy Seward had
run away from a regimented life in New England and had
eventually become a school teacher in the Phoenix section
of Putnam County. He had hoped to see the Southern slave
economy reformed but became disillusioned about Southern
aristocratic customs when the Gatewood family refused to
let him marry their daughter Mary. He left the South and
went North forever. Like Seward, Harris hated affected
people.

3   ENGLISH, THOMAS H., ed. "Introduction," to Qua: A Romance of
    the Revolution, by Joel Chandler Harris. Emory University
    Sources and Reprints Vol. 3, no's 2-3. Atlanta: Emory
    University, pp. 5-12.
        In the first half of 1900 William Dean Howells wrote to
    several American and English authors outlining his plans
    for the syndicated publishing of serialized novels in news-
    papers. Harris was solicited, too, and responded on 1 June
    1900 that he had two stories in mind. One was "One Mile to
    Shady Dale," which became Tolliver, and the other "Qua: A
    Romance of the Revolution." "Qua" was probably begun that
    year but only seven chapters were completed, and meanwhile
    Howells had dropped his project. Harris probably got in-
    terested in Qua, an African prince who died at the age of
    96 in 1826, when he was boning up on Georgia history for
    his Stories of Georgia textbook (1896). The manuscript was
    rapidly and smoothly written, with few false starts or
    revisions.

4   ENGLISH, THOMAS H. "Joel Chandler Harris's Earliest Literary
    Project." Emory University Quarterly, 2 (October), 176-85.
        Some Harris letters at Emory from 1864 to 1868 reveal
    young Joe's interest in Henry Lynden Flash (1835-1914), a
    Southern poet from Macon, Georgia, later featured in an
    eight-column biographical-critical essay by Harris for
    Turner's The Countryman. Harris also planned to publish a
    collection of Southern verse, probably to be entitled "Gems
    of Southern Poetry." Harris had fifty-one authors in his
    planned collection, and it may be that James Wood Davidson,
    in The Living Writers of the South (1869), made use of bio-
    graphical and critical material that Harris had been col-
    lecting; Harris had been corresponding with him during this
    period. Harris also served as an intermediary between
    Davidson and Sidney and Clifford Lanier. Harris's "Gems"
    was never published.

1946

5 HERSKOVITS, MELVILLE J. "African [Negro Folklore]," in
   Encyclopedia of Literature. Edited by Joseph T. Shipley.
   Vol. 1. New York: Philosophical Library, pp. 4–5, 8.
   The popularity of Harris's Uncle Remus stories has helped
   to make animal tales among the best known Negro folk
   stories. "These tales are in many cases regarded as the
   type-forms of the Negro animal trickster tale," and reference is so frequently made to them in identifying African
   material that animal-trickster stories "have been sought
   out to the exclusion of other types." Tar-baby, riding-
   horse, and rope-pulling tales are widely distributed, for
   example. Yet non-animal stories are also frequently told
   in Africa.

6 LASH, JOHN S. "The Study of Negro Literary Expression."
   Negro History Bulletin, 9 (June), 207, 210, 211.
   Quotes Thomas Dickinson that white authors, such as
   Harris, exploited Negro literary tradition and served as
   spokesmen for Negroes in literature until they themselves
   took over the responsibility. Negro scholars repudiate
   representation by such dialect writers as Page and Harris
   in textbooks and the classroom. Though skillful in dialect
   writing, these local colorists do not accurately portray
   plantation Negro life.

7 MANRY, JAMES F. "Former 'Devil' Recounts Early Days in
   Forsyth." Atlanta Journal (10 November), p. 17-C.
   Manry, ninety-six at the time of this interview, recalls
   the days when he worked as a printer's devil under Harris,
   on a Forsyth, Georgia newspaper [the Monroe Advertiser].
   Harris was quiet and timid and would stammer and blush
   around strangers. Fond of Dickens, he selected books for
   young Manry to read. Manry remembers talking with Harris
   about the tar-baby story in 1868 and believes that "Free
   Joe" grew out of a story about Free Sam that Manry related
   to him.

8 MEINE, FRANKLIN J., ed. Tall Tales of the Southwest: An
   Anthology of Southern and Southwestern Humor 1830–1860.
   New York: Alfred A. Knopf, p. xvi.
   Harris thought Georgia wit and humor were unique and
   incomparable, like Georgia watermelons.

9 ROGERS, ERNEST. "Uncle Remus ... Movie Star." Atlanta
   Journal Magazine (10 November), pp. 10–11.
   In his movie version of the Uncle Remus stories, "The
   Song of the South," Disney sought to make the wisdom and
   humor of Harris's character intelligible to all. "'Fables,'"

1946

Disney observed in an interview, "'have a stinger as well
as a laugh in them. Their shrewd comment on common human
faults is never entirely dispassionate, even though always
entertaining. Under the disarming humor are the teeth of
the purposeful moral. The very power of the fable, indeed,
is this attack by misdirection. And the relish, too.'"

10   ROWSEY, MARY HARRIS. "Brer Rabbit's Laughin' Place Was
      Shared by His Creator." Atlanta Journal (10 November),
      p. 16-C.
          Harris's granddaughter shares some anecdotes from her
      father, Lucien's, childhood. Joel Chandler loved Christmas
      and used to play Santa Claus. He once told his son, in
      response to an inquiry about how to grow rich, that putting
      on the left shoe and sock first would ensure wealth.
      Lucien has faithfully been doing this for fifty-six years.

11   _____. "Creator of Uncle Remus Loved a Good Joke--Even on
      Himself." Atlanta Journal (20 October), p. 16-A.
          Harris's granddaughter recalls the nicknames that news-
      papermen gave to Harris when he was a paragrapher--"Pink-
      Top," "Torchlight," "Sorrel-Top," "Vermilion Pate," and
      "Molasses-haired Humorist and Burning Bush of Georgia
      Journalism." Eugene Field spoofed Harris, and Harris sub-
      sequently spoofed Field by naming his Atlanta home "Snap-
      Bean Farm," a parody of Field's own "Sabine Farm." Harris
      regularly took over the reins from the driver of the mule-
      drawn streetcar that brought him home, allowing the driver
      to eat his basket lunch. Harris once caused an overly
      garrulous and boring passenger to spill a bag of grits,
      which Harris later replaced, with apologies.

12   _____. "[Untitled essay included in] Uncle Remus Lives
      Again." Think Tank, [no vol.] (October), p. 11.
          Harris's granddaughter recalls her mother's comment that
      Joel Chandler used the now-popular expression "'Be good'"
      forty-five years ago, when taking leave of his small grand-
      children. "It was not so much a caution to behave from a
      moral standpoint as a reminder to curb mischieviousness
      [sic]. For my brothers and sisters inherited from their
      grandfather an irresistable [sic] urge to tease and joke
      whenever the slightest opportunity arose."

13   ST. JOHN, WYLLY FOLK. "How Literary Detectives Found Joel
      Chandler Harris' New Novel." Atlanta Journal Magazine
      (17 March), pp. 8-9.
          The first manuscript pages for Harris's abortive novel
      "Qua: A Romance of the Revolution" were turned up by an

1946

Emory University graduate student in 1928, but positive
identification was made only after all 168 manuscript pages
and a letter to William Dean Howells about the proposed
novel were identified and analyzed. Qua was a real figure,
an African prince who died in Georgia in 1826, and some of
the other characters in the seven chapters that Harris
wrote, in 1900, figure in Georgia history. [See also
1946.B3.]

14   STAFFORD, BESSIE S.   "Harris, Painfully Shy, Dodged T. R.'s
      Reception Line." Atlanta Constitution (12 November),
      p. 12.
          When President Roosevelt visited Atlanta in October
      1905, Harris came in the side door of the Governor's Man-
      sion to avoid the feminine delegation at the front door.
      He held tightly to his umbrella and hat all day during the
      festivities. He disliked publicity so much, remembers his
      daughter Lillian, that he would go out the back door of his
      home when he saw a stranger at the front door. When asked
      what gift of nature he would most like to have, he said,
      "'The gift of gab.'"

15   STAFFORD, JOHN.   "Patterns of Meaning in Nights with Uncle
      Remus." AL, 18 (May), 89–108.
          Drawing upon Kenneth Burke's and William Empson's termin-
      ology, Stafford looks at Harris's complex literary strate-
      gies in Nights, a more unified book than Uncle Remus.
      Using overlapping strategies, Harris speaks to his readers
      from the point of view of the Southern white man, from that
      of the Negro, and from a magical-religious perspective. As
      a Southerner speaking to Southern and Northern whites, Har-
      ris wrote in the pastoral tradition, romanticizing the
      feudal past and flattering the North. Simultaneously, Har-
      ris appreciated the ironic mocking and parodying of white
      social structure and civilization inherent in Brer Rabbit's
      tricks and in the relationships, humorously displayed,
      among Uncle Remus, Sis Tempy, 'Tildy, and Daddy Jack. Brer
      Rabbit also served priestly and godlike functions at times.
      Harris was clowning about the Negro problem in his tales,
      "in order to restore health to the mind and conscience of
      the North and the South."

16   THOMPSON, STITH.   The Folktale. New York: Dryden Press,
      pp. 222, 222 n.14.
          Animal fables and epics arose in northern and western
      Europe in the Middle Ages and eventually spread to Africa
      and the New World on slave ships. Generally, the dupe is
      the bear or the wolf, and the clever animal the fox. But

as the tales spread, the fox gave way to the lowly spider
or to the rabbit, as found in Harris's Uncle Remus cycle.

1947 A BOOKS - NONE

1947 B SHORTER WRITINGS

1   [ADAMS, FREDERICK B., JR., et al., eds.]. One Hundred
    Influential American Books: Printed before 1900.
    New York: Grolier Club, p. 114.
         Uncle Remus is a "photographic reproduction of negro
    folk-lore," and the book's popularity caused the great
    flood of American dialect literature. After the success
    of Uncle Remus, Century was willing to publish Page's
    "Marse Chan," which they had held for four years. A brief
    textual history of Uncle Remus is included.

2   ASWELL, JAMES R., ed. Native American Humor. New York:
    Harper & Brothers, p. 390.
         Harris has the distinction of recognizing the mass of
    neglected oral literature of the South and raising it into
    the realm of art. Despite Remus's warm humanity, these
    stories have fallen into neglect today, perhaps because of
    the heavy dialect or the "absurd" dogma of some of our
    literati: "that only Negroes have any business writing
    about Negroes." Anthologizes "Brer Rabbit and Brer Fox."

3   BROOKS, VAN WYCK. "The South: Lanier and Joel Chandler
    Harris," in his The Times of Melville and Whitman.
    New York: E. P. Dutton and Co., pp. 351-77 passim. Also
    see pp. 53, et passim.
         Harris retold Negro tales that were universally known
    in the South, but, as Teddy Roosevelt observed, Harris's
    "genius" made them immortal. Harris "forgot to be shy"
    with the Negroes and made friends with them. Summarizes
    Harris's life, emphasizing his years at Turnwold, and com-
    ments briefly on several works. Brer Rabbit was the mythi-
    cal "Negro Hercules," and in the Uncle Remus stories the
    black man got even with his master and overseer. Re-
    printed: 1953.B2.

4   BURGUM, EDWIN BERRY. The Novel and the World's Dilemma.
    New York: Oxford University Press, p. 264.
    Reprint of 1944.B4.

5   CHRISTY, ARTHUR E. and HENRY W. WELLS. World Literature:
    An Anthology of Human Experience. New York, et al.:
    American Book Co., p. 1064.

1947

Harris is known chiefly for Nights and his Brer Rabbit
tales. Anthologizes "Brother Rabbit's Money Mint."

6 [ENGLISH, THOMAS H., ed.]. "Warm Springs in 1895: Joel
   Chandler Harris Writes Interestingly of the Warm Springs
   of Meriwether County, Georgia." Emory University Quarterly,
   3 (March), 54.
   On 26 May 1895 Harris printed a puff on Warm Springs and
   its hotel for the Atlanta Constitution; the article, here
   reproduced on pp. 54–57, was later printed up as an advertising leaflet. Warm Springs has earned an international
   reputation because of the Warm Springs Foundation for the
   study and treatment of infantile paralysis; Franklin Roosevelt was its patron.

7 FOERSTER, NORMAN, ed. American Poetry and Prose. Third
   edition. Boston: Houghton Mifflin, pp. 1051–52.
   Reprint of 1934.B5.

8 HARRIS, JULIA COLLIER. "Joel Chandler Harris: The Poetic
   Mind." Emory University Quarterly, 3 (March), 21–29.
   Although he habitually kept this private self hidden,
   Harris's more poetic, fanciful, and mystical side is revealed in his writings. In the Prélude to Tolliver and in
   Gabriel's fanciful, poetic moments in the Bermuda fields,
   in sections of the autobiographical Plantation, and in
   Wildwoods Harris develops natural images that merge with
   supernatural or purely imaginary ones. Finds the technique
   reminiscent of Hawthorne. The Remus stories are poetic,
   too, as is "Free Joe," which is a kind of prose-poem on
   the forlorn Negro.

9 HARRIS, JULIAN LaROSE. "Joel Chandler Harris as His Eldest
   Son Remembers Him." Atlanta Journal Magazine (19 May),
   p. 16.
   Remembrance corrects some mistaken notions about Harris
   and adds intimate details to the portrait of the artist.
   Contrary to what many have said, Harris was never "happier
   or more sure of himself" than when he was working on Tolliver. He did not tell or read the Uncle Remus stories to
   his children—if anything, they told him some of the
   stories—and he told Julian about tales he rejected from
   his books because he did not think they were genuine. Harris always brought magazines and books home for his children to read, from Youth's Companion and St. Nicholas to
   Scott, Cooper, Shakespeare, Dumas, and Dickens.

1947

10   HESS, M. WHITCOMB. "The Man Who Knew Uncle Remus." CathW,
     166 (December), 254–58.
          Praises Harris as a realist in his psychological por-
     trait of the Negro, although he really portrays a universal
     human type; indeed, Remus's international popularity rests
     in his revelations, through Remus and the animals, of human
     traits. "Free Joe," Harris's favorite, reveals his compas-
     sion for those not wise enough to remain with their former
     owners. Perhaps his own poverty sparked his interest in
     the Negro situation; his sympathy and understanding in-
     cluded all, however, regardless of race. Provides a brief
     biographical summary and mentions his belief in God. As a
     critic, Harris liked Newman, disliked Zola and sordid
     realism, and championed Henry James.

11   LASH, JOHN S. "What Is 'Negro Literature?'" CE, 9
     (October), 38.
          Courses in Negro literature taught at Negro colleges
     try to provide "a balance to the widely held opinion that
     Joel Chandler Harris, Irving [sic] Russell, and other 'dia-
     lect writers' are authoritative spokesmen and accurate por-
     trayers of the group tradition."

12   MOTT, FRANK LUTHER. Golden Multitudes: The Story of the
     Best Sellers in the United States. New York: Macmillan,
     pp. 162–63, 310.
          Uncle Remus was a successful "juvenile" of the 1880's
     that has probably sold 500,000 copies in its various edi-
     tions and reprints. Since the dialect is not easily read,
     versions of the Uncle Remus tales have been made periodical-
     ly for children's use. Uncle Remus "is still a good title
     from the publishers' point of view." Reprinted: 1960.B7.

13   ODUM, HOWARD W. The Way of the South: Toward the Regional
     Balance of America. New York: Macmillan, p. 116.
          Harris slipped "quietly into the good will of the
     world" through Uncle Remus. As one of the many founders
     of the New South, Harris also worked quietly to rebuild
     that part of the country.

14   PAINE, GREGORY. "Introduction," to his Southern Prose
     Writers. New York, Cincinnati, etc.: American Book Co.,
     pp. xci–xcii, xcvii, xcviii, cxxxi–cxxxii, et passim.
     See also pp. 389–90.
          Comments on Harris as a local colorist and as part of
     the plantation tradition. He was "the first faithful re-
     corder of Negro speech." Richard Watson Gilder of Century
     Magazine became a friend and gave Harris editorial advice

1947

while publishing several of his stories. Includes secondary bibliography of fifteen items. Anthologizes "Free
Joe."

15 SIMKINS, FRANCIS BUTLER. The South Old and New (A History:
    1820-1947). New York: Alfred A. Knopf, pp. 330, 334-35,
    354.
        Includes Harris in the "local color quintet" of the
    1880's, with Cable, Page, Murfree, and Allen. Harris
    faithfully represented Negro character and dialect, and ex-
    celled all other American writers both in combining accurate
    research on the Negro with artistic style, and in interest-
    ing children as well as adults. However, he never advanced
    beyond his early successes. Provides a brief biographical
    sketch. Revised and reprinted: 1953.B12; 1963.B13.

16 TIDWELL, JAMES NATHAN. "The Low Colloquial Speech of Georgia
    as Represented by Joel Chandler Harris," in his "The
    Literary Representation of the Phonology of the Southern
    Dialect." Ph.D. dissertation, Ohio State University,
    pp. 221-37, et passim.
        Discusses Harris's phonological representation of low
    colloquial white speech, only, in "Trouble on Lost Mountain"
    [Free Joe]; linguistic atlas field records "do not include
    any transcriptions of Negro speech from inland Georgia."
    Provides analysis of Southern, and Southern and Eastern
    features; Harris does not represent Southern and Midwestern
    features. He re-spells frequently to show low colloquial
    speech and uses eye-dialect. Other authors included in the
    dissertation are Page, Chesnutt, Simms, Murfree, Longstreet,
    and Richard Malcolm Johnston.

17 [WINTERICH, JOHN T.]. "The Committee's Selections: Assailed
    by John T. Winterich," in One Hundred Influential American
    Books: Printed before 1900. [Edited by Frederick B.
    Adams, Jr., et al.]. New York: Grolier Club, p. 21.
        [Compare 1947.B1.] Winterich would have included some
    "pure humor," such as Artemus Ward: His Book, in place of
    works on Grolier's list by Irving, James Russell Lowell,
    and Twain, and in place of Uncle Remus.

18 WITHAM, W. TASKER. Panorama of American Literature.
    [New York]: Stephen Daye Press, pp. 137, 172-74.
        The Uncle Remus stories are "authentic Negro folk tales
    told in authentic Negro dialect." Harris's fiction about
    aristocrats and poor whites adds to his importance as a
    local color writer but has never been as popular as the
    Remus stories.

1948

1948 A BOOKS

1 ANON. "J. C. Harris Celebration Underway." Eatonton
   Messenger (9 December), [4pp.].
   Special issue commemorates the centennial of Harris's
   birth and describes the festival planned for Eatonton.

1948 B SHORTER WRITINGS

1 BENET, WILLIAM ROSE, ed. "Harris," in The Reader's
   Encyclopedia: An Encyclopedia of World Literature and the
   Arts. New York: Thomas Y. Crowell, p. 482.
   Brief biographical and critical sketch and checklist of
   works. Harris is best known for his "humorous adaptations
   of native Negro folk-legends," which are marked by "authentic approximations" of Negro dialect.

2 BRIDGERS, EMILY. The South in Fiction. University of North
   Carolina Extension Bulletin, Vol. 13, No. 6. Chapel Hill,
   NC: University of North Carolina Press, pp. 14-15.
   The romantic plantation tradition produced several clas-
   sics, including the Uncle Remus stories. Though sentimen-
   tal, the stories are perfect for their fictional mode.
   Provides a brief biographical sketch and cites Uncle Remus
   in bibliography of plantation writings.

3 CANBY, HENRY SEIDEL and ROBESON BAILEY, eds. The Book of the
   Short Story. New and enlarged edition. New York and
   London: Appleton-Century-Crofts, pp. 401-402.
   Includes Uncle Remus and Nights under "Representative
   Tales and Short Stories." [See 1922.B7 for earlier
   edition.]

4 DAUNER, LOUISE. "Myth and Humor in the Uncle Remus Fables."
   AL, 20 (May), 129-43.
   Harris's fables have unique imaginative and dramatic
   vitality and mythic and comic implications; behind their
   naiveté lies psychological, symbolical, and metaphysical
   profundity. As myth and magic, they suggest both the supra-
   rational and the subrational; as Yeats says of magic, they
   embody "'the visions of truth in the depths of the mind
   when the eyes are closed.'" Harris was a careful and self-
   conscious artist, but he probably was not aware of the pro-
   fundities of his tales. Mythologically, the rabbit represents the Demiurge or the Trickster; "aesthetically, he is
   Irony" and the personified Irrational. Amidst the humor
   and badinage, mischief often becomes malice in the tales,

209

1948

and injury or death can lie in the balance. The question-
ing young boy auditor represents an emerging morality; he
is "Child-Man in the first impulse of naming and ordering
his worlds," and Uncle Remus is the realistic Wise Man of
his tribe. Harris's humor is that of irrationality, irony,
paradoxical contrast, language distortion, and onomatopoeia.

5   [ENGLISH, THOMAS H., ed.]. "Mr. Billy Sanders, Detective."
Emory University Quarterly, 4 (December), 194–216.
        A relatively clean first draft of this unpublished Billy
Sanders story, English explains in a headnote, was found
among the manuscripts in the Harris Collection at Emory.
It was apparently written after "The Kidnapping of President
Lincoln" (composed in early or middle 1900), where Sanders
is first introduced, and it could be that Harris's struggles
with Tolliver (published in 1902) caused him to cast aside
this tale of homely realism.

6   ENGLISH, THOMAS H. "The Twice-Told Tale and Uncle Remus."
GaR, 2 (Winter), 447–60.
        The best tales are the twice-told, traditional tales of
the human race. Harris's Uncle Remus is both a masterful
representative of the old plantation era and a great teller
of twice-told tales. Remus's range of action is one of
the narrowest possessed by any major character in fiction,
yet Harris brings him into full life. Uncle Remus is the
real hero of the tales of Brer Rabbit: "The craft and the
humor of the folk mind went into the making of Brer Rabbit
and the creeturs, but in Uncle Remus are portrayed the wisdom and the poetry of the race who found spiritual liberation before they did political emancipation."

7   GAYLE, MARGOT. "Georgia's Aesop." Holland's, 67 (December),
8–9.
        Biographical sketch recalls Harris's reluctance to ap-
pear in public, even when requested to do so by the President. When Teddy Roosevelt and his wife visited Atlanta in
1905 and asked to meet Harris, Clark Howell, publisher of
the Atlanta Constitution, appointed several friends to es-
cort Harris to the train station and to "'see that he's
there if you have to hog-tie him.'" Harris shook hands but
when the band played "Hail to the Chief" quickly disappeared
into the crowd. Harris was found and taken to the Presi-
dential luncheon, where Roosevelt observed that Georgia
never did more for the Union than "'when she gave Mr. Joel
Chandler Harris to American literature.'"

1948

8   GEORGE, DANIEL. "Uncle Remus and his Creator." <u>Listener</u>, 40
    (16 December), 936-37.
        In this BBC weekly Harris is recalled as being "immedi-
    ately popular" in England. Harris favorably reviewed Kip-
    ling's <u>Second Jungle Book</u> in 1895 and Kipling wrote back
    to thank him, saying, "'This makes me feel some inches
    taller in my boots, for my debt to you is of long standing.
    I wonder if you realize how Uncle Remus and his sayings and
    the sayings of the noble beasties ran like wild fire
    through an English public school when I was fifteen.'"
    Kipling then recalls that a fag who was nicknamed Rabbit
    was appropriately dumped into a furze-bush, the nearest
    English substitute for a briar patch. George believes that
    the Remus stories are more intelligible to the young than
    <u>Alice in Wonderland</u> or <u>Through the Looking-Glass</u>.

9   GLOSTER, HUGH M. <u>Negro Voices in American Fiction</u>. Chapel
    Hill, NC: University of North Carolina Press, pp. 15,
    24-25, 261, et passim.
        Two of Harris's stories number among the few instances
    outside of Louisiana settings where a mulatto appears in
    literature. "Where's Duncan?" [<u>Balaam</u>] is a "grim and
    bloody tale" about a mulatto slave's hatred for his white
    father, whereas "The Case of Mary Ellen" [<u>Aunt Minervy Ann</u>]
    follows the rise to artistic fame of a near-white girl,
    offspring of an aristocrat and a mulatto slave woman.
    Charles Chesnutt admitted the similarity between his Uncle
    Julius, narrator in <u>The Conjure Woman</u>, and Uncle Remus, but
    said that his own tales were original works. Unlike Harris,
    Chesnutt showed "cruelty and oppression as occasional prac-
    tices in slave life." Paul Laurence Dunbar, however, "imi-
    tated the idyllic romancing of Page and Harris" in his
    short stories.

10 HARRIS, ISABELLA D. "The Southern Mountaineer in American
    Fiction 1824-1910." Ph.D. dissertation, Duke University,
    pp. 122-23.
        Harris had only a "summer vacationer's superficial ac-
    quaintance with highlanders." His mountaineers were hardly
    distinguishable from Georgia crackers.

11 LEVERETTE, [FANNIE] L. "Odds and Ends About Joel Chandler
    Harris." Eatonton <u>Messenger</u> (9 December), p. 2.
        Harris once told this writer that George Terrell, a
    Negro who was a famous maker of ginger cakes, was the model
    for Uncle Remus; as a boy Harris would tote wood chips to
    "Uncle George," for his cook fire. Harris's mother ex-
    plained to Miss Leverette that Joe was born in a cottage on
    the Monticello road, where a canning factory now stands.

1948

12   MEINE, FRANKLIN J. "The Sage of Shady Dale: A Glance at
     Georgia's Humorous Hero, Billy Sanders, in the Tales of
     Joel Chandler Harris." Emory University Quarterly, 4
     (December), 217-28.
        Examines Billy Sanders' characteristics across three
     short stories and three novels written between 1900 and
     1907: "The Kidnapping of President Lincoln," "Billy
     Sanders, Detective," "A Child of Christmas," Tolliver,
     Shadow, and Bishop. Billy's cheerfulness and youthful
     spirit, wit, mischievousness, sympathy for humanity, horse
     sense, and uncommon ability as a storyteller contribute to
     his three-dimensional personality; he is a complex figure
     who deserves more attention in America's literary history.

13   MENCKEN, H.[ENRY] L.[OUIS]. The American Language:
     Supplement II. New York: Alfred A. Knopf, pp. 106, 262n,
     265, 270n, 376, 377.
        Representation of Negro speech in literature has always
     been imperfect. No Southern Negro actually uses Harris's
     brer; when he attempts brother he says bruh-uh or bruh,
     perhaps with a faint r on the end. Harris uses Gullah less
     effectively than his upland Georgia Negro dialect. [See
     also 1945.B12.]

14   REMENYI, JOSEPH. "American Writers in Europe." GaR, 2
     (Winter), 462.
        Bryant, Harris, Whittier, Frank Norris, O. Henry, and
     Lafcadio Hearn were only occasionally mentioned in European
     literary lexicons; some of their works were published in
     translation.

15   [SCRUGGS, ANDERSON M.]. "Editorial: The Quietness of Genius."
     Emory University Quarterly, 4 (December), 244-45.
        Harris could not have written what he did had he not
     kept himself aloof from the world; his modesty and shyness,
     and the relative quietness of his life, were signs of the
     "psychic detachment" that he needed to free his mind for
     its literary work.

16   SPARKS, ANDREW. "Joel Chandler Harris' 100th Birthday."
     Atlanta Journal Magazine (5 December), pp. 10-11.
        Eatonton, Georgia, plans a festival to honor Harris's
     birthday, and the U. S. Government will issue a 3-cents
     Harris stamp, with 400,000 first-day covers to be canceled
     through the Eatonton post office. The State Highway De-
     partment has put up 1000 permanent signs to designate
     Route 441 as the Uncle Remus Highway.

17 SPILLER, ROBERT E., et al. <u>Literary History of the United</u>
    <u>States: History</u>. New York: Macmillan, pp. 748, 852–54,
    1468, et passim.
        In <u>Uncle Remus</u> Harris "gave America one of its half-
    dozen finest humorous characters and its best example of
    artistically treated folklore." He instructs through the
    humor of his trickster tales but, unlike Twain, "did not
    despair of the 'damned human race.'" The Remus volumes
    demonstrate "a skillful variation of materials, a love of
    ironic implication, a mastery of the short dramatic form,
    and a sure grasp of humorous idiom and the natural rhythms
    of folk speech." Harris wrote with truthfulness and natur-
    alness of the Middle Georgia society he knew so well in
    creating a whole gallery of vital and authentic characters:
    Uncle Remus, but also Abe Hightower, Mingo, Aunt Fountain,
    Balaam, Free Joe, and Blue Dave. Revised: 1974.B13.

1949 A BOOKS - NONE

1949 B SHORTER WRITINGS

 1 [BOTKIN, BENJAMIN ALBERT]. "Brer Rabbit," in <u>Funk & Wagnalls</u>
    <u>Standard Dictionary of Folklore, Mythology, and Legend</u>.
    Vol. 1. New York: Funk & Wagnalls Co., p. 163.
        The hare has played a significant role in the folklore
    of India, Burma, Tibet, and African countries, and that of
    American Indians and Negroes. He is often cast as the
    trickster outwitting stronger animals. The Negro's "own
    role in slavery, where cunning and deception ('hitting a
    straight lick with a crooked stick') were often his only
    weapons against oppression," is associated with the rabbit-
    trickster. This pattern is "in line with the universal
    tendency on the part of oppressed people to identify them-
    selves with the weaker and triumphant animal in the pitting
    of brains against brute force and superior strength." Har-
    ris's tales of Brer Rabbit, which have degenerated into a
    host of trickster animal comics, "are closer to literature
    than to folklore," but Harris's artistry has made the tales
    classics. Uncle Remus fulfills "the social function of the
    Negro nurse or house-servant as story-teller to his master's
    children."

 2 BOTKIN, B.[ENJAMIN] A., ed. <u>A Treasury of Southern Folklore:</u>
    <u>Stories, Ballads, Traditions, and Folkways of the People of</u>
    <u>the South</u>. Foreword by Douglas Southall Freeman.
    New York: Crown Publishers, pp. 471, 645.

1949

Despite Harris's statement to the contrary, writing folktales is creative literature. Often a compromise is needed when writing dialect: truth to idiom is more important than truth to pronunciation. Dialect writing can also seem unintentionally grotesque or humorous; implies that Harris avoids these problems. Literary interest in making the uneducated "talk naturally" goes back before Cable, Harris, and Craddock to George Washington Harris. Anthologizes "Brer Rabbit and the Little Girl" and "Plantation Proverbs."

3 BROWN, WENZELL. "Anansi and Brer Rabbit." American Mercury, 69 (October), 438-43.
 The Uncle Remus stories are the "most famous offspring" of the Anansi stories, brought to the West Indies and America from the African east coast. In these African stories, the spider is most frequently the hero; he is a likable, clever scamp like Brer Rabbit, prefers stealing to working, and loves to eat. A tar-baby story is found in an earlier form than Remus's among Jamaican Anansi tales. The humorous Anansi stories are the real forerunners of the American comic strip and animated cartoon.

4 EATON, CLEMENT. A History of the Old South. New York: Macmillan, p. 514.
 The antebellum humorists seldom used the Negroes as a source of literary material until Russell and Harris. The Countryman was one of the most attractive Georgia periodicals of the time.

5 FREEMAN, DOUGLAS SOUTHALL. "Foreword," to A Treasury of Southern Folklore: Stories, Ballads, Traditions, and Folkways of the People of the South. Edited by B.[enjamin] A. Botkin. New York: Crown Publishers, pp. vii, ix.
 Cunning is a primal quality in folklore. In Harris's "delightsome tales" of the fox, was cunning learned from the fox or a quality transferred from humans? The red hills of Georgia provided an ideal setting and climate for folklore; Uncle Remus could not have understood Brer Fox if he had been wearing ear muffs.

6 HARRIS, EVELYN. A Little Story About My Mother Esther LaRose Harris. Atlanta: privately printed, 65pp., passim.
 Written for the "information and interest" of Mrs. Harris's great grandchildren by her son Evelyn, this booklet mentions Esther's "constant and effective influence" on Joel Chandler and her "good humor, determination and rare mental poise" that made her an ideal mate for a "shy,

1949

retiring, home-loving ·man." Esther was born of French-
Canadian parents and attended a Catholic convent school in
St. Hyacinthe, Quebec, before meeting Joel in Savannah in
1872; they were married in 1873, when Esther was eighteen.
Esther and Joel had nine children. Mrs. Harris's affec-
tionate name for Harris was "'Cephas,'" probably a contrac-
tion of Josephus; Harris signed many of his family letters
"'Cephas.'" Esther suffered an incapacitating stroke in
1925; she died in 1938. Esther retained a trace of French-
Canadian accent throughout her life.

7   HESSELTINE, WILLIAM B. The South in American History.
New York: Prentice-Hall, pp. 630-31.
    Irwin Russell and Harris created a new Negro and Remus
supplanted Uncle Tom in the nation's list of stock characters.

8   MENCKEN, H.[ENRY] L.[OUIS]. "The Sahara of the Bozart," in
A Mencken Chrestomathy. New York: Alfred A. Knopf, p. 187.
    Reprinting of 1920.B6, with Mencken's footnote that the
reference is to Harris.

9   NICHOLS, CHARLES H., JR. "Slave Narratives and the
Plantation Legend." Phylon, 10 (Third Quarter), 202, 203.
    After the Civil War, Harris, Page, Grace King, Thomas
Dixon, and others revived the nostalgic and romantic pictures of the Old South and the plantation myth portrayed
earlier by J. P. Kennedy, Mrs. Schoolcraft, and Mrs. Eastman. Slave narratives, however, reveal the grimness and
brutality of the slave's existence.

10   POCHMANN, HENRY A. and GAY WILSON ALLEN, eds. "Introduction,"
to their Masters of American Literature. Vol. 2.
New York: Macmillan, pp. 5, 8.
    Charles H. Smith, or "'Bill Arp,'" used both Negro and
cracker dialect and may have influenced Harris. Harris
wrote cracker stories but will be best remembered for the
classic Uncle Remus tales.

11   ROSE, ARNOLD M. The Negro's Morale. Minneapolis, MN:
University of Minnesota Press, pp. 19-20.
    Slaves identified with Harris's Brer Rabbit and saw Brer
Fox as the white man. As Bernard Wolfe suggests [see
1949.B15], Harris was aware of these identifications but
camouflaged Negro hatred with the stereotyped Uncle Remus
and with the comment that the stories were of African
origin.

1949

12 SPILLER, ROBERT E., et al. Literary History of the United
    States: Bibliography. New York: Macmillan, pp. 540-41.
    Includes a full list of Harris's primary works and
    edited texts and reprints, and twenty-six biographical or
    critical books and articles on Harris. [Supplement:
    1959.B10.]

13 VAN SANTVOORD, GEORGE and ARCHIBALD C. COOLIDGE. "Preface,"
    in their The Essential Uncle Remus. London: Jonathan
    Cape, pp. 5-6.
    A collection of sixty tales from the seven Remus volumes
    designed to illustrate Harris's emphasis on the characteris-
    tic Negro fable, where the weaker animal uses his wits and
    his mischievousness to triumph over a stronger foe. Har-
    ris's text has been "condensed" and the spelling "standard-
    ized to some extent."

14 WANN, LOUIS, ed. The Rise of Realism: American Literature
    from 1860 to 1900. Revised edition. New York: Macmillan,
    pp. 12, 841-42.
    Revised edition of 1933.B11. Harris commentary identi-
    cal, with slightly enlarged bibliography.

15 WOLFE, BERNARD. "Uncle Remus and the Malevolent Rabbit."
    Commentary, 8 (July), 31-41.
    Commercial as well as folkloric and literary images of
    the Negro picture him as smiling servilely, but hidden be-
    hind that smile may be feelings of resentment or even re-
    venge. Beneath Uncle Remus's smiling countenance was
    malevolence towards the white race. Allegorically, the
    weaker Brer Rabbit triumphs repeatedly, and often viciously,
    over the stronger animals; in the world of sexual affairs,
    too, the Rabbit outshines or humiliates the other creatures.
    Also, the possibilities of sitting down at the communal
    table, and hopes for equality and fraternity among the ani-
    mals, are repeatedly denied. The crafty Rabbit has a top-
    dog air, which a slave can only dream of having, and a
    cynical view of the social world; life for him is a jungle.
    Harris, although he identified with the creativity and the
    social struggle of the Negro, was reluctant to face the
    American racial themes of the tales; instead, he insisted
    on their African origins. The tales may have been Negro
    versions of Reynard the Fox stories learned from blacks who
    came to America from Western Europe, with the seemingly
    weak Rabbit substituted for Reynard. Reprinted: 1968.B20,
    1973.B15.

1950 A BOOKS

1   BROOKES, STELLA BREWER. <u>Joel Chandler Harris--Folklorist</u>.
    Athens, GA: University of Georgia Press, 182pp.
    Some material in the body of the dissertation was moved
    to an appendix; otherwise Brookes's book is substantively
    equivalent to her dissertation. [<u>See</u> 1946.A3.]

2   IVES, SUMNER ALBERT. "The Negro Dialect of the Uncle Remus
    Stories." Ph.D. dissertation, University of Texas at
    Austin, 244pp. with 47pp. supplement.
    Includes a brief biographical sketch, a history of Put-
    nam County dialects, a review of research methods and dia-
    lect theory used in the study, and discussion of Harris's
    phonology and spelling. Harris successfully differentiated
    the speech of Southern Negroes from that of lower class
    whites, and his literary dialect is consistent with data
    in the <u>Linguistic Atlas</u>. Primary and secondary bibliog-
    raphies are included. [Portions of this dissertation ap-
    pear in revised form in 1950.B6, 1954.A1, and 1955.B2.]

1950 B SHORTER WRITINGS

1   BROWN, STERLING A. "Negro Folk Expression." <u>Phylon</u>, 11
    (Fourth Quarter), 318, 320, 322, 323, 325.
    For a long time, "Uncle Remus and his Brer Rabbit tales
    stood for the Negro folk and their lore." Disney's "Song
    of the South" made it clear, however, that Uncle Remus be-
    longed to white people rather than to Negroes. There is
    an abundance of authentic Negro folk material, aside from
    the Remus tales, that must be studied in order to reevaluate
    the Negro folk: the folk character Huddie Ledbetter, the
    tales of Zora Neale Hurston, Library of Congress music
    holdings, African, European, Caribbean, and ancient Indian
    lore, the Master and John cycle, and so on. Apparently,
    the American Negro did take Brer Rabbit for hero--making
    him "a practical joker with a streak of cruelty, a daring
    hunter of devilment, a braggart, a pert wit, a glutton, a
    lady's man, a wily trickster"--as a type of wish-fulfillment
    of an oppressed people.

2   CHEW, SAMUEL C., ed. <u>Fruit Among the Leaves: An Anniversary
    Anthology</u>. New York: Appleton-Century-Crofts, pp. 34-37,
    350, 473-74, 534.
    Recounts D. Appleton and Company's publication of Har-
    ris's writings. Harris's self-depreciation is illustrated

1950

by his letter to Appleton's in which he apologized for not
having visited their offices in the summer of 1882; he was
afraid he would prove a bore. Harris's works were later
published by the merged operations of Appleton's and the
Century Company; press archives record the ways in which
the company and Harris's son Lucien protected the Uncle
Remus copyright after Harris's death. "A Story of the War,"
"Uncle Remus and the Savannah Darkey," "The Tar-Baby Story,"
and "Revival Hymn" are reprinted with explanatory notes on
pp. 350–58, 473–79, and 534–35. "The Story of the War"
reveals Harris's charitable spirit of reconciliation after
the Civil War, and "The Savannah Darkey" shows his prefer-
ence for up-state Negroes from the cotton plantations. The
most characteristic Uncle Remus tales were brought from
Africa but Brer Rabbit's cleverness and "infinite resource"
reflect the situation on the slave plantation and reveal
him to be far from "harmless."

3   CRAVEN, AVERY and WALTER JOHNSON. The United States:
     Experiment in Democracy. Boston: Ginn and Co., p. 438.
     The Gilded Age led to a worship of wealth and decline in
     literary taste. A few local color writers, including Har-
     ris, produced sketches of enduring value, however.

4   HARWELL, RICHARD B. Confederate Music. Chapel Hill, NC:
     University of North Carolina Press, p. 81.
     Harris rightly concluded that Mrs. Ethel Lynn Eliot
     Beers of Massachusetts, not Lamar Fontaine of Mississippi,
     was the author of "All Quiet Along the Potomac To-night."

5   HERSKOVITS, M.[ELVILLE] J. [and ERMINE W. VOEGELIN]. "Tar
     Baby," in Standard Dictionary of Folklore, Mythology, and
     Legend. Vol. 2. New York: Funk & Wagnalls Co., p. 1104.
     The tar-baby story so familiar among American Negroes
     has its widest distribution in western Africa, from whence
     the American versions probably came, but also appears in
     Europe and India. Negroes and Spanish storytellers may have
     helped to diffuse the story among Southeastern and South-
     western American Indians as well.

6   IVES, SUMNER. "A Theory of Literary Dialect." Tulane Studies
     in English, 2 (1950), 137–82.
     [Reprints portions of 1950.A2.] Literary dialects are
     found from Chaucer through modern writers, but a study of
     Harris's use of dialect in the Remus stories can help to
     formulate principles by which American English dialects in
     literature may be evaluated. Although at times Harris may
     exaggerate, for purposes of humor or social commentary, the

1951

sounds in the speech community he portrays and the dialectical patterns of his own regional speech precondition his
ear. Thus, for example, H. L. Mencken [see 1948.B13]
should not fault Harris's use of "Brer" as dialectically
inaccurate, for in Middle Georgia it was probably pronounced
[brə] or [brʌ], like Mencken's preferred "Bruh."

7   LEISY, ERNEST E. The American Historical Novel. Norman, OK:
    University of Oklahoma Press, pp. 184-85.
       Harris did much to foster an understanding between North
    and South in his writings. In his Reconstruction novel
    Tolliver, Harris "laughs alike at 'fire-eating colonels'
    and 'pestiferous reformers'" and uses the wit of Billy
    Sanders to help soften "his recital of the real cruelties
    inflicted upon the South."

8   MYRICK, MARY ROBINSON. "'The Sign of the Wren's Nest.'"
    Garden Gateways, 20 (October), 1.
       In 1946 the Ivy Garden Club of Atlanta undertook to re-
    store the large garden that Harris had planted next to "The
    Wren's Nest." The task was completed by 12 November 1946
    when the premiere of Disney's "The Song of the South" and
    related activities occurred. Harris called his garden
    "Snap Bean Farm," and in his imagination it was the home
    of the various "'critters'" in his tales.

1951 A BOOKS - NONE

1951 B SHORTER WRITINGS

1   CANBY, HENRY SEIDEL. Turn West, Turn East: Mark Twain and
    Henry James. Boston: Houghton Mifflin, pp. 7, 225.
       The "pure folklore" of Miss Watson's Jim, the runaway
    slave in Huckleberry Finn, is from Twain's own memory "and
    belongs with the best of Uncle Remus." As anecdotist,
    Twain is in the line of Uncle Remus rather than Hawthorne
    and Poe. Reprinted: 1965.B1.

2   COWIE, ALEXANDER. The Rise of the American Novel. New York:
    American Book Co., pp. 245, 460, 592.
       Praises Harris's "enlightened view" of loving the South
    while deploring sectionalism, his mastery of the Negro dia-
    lect, and his part in winning Northern recognition for the
    South. Contrasts Stowe's limitations in treating Negro
    dialect with Harris's skill.

1951

3 CURTI, MERLE. The Growth of American Thought. Second
   edition. New York: Harper & Brothers, p. 432.
   Reprint of 1943.B4.

4 ESPINOSA, AURELIO M. Review of Folklorist. JAF, 64 [no
   number indicated]:334-36.
   Chapter-by-chapter summary of and commentary on Brookes's
   Folklorist [see 1950.A1]. Her book is original because it
   does not rehash scholarly analyses of Harris's folklore.
   "In this book it is possible to find Harris himself with
   his books." Her bibliography is welcome.

5 HOFFMAN, DANIEL G. "Joel Chandler Harris--Folklorist. Stella
   Brookes [review]." Midwest Folklore, 1 (Summer), 134.
   Still deserving study is the degree to which Harris's
   wit transformed the folktale motifs he heard, and the origin
   of the Uncle Remus tales. The rabbit is surely "a masked
   self-portrait of the slave; how successfully the droll features hid the hopes, resentments, and imaginative triumphs
   of the Negro may be measured by the popularity of these
   stories with the whites; the first Uncle Remus book alone
   sold 80,000 copies in twenty years." One wonders how aware
   Harris was of the meanings of the tales for the Negro.

6 KARDINER, ABRAM and LIONEL OVESEY. The Mark of Oppression:
   A Psychosocial Study of the American Negro. New York:
   W. W. Norton, pp. 340-41.
   Though told by Remus, a white stereotype of the compliant
   Negro, the pattern of the Uncle Remus stories is similar to
   that of aboriginal American and African tales. The tales
   are a fantasy of aggressive attitudes with great release
   value for the slave. The protagonists Brer Rabbit and
   Coyote are seen in today's Mickey Mouse and Donald Duck
   images.

7 McDAVID, RAVEN I., JR. and VIRGINIA GLENN McDAVID. "The
   Relationship of the Speech of American Negroes to the Speech
   of Whites." American Speech, 26 (February), 6-7, 7 n.17.
   Criticizes Cleanth Brooks's study of the Uncle Remus dialect [see 1935.B2]. Uncle Remus says he was raised in Virginia; his dialect may not represent Georgia-Alabama speech.
   Reprinted: 1971.B10.

8 QUINN, ARTHUR HOBSON, et al. The Literature of the American
   People: An Historical and Critical Survey. New York:
   Appleton-Century-Crofts, pp. 655-56, 1057, et passim.
   Harris read widely among the classic authors and wrote
   editorials in "clear and vigorous English" on literary

1951

subjects and on social issues; among other things, "he tact-
fully argued that the property and intelligence of the South
should not be put in the charge of those who had neither
property nor intelligence." The Remus volumes "constitute
a precious body of distinctive work and prove that the old
fascination of the Beast Epic could be revived in an age of
McCormick reapers and street cars." The best of Harris's
stories, "The Tar-Baby," "The Story of the Deluge," or "The
Awful Fate of Brer Wolf," are "marvels of the art that con-
ceals art," but Mingo and Free Joe by themselves would have
won Harris an enduring reputation. A bibliographical checklist is included.

9   [ROOSEVELT, THEODORE]. The Letters of Theodore Roosevelt.
    Edited by Elting E. Morison, with John M. Blum and John J.
    Buckley. Vol. 1. Cambridge, Mass.: Harvard University
    Press, p. 277.
        Letter #355 to Cecil Arthur Spring Rice (3 May 1892):
    Harris's Plantation is very good. [See also 1951.B10,
    1952.B7, 1954.B12.]

10 _____. The Letters of Theodore Roosevelt. Edited by Elting E.
    Morison, with John M. Blum, Hope W. Wigglesworth, and Sylvia
    Rice. Vol. 4. Cambridge, MA: Harvard University Press,
    pp. 857, 1155.
        Letter #3124 to Silas McBee (14 July 1904): Harris is
    not only a great writer but a great moral teacher. Letter
    #3501 to Richard Watson Gilder (31 March 1905): Harris
    has done good work because he remained in Atlanta instead
    of going to New York. [See also 1951.B9, 1952.B7,
    1954.B12.]

11 SPENCER, BENJAMIN T. "Regionalism in American Literature,"
    in Regionalism in America. Edited by Merrill Jensen.
    Madison: University of Wisconsin Press, pp. 229-30, 231,
    234, 236, 238.
        Recounts Harris's criticism of sectionalism in literature
    and Garland's praise of Harris's localism. Garland incor-
    rectly assumed that Harris, and others, adhered to the
    principle of provincialism unconsciously; Harris's adherence
    was explicit. Harris saw the universal in rural characters.
    He is part of the addiction to dialect and short stories
    evident in the last decades of the century. The picturesque
    dialect in the Southern highlands "could not entirely allay
    the bleakness which formed the substratum" of the Harris
    stories.

1951

12   WOODWARD, C.[OMER] VANN. Origins of the New South: 1877-
     1913. Vol. 9 in A History of the South. Edited by Wendell
     Holmes Stephenson and E. Merton Coulter. Baton Rouge:
     Louisiana State University Press, The Littlefield Fund for
     Southern History of the University of Texas, pp. 158, 166,
     168-69, 432-33.
        Harris's work for Grady revealed "no consciousness of
     serving two masters"--the Old and New South. A part of the
     Southern revival of the 1880's, Harris's success with Negro
     dialect "precipitated a national flood of dialect litera-
     ture." Harris's literary criticism truthfully addressed
     the disgrace of Southern literature and called for regional-
     ism. The Southern writers of the 1880's did not provide a
     realistic portrayal of their times. Harris knew better but
     clung to the belief of neighborly love, as seen in Middle
     Georgia, as the "talisman against all evil." He tried to
     believe Atlanta was but an enlargement of Snap Bean Farm.
     Tolliver is part of the historical vogue popular at the end
     of the century, but it did not fit the stereotype pattern
     for Reconstruction books. Reprinted: 1971.B18.

1952 A BOOKS

1   RAY, CHARLES ARTHUR. "A Study of Realism in the Writings of
     Joel Chandler Harris." Ph.D. dissertation, University of
     Southern California, 243pp.
        Drawing definitions from Louis Wann's The Rise of Realism
     [1933.B11] and assessing Harris's own literary perspectives
     in his editorials, essays, and introductions, Ray compares
     Harris's brand of realism to the literary attitudes of the
     South and of the nation. Harris sought "honesty," "sincer-
     ity," "simplicity," and the picturesque in his works.
     Primarily, he attempted to "be true" to his own vision and
     avoided naturalism or photographic realism. He was a "mod-
     erate realist" who brought the Negro into fiction through a
     sympathetic portraiture, achieved dialectical accuracy, and
     relied on the oral tradition. Includes a discussion of
     realism in the editorials of the Atlanta Constitution and
     a twelve-page primary and secondary bibliography.

1952 B SHORTER WRITINGS

1   BEATTY, RICHMOND CROOM; FLOYD C. WATKINS; THOMAS DANIEL YOUNG;
     and RANDALL STEWART. The Literature of the South.
     Chicago, et al.: Scott, Foresman, pp. 438-39, 443-45,
     545-46, et passim.

1952

Discusses the characteristics of the New South movement
and mentions Harris's concern for problems caused by emancipation. Critics agree Harris has given the most authentic
and artistic reproduction ever of the Middle Georgia Negro
dialect. As a whole, his writing "did much to reduce the
sectional hostility" after the War. Gives brief biographical summary, and anthologizes selected Remus stories and
"Free Joe."

2   BROOKS, VAN WYCK. The Confident Years: 1885-1915. New York:
    E. P. Dutton & Co., pp. 42, 366, et passim.
        Many contemporary Southern writers could accept neither
    nationalism nor industrialism; however, some, like Harris
    and Lanier, did agree with the concepts of Union. In fact,
    General Garwood [in "Azalia"] represented those Southerners
    who felt that their duty now lay in restoring the Union.
    Harris showed a "touch of genius" in his Uncle Remus
    stories.

3   CURRENT-GARCIA, EUGENE and WALTON R. PATRICK, eds. "Preface,"
    and headnote, in their American Short Stories: 1820 to the
    Present. Chicago, et al.: Scott, Foresman, pp. xxviii,
    239-40.
        The stories of Cable, Murfree, Jewett, Harris, and others
    were realistic only in externals; they were more like folk
    idylls. Headnote to "Free Joe," here anthologized, gives
    a biographical sketch and points out that the popularity of
    the Uncle Remus stories tends to obscure "the variety and
    excellence" of his local color stories. Free Joe is vividly
    drawn and employs Harris's typically accurate dialect. Re-
    vised edition: 1964.B7.

4   DARGAN, MARION. "Harris," in Guide to American Biography:
    Part II--1815-1933. Albuquerque, NM: University of New
    Mexico Press, p. 326.
        Cites eleven articles and books containing biographical
    material on Harris.

5   DIKE, DONALD A. "Notes on Local Color and Its Relation to
    Realism." CE, 14 (November), 85.
        Much of post-Civil War Southern literature sentimen-
    talizes or idealizes the Southern way of life and seems
    motivated by "resistance to northern industrialism, cen-
    tralization, and Negro suffrage." Cites Stafford's essay
    [1946.B15] to illustrate how Harris conceals pro-South
    attitudes in his Uncle Remus stories. "Aunt Fountain's
    Prisoner" [Free Joe] even more overtly marries a Northerner
    to a Southerner and promotes North-South friendship--but on
    the South's terms.

1952

6   LOCKE, ALAIN. "The Negro in American Literature," in New
     World Writing. First Mentor Selection. New York: The
     New American Library of World Literature, p. 26.
     In his Remus stories, Harris "rendered as much poetic
     justice to the Negro as an orthodox Southerner could." [For
     revision, see 1956.B5.]

7   [ROOSEVELT, THEODORE]. The Letters of Theodore Roosevelt.
     Edited by Elting E. Morison, with John M. Blum, Alfred D.
     Chandler, Jr., and Sylvia Rice. Vol. 6. Cambridge, MA:
     Harvard University Press, pp. 1108-11.
         Letter #4759 to Joel C. Harris (15 June 1908): Requests
     that Harris print his letter in Uncle Remus's Magazine pro-
     moting "The Battle Hymn of the Republic" as a national
     treasure. Letter #4793 to Julian Harris (6 July 1908):
     Feels the continuation of Uncle Remus's Magazine can do the
     most to promote Harris's memory. It gives the South recog-
     nition through its unbiased, broad reflections of national
     sentiment. Roosevelt offers to have his own letters pro-
     moting the magazine published. Letter #4794 to Julian
     Harris (6 July 1908): Uncle Remus is one of the few undy-
     ing characters. However, the Remus stories only represent
     a small part of Harris's important work. Believes Harris's
     ethical values to be as great as his literary quality.
     Without being didactic, Harris encouraged his readers to
     be courageous, honest, and generous. Compliments Uncle
     Remus's Magazine for its broad reflection of national sen-
     timent and its criticism of America's faults. [See also
     1951.B9, B10, 1954.B12.]

8   WISH, HARVEY. Society and Thought in Modern America: A
     Social and Intellectual History of the American People from
     1865. Vol. 2 of Society and Thought in America. New York:
     Longmans, Green and Co., pp. 24, 39, 40-42.
         It took Appleton's manuscript scout to make Harris a
     national idol with Uncle Remus. A democratic spirit, he
     sympathized with the Negro and the North, although he did
     not go beyond the happy "darky" stereotype in the Remus
     stories. His poor white tales like "Mingo" are more realis-
     tic, but he still colored his stories with sentimental
     situations in which pity dominates; he retained a respect-
     able middle class American attitude. Also discusses the
     tar-baby story and its numerous versions, particularly the
     American Indian (Cherokee) origin.

1953 A BOOKS

1 ENGLISH, THOMAS H., ed. <u>Mark Twain to Uncle Remus:</u> <u>1881–</u>
   <u>1885.</u> Emory University Sources and Reprints, Vol. 7,
   no. 3. Atlanta: Emory University, pp. 5–7, et passim.
   Fully transcribes five letters to Harris from Twain.
   Also reprints Harris's review of <u>The Prince and the Pauper</u>,
   published in the Atlanta <u>Constitution</u> for 25 December 1881.
   Both Twain and Harris as boys had heard Negro folktales
   narrated by older Negro men. Twain shared his own transcription of "De Woman wid de Gold'n Arm" with Harris and
   before and after their meeting in New Orleans in 1882 gave
   him advice on publishing his Uncle Remus tales in book form;
   Harris's shyness led him to decline Twain's proposal of a
   joint lecture tour. Harris admired <u>Huckleberry Finn</u> as much
   as Twain did <u>Uncle Remus</u>.

1953 B SHORTER WRITINGS

1 BECK, LEWIS H. "Snap Bean Farm." <u>AH</u>, NS 4 (Spring), 11.
   Describes the Wren's Nest and the garden at Snap Bean
   Farm where the Uncle Remus characters cavorted. A gifted
   writer of the immortal Remus stories, Harris was a "kindly
   spirit."

2 BROOKS, VAN WYCK. "The South: Lanier and Joel Chandler
   Harris," in his <u>The Times of Melville and Whitman</u>.
   New York: E. P. Dutton and Co.; London: J. M. Dent and
   Sons, pp. 360–87 passim. [<u>See also</u> pp. 66, et passim.]
   Reprinting of 1947.B3.

3 BROWN, STERLING. "Backgrounds of Folklore in Negro
   Literature." <u>Jackson College Bulletin</u>, 2 (September), 27,
   28.
        Excerpt from an address on the theme "Seventy-Five Years
   of the Negro in Literature." Negro writers, as well as
   publishers and readers, have been influenced positively and
   negatively by white authors who have set up stereotypes of
   Negro life. Harris praised Irwin Russell for his "perfect"
   knowledge of Negro character; but no writer, including Harris, who did have more knowledge than Russell, has such
   perfect understanding. Harris altered the folktales he
   heard, but at least he saved the valuable Uncle Remus tales
   for blacks and his heart was right.

4 _____. "Negro Folk Expression: Spirituals, Seculars, Ballads
   and Work Songs." <u>Phylon</u>, 14, no. 1 (1953), 61.

1953

"With varying authenticity and understanding," Harris,
DuBose Heyward, Julia Peterkin, Roark Bradford, Marc Connelly, E. C. L. Adams, Zora Neale Hurston, and Langston
Hughes have all made rewarding use of Negro folk life and
character.

5   BURRELL, ANGUS and BENNETT CERF, eds. An Anthology of Famous
    American Stories. New York: Modern Library, p. 1315.
        Although a "brilliant" newspaperman, Harris's fame comes
    from the Remus tales. Quotes Carl Van Doren that, besides
    Twain, the nineteenth century "'left hardly a single last-
    ing folk-hero except Uncle Remus and the animals of his
    bestiary.'" Anthologizes "The Tar-Baby."

6   COOK, DOROTHY E. and ISABEL S. MONRO, eds. Short Story Index:
    An Index to 60,000 Stories in 4,320 Collections. New York:
    H. W. Wilson Co., pp. 581-82.
        Lists ninety-four folktales and short stories collected
    in Harris's books and in subsequent gatherings. Two
    stories by Frank Harris are erroneously included.

7   DAY, ARTHUR GROVE and WILLIAM F. BAUER, eds. The Greatest
    American Short Stories: Twenty Classics of Our Heritage.
    New York, Toronto, London: McGraw-Hill Book Co., p. 105.
        Headnote to "The Tar-Baby Story" calls Harris the "great
    Southern humorist, editor, and taleteller."

8   DOBIE, J. FRANK. "The Traveling Anecdote," in Folk Travelers:
    Ballads, Tales, and Talk. Edited by Mody C. Boatright,
    Wilson M. Hudson, and Allen Maxwell. Publications of the
    Texas Folklore Society, No. 25. Dallas, TX: Southern
    Methodist University Press, p. 8.
        Treatises on Harris's immortal tar-baby story trace its
    origins to ancient India, to Europe, to Africa, and to
    American Indian tribes; behind the curtain of antiquity,
    "all is speculation."

9   FALK, ROBERT P. "The Rise of Realism, 1871-1891," in
    Transitions in American Literary History. Edited by Harry
    Hayden Clark. Durham, NC: Duke University Press,
    pp. 430-31.
        Hamlin Garland [see 1929.B6] cites Harris as part of the
    local color movement, a movement which gave us a vital,
    original, and democratic literature. Localism is seen as
    the key to the realistic trend.

10 HOPKINS, J. G. E., ed. The Scribner Treasury: 22 Classic
    Tales. New York: Charles Scribner's Sons, [p. 140].

1954

Headnote to "Free Joe" summarizes Harris's career and
stresses his achievement in letting his Negro characters
live as men, not as accessories to white masters. Harris
refused to condescend to the Negro or to the poor white
cracker. In "Free Joe" Harris's intuitive democracy,
honesty, pity for the weak, and narrative force are "displayed in their finest form."

11   LEASE, BENJAMIN, ed. "A Newly-Discovered Joel Chandler Harris
     Letter." Georgia Historical Quarterly, 37 (December),
     345-46.
        Harris shows his characteristic wit in a letter of 2
     March 1885, printed here, to James R. Osgood, the Boston
     publisher. Harris humorously complains about the request
     of Osgood's partner, Benjamin H. Ticknor, for a personal
     photograph and, more seriously, urges that Osgood publish
     James Whitcomb Riley's dialect poetry.

12   SIMKINS, FRANCIS BUTLER. A History of the South. Second
     edition, revised and enlarged. New York: Alfred A. Knopf,
     pp. 428, 432-33.
        Substantively equivalent to 1947.B15. Revised and re-
     printed: see 1963.B13.

1954 A BOOKS

1   IVES, SUMNER. The Phonology of the Uncle Remus Tales.
     Publication of the American Dialect Society, No. 22
     (November). Gainsville, FL: American Dialect Society,
     59pp.
        [Based upon 1950.A2.] An interpretation of the spellings
     of the dialect in the Remus stories reveals that Harris used
     a consistent phonology, one based clearly "on accurate ob-
     servation of a genuine folk speech." Harris made no signi-
     ficant changes in his dialect when his audience became a
     national one. All available linguistic field records for
     the Southeast were consulted in this analysis of forty-six
     phonemes in the Remus dialect.

1954 B SHORTER WRITINGS

1   BROWN, GLENORA W. and DEMING B. BROWN. A Guide to Soviet
     Russian Translations of American Literature. New York:
     King's Crown Press, Columbia University, pp. 15, 39, 84-85.
        Harris's books and other works on the Negro were espe-
     cially popular in Russia in the 1930's, following the period

of the New Economic Policy. Two editions of Uncle Remus
tales are listed; with reprintings, the total number of
copies published in Russia in the 1930's exceeds 400,000.

2 [CALLAWAY, H. L.]. "Harris," in Cassell's Encyclopaedia of
World Literature. Edited by S. H. Steinberg. Vol. 1.
New York: Funk and Wagnalls, p. 998.
Biographical sketch and seven-item checklist of primary
and secondary works. Harris recorded the Old South Negro
and Georgia plantation folklore with "realism and homely
humour." [For minor revision, see 1973.B3.]

3 COULTER, ELLIS MERTON; ALBERT BERRY SAYE; SPENCER BIDWELL
KING, JR.; and W. W. LIVENGOOD. History of Georgia.
New York, et al.: American Book Co., pp. 218-20, 403.
Harris is the best known of Georgia writers; he created
the lovable Remus straight from Georgia life, complete with
everyday Georgia animals. Provides brief biographical
sketch.

4 CUNLIFFE, MARCUS. The Literature of the United States.
Melbourne, London, and Baltimore: Penguin Books, pp. 171,
175-76.
Provides a brief biographical sketch. Though he wrote
too many Remus volumes and was "emphatically a Southerner,"
Harris did not propagandize. He showed a profound sympathy
with the underdog. The philosophy of the gentle and the
poor in Remus makes the stories timeless and universal.

5 [ENGLISH, THOMAS H.]. "An Uncollected Uncle Remus Sketch."
Emory University Quarterly, 10 (December), 266-70.
A widely popular way of advertising patent medicines in
the nineteenth century was the comic almanac, although few
of these survive. Almanacs published by the Charles A.
Vogeler Company of Baltimore, proprietors of St. Jacobs Oil,
included contributions by several American authors; recently, a Harris sketch, "Uncle Remus' 'Little Red Speckle
Steer,'" was found in an 1883-84 St. Jacobs almanac. It is
especially important because it portrays the "other" Uncle
Remus, who lived in Atlanta and reported his opinions and
accounts of the Negro community there.

6 GARRETT, FRANKLIN M. Atlanta and Environs: A Chronicle of
Its People and Events. Vol. 2. New York: Lewis Historical
Publishing Co., pp. 532-34, 943, et passim.
Contains a brief biographical summary. Harris started
on the Constitution as an editorial paragrapher at $25 per
week. The Remus books were famous for their dialect, humor,

and lore. Describes the Harris memorials, the Frost dedi-
cation, and the Wren's Nest.

7 GOLDSTONE, HERBERT. "From Uncle Remus to Mark Twain." SFQ,
   18 (December), 242–43.
      Publishes a letter of 6 December 1881 from Harris to
   Twain, thanking Twain for sending him the Golden Arm legend
   and complimenting The Prince and the Pauper and other works.
   The headnote provides background details.

8 HUBBELL, JAY B. The South in American Literature 1607–1900.
   Durham, NC: Duke University Press, pp. 782–95, et passim.
      Harris was less an "accidental author" than he claimed.
   As a youth he filled notebooks with his writings, and he
   received extensive training and experience as an apprentice
   journalist under Joseph Addison Turner. He was indebted to
   the Georgia humorists, but he did not like to be thought of
   only as a humorist and made his most significant achievement
   as a writer of character sketches. Harris had a full career
   as a journalist, social critic, and promoter of Southern
   letters, yet he recognized that he was happiest when "'the
   other fellow,'" who understood the old plantation Negro and
   the Georgia cracker and spoke their language, was given a
   free hand to write. Harris's "'other fellow'" produced the
   Uncle Remus tales, which tend to glorify the plantation regime, "Free Joe," his best story, and Billy Sanders, the
   cracker humorist and social philosopher. A checklist of
   books and articles on Harris is included on pp. 934–35.

9 LEARY, LEWIS, ed. Articles on American Literature 1900–1950.
   Durham, NC: Duke University Press, pp. 125–26.
      Lists thirty-four articles on Harris. [For supplement,
   see 1970.B15.]

10 LOGAN, RAYFORD W. The Negro in American Life and Thought:
   The Nadir 1877–1901. New York: Dial Press, pp. 162–63,
   254.
      Harris was "the famed exponent of friendship for the
   Negro"; his interpretations of the Southern Negro have been
   generally accepted as the kindliest and most authentic. He
   reanimated the plantation tradition in Harper's and Century.
   Revised edition: 1965.B10.

11 RICE, GRANTLAND. The Tumult and the Shouting: My Life in
   Sport. New York: A. S. Barnes & Co., pp. 14, 36–37.
      Speaks of his friendship with Harris. "Perhaps the un-
   stuffiest man I ever knew," Harris refused to meet Stanley,
   the man who found Dr. Livingston, because he didn't like

1954

beards and because he was older than Harris: "'I like
youngsters. They're more my kind.'" Harris's death jarred
Rice and he wrote a poem on "Uncle Remus" for the paper the
day afterwards. The poem is reproduced.

12   [ROOSEVELT, THEODORE]. The Letters of Theodore Roosevelt.
     Selected and edited by Elting E. Morison, with John M. Blum,
     Alfred D. Chandler, Jr., and Sylvia Rice. Vol. 7.
     Cambridge, MA: Harvard University Press, p. 584.
         Letter #5749 to Julian LaRose Harris (1 August 1912):
     Harris possessed genius, but also a gentle soul and a sym-
     pathy with others. His life and work brought the North and
     South closer together, and, as the author of Uncle Remus
     and "Free Joe," he felt a deep interest in the welfare of
     the Negro. [See also 1951.B9, B10; 1952.B7.]

13   THORP, WILLARD; MERLE CURTI; and CARLOS BAKER, eds. American
     Issues. Vol. 2 of The Literary Record. Revised and
     enlarged. Chicago, Philadelphia, and New York: J. B.
     Lippincott, pp. 665-66.
         Substantively equivalent to 1941.B12.

1955 A BOOKS

1   [LARWOOD, JAMES]. Georgia 1800-1900: A Series of Selections
    from the Georgiana Library of a Private Collector. Joel
    Chandler Harris: Folklore in the Deep South. Atlanta:
    Atlanta Public Library, 12pp.
        Following a three-page biographical and critical sketch
    of Harris, the publication history of items 148-167 in the
    collector's library is given. A facsimile of a number of
    Joseph Addison Turner's weekly journal, The Countryman,
    faces a sketch of Harris's experiences as a printer's devil
    for Turner for four years; among other items, he contributed
    to The Countryman a recipe for making black ink and a dispu-
    tation upon "'Grumblers.'"

1955 B SHORTER WRITINGS

1   CHASE, RICHARD, ed. "Foreword," to The Complete Tales of
    Uncle Remus. Boston: Houghton Mifflin, pp. xi-xiii.
        Chase acknowledges the influence of Harris in teaching
    him to "learn how to write with the Southern mountain idiom"
    in his ears. The Uncle Remus tales are a "treasure" of race
    and tradition that come "from the soul of a people," and
    they "embody a serenity and a simplicity that keep us close

to the Earth." They endure, in spite of any difficulties
of dialect, "by simply being what they are: the recording
of one man's joy in the spirited genuineness of 'the old
times.'" Chase includes a glossary of footnotes by Harris
on word definitions, along with Chase's own definitions.

2 IVES, SUMNER. "Dialect Differentiation in the Stories of
   Joel Chandler Harris." AL, 27 (March), 88-96.
      [Based upon 1950.A2.] Harris skillfully indicated dif-
   ferences in speech patterns among the various social classes
   in Middle Georgia, and he also differentiated regional
   speech patterns effectively. He distinguished among several
   white dialects, but, accurately, noted few differences between rural black and rural white speech.

3 PENROD, JAMES H. "Folk Motifs in Old Southwestern Humor."
   SFQ, 19 (March), 118.
      Passing reference. Universal folk motifs as identified
   by Stith Thompson treating the origin of the colored race,
   speaking animals, giant animals, and remarkable persons are
   broad patterns in Old Southwestern humor. Harris also includes tales about the Negro's origin and humanized animals
   among his Uncle Remus stories.

4 SPILLER, ROBERT E. The Cycle of American Literature: An
   Essay in Historical Criticism. New York: Macmillan,
   pp. 145, 146.
      More "mellow and restrained" than the local color writ-
   ings of the Middle and Far West, Uncle Remus used a "mix-
   ture of realism in dealing with the present and romance in
   dealing with the past." Harris felt a sense of social
   injustice about former slaves.

5 THORP, WILLARD, ed. A Southern Reader. New York: Alfred A.
   Knopf, pp. 674-75.
      "Harris was shrewd enough to realize that behind the
   tricks of Brer Rabbit and the defeats of Brer Fox were con-
   cealed the Negro's desire to triumph over the white man--in
   fiction at least." But he would have been shocked at recent speculations [refers to Wolfe's essay; see 1949.B15]
   about "the particular ways in which the Negro animus against
   the white man is projected through the stories that Harris--
   in this view--so innocently took down as amanuensis." "Mr.
   Rabbit Nibbles Up the Butter" is anthologized.

6 WALKER, RAYMOND J. "The Countryman: A Georgia Journal."
   Hobbies, 60 (August), 110.

231

1956

Sketches Harris's life at Turnwold Plantation as a printer's apprentice. Harris dedicated Plantation to Joseph
Addison Turner, his mentor during his apprenticeship.

1956 A BOOKS - NONE

1956 B SHORTER WRITINGS

1   ANON. "Joel Chandler Harris: 75th Anniversary." News from
    Home, 17 (Spring), 14-16.
    Article in the Home Insurance Company's magazine com-
    memorates the seventy-fifth anniversary of the publication
    of Harris's first book, Uncle Remus. The first edition was
    priced at $1.50 and contained 231 pages of text and eight
    pages of advertising; it was an immediate success. Harris
    had explained to his illustrator, Frederick S. Church, that
    the fox in the tales was the grey fox, not the red fox, and
    that the common American hare was the rabbit he had in mind;
    the bear was the smallest species of black bear, common in
    Florida and Georgia. Later, A. B. Frost would make the
    book "his own," with his sensitive drawings.

2   BAKER, AUGUSTA. Review of Complete Tales. Saturday Review,
    39 (18 February), 54.
    Reviewed among "Books for Young People." The dialect of
    the Uncle Remus tales is "extremely difficult" for young
    children to read, so Chase's edition is necessarily for the
    storyteller. This volume belongs on the folklorist's shelf.
    "These stories are as American as the stars and stripes,
    even though they have some of their origins in Africa."

3   BRADLEY, SCULLEY; RICHMOND CROOM BEATTY; and E. HUDSON LONG.
    Whitman to the Present. Vol. 2 of The American Tradition
    in Literature. Revised. New York: W. W. Norton & Co.,
    pp. 512-14.
    The Uncle Remus tales are the "first dependable repre-
    sentation of the Negro dialects" and are the only lasting
    literary record of American Indian and Negro folktales in
    which animals "reflect the comedy of mankind." Harris cre-
    ated a regional literature of "impressive reality, depth,
    and permanence." While Uncle Remus and Nights are the best
    works in Negro characterization, dialect, and folklore, the
    success of Uncle Remus has obscured Harris's achievement in
    his other books, such as Free Joe. Plantation and Tolliver
    are also noteworthy. Anthologizes "The Story of the Deluge
    and How It Came About" and "Free Joe."   .

1956

4   BROOKS, VAN WYCK and OTTO L. BETTMANN. Our Literary Heritage,
    A Pictorial History of the Writer in America. New York:
    E. P. Dutton & Co., pp. 136-37.
        Writers began exploring the richness of Negro lore
    "largely because of the curiosity the Negroes were exciting
    in these years of their emancipation after the war." Har-
    ris's firsthand experiences with the Negro during his early
    life led to the Remus stories. The animals represented the
    Negroes and Brer Rabbit was the "Negro Hercules," a mythical
    hero. The motto for the tales may be St. Augustine's to
    "'spare the lowly and strike down the proud.'" These tales
    were universally known in the South, but it took Harris's
    genius to make them immortal.

5   BUTCHER, MARGARET JUST. The Negro in American Culture.   .
    New York: Alfred A. Knopf, pp. 33, 38, 47-48, 114, 158-60,
    et passim.
        Revision of 1952.B6; based on materials left by Alain
    Locke. A discerning Southern writer, Harris preserved the
    "most organic body of Negro folk tale [sic] American litera-
    ture possesses," but Butcher wishes he had been more accu-
    rate and less improvising. One means of survival as a
    slave is the emotional release of laughter, ridicule, and
    mockery: Remus is a good example. The stories tell a
    "sly, meaningful allegory" and provide "crafty comic conso-
    lation." Harris handles dialect well but has been criti-
    cized severely for making the narrators too important, for
    treating bad-good Negro stereotypes, and for portraying the
    slave's loyalty to his white master. Harris modified orig-
    inal folk materials to "suggest universality," as did
    Stephen Foster, thus creating an unrealistic, one-sided,
    and sentimental view of the folk Negro. Yet Harris should
    be praised for his thorough, though embellished, study of
    folklore: Uncle Remus and Nights are American classics.
    Later volumes have Remus speaking as an apologist for the
    Old South; these stories are "strained and artificial."

6   COAN, OTIS W. and RICHARD G. LILLARD. America in Fiction: An
    Annotated List of Novels That Interpret Aspects of Life in
    the United States. Fourth edition. Stanford, CAL:
    Stanford University Press, pp. 48, 127, 165.
        Revision of 1945.B8. [See 1966.B4 for later revision.]
    The only substantive variation from 1945.B8 is the inclusion
    of Tolliver under "The Civil War and Reconstruction." Plot
    and theme are briefly described. The novel is more like an
    essay than "the present-day historical novel."

233

1956

7   COOK, DOROTHY E. and ESTELLE A. FIDELL, eds. Short Story
    Index: Supplement 1950-1954. An Index to 9,575 Stories
    to [sic] 549 Collections. New York: H. W. Wilson Co.,
    p. 141.
        Lists two Harris tales appearing in anthologies. [See
    1960.B3 and 1965.B5 for supplements.]

8   DORSON, RICHARD M., ed. Negro Folktales in Michigan.
    Cambridge, MA: Harvard University Press, pp. 31-33, 49.
        Harris thought that the Uncle Remus tales were clearly
    of African origin, but it seems now that there are European
    and Anglo-American sources for the animal fables as well as
    African origins. Also, Harris misrepresents the body of
    Negro folklore in relating almost exclusively animal stories
    told by a faithful retainer who thinks nostalgically of
    antebellum days. The Negro did use the rabbit as a trick-
    ster and schemer figure, and there may be "ego projection"
    by the underdog Negro onto the rabbit, but other folk nar-
    rative traditions and motifs are also important. For in-
    stance, Harris only includes one example of the "Old Marster
    and John" cycle, which treats the duplicities of a slave
    and his master's typically good-humored responses. [For
    revision, see 1967.B5.]

9   FURNAS, J.[OSEPH] C. Goodbye to Uncle Tom. New York:
    William Sloane Associates, pp. 121, 171.
        Comments that, in Harris, the Negroes who followed Sher-
    man were largely fieldhands and not on familiar terms with
    their owners. Remus's "Sis Cow" and "Br'er Rabbit" in imi-
    tation of white usage "show how important to Negroes was
    the evangelical notion of fellowship among the saved."

10 JOHNSON, SIDDIE JOE. Review of Complete Tales. LJ, 81
    (15 January), 238.
        Chase's Complete Tales is a good collection "for the
    storyteller, the scholar, and for family sharing." Librar-
    ies will need other less comprehensive editions, but they
    will want this one, also.

11 LEYBURN, ELEANOR DOUGLASS. Satiric Allegory: Mirror of Man.
    New Haven: Yale University Press, pp. 57, 60-66.
        Harris is a gifted allegorist because the reader can
    appreciate both the human and the animal traits in the
    Remus tales. Harris wisely emphasizes one trait in Brer
    Rabbit at a time (usually mischievousness or craftiness)
    and focuses on only one major failing in his opponents:
    cruelty, greed, or vanity. While we are meant to admire
    Brer Rabbit, the baseness, evil, and cold-blooded cruelty

1956

of Caxton's Reynard the Fox is supposed to shock us. Harris's, Caxton's, and Orwell's animal allegories are more
successful in art and point of view than Spenser's Mother
Hubberd's Tale.

12 MacDOUGALD, DUNCAN, JR. Review of Complete Tales. New York
    Times Book Review (5 February), p. 24.
        Charles Alphonso Smith included Harris among the ten
    American authors he lectured on at the University of Berlin
    in 1910. Chase's edition is timely because children have
    been neglecting these classic tales in recent years. Fifty
    of the 175 stories are largely unknown to the public. The
    stories are of major folkloristic value, but they are also
    important literary works of great dialectical skill and
    satiric force. Although the introduction and glossary are
    inadequate, the book is one of the greatest folklore and
    literary bargains of our time.

13 POLLOCK, EILEEN and ROBERT MASON. "The Magic of Uncle Remus."
    Saturday Review, 39 (18 February), 13, 47.
        Harris enjoys enthusiastic audiences around the world.
    In Norway there is even a children's radio series based on
    his stories. Some of his stories have been translated into
    Swedish, French, Bengali, Dutch, Spanish, Japanese, and a
    number of African dialects. Recounts Harris's life and
    quotes from the Remus tales to illustrate his humor and
    eternal charm. [Reprinted in condensed version: 1956.B14.]

14 _____. "Uncle Remus: Storyteller to the World." Reader's
    Digest, 68 (March), 212–14.
        Condensation of 1956.B13.

15 PRITCHARD, JOHN PAUL. Criticism in America: An Account of
    the Development of Critical Techniques from the Early
    Period of the Republic to the Middle Years of the Twentieth
    Century. Norman, OK: University of Oklahoma Press,
    pp. 196–97, 198.
        Harris encouraged Southern writers to use local literary
    materials, but to avoid sectionalism and romanticizing. He
    was evidently unsuccessful, for Southern writers still faced
    the same problems in 1902: poverty, lack of public interest
    in literature, and even scorn of postwar Southerners towards
    writers.

16 SELBY, JOHN; BERNARD WOLFE; and LYMAN BRYSON. "Joel Chandler
    Harris: The Uncle Remus Stories," in The Invitation to
    Learning Reader. Edited by Ralph Backlund. New York:
    Herbert Muschel, pp. 346–53.

1956

Reprint of CBS radio broadcast of 14 August 1955. Wolfe
tends to dominate this free-wheeling discussion, arguing
that Harris was a compiler, not an author, and that he was
condescending toward the Negro because he had been condi-
tioned by plantation life. Bryson and Selby, however, see
literary merit in the tales and feel that for modern audiences, and perhaps for the Negro storytellers as well, the
Remus fables about the rabbit's triumph over stronger creatures are racially symbolic.

17   VANSTORY, BURNETTE. Georgia's Land of the Golden Tales.
     Athens, GA: University of Georgia Press, pp. 49–50.
        Talks of Bu Allah, or Ben Ali, the Mohammedan slave on
     the Spalding plantation, stressing his reputation for wis-
     dom and curing illness. The diary mentioned by Harris in
     Aaron was given to Francis Goulding by Ben Ali and later
     presented to the Georgia State Library. It is believed to
     be the only existing example of African-American writing.

1957 A BOOKS - NONE

1957 B SHORTER WRITINGS

1   BECKER, ALLEN W. "The Period 1865–1925." GaR, 11 (Summer),
    151.
       Part two of a four-part symposium on "Agrarianism in
    Southern Literature." Page and Harris actively defended
    the passing Southern civilization. Harris made the Negro
    his special theme, and agrarianism appears in his fiction
    in his portraits of the ex-slave's loyalty to his former
    master.

2   DORSON, RICHARD M. "The Identification of Folklore in
    American Literature." JAF, 70 (January–March), 3–4, 5–6.
       Folklore collectors as well as literary critics often
    publish materials without sufficient research into folk
    backgrounds. In the Uncle Remus tales Harris portrays
    "only one segment of a richly diversified lore"; Brer Rabbit
    tales do not constitute the entirety of Negro folk stories.
    But Harris's stories are "vitally linked" to Negro folklore,
    for he gathered them directly from the Negroes; Longfellow's
    Indian material, though, possesses no ethnographic value.

3   [ENGLISH, THOMAS H.]. "Boyhood Verses by Joel Chandler
    Harris." Emory University Quarterly, 13 (December), 245–46.
       After a year as a printer's devil for The Countryman
    Harris had seen four of his own signed compositions appear.

1957

A year later he developed an enthusiasm for the romantic
poetry of Henry Lynden Flash (1835–1914), editor of the
Macon Daily Confederate, and on 5 May 1864 published "I Saw
Her To-Day," a sentimental poem about the possible separa-
tion of the lover from his beloved. Harris later wrote a
long biographical-critical essay on Flash for The Countryman. Coincidentally, a news story, "Alleged Plot to Assas-
sinate or Kidnap President Lincoln," appeared directly
below the poem. This article may have been the germ out of
which grew "The Kidnapping of President Lincoln," published
in The Saturday Evening Post in 1900 and collected in Occasions. This story is the finest of the Billy Sanders tales.

4   HOWELLS, WILLIAM DEAN. Prefaces to Contemporaries (1882–1920).
    Facsimile Reproductions, with introduction and bibliographi-
    cal note by George Arms, William M. Gibson, and Frederic C.
    Marston, Jr. Gainesville, FL: Scholars' Facsimiles &
    Reprints, pp. 196, 198.
        Reprint of 1920.B4.

5   LIVELY, ROBERT A. Fiction Fights the Civil War: An Unfinished
    Chapter in the Literary History of the American People.
    Chapel Hill, NC: University of North Carolina Press,
    pp. 12, 42, 48, 59, 60.
        Lists Plantation as a representative Civil War novel,
    though not one of the best. Harris's Negro is a stereotype
    Southern view of the former slave: loyal; "shrewd, with
    the wisdom of a contented and rooted peasant; and carefree,
    happily confident" in plantation security. Comments on the
    "harmless and reasonably accurate story-telling" in Shadow.

6   MacDOUGALD, DUNCAN, JR. "The Complete Tales of Uncle Remus."
    JAF (April–June), 188–90.
        Chase's compilation of the Remus tales is valuable, for
    these stories are a vast storehouse of linguistic, literary,
    artistic, psychological, historical-sociological, and folk-
    loristic materials. However, the apparatus of the edition
    (a perfunctory Foreword and too-selective Glossary) is vir-
    tually useless. Desperately needed here is an account of
    the origins of Negro dialect (transplanted forms of pro-
    vincial dialects from Southwest England), of Harris's
    phonological method, and of the actual folkloristic, as com-
    pared to literary, content of the tales. For, as English
    has pointed out [see 1948.B6], the Remus stories are twice-
    told, not quite as "uncooked" as Harris said they were; a
    ten-line tale from a Negro correspondent could become a
    four-page story.

1957

7 MacDOUGALD, DUNCAN, JR. "The 'Uncle Remus Stories.'" Fabula,
   1 (1957), 159-61.
   Review-article of Chase's Complete Tales. Culturally,
   the most important subject matter of the world's folk tales
   is anthropomorphic, involving the attribution of human
   traits to non-human things, chiefly animals. Harris's
   Uncle Remus stories are the most "human," and perhaps the
   most endearing, of all delineations of animals in world
   literature. Remus's tales do not merely show up man's
   weakness or stupidity, but his sense of humor, feelings of
   frustration, and perception of reality, including emotional
   reality. Additionally, Harris's tales are valuable dialectical studies and documents on Southern social history.

8 MOTT, FRANK LUTHER. A History of American Magazines: 1885-
   1905. Cambridge, MA: Harvard University Press, Belknap
   Press, pp. 361, 451, 544, 592, 689, 721, 774.
   Lists Harris as among contributors to The Chap-Book,
   Ladies' Home Journal, McClure's, Saturday Evening Post,
   Scribner's, and The World's Work. The Home Magazine merged
   with Uncle Remus's Magazine.

9 SMITH, GUY E. American Literature: A Complete Survey.
   Ames, IA: Littlefield, Adams & Co., pp. 103-104, 157, 215.
   Harris dealt with Georgia cracker dialect, but his great
   success came with the Uncle Remus stories. Wise and good-
   natured Uncle Remus became a national institution, and no
   American in the last three generations "has failed to come
   in contact" with the Uncle Remus lore. Regrettable as it
   may be that a "world concept" of the Southern Negro should
   be based upon the "childlike simplicity" and dialect of
   Uncle Remus, Harris's lovable creation will continue to
   carry his message for years to come. For better or worse,
   Harris and Bret Harte have survived as "the two most read
   and dramatized of the local-colorist contributors." A
   plot-summary of the tar-baby story is included.

10 SPENCER, BENJAMIN T. The Quest for Nationality: An American
   Literary Campaign. Syracuse, NY: Syracuse University
   Press, pp. 258-59, 261-63, 278, et passim.
   Avoiding sectionalism and nationalism, Harris opted for
   the "politically neutral" world of Brer Rabbit, and portrayed the universal through the local. Part of the local
   realism movement, Harris expounded on the values of provin-
   cialism. "Thus provincial realism, with its tendency to
   ignore the dominant social and political forces of the
   national life in a single leap from the local to the universal," was a product of national concern for stability

after the War. Localism was soon criticized by Walt Whitman and others for not revealing or for misrepresenting the
true national picture. James Lane Allen wanted to "redress
what he regarded as the exploitation and the misrepresenta-
tion of the South in the odd and freakish portrayals which
Cable, Harris, and Craddock had irresponsibly supplied for
urban taste."

11   STEGNER, WALLACE and MARY STEGNER, eds. Great American Short
     Stories. New York: Dell, pp. 17-18, 19-20.
          At times Harris's Georgia mountain stories "approximate
     the leisurely method and the almost legendary intention of
     a Washington Irving." Although not short stories, the
     Uncle Remus tales are superb and "have affected the true
     short story with their wisdom and their humor." These beast
     stories put Harris in a tradition which looks back to La
     Fontaine and Aesop and which looks forward to the Walt Dis-
     ney cartoons and James Thurber's stories of the 1940's and
     1950's. In fact, in Thurber's "The Catbird Seat" Mr. Martin
     parallels Brer Rabbit, while Mrs. Barrows serves for Brer
     Fox.

1958 A BOOKS - NONE

1958 B SHORTER WRITINGS

1   ANON. "The Author of Uncle Remus: Joel Chandler Harris and
     His Tales of Brer Rabbit." London Times (2 July), p. 12.
          Tomorrow marks the fiftieth anniversary of Harris's
     death. He was perhaps the best-loved American of his day.
     His writing for the Atlanta Constitution was compared to
     Harte's and Lamb's, and he sought to exalt the South with-
     out bitterness toward the North. Brer Rabbit was a favorite
     with the slaves because he personified the triumph of the
     underdog. Harris also wrote many other stories.

2   BAIRD, DON. "Joel Chandler Harris, Briar Patch Philosopher."
     Atlantan Magazine, 1 (14 June), 10-12, 58.
          Over 12,000 people visited the Harris Memorial at "The
     Wren's Nest," West End Atlanta, in 1957. Harris's personal
     effects have been left as they were found when he died on
     3 July 1908. His books have been translated into seventeen
     languages.

3   BROWNING, D. C., ed. "Harris," in Everyman's Dictionary of
     Literary Biography: English & American. London: J. M.
     Dent & Sons; New York: E. P. Dutton & Co., p. 304.

1958

Biographical sketch lists the Uncle Remus books and mentions that Harris "also wrote a number of novels of life in
the plantations."

4   CABLE, GEORGE W. The Negro Question: A Selection of Writings
     on Civil Rights in the South. Edited by Arlin Turner.
     Garden City, NY: Doubleday & Co., Doubleday Anchor Books,
     pp. xvii, 40.
          Turner explains in the introduction that Harris gave
     Cable partial support only in his views on the Freedman.
     Such spokesmen for progress as Grady, Harris, and Watterson
     wanted better treatment for the Freedman eventually, but
     they would not compromise on the doctrine of race supremacy.
     In an 1882 address on "Literature in the Southern South"
     Cable concurs with Harris in the need for a national, rather
     than sectional, literature.

5   DABBS, JAMES McBRIDE. The Southern Heritage. New York:
     Alfred A. Knopf, p. 128.
          Alludes to Harris's depiction of the happy Negro: he
     was the "faithful servant and loyal friend, best product of
     the Old South. The picture was overdrawn. But we were
     desperate." After the Civil War only the Negro stayed in
     his place; all else changed. In Reconstruction times the
     South depended on the Negro.

6   DOWNS, ROBERT C. "Apocryphal Biology: A Chapter in American
     Folklore," in The Family Saga and Other Phases of American
     Folklore, by Mody C. Boatright, Robert B. Downs, and John T.
     Flanagan. Urbana: University of Illinois Press, p. 27.
          Man has a tendency to create animals in his own image,
     hence the universality of such animal tales as Remus's
     Brer Rabbit.

7   FLANAGAN, JOHN T. "Folklore in American Literature," in The
     Family Saga and Other Phases of American Folklore, by Mody
     C. Boatright, Robert B. Downs, and John T. Flanagan.
     Urbana: University of Illinois Press, p. 58.
          In the nineteenth century many American newspaper humor-
     ists used the proverb or wisecrack. Cites two examples of
     Harris's plantation sayings in the Remus tales as unfor-
     gettable.

8   GREEN, DAVID BONNELL. "A New Joel Chandler Harris Letter."
     Georgia Historical Quarterly, 42 (March), 106-109.
          A letter of 12 November 1883 to James R. Osgood, the
     Boston publisher, discloses that Harris did not want a note
     explaining the setting of Nights included in the book's

1958

front-matter and indicates Harris's interest in seeing the
book promoted in New York. The headnote briefly recounts
Osgood's biography.

9   HERSKOVITS, MELVILLE J. The Myth of the Negro Past. Boston:
    Beacon Press, p. 75.
    Reprint of 1941.B6.

10 HOLLIS, CHRISTOPHER. "Brer Rabbit and White Rabbit."
    Spectator, 201 (18 July), 82.
        It would not be much of an exaggeration to say that the
    two best-known characters in nineteenth-century fiction were
    Harris's Brer Rabbit and the White Rabbit [of Lewis Car-
    roll]. Harris's animals, unlike earlier talking animals,
    are "real" characters who have sense but who also reveal
    the "ceaseless and pitiless warfare" of the animal kingdom.
    As Uncle Remus points out, Brer Rabbit and the other crea-
    tures do not have pity or morality; some of Brer Rabbit's
    acts are revolting. Uncle Remus's philosophy of acceptance,
    to some, seems a case of the white man's putting his own
    words into the mouth of the black man. But one should re-
    member that Harris was once himself a very poor white man.

11 HUGHES, LANGSTON and ARNA BONTEMPS, eds. "Introduction," in
    their The Book of Negro Folklore. New York: Dodd, Mead,
    pp. vii, viii, ix-x.
        The Uncle Remus stories contributed significantly to the
    popularity of Negro folklore and to the vogue of Brer Rabbit
    as a folk hero, although Harris's were not the first or the
    last collections of Negro lore. "Much of the special appeal
    of his versions may be attributed to the setting in which
    the old Uncle entertains the Young Master," but this setting
    is technically not folkloristic.

12 HYMAN, STANLEY EDGAR. "The Negro Writer in America: An
    Exchange. I. The Folk Tradition." PR, 25 (Spring), 201.
        Hyman's portion of an exchange with Ralph Ellison in the
    same number. The "darky act," the performance of a Negro
    who is an illusionist around whites, is developed most fully
    in Ellison's Invisible Man. But the origins of this figure
    lie in Negro folklore; in one form he is Brer Rabbit, and
    in another, John, the seemingly ignorant and servile slave.

13 LEVIN, HARRY. The Power of Blackness. New York: Random
    House, p. 15.   ·
        Levin mentions Harris's writings as a variation of Emer-
    son's metaphysics in Nature, that natural facts and appear-
    ances are symbols of spiritual facts and that traits in

1958

humans are at times compared to those in animals. "Animals,
of course, may be treated anthropomorphically; Brer Rabbit
would be endowed with all the patient sagacity of Uncle
Remus."

14 LYNN, KENNETH S., ed. The Comic Tradition in America.
Garden City, NY: Doubleday & Co., Doubleday Anchor Books,
pp. 319-21.
   Though the Constitution advocated the New South, Harris
was disturbed by the "blatant materialism of the age."
Contrasts Harris's manner and philosophy with Grady's.
Harris wanted to preserve the sense of mystery in life that
machines and the emphasis on facts had crushed. This mystery draws the child and Negro together: both Remus and
the boy are "alienated from the prosaic world of white
adults." In his "nighttime" personality, Harris himself is
a child: "What the child in Harris wished to believe was
that the bears and wolves of the adult world, the ruthless
competitors so frighteningly praised by Henry Grady, could
somehow be outsmarted." Anthologizes "Uncle Remus Initiates
the Little Boy" and "Uncle Remus's Wonder Story."

15 ____. "Introduction," in The Octopus: A Story of California,
by Frank Norris. Boston: Houghton Mifflin, Riverside
Press, p. ix.
   After the Civil War there was an astounding proliferation
of books about children, perhaps to evade the psychological
penalties the writer faced in the Gilded Age. Twain and
Harris sought for Wordsworthian freshness in children,
which the adults had lost. Reprinted: 1973.B10.

16 MAGILL, FRANK N. and DAYTON KOHLER. "Harris," in Cyclopedia
of World Authors. New York: Harper and Brothers,
pp. 481-82.
   Primary and secondary bibliographical checklists accom-
pany biographical and critical sketch. Harris was the first
to create lasting local color tales out of Negro and dialect
stories in the South. Harris and Uncle Remus were similar
in temperament. Harris's syntax, story frames, and philosophy make his Uncle Remus tales delightful reading.

17 STEGNER, WALLACE, ed. "Introduction," in his Selected
American Prose 1841-1900: The Realistic Movement.
New York: Holt, Rinehart and Winston, p. xi.
   The Negro came to local color literature under the "best
of guides": Harris and Twain. Harris's stories are endur-
ing. Anthologizes "The Tar-Baby" and "Mr. Fox Goes
A-Hunting."

1959

18 TURNER, ARLIN. "Realism and Fantasy in Southern Humor."
    GaR, 12 (Winter), 451.
        Harris was probably thinking back to "Yankee Doodle" of
    colonial days, or to bumpkin characters in American news-
    papers and history, when he once observed that the American
    characteristically views both work and events with a sense
    of humor. In his Constitution editorials he more than once
    declared that the Old South had produced no real literature,
    so Harris would probably not have cited authors of the Old
    South to support his statement. Yet in fact in the Old
    Southwest, in the works of Longstreet, Thorpe, Baldwin,
    G. W. Harris, and W. T. Thompson, American humor had its
    beginnings.

1959 A BOOKS

1 TAYLOR, CELIA BLACKMON. "Cherokee and Creek Folklore Elements
   in the Uncle Remus Stories: A Comparison of the Tales by
   Joel Chandler Harris and Legends of the Southeast."
   Master's Thesis, Alabama Polytechnic Institute [Auburn
   University], vii, 84pp.
        Analyzes parallels in plot, narrative framework, lan-
   guage, characterization, and motif between Harris's tales
   and the Cherokee and Creek folklore collections of J. R.
   Mooney and W. O. Tuggle. Evaluates evidence that Southern
   Negroes borrowed folklore from Indians in the region, as
   Mooney and Tuggle contended, but also, as Harris believed,
   that the Indian borrowed materials from the Negro. Thirty-
   three of Harris's stories are found in similar form among
   Indian legends. [See Dundes, 1965.B4, for commentary on
   this thesis.]

1959 B SHORTER WRITINGS

1 BLANCK, JACOB. Bibliography of American Literature. Vol. 3.
   New Haven: Yale University Press; London: Oxford
   University Press, pp. 387-401.
        Cites and describes all known books, contributions to
   books, and reprints, and gives dates of deposit. [For
   addendum, see 1967.B1.]

2 CARTER, HODDING. The Angry Scar: The Story of Reconstruction.
   Mainstream of America Series. Edited by Lewis Gannett.
   Garden City, NY: Doubleday & Co., pp. 391, 393.
        Few Southerners, besides Cable, Harris, and Lanier, called
   for a realistic national viewpoint, although Harris endeared

1959

himself with his loving Negro tales. Praises Grady and
Harris in a list of the few outstanding Southern journalists
of the period.

3 [CLEMENS, SAMUEL LANGHORNE]. The Autobiography of Mark Twain:
Including Chapters Now Published For the First Time.
Edited by Charles Neider. New York: Harper & Brothers,
pp. 14, 47, 360.
    Twain reminisces about hearing the "immortal tales which
Uncle Remus Harris was to...charm the world with" as a child
in Uncle Dan's kitchen; he especially liked the "creepy joy"
of the "Golden Arm" story. Harris visited Twain's home in
Hartford and impressed his girls--who knew the tales by
heart--by saying he was a "whitewashed" Remus so he could
go in the front door. "He was the bashfulest grown person
I have ever met. When there were people about he stayed
silent and seemed to suffer until they were gone. But he
was lovely nevertheless, for the sweetness and benignity of
the immortal Remus looked out from his eyes and the graces
and sincerities of his character shone in his face." Harris's death was a "heavy loss."

4 DONALD, DAVID. "Introduction," in A Rebel's Recollections,
by George Cary Eggleston. Civil War Centennial Series.
Bloomington: Indiana University Press, p. 16.
    In his introduction Donald classifies Harris as a roman-
ticizer of the Civil War. He, Page, George Washington Harris, and Eggleston minimized the horrors of war and "forgot
the darker aspects of ante-bellum Southern life."

5 DORSON, RICHARD M. American Folklore. Chicago: University
of Chicago Press, pp. 174, 175-76, et passim.
    With the publication of Slave Songs of the United States
in 1867 and Harris's Uncle Remus in 1880, Negro folklore
found a "conspicuous place" in American music, popular entertainment, and scholarly studies. Harris had no prior
knowledge of folklore but transformed the folk materials he
stumbled across into artistic fiction. Influenced by Harris, C. C. Jones and Mrs. A. M. H. Christensen gathered
other Negro tales [see 1888.B18 and 1892.B20]. The "benign,
autocratic figure of Uncle Remus" spinning fables to the
little white boy and "dodging his troublesome questions with
a pontifical authority" won over the reader as effectively
as the tales themselves.

6 HOWELLS, W.[ILLIAM] D.[EAN]. Criticism and Fiction and Other
Essays. Edited by Clara Marburg Kirk and Rudolf Kirk.
New York: New York University Press, pp. 324-25.
Reprint of 1901.B15.

1959

7   JONES, LAURENCE C. "The Negro," in <u>This Is the South</u>.
     Edited by Robert West Howard. Chicago, New York, San
     Francisco: Rand McNally & Co., p. 62.
          Negro music and folktales make up a substantial portion
     of the native American art forms. The tales provided an
     emotional exhaust through laughter, ridicule, and mockery;
     Harris's Remus stories are among the best.

8   LYNN, KENNETH S. <u>Mark Twain and Southwestern Humor</u>. Boston:
     Little, Brown, pp. 111, 184-85, 189, 240, 241-42.
          Uncle Tom represents a Black Christ figure, a stereotype
     to be seen in Uncle Remus. In going back to childhood,
     post-Civil War Americans sought to recapture the Words-
     worthian freshness of experience, a return to nature in an
     increasingly industrial society. Though Harris stood for
     the New South, he lamented the loss of childlike imagina-
     tion. Twain also shared Harris's misgivings about a narrow,
     sterile business civilization. Recounts Twain's praise of
     Harris, particularly the frame of the little boy and slave.
     Both Twain's and Harris's boy-heroes looked to the black
     for refuge and for a quality missing in their white lives.
     A mythical figure, this Negro was "passionate, loyal, im-
     mensely dignified--A Black Christ...but with a very human
     sense of humor."

9   OREN, ARNOLD. "Laughter Is to Live," in <u>This Is the South</u>.
     Edited by Robert West Howard. Chicago, New York, San
     Francisco: Rand McNally & Co., p. 178.
          The Remus tales hold adventure laced with humor. Humor
     is the "meat" of life and literature, and no "Southern
     darky" can tell a story without it.

10   SPILLER, ROBERT E., et al. <u>Literary History of the United</u>
     <u>States: Bibliography Supplement I</u>. New York: Macmillan,
     pp. 132-33.
          Lists edited texts and correspondence and seven books
     and articles on Harris. [Supplement to 1949.B12; <u>see also</u>
     1972.B12.]

11   WELDON, FRED O., JR. "Negro Folktale Heroes," in <u>And Horns on</u>
     <u>the Toads</u>. Edited by Mody C. Boatright et al. Dallas, TX:
     Southern Methodist University Press, pp. 172, 176, 178, 179.
          No specific reference to Harris but discusses trickster-
     heroes in Negro folktales, particularly the Rabbit and John
     cycles, and mentions the tar-baby story as representing the
     Negro's disguising of his desires to do violence to white
     masters.

1960

1960 A BOOKS - NONE

1960 B SHORTER WRITINGS

1 BASLER, ROY P. [director]; DONALD H. MUGRIDGE; and BLANCHE P.
   McCRUM. A Guide to the Study of the United States of
   America: Representative Books Reflecting the Development
   of American Life and Thought. Washington: U. S. Library
   of Congress, General Reference and Bibliography Division,
   Reference Department, pp. 80-81.
      Uncle Remus revealed the vitality of Southern literature
   even after the War, and the Remus volumes reflect a modern
   treatment of animal mythology, a gentle humor, and popular
   philosophy. Harris's local color writing shows an authentic
   and democratic strain. Checklists representative Harris
   works and collections and two critical studies.

2 DURHAM, PHILIP and TAUNO F. MUSTANOJA. American Fiction in
   Finland: An Essay and Bibliography. Mémoires de la
   Société Néophilologique de Helsinki, No. 24. Helsinki:
   Société Néophilologique, pp. 68, 103, 105, 146, 180.
      The Uncle Remus tales are better known in Finland than
   Uncle Tom's Cabin. In 1911 Anni Swan translated a small
   collection of Remus stories, Tales of Uncle Remus, which
   has now gone through sixteen large editions. These tales
   were the only genuine American contribution to juvenile
   folklore popular in Finland.

3 FIDELL, ESTELLE A. and ESTHER V. FLORY, eds. Short Story
   Index: Supplement 1955-1958. An Index to 6,392 Stories
   in 376 Collections. New York: H. W. Wilson Co., p. 124.
      Lists one Harris story in one anthology. [Supplement
   to 1956.B7.]

4 HARTE, BRET. "The Rise of the Short Story," in American
   Literary Essays. Edited by Lewis Leary. New York:
   Thomas Y. Crowell, p. 244.
      Reprint of 1899.B22.

5 HUBBELL, JAY B. Southern Life in Fiction. Athens, GA:
   University of Georgia Press, pp. 29, 70, 82, 83-85, 86-90,
   et passim.
      Middle Georgia produced most of what is memorable in
   Georgian literature, although this region owed a lot to
   settlers from the Carolinas and Virginia. "Perhaps the
   circumstances attending Harris's birth and boyhood helped
   to give him a deeper insight into the minds of the poorer
   whites and the Negro field hands than Thomas Nelson Page or

1960

James Lane Allen ever acquired," but Harris was too shy to
send his writings to Northern publishers so they had to
seek him out. Nights and Page's In Ole Virginia were tre-
mendously popular in the North in the 1880's and 1890's.
Harris wrote "fine tales and episodes," and Uncle Remus and
Billy Sanders are his best characters. His descriptions of
rural Georgians are "vivid and accurate," but his stories
of poor whites are often poorly constructed and too senti-
mentalized.

6   JONES, JOSEPH, et al., eds. American Literary Manuscripts:
    A Checklist of Holdings in Academic, Historical and Public
    Libraries in the United States. Austin: University of
    Texas Press, p. 160.
        Lists thirty-three libraries that have Harris manuscript
    holdings.

7   MOTT, FRANK LUTHER. Golden Multitudes: The Story of the Best
    Sellers in the United States. New York: R. R. Bowker,
    pp. 162-63, 310.
        Reprint of 1947.B12.

8   SIMPSON, CLAUDE M., ed. The Local Colorists: American Short
    Stories, 1857-1900. New York: Harper and Brothers, pp. 10,
    19, 227-28.
        Anthologizes "Free Joe" and "Aunt Fountain's Prisoner"
    to illustrate the considerable body of Harris's writing
    that did not treat Uncle Remus's folktales and the "somewhat
    idealized features of plantation life." In Mingo, Free Joe,
    Balaam, and Home Folks Harris focused on slavery, the Civil
    War, and Reconstruction. Rather than stereotyping, he in-
    dividualized his portraits of poor whites, small farmers
    and the yeoman class. "Aunt Fountain's Prisoner" is the
    final story in a series of tales about "pride and prejudice"
    and features a "symbolic union" of Southerner and Northerner.
    "If his fiction tends to sprawl because of his interest in
    detail, his leisureliness reflects the fashion of a period."

9   TURNER, ARLIN, ed. "Introduction," in his Southern Stories.
    New York: Rinehart & Co., pp. xii-xiii, xviii, xix, xx,
    xxi.
        Along with Cable and Page, Harris helped to make the
    Negro a "full-scale character" in literature. Harris's
    humor, his natural dialect, and his ability to display uni-
    versal human elements in the animals and the old plantation
    Negro led to world-wide recognition. Although Harris
    "caught with undoubted accuracy such externals as the lan-
    guage of the unsophisticated rural Negro and his way of

1960

dealing with his white folks," he nevertheless could portray "the essential character of the Negro only as the white
man thought him to be." "Mr. Terrapin Shows His Strength"
and "Old Mr. Rabbit, He's a Good Fisherman" are anthologized, and Harris's major works are listed in "A Southern
Chronology" of history and literature from 1565-1959.

10   UNTERMEYER, LOUIS, ed. The Britannica Library of Great
     American Writing. Vol. 1. Chicago: Britannica Press,
     pp. 859-60.
         Provides a brief biographical sketch. The Remus tales
     were as naive as they were endless, and the childlike
     stories had universal appeal. Harris was a folklorist, not
     a social historian, and he captured nuances of dialect and
     humor. Anthologizes "The Tar-Baby" and "How Mr. Rabbit Was
     Too Sharp for Mr. Fox."

1961 A BOOKS - NONE

1961 B SHORTER WRITINGS

1   ÅHNEBRINK, LARS. The Beginnings of Naturalism in American
    Fiction. A Study of the Works of Hamlin Garland, Stephen
    Crane, and Frank Norris with Special Reference to Some
    European Influences: 1891-1903. Essays and Studies on
    American Language and Literature, No. 9. Edited by S. B.
    Liljegren with O. S. Arngart, Frank Behre, and Eilert
    Ekwall (The American Institute in the University of Upsala).
    New York: Russell & Russell, p. 447.
        Prints extracts from a Hamlin Garland manuscript of a
    lecture on "The Modern Novel in Germany and America." Gar-
    land praises local color writers, including Harris's depic-
    tion of the Negro quarters: "These men are soaked in the
    aroma of their surroundings for it produced them!!!" Harris
    has "great value."

2   EATON, CLEMENT. The Growth of Southern Civilization: 1790-
    1860. New York and Evanston: Harper & Row, p. 94.
        Comments on the plight of the free Negroes. "Free Joe"
    indicates that the free Negro was not as happy as the slave.

3   FISHWICK, MARSHALL. "Uncle Remus vs. John Henry: Folk
    Tension." WF, 20 (April), 77-85.
        Harris, whose illegitimacy may have contributed to his
    compassion for the underdog, created in Uncle Remus a moral-
    ist counseling his people through parables to accept life
    rather than revolt. Like Faulkner's Dilsey, Uncle Remus

1961

endures. However, John Henry, who may have come into Negro folklore in West Virginia during the construction of the Big Bend Tunnel in the 1870's, defied rather than demurred. Booker T. Washington's message of submission and patience echoes Uncle Remus's, while W. E. B. DuBois's advocacy of social, educational, and civil advancement suggests the John Henry legend. The rabbit-figure may have been borrowed from the Cherokees, who intermarried with the Negroes.

4   GROSS, THEODORE L. "The Negro in the Literature of Reconstruction." Phylon, 22 (First Quarter), 5-14 passim. Reconstruction authors like Harris, Page, Woolson, and J. W. DeForest offered superficial and stereotyped descriptions of the postbellum period, "for they were obviously propagandists, legislating for peace." Typically, the carpetbagger is the villain and the Ku Klux Klan a defense against "'pothouse politicians.'" The Southern gentleman in Tolliver respects Negroes who do not come under the carpetbagger's control. Harris did share the "fears and laughter and anger" of the Negro and contributed "the most popular Negro characters to American fiction--Uncle Remus, Balaam, Ananias, and Mingo." But in Tolliver he depicted as misguided children the Negroes who supported the Union League, and for him Reconstruction was a tragedy. [Simultaneous printing: 1961.B5.]

5   _____. "The South in the Literature of Reconstruction." MissQ, 14 (Spring), 68-77 passim. See 1961.B4.

6   HART, JAMES D.[AVID]. The Popular Book: A History of America's Literary Taste. Berkeley and Los Angeles: University of California Press, p. 202. Harris's Uncle Remus volumes, and F. Hopkinson Smith's novelette, Colonel Carter of Cartersville (1891), "though not orthodox romances, helped set the tone for later fiction, and their leading characters became prototypes for a new conception of slave and master to replace Uncle Tom and Simon Legree."

7   HATFIELD, DOROTHY BLACKMON and EUGENE CURRENT-GARCIA. "William Orrie Tuggle and the Creek Indian Folk Tales." SFQ, 25 (December), 238, 242, 245, 249. Tuggle's collection of Creek Indian folktales and other material was admired by Harris, who predicted in 1883 that it would be published by the Smithsonian Institution; Tuggle died in 1885, leaving his collection in manuscript form. Harris may have used some of Tuggle's Creek tales in Nights.

1961

8   HAYWOOD, CHARLES. A Bibliography of North American Folklore
    and Folksong. Second Revised Edition. Vol. 1. New York:
    Dover Publications, pp. 255, 432, 436, 437-38, 441, 445,
    524.
        Several of Harris's books and essays are listed, under
    subheadings, in sections titled "Georgia Folklore" and "The
    Negro."

9   HILL, HAMLIN L. "Archy and Uncle Remus: Don Marquis's Debt
    to Joel Chandler Harris." GaR, 15 (Spring), 78-87.
        The Archy and Mehitabel stories used techniques and meth-
    ods of native American humor, especially the humanization of
    animals and the dramatic monologue, that Marquis learned
    from Harris.

10 HOFFMAN, DANIEL G. Form and Fable in American Fiction.
    New York: Oxford University Press, p. 341.
        Uncle Remus remains a minstrel in blackface, and the po-
    etic irony in the Remus books "is one of which Harris was
    probably unaware: the Negro's human dignity survives the
    minstrel mask not in Uncle Remus's character but in the
    satirical stories he tells the white boy." Harris's "con-
    scious literary strategy" was to "palliate Northern antago-
    nism of the South by idealizing ante-bellum plantation
    life," and he did not see the "thinly veiled avowals of the
    Negro's pride and dignity and refusal to submit his spirit
    to the unjust yoke of custom." Twain admired Uncle Remus,
    but he tried, with only partial success, to portray Jim not
    as a minstrel but in his manhood.

11 THORP, WILLARD; CARLOS BAKER; JAMES K. FOLSOM; and MERLE CURTI,
    eds. The American Literary Record. Enlarged edition.
    Chicago, Philadelphia, New York: J. B. Lippincott,
    pp. 665-66.
        Reprint of 1941.B12.

12 THORPE, EARL E. The Mind of the Negro: An Intellectual
    History of Afro-Americans. Baton Rouge, LA: Ortlieb
    Press, pp. xiv, 83-84, 279, 452.
        Harris began the big interest in collecting black folk
    literature. Discusses the revenge motif in black tales,
    citing Wolfe [1949.B15] and Rose [1949.B11] on Harris. The
    blacks could siphon off their hatred through the Remus
    tales. Remus's docility fit well with the Romantic penchant
    of postbellum Southern writers in their idolization of the
    Old South. A "concomitant degrading of the Negro personal-
    ity" is found in such writers as Harris.

13 UTLEY, FRANCIS LEE. "Folk Literature: An Operational
    Definition." JAF, 74 (July-September), 203, 206 n.41.
    Harris, like Rabelais and Boccaccio, was a popularizer
    of folklore, but all three were distinguished artists. Har-
    ris poses a typical problem. "Probably no collection in
    America reflects more genuine American Negro folklore than
    The Complete Tales of Uncle Remus [1955]," although Harris
    probably included tales from American Indian and European
    sources that were similar to the Negro tales he heard. One
    must treat his collection as literary; a type and motif-
    index of American Negro folklores might help solve the prob-
    lem of Harris's sources. Reprinted: 1965.B13.

1962 A BOOKS - NONE

1962 B SHORTER WRITINGS

1   ABRAHAMS, ROGER [D.]. "The Changing Concept of the Negro
    Hero," in The Golden Log. Edited by Mody C. Boatright,
    Wilson M. Hudson, and Allen Maxwell. Dallas: Southern
    Methodist University, pp. 121, et passim.
       Perhaps because of a "real prevalence" of the type in
    Negro lore, or because Harris's stories about tricksters
    may have influenced future collections of the same type,
    the trickster figure "has been the most identified hero in
    Negro lore throughout this country and the West Indies."
    In contemporary lore, the trickster takes the form of the
    "Signifying Monkey," the "colored man," "John," and some-
    times "the preacher." On the sociological level, the
    trickster may be reacting against overdomination.

2   ANTHONY, EDWARD. O Rare Don Marquis. A Biography. Garden
    City, NY: Doubleday and Co., pp. 87, 95-99, 113-14.
       For Marquis, Harris was "the first great man he'd ever
    met," and he gladly accepted Harris's offer of an editorial
    position on Uncle Remus's Magazine. Next to Twain, Marquis
    thought Harris to be America's foremost living humorist and
    an outstanding editorial-writer. Marquis was also impressed
    by Harris's thorough knowledge of natural history. Harris
    had to edit out occasional Marquis ribaldry in his writings
    for Uncle Remus's Magazine.

3   DORNBUSCH, CLYDE H. "Joel Chandler Harris Visits the White
    House." Georgia Historical Quarterly, 46 (March), 41-43.
       Records the warm relationship between Harris and Theodore
    Roosevelt and his family. Roosevelt had admired Harris be-
    fore they met in 1902, and Harris had sent young Ethel

1962

Roosevelt an autographed copy of Uncle Remus in 1901, and
Kermit a copy of Daddy Jake in 1902. Harris had a genial
visit with the Roosevelts at the White House in the summer
or fall of 1902, and Roosevelt later endorsed Uncle Remus's
Magazine.

4   HALL, WADE H. Reflections of the Civil War in Southern Humor.
    University of Florida Monographs: Humanities No. 10.
    Gainesville, FL: University of Florida Press, pp. 2, 17-18,
    65-67, 70, 78.
        Harris was "the great humorist-conciliator of the post-
    war period," but he could not always remain objective about
    the Civil War. His youthful unfinished play written during
    the War, "Butler the Beast," was a piece of propaganda di-
    rected against the Union general Ben Butler. Harris's later
    Civil War stories, Union Scout, Home Folks, and Shadow,
    "were written to show both North and South that the adver-
    saries had been people who were kind and honorable and had
    fought for what they thought was right." The marriage of
    a Northern soldier and a Southern woman rounds out "A Story
    of the War," and Plantation and "At Teague Poteet's" sym-
    pathetically portray deserters from the Confederate army.
    [See also 1965.B7.]

5   HARWELL, RICHARD B. "Gone with Miss Ravenel's Courage: or
    Bugles Blow So Red: A Note on the Civil War Novel." NEQ,
    35 (June), 257.
        Harris's Plantation, T. C. DeLeon's John Holden, and
    Page's Meh Lady are Civil War novels of "more than regional
    interest."

6   HERZBERG, MAX J., ed. "Harris," in The Reader's Encyclopaedia
    of American Literature. New York: Thomas Y. Crowell,
    pp. 432-33, 742, 1166-67.
        Biographical sketch emphasizes Harris's artistic render-
    ing of plantation lore in Uncle Remus and Uncle Remus's
    warmth, humor, and shrewdness as a character. "Free Joe"
    and "At Teague Poteet's" were among his best local color
    stories; his novels were less successful. Four critical
    and biographical studies are listed and Uncle Remus and
    Mingo summarized.

7   HUFF, LAWRENCE. "The Literary Publications of Joseph Addison
    Turner." Georgia Historical Quarterly, 46 (September),
    223, 231, 234.
        Harris, mentioned in passing, served as an apprentice
    printer under Turner. Also, Turner "taught a sound theory
    of literature which bore fruit in the career of his dis-
    ciple," Harris.

1962

8   MOTT, FRANK LUTHER. American Journalism: A History: 1690–
    1960. Third edition. New York: Macmillan, p. 485.
    Recounts Harris's newspaper experiences, his encourage-
    ment of Frank L. Stanton, and the fame of his Remus stories.

9   PARKS, EDD WINFIELD. Ante-Bellum Southern Literary Critics.
    Athens, GA: University of Georgia Press, pp. 258, 344.
    Paul Hamilton Hayne had only praise for Harris and felt
    that his genius, particularly in delineating Negro charac-
    ter, was absolute.

10 SHUMAN, R. BAIRD. "Irwin Russell's Christmas." MissQ, 15
    (Spring), 81, 82.
    Harris saw the potential of the young Mississippi writer
    Irwin Russell and in 1888 compiled a volume of verse titled
    Poems by Irwin Russell. A letter by Russell dated 30 De-
    cember 1877 contains an anecdote about a Negro and a mule
    that suggests Harris's writings.

11 WEBER, BROM, ed. An Anthology of American Humor. New York:
    Thomas Y. Crowell, p. 405.
    Harris's local color writing does not vitiate authentic
    local details with excessive sentimentality or condescen-
    sion. The Remus world is only superficially peaceful; un-
    derneath is a contest for survival. Remus's irony, wisdom,
    and imagination triumph over the happy slave stereotype,
    though Harris himself partially believed in this image.
    Anthologizes "How Mr. Rabbit Succeeded in Raising a Dust"
    and "The Tar-Baby Story."

12 WILSON, EDMUND. Patriotic Gore: Studies in the Literature of
    the American Civil War. New York: Oxford University Press,
    p. 639.
    Quotes Twain's passage in Life on the Mississippi [see
    1883.B8] praising Harris as one of the few Southern writers
    not writing in the obsolete Southern style.

13 WOODRESS, JAMES. Dissertations in American Literature 1891–
    1955: with Supplement 1956–1961. Durham, NC: Duke
    University Press, p. 21.
    Lists four dissertations.

1963

1963 A BOOKS - NONE

1963 B SHORTER WRITINGS

1   ABEL, DARREL. Masterworks of American Realism: Twain,
    Howells, James. Vol. 3 of American Literature. Woodbury,
    NY: Barron's Educational Series, p. 72.
        Twain criticized most Southern writers for romanticizing
    the past; he commended his friends Harris and George Cable,
    however, for their realism and humor.

2   ANON. "Fact of Museum Becomes Answer to Many Dreams."
    Eatonton Messenger (6 June), p. 1.
        The Uncle Remus Museum was recently built in Eatonton,
    Georgia, to honor Joel Chandler Harris.

3   BARO, GENE, ed. After Appomattox: The Image of the South in
    Its Fiction 1865-1900. New York: Corinth Books, pp. 20,
    148-49.
        After the War the North was ready for a wider view of
    Southern life; Harris was one of the "instruments" revealing
    the Georgia mountain people and the Negro. Tolliver is one
    of the forthright Reconstruction novels on Southern social
    conditions. Provides brief biographical sketch of Harris
    and cites his major works. While the Remus volumes have
    made Harris and his characters household words, Mingo, Free
    Joe, Home Folks, Statesman, Sister Jane, and Tolliver are
    more realistic approaches to Southern life. Anthologizes
    "Free Joe."

4   DANIEL, FRANK. "Treasures for Joel Chandler Harris Collection."
    Atlanta Journal and Constitution Magazine (1 December),
    40-42, 44.
        Among recent valuable items acquired by Emory University
    for the Harris Collection are autographed presentation
    copies of books from Sherwood Anderson, H. L. Mencken, and
    other writers, and hundreds of books, manuscripts, and let-
    ters from the library of his son Julian and daughter-in-law
    Julia Collier Harris. A letter to Ambrose Bierce protests
    that Harris is only a "cornfield 'journalist'"; a Harris
    review for the Constitution terms Bierce's tales the most
    original short stories since Poe. Harris once considered
    turning Uncle Remus into a comic opera and had enlisted Paul
    Tietjens to compose the music.

5   EZELL, JOHN SAMUEL. The South Since 1865. New York:
    Macmillan, pp. 284, 298-99, 304.

1963

Speaks of Harris in connection with the Southern domi-
nance of literature in the late 1880's. The greatest writer
to follow Page, Harris's best work was Uncle Remus; a more
authentic and accurate reproduction of the pre-Civil War and
post-Civil War South has never been achieved. Grady and
Harris made the Constitution one of the most liberal papers
in the South. With Harris's death the Uncle Remus Magazine
lost its primary appeal; a purely Southern magazine could
not survive after the 1880's.

6   FALK, ROBERT. "The Search for Reality: Writers and Their
     Literature," in The Gilded Age: A Reappraisal. Edited by
     H. Wayne Morgan. Syracuse, NY: Syracuse University Press,
     pp. 197, 202, 209.
         Harris was an artful practitioner of regional fiction
     whose Uncle Remus tales became a force for reconciliation
     and compromise in the 1870's and 1880's. Reprinted:
     1970.B5.

7   GROSS, THEODORE L. Albion W. Tourgée. New York: Twayne
     Publishers, pp. 88–90, 121, et passim.
         Harris painted the carpetbagger Hotchkiss, in Tolliver,
     as fanatical, self-centered, and unscrupulous, not truly
     interested in improving the Negroes' conditions. Southern
     writers were condescending towards the blacks. Even though
     Harris shared "the fears and laughter and anger of the Ne-
     gro" and created some of the most popular fictional charac-
     ters--Remus, Balaam, Ananias, and Mingo--in Tolliver he
     opposed immediate reconstruction and the manipulation of
     the average Negro by black and white leaders. Harris con-
     tributed to the magazine, Our Continent, edited by Tourgée,
     but criticized his fanaticism. Because he could not see
     the South in realistic terms and because of his attraction
     to eighteenth and nineteenth century English authors, Har-
     ris rejected James, Howells, and Emerson in favor of Scott
     and Cooper. Page, Harris, and Thomas Dixon used their
     youthful recollections and unreliable journalistic accounts
     in their treatment of Radical Republicanism; they thus per-
     petuated a bias.

8   HOROWITZ, FLOYD R. "Ralph Ellison's Modern Version of Brer
     Bear and Brer Rabbit in Invisible Man." Midcontinent
     American Studies Journal, 4 (Fall), 21–27 passim.
         A pattern of images in Ellison's Invisible Man is based
     upon the folklore of Brer Bear and Brer Rabbit. Ellison's
     "rich language play" at times seems to equate the two ani-
     mals, but "we know from Uncle Remus" that the two creatures
     are "naturally irreconcilable" and must eventually demon-
     strate it. The narrator of the novel, often portrayed as

255

1963

a bear in a state of hibernation, encounters a series of
wily Brer Rabbit blacks who show him the keys to power in
a white world.

9   HUFF, LAWRENCE. "Joseph Addison Turner: Southern Editor
During the Civil War." Journal of Southern History, 29
(August), 469, 472, 477, 478.
Harris contributed thirty-three signed book reviews, es-
says, and poems to Turner's newspaper, The Countryman, and
received instruction and criticism from Turner.

10   McGARRY, DANIEL D. and SARAH HARRIMAN WHITE, eds. Historical
Fiction Guide: Annotated Chronological, Geographical and
Topical List of Five Thousand Selected Historical Novels.
New York: Scarecrow Press, p. 405.
One-sentence summary of Union Scout is given under the
heading "Civil War Period (1861-1865)." [Entry reprinted
in 1973.B11.]

11   McGILL, RALPH. The South and the Southerner. An Atlantic
Monthly Press Book. Boston: Little, Brown, p. 214.
Eatonton was almost a storybook Old South center when
cotton was king. Settled by large plantation owners, it
became a small, self-contained seat of antebellum culture.
Harris drew Remus as a composite from ex-slaves he knew
there.

12   SIMKINS, FRANCIS BUTLER. The Everlasting South. [Baton
Rouge]: Louisiana State University Press, p. 14.
One should not be ashamed of illiteracy: the unschooled
Remus was among the wisest of Southerners.

13   _____. A History of the South. Third edition. New York:
Alfred A. Knopf, pp. 428, 432-33.
Substantively equivalent to 1947.B15 and 1953.B12.

14   SMITH, HERBERT F. "Joel Chandler Harris's Contributions to
Scribner's Monthly and Century Magazine." Georgia
Historical Quarterly, 47 (June), 169-79.
Scribner's Monthly, which became Century Magazine in
1881, was the first nationally circulated magazine to soli-
cit contributions from Harris. Editors Richard Watson
Gilder and Robert Underwood Johnson published several of
Harris's plantation poems and stories, as well as "At
Teague Poteet's," "Free Joe," "Trouble on Lost Mountain,"
"Little Compton," and "Azalia." Gilder and Johnson sought
to boost Harris's confidence, publishing stories that their
author was ashamed of, and encouraged Harris to make needed
stylistic and structural revisions.

1964

1964 A BOOKS

1   WEDDLE, ETHEL H.   Joel Chandler Harris: Young Storyteller.
    Indianapolis, IN: Bobbs-Merrill, 200pp.
    Fictionalized biography for young people improvises free-
    ly around the major events in Harris's life, giving primary
    emphasis to Harris's youth in Eatonton and on Turnwold Plan-
    tation.   Displays his characteristic shyness and modesty in
    dramatized incidents.

1964 B SHORTER WRITINGS

1   ABRAHAMS, ROGER D.   Deep Down in the Jungle ... Negro Narrative
    Folklore from the Streets of Philadelphia.   Hatboro, PA:
    Folklore Associates, pp. 66, 73-77, 222.
    Harris's gathering of Negro trickster tales may have
    helped bring such stories into prevalence with other collec-
    tors.   In Philadelphia street lore the rabbit becomes the
    "hard man" of agility, masculinity, and "style."   Revised
    edition: 1970.B1.

2   ALEXANDER, HARTLEY BURR.   North American [Mythology], Vol. 10
    in The Mythology of All Races.   Edited by Louis Herbert
    Gray.   New York: Cooper Square Publishers, pp. 67, 121,
    297 n.47.
    Reprint of 1916.B1.

3   BLAIR, WALTER; THEODORE HORNBERGER; and RANDALL STEWART.
    American Literature: A Brief History.   Chicago, et al.:
    Scott, Foresman, pp. 151-52, 175, 180, 293.
    The local color writers sought to dispel sectional and
    social differences after the War.   "More effectively than
    any other single writer, Joel Chandler Harris reassured the
    world of the essential kindliness which existed between mas-
    ter and slave in the ante bellum plantation and implied that
    not even emancipation and reconstruction could destroy the
    friendly relations of the two races."   The "infectious
    laughter" of Uncle Remus and Harris's kindliness worked to
    relieve North-South ill will.   Harris helped to make the
    Atlanta Constitution "the most influential newspaper ever
    published in the South."

4   BLOTNER, JOSEPH.   William Faulkner's Library--A Catalogue.
    Charlottesville, VA: University Press of Virginia, pp. 35,
    50.
    Sister Jane and the edition of Irwin Russell's poems in-
    troduced by Harris were among Faulkner's books.

1964

5   BOGER, LORISE C., ed. <u>The Southern Mountaineer in Literature:</u>
    <u>An Annotated Bibliography.</u> Morgantown, W. VA: West
    Virginia University Press, pp. 37–38.
        Harris's four stories about mountaineers, "At Teague
    Poteet's," "The Cause of the Difficulty," "A Conscript's
    Christmas," and "Trouble on Lost Mountain," are briefly
    summarized.

6   COHEN, HENNIG and WILLIAM B. DILLINGHAM, eds. "Introduction,"
    in their <u>Humor of the Old Southwest.</u> Boston: Houghton
    Mifflin, pp. xiv–xv.
        In contrast to the bawdy Southwestern humorists, Harte,
    Harris, Page, and other local colorists would not have of-
    fended the taste of young women in nineteenth century
    seminaries.

7   CURRENT-GARCÍA, EUGENE and WALTON R. PATRICK, eds. <u>American</u>
    <u>Short Stories: 1820 to the Present.</u> Revised edition.
    Chicago, et al.: Scott, Foresman, pp. xxviii, 245–46.
        Reprints comments in 1952.B3.

8   CURTI, MERLE. <u>The Growth of American Thought.</u> Third edition.
    New York and Evanston: Harper & Row, pp. 419–20, 422, 475.
        Revision of 1951.B3. The Negro's lore reflected his
    African cultural heritage and views on "many matters," but
    these myths did not become generally accessible until Harris
    recorded the dialect lore in post-bellum days. Negro folk-
    lore was recorded largely through whites. Southern local
    color writers, including Page and Harris, believed in white
    supremacy; Cable was the exception.

9   DABBS, JAMES McBRIDE. <u>Who Speaks for the South?</u> New York:
    Funk & Wagnalls Co., pp. 269–70.
        The South tried to put the Negro in his place, partially
    with the myth of the loyal, happy Negro servant. Page and
    Harris claim that "the Negro in his place is where he longs
    to be; that he is happy to be the Atlas of the South."

10 EATON, CLEMENT. <u>The Mind of the Old South.</u> Kingsport, TN:
    Kingsport Press, Louisiana State University Press, p. 105.
        The Negro "darky" did not assume a prominent place in
    Southern humor until the time of J. C. Harris. The aristo-
    cratic Old South humorists had enough detachment to see the
    ludicrous side of the poor white, but they regarded the
    black as property and, unlike the cracker, as a congruous
    part of the plantation regime.

1964

11 ENGLAND, KENNETH. "Sidney Lanier in C Major," in <u>Reality and</u>
    <u>Myth: Essays in American Literature in Memory of Richmond</u>
    <u>Croom Beatty</u>. Edited by William E. Walker and Robert L.
    Welker. Nashville, TN: Vanderbilt University Press, p. 61.
        Lanier and Harris sympathized primarily with the old
    ways, although with a tone of amelioration towards the
    North. Harris was disillusioned with the New South and
    nostalgic for the Old at the turn of the century.

12 GREEN, CLAUD B. "The Rise and Fall of Local Color in Southern
    Literature." <u>MissQ</u>, 18 (Winter), 1, 2, 4, 6.
        In no area of the country did local color writing flour-
    ish more vigorously than it did in the South. The term
    local color, however, implies a secondary order of merit;
    it should be an historical rather than a critical term,
    which is not to say that Cable, Harris, and Page would be
    better writers if we labeled them some other way.

13 LOGGINS, VERNON. <u>The Negro Author: His Development in</u>
    <u>America</u>. Port Washington, NY: Kennikat Press, pp. 255,
    309-11, 312, 314-15, 349, 360.
        Reprint of 1931.B11.

14 NORRIS, FRANK. "New York as a Literary Center," in <u>The</u>
    <u>Literary Criticism of Frank Norris</u>. Edited by Donald Pizer.
    Austin, TX: University of Texas Press, p. 38.
        Reprint of 1903.B12.

15 QUARLES, BENJAMIN. <u>The Negro in the Making of America</u>.
    New York and London: Collier-Macmillan, p. 200.
        The authors of the Negro renaissance agreed that dialect-
    writing was taboo, even though well-known whites like Harris
    and Page had given the dialect school respectability. These
    dialect writers, while masterfully blending humor with pa-
    thos, "generally put a comic mask on the Negro" and created
    caricatures. Dunbar was the best-known Negro practitioner
    of the dialect school.

16 RUBIN, LOUIS D., JR. "The Literature of a Changing South," in
    <u>The Deep South in Transformation: A Symposium</u>. Edited by
    Robert B. Highsaw. University, AL: University of Alabama
    Press, pp. 152, 156, 166.
        The Negro is a symbol for the changing South; a study of
    the Southern literary image of the Negro, from Uncle Remus
    to Joe Christmas, would produce a moral history of the
    region.

1964

17 STEPHENSON, WENDELL HOLMES. Southern History in the Making:
    Pioneer Historians of the South. [Baton Rouge, LA]:
    Louisiana State University Press, p. 90.
        William P. Trent enthusiastically praised Harris and
    Lanier but wondered if they were unique or typical of a new
    literary awakening; most Southern writers were too sensitive
    to criticism to provide enduring literature.

18 TANDY, JENNETTE. Crackerbox Philosophers in American Humor
    and Satire. Port Washington, NY: Kennikat Press, pp. 69,
    95.
        In Free Joe and Mingo Harris "invested with sentiment and
    pathos" the lives of the poor whites. In the Remus tales he
    used the convention of the framework that introduces the
    narrator; G. W. Harris, T. B. Thorpe, and other predecessors
    had employed it, too.

19 THORP, WILLARD. American Humorists. University of Minnesota
    Pamphlets on American Writers, No. 42. Minneapolis:
    University of Minnesota Press, pp. 24–25.
        Remus combines the usual Uncle Tom image with the Negro's
    desire to triumph. In Harris are two "partially concealed
    strains": doubts about New South industrialization (prog-
    ress), and the Negro's ability to deceive or escape punish-
    ment. Most readers missed these themes and saw a sentimen-
    tal picture of plantation life; the "modern" Negro dislikes
    them for this reason, and the Remus stories may not survive.

20 WARD, MARTHA E. and DOROTHY A. MARQUARDT, eds. Authors of
    Books for Young People. New York and London: Scarecrow
    Press, p. 99.
        Ten-line biographical sketch and checklist of works.

21 WERNER, ALICE. African [Mythology], Vol. 7 in The Mythology
    of All Races. Edited by John Arnott MacCulloch. New York:
    Cooper Square Publishers, pp. 283–84, 292, 307.
        Reprint of 1925.B10.

22 YATES, NORRIS W. The American Humorist: Conscience of the
    Twentieth Century. Ames, IA: Iowa State University Press,
    pp. 23, 197, 209.
        Refers to the crackerbox philosopher: the wise fool is
    an effective disguise when he is a member of the minority
    group as is Uncle Remus. Harris is "one of the great crack-
    erbox humorists." Harris's philosophy influenced Don
    Marquis.

1965

1965 A BOOKS – NONE

1965 B SHORTER WRITINGS

1 CANBY, HENRY SEIDEL. <u>Turn West, Turn East: Mark Twain and Henry James</u>. New York: Biblo and Tannen, pp. 7, 225. Reprint of 1951.B1.

2 CHURCH, MARY L. <u>Living in Georgia</u>. Ann Arbor, MI: Edwards Brothers, pp. 45–46.
Provides a biographical sketch, emphasizing Harris's Turnwold experiences. Harris loved animals, particularly horses.

3 CUNNINGHAM, HORACE H. "The Southern Mind Since the Civil War," in <u>Writing Southern History: Essays in Historiography in Honor of Fletcher M. Green</u>. Edited by Arthur S. Link and Rembert W. Patrick. [Baton Route, LA.]: Louisiana State University Press, p. 404.
There is no satisfactory biographical study of Harris, although Julia Collier Harris's <u>Life and Letters</u> [<u>see</u> 1918.A1] is an interesting record.

4 DUNDES, ALAN. "African Tales among the North American Indians." <u>SFQ</u>, 29 (September), 207–19 passim.
Reviews the controversy about African versus American Indian origins for Negro folktales, specifically Harris's Uncle Remus tales. Crane [1881.B14], Harris himself, Vance [1888.B22], Ellis [1895.B17], and Gerber [1893.B19] argued for African origins; Mooney [1888.B19], Chamberlain [1891.B16], Alexander [1916.B1], and C. B. Taylor [1959.A1] and others made the case for American Indian influences. The evidence seems to suggest that the Indians borrowed African tales from the Negroes.

5 FIDELL, ESTELLE A. <u>Short Story Index: Supplement 1959–1963. An Index to 9,068 Stories in 582 Collections</u>. New York: H. W. Wilson Co., p. 181.
Lists two stories anthologized in two collections. Supplements 1960.B3.

6 GASTON, PAUL M. "The New South," in <u>Writing Southern History: Essays in Historiography in Honor of Fletcher M. Green</u>. Edited by Arthur S. Link and Rembert W. Patrick. [Baton Rouge, LA.]: Louisiana State University Press, pp. 327, 333 n.
The Agrarians wrote no historical studies of the political "Redeemers" of the post-Reconstruction period, except

261

1965

for occasional essays such as those by John Donald Wade on
Grady (1938) and on Harris [see 1932.B19]. Harris deserves
a new biographical study.

7   HALL, WADE. The Smiling Phoenix: Southern Humor from 1865 to
    1914. Gainesville, FL: University of Florida Press,
    pp. 77-78, 113-14, 116-17, 128-29, 157-58, 212-15, 221-24,
    325-26, et passim.
        Uncle Remus "reflects the idealized image of the ante-
    bellum regime"; the aristocratic Remus "gives advice to up-
    start young Negroes who mistake freedom for license."
    Harris's folk tales at times have racial allegorical impli-
    cations: the sly Rabbit is a mask for the Negro and the
    Rabbit's adversaries may symbolize threats from the white
    world. Harris's portrait of the old plantation and slavery
    was not entirely nostalgic and glamorous, as "Free Joe"
    demonstrates, nor did he romanticize the War. "The Comedy
    of War" sketches illustrate the War's absurdity; Union
    Scout and "Aunt Fountain's Prisoner" use marriage between
    Northerners and Southerners as emblems of reconciliation.
    Tolliver is a realistic Reconstruction novel that shows
    Harris's impatience with radicals and carpetbaggers. Billy
    Sanders is critical of the rise of corruption and material-
    ism in the later nineteenth and early twentieth century.
    Bibliography on Southern humor includes works on Harris.
    [See also 1962.B4.]

8   HART, JAMES D. "Harris," in his The Oxford Companion to
    American Literature. Fourth edition. New York: Oxford
    University Press, p. 351.
        Harris's Remus tales "remain the greatest in the school
    of Negro folk literature." The tales are "told with a
    simple humor and authentic dialect that is in perfect har-
    mony with the thing said and the way of saying it." Harris
    also sensitively portrayed Georgia aristocrats, poor whites,
    and ex-slaves in Mingo, Free Joe, Sister Jane, and other
    volumes. Includes biographical sketch.

9   HUBBELL, JAY B. South and Southwest: Literary Essays and
    Reminiscences. Durham, NC: Duke University Press, pp. 53,
    77, 104, et passim.
        Comments on Harris's indebtedness to the humorists of
    the Old South and the fact that in the 1930's few realized
    the influence of the Southern local colorists on twentieth-
    century regionalists. Harris and his contemporaries pro-
    duced a "notable body of poetry and fiction" which attracted
    wide Northern recognition and helped with reconciliation.
    Traces of Dante's and Petrarch's attitude towards women are
    found in Harris's novels and stories.

1966

10 LOGAN, RAYFORD W. <u>The Betrayal of the Negro: from Rutherford
    B. Hayes to Woodrow Wilson.</u> London: Collier-Macmillan,
    pp. 167, 168, 256-57.
       The commentary on Harris is identical to 1954.B10.

11 MENCKEN, H.[ENRY] L.[OUIS]. "The Sahara of the Bozart," in
    <u>The American Scene: A Reader.</u> Edited by Huntingdon Cairns.
    New York: Alfred A. Knopf, p. 160.
       Reprinting of 1920.B6, with Mencken's footnote explaining
    that the reference is to Harris.

12 ST. JOHN, WYLLY FOLK. "Long-Lost Harris Letters To His Uncle
    Remus Artist." Atlanta <u>Journal and Constitution Magazine</u>
    (28 November), pp. 8-10, 20.
       Emory University Library has recently acquired twelve
    unpublished letters from Harris to A. B. Frost, his favorite
    illustrator, and twelve of Frost's pen-and-ink and wash
    drawings. Emory already owns Frost's letters to Harris.
    One Harris expert feels Frost may be the most sympathetic
    and effective delineator of Negro character that America
    has ever had. The letters by both men are warm and enthusi-
    astic, and Harris would later write an introduction to a
    volume of Frost's drawings.

13 UTLEY, FRANCIS LEE. "Folk Literature: An Operational
    Definition," in <u>The Study of Folklore.</u> Edited by Alan
    Dundes. Englewood Cliffs, NJ: Prentice-Hall, pp. 22,
    22n. 43.
       Reprint of 1961.B13.

1966 A BOOKS

1 COUSINS, PAUL MERCER. "Joel Chandler Harris: A Study in the
   Culture of the South, 1848-1908." Ph.D. dissertation,
   Columbia University, 433pp.
      This biography emphasizes the importance of Harris's
   youthful experiences at Turnwold Plantation, under the tute-
   lage of Joseph Addison Turner, in shaping the attitudes and
   writings of the mature man. After a "journalistic odyssey"
   from the plantation to Macon, New Orleans, Forsyth, and
   Savannah, Harris found challenge and fulfillment as a news-
   paperman on the Atlanta <u>Constitution,</u> where his editorials
   and Uncle Remus tales helped to create a new style of
   Southern literature. The Uncle Remus tales were unstudied
   art based on familiar but hitherto neglected folk materials.
   Harris stressed the theme of reconciliation and understanding between North and South in his local color stories and

1966

in Tolliver; his persona Billy Sanders speaks out against
materialism, dishonesty, and political corruption at the
turn of the century. During his lifetime Harris earned an
international reputation as a folklorist and local color
writer, but he remained painfully shy, sensitive, and modest
to the last. Cousins includes material from interviews,
made forty years earlier, with some of Harris's acquaintances. [For published version of this dissertation, see
1968.A2.]

2 HERNDON, JERRY ALLEN. "Social Comment in the Writings of Joel
Chandler Harris." Ph.D. dissertation, Duke University,
233pp.
Harris's social views changed little over the years. He
felt that the South should be left to solve its own problems
and in its own time, and that the Negro should be encouraged
"to improve himself educationally and economically, though
in a segregated condition." Harris was a "progressive conservative" who supported the Negro when other Southerners
did not. Harris's social views are compared to those of
Twain, Cable, Booker T. Washington, Tom Watson, the "agrari-
an rebel," and others. The last part of the study surveys
Harris's fiction, giving particular attention to Stories of
Georgia where Harris's conservatism is controversial by
modern standards.

1966 B SHORTER WRITINGS

1 BRIDGMAN, RICHARD. The Colloquial Style in America.
New York: Oxford University Press, pp. 51, 116.
Accurate dialect writing is too exasperating for a long
work: "An Uncle Remus novel is unthinkable." Criticizes
the Remus tales for forcing the reader into "incessant surface activity." Their "orthography may be an excellent
guide to oral reading, but...[it] makes silent reading
arduous."

2 BROWN, STERLING. "A Century of Negro Portraiture in American
Literature." MR, 7 (Winter), 76-78.
Page and Harris were the most persuasive of the authors
who established the plantation tradition, and they "invested
the Lost Cause with the glamor of the defeated and the departed." Harris showed more harshness in his portraits of
the antebellum South, "but his picture remains one of mutual
affection and kindness." Blue Dave finds another master,
and Free Joe dies free, although "disconsolate, and ineffec-
tual" among the happier slaves. Harris's Uncle Remus

1966

plantation tales are a "rich yield," but the Atlanta Uncle
Remus sounds like a Georgia politician as when he deplores
the education of Negroes.

3   CAMPBELL, F. C. "An Ontological Study of the Dynamics of
    Black Anger in the United States." New South, 21 (Spring),
    30, 32.
        An essay written as a social drama in three acts. The
    Negro hides behind his mask. The white master has night-
    mares about being slain by kindly Uncle Remus; in the sub-
    urbs, behind the riots and street crimes, stands Uncle
    Remus, his kindly old smile dripping with gore.

4   COAN, OTIS W. and RICHARD G. LILLARD, eds. America in Fiction:
    An Annotated List of Novels That Interpret Aspects of Life
    in the United States, Canada, and Mexico. Fifth edition.
    Palo Alto, CA: Pacific Books, pp. 51, 139, 188.
        Identical to 1956.B6.

5   ESTES, DAVID E. "The Joel Chandler Harris Collection." Emory
    Magazine, 42 (January), 6-15.
        The Harris Collection at Emory was started in 1927, at
    the suggestion of a graduate who knew that Harris's son
    Lucien had a trunk of manuscripts in his attic. Over the
    years Thomas H. English, now honorary curator of the Collec-
    tion, has guided the Library's acquisition of materials.
    The Collection is described in some detail.

6   GROSS, SEYMOUR L. "Introduction: Stereotype to Archetype:
    The Negro in American Literary Criticism," in Images of the
    Negro in American Literature. Edited by Seymour L. Gross
    and John Edward Hardy. Chicago: University of Chicago
    Press, p. 11.
        Quotes Nelson, Rollins, and Brawley on Harris and men-
    tions the "'Uncle Remus Syndrome'": critics came from
    praising Harris's accuracy [Moses; see 1910.B8] to condemn-
    ing his misrepresentation [Redding; see 1939.B11].

7   GROSS, THEODORE L. "The Negro in the Literature of the
    Reconstruction," in Images of the Negro in American
    Literature. Edited by Seymour L. Gross and John Edward
    Hardy. Chicago: University of Chicago Press, pp. 71-83
    passim.
        Reprinting of 1961.B4.

8   LEACH, MacEDWARD. "Folklore in American Regional Literature."
    JFI, 3 (December), 388.

265

1966

Harris demonstrated how Negro lore, folk-say, songs, and
stories could be made meaningful in a popular culture. His
device of allowing the reader to overhear kind old Uncle
Remus tell his folk stories to the little boy "is the best
possible way a folktale can be socialized for a reading
audience." The tales have an "authentic Negro folk ring,"
but there is "editing, selection, and sentimentalization,
all necessary for acceptance by the regional popular culture
of Harris' time."

9 [WALTON, DAVID A.]. "Folklore as Compensation: A Content
   Analysis of the Negro Animal Tale." <u>Ohio Folklore Society
   Journal</u>, 1 (October), 1–10.
       Folklorists now believe that the original versions of
   Negro tales recorded as the Uncle Remus stories were more
   than light entertainment for the slave. They served a psychological and symbolic need by allowing the slave to fan-
   tasize about the triumph of an oppressed people over a
   stronger race. The tales were a form of psychological compensation for the Negro. <u>Uncle Remus</u> is used as the source
   for the tales discussed.

10 _____. "Joel Chandler Harris as Folklorist: A Reassessment."
    <u>KFQ</u>, 11 (Spring), 21–26.
        Harris had a background in Negro folklore equal to that
    of the best collectors and in his first two or three vol-
    umes of tales remained admirably close to the oral tradi-
    tion; later collections, which are more derivative and
    secondhand, are of less value. His dialectical usage was
    accurate; however, his framing devices are too consciously
    literary and should be ignored by folklorists, although the
    meaning of the tales remains intact. Also, Harris dealt
    primarily with only one phase of Negro folklore--animal
    fables--omitting the Old Master-John tales, for example.
    Despite his limitations, Harris's work is still a valuable
    tool for the researcher.

11 WOODWARD, C.[OMER] VANN. <u>The Strange Career of Jim Crow</u>.
    Second revised edition. New York: Oxford University
    Press, p. 93.
        In all but his <u>Constitution</u> editorials, Harris may have
    been patronizing, sentimentalized, and paternalistic, but
    not venomous or bitter toward the Negro. His writing, as
    reflected in Uncle Remus, elicited respect, sympathy, and
    even an indulgent affection. Reprinted: 1974.B14.

12 WRIGHT, LYLE H. <u>American Fiction 1876-1900: A Contribution
    Toward a Bibliography</u>. San Marino, CA: Huntington Library,
    pp. 251–52.

1967

Lists a reprinting of "Aunt Fountain's Prisoner," six volumes of short fiction, and Plantation and Sister Jane.

1967 A BOOKS - NONE

1967 B SHORTER WRITINGS

1   BLANCK, JACOB. "BAL Addendum: Joel Chandler Harris--entry No. 7115." PBSA, 61 (Third Quarter), 266. Addendum to 1959.B1. Blanck cites three printings of The Young Marooners on the Florida Coast (1887) by F. R. Goulding with an introduction by Harris.

2   BYRD, JAMES W. J. Mason Brewer: Negro Folklorist. Southwest Writers Series, No. 12, with James W. Lee, general editor. Austin, TX: Steck-Vaughn Co., pp. 11-12, 27, 36-37, 39, 41-42.
    In Negro folklore most think only of Harris's animal tales. During the antebellum day readers missed the fact that the tales were projections of Negro experiences. Harris's animal tales are compared with Brewer's John tales; Brewer's "Tales of Animals and Ranch Life," in Dog Ghosts, is also in the Remus tradition. Brewer's dialect is more genuine and colorful than Harris's. Brewer and Harris leave folklore scholarship to others, though they insured direct Negro sources for their tales.

3   CLARK, THOMAS D. and ALBERT D. KIRWAN. The South Since Appomattox: A Century of Regional Change. New York: Oxford University Press, pp. 208, 212, 216.
    Trained in a country newspaper office, Harris was one of the more compassionate and perceptive of the Southern writers. He earned an international reputation. Almost as much the spirit behind the Constitution as Grady, Harris's chief fame rests in his Southern and African folklore. With humanity and humility he understood and portrayed the nuances of Southern and Negro folkways. Remus stood for the wisdom of the white and black, while Free Joe represented the tragedy attending the baffling changes in the postwar South.

4   CLEGHORN, REESE. "A Few Parental Thoughts about the Future of Uncle Remus." Atlanta, 6 (April), 32, 34, 97, 98-99.
    When one learns more about Harris's life and the "prospecting and authenticity" of his stories, one appreciates his work even more. The stories themselves are timeless, and A. B. Frost's illustrations show a lot more of the

1967

character of Remus's animals than Disney's drawings. Harris's creations are so much a part of American culture now
that people even use his expressions: someone is as big as
life and twice as natural, or is as sassy as a jaybird. As
a "non-accusatorial" old Negro, Uncle Remus may come across
to modern readers as an Uncle Tom, and at least one Negro
maid the author knows of vigorously slams doors around the
house when the white father starts to read Remus tales to
his children. Harris and his Uncle Remus need a little in-
terpreting; one needs to remember the other Uncle Remus who
lived in Reconstruction Atlanta and worried about voting,
economics, and social change, and one should recall that
Harris was adamant about uplifting both races and making
justice prevail. Atlanta should do more to preserve the
heritage of the South that Harris saw and interpreted.

5   DORSON, RICHARD M., ed. <u>American Negro Folktales</u>. Greenwich,
     CN: Fawcett Publications, pp. 16-17, 66-67, 124, et passim.
     Commentary slightly revised version of 1956.B8.

6   ENGLISH, THOMAS H. "The Other Uncle Remus." <u>GaR</u>, 21 (Summer),
     210-17.
          In 1876, three years before Uncle Remus the plantation
     storyteller was introduced to the public, Harris brought to
     life in the pages of the Atlanta <u>Constitution</u> Uncle Remus
     the "elder statesman of Atlanta's Negro community"; Remus
     appears in his dual role in <u>Uncle Remus, Friends</u>, and the
     posthumous <u>Returns</u>. The first Uncle Remus had left the
     plantation in Putnam County to live in the city with Mars
     John and Aunt Sally as servant of sorts and gardener, and
     enjoys dropping by the <u>Constitution</u>'s office for chats with
     the staff. Remus is impatient with carpetbaggers, theories
     of social equality, and lazy and dishonest city Negroes and
     is critical of the latter's "thin veneer of culture"; he
     longs for the "'ol' farmin' days'" down in "'Putmon.'"
     Much can be learned of Harris's "more intimate" views of
     the Negro in the Reconstruction South through a study of
     the "other" Uncle Remus.

7   GROSS, THEODORE L. <u>Thomas Nelson Page</u>. New York: Twayne
     Publishers, pp. 41, 52, 107, 112.
          Cites Page's reactions to Harris as an important local
     colorist who depicted a friendly, idealistic South for nos-
     talgic Northern readers. Like Harris and Thomas Dixon,
     Page's view of the Reconstruction Negro reveals pious
     condescension.

1967

8   HAMPTON, BILL R. "On Identification and Negro Tricksters."
     SFQ, 31 (March), 55-63 passim.
     Discusses the Negro's identification with the Brer Rabbit
     trickster figure and with John and Stackolee as a cultural
     projection of power and hope.

9   HARRIS, JULIA COLLIER. "Joel Chandler Harris: Constructive
     Realist," in Southern Pioneers in Social Interpretation.
     Edited by Howard W. Odum. Freeport, NY: Books for
     Libraries Press, pp. 143-64.
     Reprint of 1925.B5.

10   HICKS, GRANVILLE. The Great Tradition: An Interpretation of
     American Literature Since the Civil War. Revised edition.
     New York: Biblo and Tannen, p. 57.
     Reprint of 1935.B6.

11   JACKSON, BRUCE, ed. The Negro and His Folklore in Nineteenth-
     Century Periodicals. Austin & London: University of Texas
     Press, pp. 177, 243.
     Reprints with background commentary Harris's essays
     "Plantation Music" (1883) and "An Accidental Author" (1886).
     Harris was more than just the journalist he pretended to be.
     Mingo and Free Joe alone would have secured his reputation
     as an author, but the Remus folktales reveal him to be a
     "skillful and sensitive creator" and American literature
     would be the poorer without them. Nevertheless, while the
     Remus stories were "influential," they "created a fallacious
     conception of the form those stories should take and the
     themes they should cover" that was not corrected until after
     Parsons began her collections in 1923.

12   JOHNSON, AMANDA. Georgia as Colony and State. Ann Arbor, MI:
     University Microfilms, pp. 971-72.
     Reprint of 1938.B5.

13   KRAUSE, SYDNEY J. Mark Twain as Critic. Baltimore: Johns
     Hopkins Press, pp. 176, 179, 181, 188.
     Chapter 42 in Life on the Mississippi [see 1883.B8] re-
     counts Twain's meeting with Harris and Cable, "writers whose
     vital regionalism forecast the rebirth of a bona-fide South-
     ern literature." Twain saw the "tradition of the vernacular
     character" as a remedy for Scott's influence. Quotes Twain
     that Harris and Cable did not write in the "Southern style."
     By leaving the South or publishing in Northern journals,
     however, the regionalists--Twain, Cable, and Harris--who
     "placed craft above sentiment" left the South to the his-
     torical romancers.

1967

14   MARTIN, JAY.   <u>Harvests of Change: American Literature 1865-</u>
     <u>1914</u>.   Englewood Cliffs, NJ: Prentice-Hall, pp. 28,
     96-100, et passim.
          More than Stowe's Uncle Tom, Stephen Foster's songs and
     Harris's Uncle Remus tales "gave Americans their sense of
     the lost South."   Professionally, Harris was a jovial "corn-
     field journalist" and later the major editorial writer for
     the Atlanta <u>Constitution,</u> but gradually the "other fellow,"
     the creative writer, came to play a larger role.   Harris's
     stuttering, avoidance of novel situations, and refusal to
     change his style of apparel were signs of his split psyche.
     Although Harris publicly espoused the cause of the New,
     industrialized South, his stories celebrated the "primitive,
     Edenic world of Uncle Remus" and the pastoral plantation
     days.   Through the personae of Uncle Remus, Billy Sanders,
     and "the Sage of Snap-Bean Farm," Harris rebelled against
     Grady's industrial programs and "satirized the South emerg-
     ing in his time by questioning all of the values it was de-
     veloping."   The Remus stories are "largely allegorical
     assertions of the superiority of the weak against the
     strong--of the power of the Old Plantation against the New
     Industry; of the primacy of the primitive over the modern,
     of wisdom over power."

15   PATRICK, REMBERT W.   <u>The Reconstruction of the Nation</u>.
     New York, London, Toronto: Oxford University Press,
     pp. 292-93.
          Harris was the only author to surpass Page in the use of
     Negro dialect, and his Uncle Remus tales and local color
     stories "did much to placate northern hostility toward the
     South."

16   REED, HENRY M.   "'Brer Rabbit' and 'Uncle Remus,'" in his <u>The</u>
     <u>A. B. Frost Book</u>.   Rutland, VT: Charles E. Tuttle Co.,
     pp. 59-68.
          A. B. Frost became Harris's favorite illustrator.   His
     first pen-and-ink drawings for Harris appeared in the <u>Cen-</u>
     <u>tury</u> magazine publication of "Free Joe."   The two men met
     in 1886, and warm correspondence between them continued
     from that year until 1904.   The men were kindred spirits;
     both were even red-headed.   They shared the characteristic
     of self-criticism and apology, but they were enthusiastic
     about their mutual involvement in <u>Friends</u> (1892), in the
     new, Frost-illustrated edition of <u>Uncle Remus</u> (1895), and
     in other works that Frost would illustrate.   Harris con-
     tributed a warm introduction to <u>A Book of Drawings by A. B.</u>
     <u>Frost</u> (1904).   Harris always wanted Frost to draw the Remus
     "'critters'" in his own way; Frost's sketchbooks for the

1967

period are full of rabbit-studies, particularly, in various
poses and clothing.

17   RUBIN, LOUIS D., JR.   "William Styron and Human Bondage:
     The Confessions of Nat Turner." HC, 4 (December), 5, 6.
          Thomas Nelson Page displayed stereotyped Negro charac-
     ters; Harris's darky knew his place, and Harris, like Page,
     thought it was relatively easy to create a Negro narrator.
     Even Faulkner shows the white man trying to see the Negro,
     rather than the Negro himself. But Styron sought to become
     Nat Turner in writing The Confessions of Nat Turner. Re-
     printed: 1971.B14; 1975.B19.

18   RULAND, RICHARD.   The Rediscovery of American Literature:
     Premises of Critical Taste, 1900-1940. Cambridge, MA:
     Harvard University Press, p. 202.
          Tate, in "The Cornfield Journalist" [see 1932.B18], feels
     Harris's advocacy of the provincial made him "the successful
     prophet of a national literature." This overlooked virtue
     deserves serious consideration.

19   SMITH, HENRY NASH, ed.   Popular Culture and Industrialism
     1865-1890. Documents in American Civilization Series.
     [New York]: New York University Press, p. 231.
          Uncle Remus is a familiar stock figure representing the
     loyal servant faithful through the Reconstruction and a
     celebrant of the prewar Southern plantation myths. Compares
     Remus with Page's characters and Foster's "Way Down Upon the
     Suwannee River."

20   WOODS, GEORGE A.   "In Uncle Remus Land." New York Times Book
     Review (17 December), p. 18.
          Harris's "700 [sic] Negro folktales" made his worldwide
     reputation, although he also wrote important short stories
     and novels. His Uncle Remus tales are dialectically diffi-
     cult for younger readers and have been made available in
     many versions; some readers have criticized them for per-
     petuating Negro stereotypes, yet their "essential wit and
     wisdom" continue to be praised. Harris argued for ration-
     ality and sanity and scorned prejudice, yet ironically the
     Wren's Nest, his West End home, has remained segregated
     since 1909, despite a suit filed under the 1964 Civil Rights
     Act and despite community pressure by the Atlanta Community
     Relations Commission, the mayor, and the school board. An
     elderly hostess who showed the author through the home jus-
     tified the segregated policy by saying that "'if you let one
     in they will all come in'" and that it was for the protec-
     tion of two ladies who lived alone upstairs.

1968

1968 A BOOKS

1 BURRISON, JOHN A. "The Golden Arm": The Folk Tale and Its
   Literary Use by Mark Twain and Joel C. Harris. Atlanta, GA:
   Georgia State College School of Arts and Sciences Research
   Paper No. 19 (June), 67pp.
       "The Golden Arm," a variant of which Mark Twain outlined
   for Harris in 1881, has been widespread in American folk
   tradition since the early 1800's. It is one of "The Man
   from the Gallows" tale-types listed in Aarne-Thompson's The
   Types of the Folk-Tale (1961) and indexed in Thompson's
   Motif-Index (1955-58). The basic pattern of the tale is
   that a dead man or animal cannot rest in the grave until it
   recovers a missing extremity. Twain had heard the golden
   arm tale from Uncle Dan'l, a Negro, when he was a child in
   Missouri; Harris watched for the tale after Twain wrote him
   and soon had heard another variant from a black preacher in
   Atlanta. Harris printed his version, in which stolen silver
   coins take the place of the missing golden arm, in Nights.

2 COUSINS, PAUL M.[ERCER]. Joel Chandler Harris: A Biography.
   Baton Rouge, LA: Louisiana State University Press, xiv,
   237pp.
       Substantively equivalent to 1966.A1. Wording revised
   and some structural changes made. Bibliography essentially
   identical.

1968 B SHORTER WRITINGS

1 ALLEN, GAY WILSON. "Roots of a Fabulist's Genius." Saturday
   Review, 51 (22 June), 76.
       Review-essay of Cousins's Harris [see 1968.A2]. He is
   the first of Harris's biographers to use the abundant manuscript materials at Emory; his book reveals the relevancy
   of Harris's writings and thought to the present age of racial tension and strife. Harris defended localism in literature but saw only harm in patriotic sectionalism and was
   deeply interested in the plight of the poor white, who was
   also a victim of slavery. After the War, some poor whites
   became exploiters themselves, and Harris's writings reveal
   a wider background for Faulkner's fiction (especially his
   portrait of the Snopses) than most readers realize. Uncle
   Remus is true to his locality, and his dialect was written
   not for comic effect but to preserve the idiom and creativ-
   ity of the black man. "The archetypes of Uncle Remus's
   fables are African, but the mutations had grown out of the
   pathos of American slavery."

1968

2   BIER, JESSE. <u>The Rise and Fall of American Humor</u>. New York:
     Holt, Rinehart and Winston, pp. 80-81, 82, 92-95, 98, 280,
     349, et passim.
         "In his depths," Harris "sets himself against the old
     southern code of gentility, honor, and pride and against
     northern victory and rapacity"; his Remus tales are "the
     most fetching and deep-leveled cynical inversions" of the
     humor of the Civil War and Reconstruction periods and "per-
     haps in the whole of American humor." The violent and
     amoral Uncle Remus tales teach "the wildest chicanery."
     They propound a "cynical ethic of success at any cost,
     placing the rabbit (the wily, unreconstructed south) against
     the fox (the predatory north)" and permitting the rabbit any
     means of survival; Uncle Remus's partisanship for the rabbit
     was Harris's, furthermore. The tales also show the enslaved
     South twice enslaved—"by the vindictive north and then by
     Negro psychology." As in Faulkner, the endurance of the
     Negro is owed to his flexibility and deviousness, which
     Southern whites also relied upon to help them endure and
     re-emerge after the War.

3   BREWER, J. MASON, ed. <u>American Negro Folklore</u>. Chicago:
     Quadrangle Books, pp. 3-4, 9, 28, et passim.
         The role that the rabbit plays in American Negro folklore
     parallels that of the African hare—the trickster who out-
     wits stronger adversaries. But, for the Negro slave, the
     rabbit "actually symbolized the slave himself. Whenever the
     rabbit succeeded in proving himself smarter than another
     animal the slave rejoiced secretly, imagining himself smart-
     er than his master." The collection includes several Uncle
     Remus tales and proverbs, and headnotes occasionally compare
     Remus tales with other legends. For example, a story about
     "'Buh Fox'" and "'Buh Rabbit,'" collected by J. Russell
     Reaver, was told in 1954 by an elderly Negro who lived a
     few miles north of Tallahassee, Florida, and had never heard
     of Harris. After the Civil War the "John" tales supplanted
     stories of Brer Rabbit among Negro narrators; like Brer Rab-
     bit, "John always comes out victorious in his contests with
     his 'boss-man.'"

4   BRUNVAND, JAN HAROLD. <u>The Study of American Folklore: An
     Introduction</u>. New York: W. W. Norton, p. 107.
         Southern Negroes have given America the best-known ex-
     amples of animal tales, which in turn have been publicized
     mainly in the "semi-literary renderings" of Harris and in
     Disney's cartoons. Both of these adaptations "are somewhat
     removed from the oral specimens of such tales as Type 175
     [in the 1961 revision of Stith-Thompson's <u>The Types of the</u>

1968

Folktale], 'The Tarbaby and the Rabbit,' which has a wide
international distribution."

5 DOYLE, BRIAN, ed. "Harris," in The Who's Who of Children's
   Literature. London: Hugh Evelyn, pp. 136-38.
   Biographical sketch mentions that the Uncle Remus stories
   are told in "authentic Southern Negro dialect and are difficult to understand at once." As soon as the dialect is mastered, "the stories are outrageously funny." Simplified
   modern retellings are available.

6 DURHAM, FRANK. "The Southern Literary Tradition: Shadow or
   Substance?" SAQ, 67 (Summer), 461.
   Literary propagandists during the New South era para-
   doxically celebrated the golden prewar days. Page, Mary
   Johnston, and, "with some reservations," Harris and Cable
   "ground out" the Plantation Legend.

7 MACKAY-SMITH, ALEXANDER. The American Foxhound, 1747-1967.
   Millwood, VA: American Foxhound Club, p. 27.
   Harris's story of Mr. Birdsong's foxhound Hodo, which
   first appeared in Scribner's in 1893, is a "classic account"
   in the annals of fox-hunting.

8 MOORE, JOHN HAMMOND. "When Brer Rabbit and Brer Fox Played
   Baseball." Atlanta Historical Bulletin, 13 (June), 49-54.
   Harris had once challenged Dr. Amos Fox, an Atlanta busi-
   nessman, to a game of baseball to prove which of the two
   men knew more about the sport; Harris had maintained that
   baseballs grew on baseball trees down on the Suwannee River,
   but Fox disagreed. The Constitution for 28 April and 14
   May 1888 carried a humorous account, reproduced here, of
   the challenge and the game between "Brer" Harris's Rabbits
   of the Constitution staff and city post office and "Brer"
   Fox's Foxes, a group of local businessmen. After several
   broken bats and humorous exchanges with the umpire, the
   Rabbits prevailed, 37 to 20. Harris himself may have
   written all or part of the newspaper account.

9 MOTT, FRANK LUTHER. A History of American Magazines. Vol. 5.
   Sketches of 21 Magazines 1905-1930. Cambridge, MA:
   Harvard University Press, Belknap Press, p. 73.
   Walter Hines Page first suggested Harris as the editor
   of Everybody's Magazine, New York, and, when he declined,
   named John O'Hara Cosgrave to the position.

10 PAINTER, F.[RANKLIN] V.[ERZELIUS]. N.[EWTON]. Poets of the
    South. Freeport, NY: Books for Libraries Press, p. 27.
    Reprint of 1903.B13.

11 STERN, MILTON R. and SEYMOUR L. GROSS, eds. American
    Literature Survey. Nation and Region. 1860-1900. Revised
    and expanded, with prefatory essay by Howard Mumford Jones.
    New York: The Viking Press, pp. 126-28.
        Harris learned from J. A. Turner "the necessity for con-
    ciseness and the urbane swift stroke of telling wit." The
    Uncle Remus stories, taken from the folk bestiaries of
    American slaves, proved Harris "unsurpassed"; indeed, Mark
    Twain called him "the only master of the Negro dialect."
    After his association with Grady and the Constitution, Har-
    ris's work took on political purposes, primarily that of
    reconciliation: for Harris, "local color is a regional in-
    strument for talking to the entire nation and, indeed, to
    every man." The poems and novels neither received nor
    merited wide attention, but Harris's Georgia cracker stories,
    such as Tolliver, pointed toward the realism of the new
    Southern local color literature. Although a "second rank"
    Southern writer, Harris is important, "not only for histori-
    cal purposes, but also for his own real achievement in his
    given genre." Anthologizes "The Moon in the Mill-Pond" and
    "Free Joe."

12 STUCKEY, STERLING. "Through the Prism of Folklore: The Black
    Ethos in Slavery." MR, 9 (Summer), 434 n. 46.
        Slave tales are often subtle in conception and illuminate
    the inner-world of the bondsman. The most memorable tales
    are those of the trickster Brer Rabbit and of John. "With-
    out understanding what humor meant to slaves themselves,
    one is not likely to rise above the superficiality of a
    Stephen Foster or a Joel Chandler Harris."

13 TURNER, ARLIN. "Joel Chandler Harris (1848-1908)." ALR, 1
    (Summer), 18-23.
        Surveys the major critical books and essays on Harris,
    listing bibliographical sources, editions, and manuscript
    collections, and reviews recent scholarly articles. Per-
    spectives for further study conclude the essay.

14 _____. "Joel Chandler Harris in the Currents of Change."
    SLJ, 1 (Autumn), 105-11.
        Review-essay on Cousins's Harris [see 1968.A2] emphasizes
    Harris's close attention in his tales to the life and lore
    of Middle Georgia. Harris's world was "caught up in change"
    after the War, and his newspaper editorials and stories re-
    veal his nostalgia for the old days on the plantation. An
    extremely shy man, Harris was a meliorist and a pragmatist
    in his writings. With the War over, Harris did not seek to
    defend the institution of slavery; he asked for toleration

1968

for the Negro's plight, but did not protest when the thorny
problem of civil rights for blacks was effectively postponed
in the 1890's with the institution of state laws on segrega-
tion and voting qualifications.

15   TURNER, DARWIN T.   "Daddy Joel Harris and His Old-Time
     Darkies." SLJ, 1 (December), 20–41.
         Harris portrayed mental, physical, and emotional differ-
     ences among Negroes in his fiction but he nevertheless dealt
     in stereotypes of "the wise, venerable old-time Negro, the
     devoted slave, the mammy, the comic darky, and the pathetic
     freedman." Additionally, Harris's male darkies are sexless.
     For Harris "clung philosophically and emotionally to the
     dream of a utopian plantation society," where the dignified
     but devoted slave would attend unobtrusively to his patriar-
     chal and paternal master's needs. Harris thought Negroes
     were inferior and were therefore suited for domestic and
     farm labor; he was reluctant to have them enter the ministry
     or the law. Harris, the collector of tales, became "Daddy
     Joe," the father of a myth.

16   _____. "Southern Fiction, 1900–1910." MissQ, 21 (Fall),
     281–82, 284.
         There is little of worth in Southern fiction from 1900
     to 1910, but here and there "gleams a source of influence
     for a subsequent writer." Tolliver, for example, "seems a
     possible source for Faulkner's myth of the founding of Jef-
     ferson, some of Faulkner's names, and possibly some of his
     characters, such as Dilsey." Although Harris earned his
     literary reputation by skillfully transforming Negro folk-
     tales into art, "he approved of Negroes only when they con-
     fined themselves to telling stories and serving their
     masters." Tolliver begins well but offers a view of Recon-
     struction "more amazing than any yarn spun by Uncle Remus."
     The only murder is committed by a Negro; the only violence
     is perpetuated by Yankee soldiers; the heroes are the
     Knights of the White Camellia who restore order to the
     South merely by parading on horseback and solemnly intoning,
     'Beware.'"

17   WAGER, WILLIS. American Literature: A World View. New York:
     New York University Press, pp. 161–62.
         Harris was an "outstanding" author of the Deep South and
     "eagerly read" in Europe. The New South writers paid a
     price for reaching the national and international audience:
     they had to present an "acceptable attitude" toward America.
     Offering too forthright a criticism or debunking local
     myths was not acceptable.

18   WARD, JOSEPH A.   "Joel Chandler Harris: A Biography.   By
      Paul M. Cousins."   Journal of Southern History, 34
      (November), 625-26.
         Reviews Cousins's Harris [see 1968.A2].   Harris seems
      "pathologically withdrawn" and, significantly, employed the
      persona of the Negro slave in his most celebrated work;
      also, he was "geographically remote from American literary
      culture."   A "more confident and aggressive Harris could
      have overcome the limitations of his provincial origins" to
      have "beneficial contact" with Northern realists.

19   WEAVER, RICHARD M.   The Southern Tradition at Bay: A History
      of Postbellum Thought.   Edited by George Core and M. E.
      Bradford.   New Rochelle, NY: Arlington House, pp. 298-301,
      385.
         Harris was a vigorous opponent of sectionalism and skep-
      tical about New South materialism, as his editorials and
      Tolliver reveal.

20   WOLFE, BERNARD.   "Uncle Remus and the Malevolent Rabbit," in
      The National Temper: Readings in American History.
      New York, et al.:   Harcourt, Brace & World, pp. 190-206.
      Reprint of 1949.B15.

21   WOODRESS, JAMES [and MARIAN KORITZ], eds.   Dissertations in
      American Literature 1891-1966.   Revised edition.   Durham,
      NC: Duke University Press, not paginated.
         Entries 1107-1111 list five dissertations on Harris.

1969 A BOOKS - NONE

1969 B SHORTER WRITINGS

1   ABRAHAMS, ROGER D.   "Joel Chandler Harris: A Biography, by
      Paul M. Cousins."   NALF, 3 (Fall), 98-99.
         Reviews Cousins's Harris [see 1968.A2].   Uncle Remus
      represents "not Negroes but a pastoral way of life that is
      common to all such old and wise figures in American regional
      literature."   Remus endures because he is willing "to live
      in harmony with cyclical nature."   He can "look upon human
      vanities with a lighthearted but pervasive irony" and see
      relationships in family terms.   This agrarian, "extended-
      family" perspective is present in Faulkner, Steinbeck,
      Cather, Rolvaag, and, "negatively speaking," in Frank
      Norris and Sinclair Lewis.

1969

2   BLAIR, WALTER; THEODORE HORNBERGER; RANDALL STEWART; and
    JAMES E. MILLER, JR. The Literature of the United States.
    Book 2. Third edition. Glenview, ILL: Scott, Foresman,
    pp. 343-44.
        Harris's supremacy as master of the Negro dialect may
    well pass unquestioned. Recent historical critics point
    out that Harris aimed at the reconciliation of the North
    and South in his Uncle Remus stories, but their "unalloyed
    humor" also makes them enjoyable as "comic masterpieces of
    their kind." Abundant humor comes from incongruity as the
    animals' behavior closely approximates that of human beings.
    Uncle Remus embodies the "primitive outlook" of the ante-
    bellum Southern Negro. Anthologizes four Remus stories.

3   BURTON, RICHARD. Forces in Fiction and Other Essays.
    Freeport, NY: Books for Libraries Press, p. 14.
    Reprint of 1902.B20.

4   CHRISTENSEN, [MRS.] A. M. H. Afro-American Folk-Lore: Told
    Round Cabin Fires on the Sea Islands of South Carolina.
    New York: Negro Universities Press, pp. ix-xiv.
    Reprint of 1892.B20.

5   GLAZIER, LYLE. "The Uncle Remus Stories: Two Portraits of
    American Negroes." Hacettepe Bulletin of Social Sciences
    and Humanities, 1 (June), 67-74.
        Article in Hacettepe University journal, Ankara, Turkey.
    Harris's portrait of the American Negro is "sophisticated
    and paradoxical," for the framework of the stories "perpetu-
    ates the Southern myth of white supremacy" while the content
    of the tales themselves reverses this myth. James Weldon
    Johnson [see 1922.B8] praised Uncle Remus as one of the four
    great artistic achievements of his race, perhaps because
    Harris seemed to "submerge his ego under the spell of an-
    cient story telling--tribal, racial (of the whole human
    race)." Harris's "Story of the War" discloses Remus's role
    as the "willing slave" devoted to the family in the "big
    house"; the animal fables, however, elicit the reader's
    sympathy for the weak and the downtrodden members of the
    human race, fighting against class-superiority myths. If
    Harris saw the parallels between the sufferings in the
    fables and the sufferings of the Negro under slavery, "he
    didn't let on," nor did the "Uncle Remus" from whom Harris
    heard his stories let his white patron in on his private
    joke about white society. Reprint: 1970.B10.

6   HURSTON, ZORA NEALE. Mules and Men. New York: Negro
    Universities Press, p. 17.
    Reprint of 1935.B8.

278

1970

7   KOLB, HAROLD H., JR. The Illusion of Life. American Realism
    as a Literary Form. Charlottesville, VA: University Press
    of Virginia, pp. 50, 138, et passim.
    "Unlike many contemporary critics, Harris realized that
    the ethical force of Huckleberry Finn and the other realis-
    tic novels was not based upon external spiritual forces but
    upon the confrontation of human beings in a humanly created
    social environment." Harris praised Twain's novel for its
    wholesome lesson in honesty, justice, and mercy. The best
    regional writers, such as Harris, Jewett, and Freeman, focus
    on ordinary people in contrast to Bret Harte's "cardboard
    characters."

8   RAY, CHARLES A. "Joel Chandler Harris (1848–1908)," in A
    Bibliographical Guide to the Study of Southern Literature.
    Edited by Louis D. Rubin, Jr. Baton Rouge, LA: Louisiana
    State University Press, pp. 212–14.
    Ray gathers and briefly annotates twenty-five articles
    and books on Harris, observing in his introductory note that
    "there is no systematic study of the precise forces that
    made [Harris] the shrewd critic of literature that some com-
    mentators say that he is," and that his cracker sketches and
    dialect deserve more scholarly attention.

9   TOULMIN, HARRY AUBREY, JR. Social Historians. Introduction
    by Charles W. Kent. Ann Arbor: University Microfilms,
    pp. 30, 133–64, 170–71.
    Reprint of 1911.B11.

1970 A BOOKS - NONE

1970 B SHORTER WRITINGS

1   ABRAHAMS, ROGER D. Deep Down in the Jungle...Negro Narrative
    Folklore from the Streets of Philadelphia. First revised
    edition. Chicago: Aldine Publishing Co., pp. 62, 70–74.
    [Revision of 1964.B1.] Philadelphia city dwellers, who
    may have been influenced by the Disney comic strip, have
    changed the trickster-rabbit's character to that of the
    "hard man" of agility, meanness, and strength; he has "the
    ability to revolt in the face of authority and possible
    death."

2   BAETZHOLD, HOWARD C. Mark Twain and John Bull: The British
    Connection. Bloomington: Indiana University Press, p. 36.
    In London in 1879 Twain met Charles Lutwidge Dodgson
    [Lewis Carroll] whose Alice in Wonderland he had long

1970

admired. Twain recalled later that Carroll was the "still-
est and shyest full-grown man I have ever met except 'Uncle
Remus' [Harris]."

3 DAVIS, RICHARD BEALE; C. HUGH HOLMAN; and LOUIS D. RUBIN, JR.,
   eds. Southern Writing 1585–1920. New York: Odyssey
   Press, p. 757.
   Biographical sketch and short bibliographical note pre-
   cede reprinting of six tales from Uncle Remus, and "Free
   Joe."

4 DAY, MARTIN S. History of American Literature From the
   Beginning to 1910. Garden City, NY: Doubleday & Co.,
   pp. 244–45.
   After a brief biographical sketch, Day states that Uncle
   Remus and Nights "bear the most authentic seal of Negro
   folklore"; subsequent stories are "good but lean increasingly upon Harris' independent imagination." Uncle Remus's
   speech is "dramatic and convincing, as is his calculated
   use of detail and suspense." Harris makes folklore live
   and avoids moral didacticism.

5 FALK, ROBERT. "The Writers' Search for Reality," in The
   Gilded Age. Edited by H. Wayne Morgan. Revised and
   enlarged edition. Syracuse, NY: Syracuse University
   Press, pp. 225, 229.
   Reprint of 1963.B6.

6 FRIEDMAN, LAWRENCE J. The White Savage: Racial Fantasies in
   the Postbellum South. Englewood Cliffs, NJ: Prentice-Hall,
   pp. 59, 59 n.10, 101.
   The Uncle Remus stories exemplified the new postbellum
   Cavalier literature the South was trying to cultivate. Harris was careful to avoid adverse comments on the North and
   to show Northern readers that "they no longer differed with
   white Southerners on vital issues, particularly racial issues." Harris told the Yankee that the Negro was content
   with Cavalier treatment, and hence that the Cavalier was
   above suspicion. Harris promoted intersectional trust and,
   like Henry Watterson, helped to head off the second Reconstruction that white Southerners feared. Brer Rabbit, superior in brain power to Brer Fox, may have represented the
   South's circumvention of Northern industrial might.

7 GALLUP, DONALD. "T. S. Eliot & Ezra Pound: Collaborators in
   Letters." Atlantic, 225 (January), 60.
   Eliot's growing more conservative during his career "was
   a factor in Pound's increasingly frequent use of the nickname

1970

'Possum' in addressing and referring to Eliot" in Pound's
letters. Pound himself was called "'Brer Rabbit'" in a
"zoological system derived from Joel Chandler Harris."

8   GASTON, PAUL M. The New South Creed: A Study in Southern
    Mythmaking. New York: Alfred A. Knopf, pp. 171, 180-82.
    The 1870's and 1880's saw an increase in Southern contri-
    butions to national periodicals. An "enormous" number of
    authors, with Harris and Page as the most prominent, pre-
    sented plantation material. Harris was more subtle and
    possibly more effective than Grady at reconciliation,
    through Remus and his short stories. Harris changed a
    story to placate the North: in the 1877 "Uncle Remus as a
    Rebel" the Yankee is killed, but in "A Story of the War" he
    loses his arm and marries a Southern girl. Harris used the
    intersectional marriage, as in "Aunt Fountain's Prisoner,"
    to indicate North-South reconciliation and prosperity. He
    also used humor and his Uncle Remus character to show the
    North the Southern viewpoint toward the slave and to mollify
    his audience; a humorous Negro could not have been mis-
    treated.

9   GERSTENBERGER, DONNA and GEORGE HENDRICK, eds. The American
    Novel: A Checklist of Twentieth Century Criticism on
    Novels Written Since 1789. Vol. 2: Criticism Written
    1960-1968. Chicago: Swallow Press, p. 144.
    Lists one article on Harris.

10 GLAZIER, LYLE. "The Uncle Remus Stories: Two Portraits of
    American Negroes." JGE, 22 (April), 71-79.
    Reprint of 1969.B5.

11 GOLDSTEIN, KENNETH S. and DAN BEN-AMOS, eds. Thrice Told
    Tales: Folktales from Three Continents. Lock Haven, PA:
    Hammermill Paper Co., pp. 69, 121, 149-54 passim.
    In their notes the editors review the studies made of
    the origins of the tar-baby tale; anthologized are the Indi-
    an Játaka tale "Prince Five-Weapons" and the Nigerian folk-
    tale "Tortoise, the Trickster," both of which feature the
    five-point stick-fast motif. Harris's stories have been
    considered prejudicial "humorous" tales about Negroes, but
    the search for "African origin-identity among black Ameri-
    cans today brings us full circle to the tales brought over
    by their ancestors." The tar-baby story is still current;
    a 1957 New Orleans version of the tale is given in the
    notes.

1970

12 HERSKOVITS, MELVILLE J. "The African Heritage," in America's
    Black Past: A Reader in Afro-American History. Edited by
    Eric Foner. New York and Evanston: Harper & Row, p. 25.
    Reprint of a chapter in 1941.B6.

13 JACOBS, JOSEPH, ed. The Fables of Aesop as first printed by
    William Caxton.... [Vol.] I. History of the Aesopic
    Fable. New York: Burt Franklin, pp. 113, 136-37.
    Reprint of 1889.B9.

14 KAY, TERRY. "'Song of The South' Shelved." Atlanta Journal
    (3 March), p. 16-A.
        Disney's "The Song of the South" was released in 1946
    and rereleased in 1956. It was withdrawn from the market
    in 1958 because the movie depicted racial bias. The Disney
    organization has now shelved the movie permanently, because
    it was impossible to edit out racial references. Many have
    objected to the tar-baby story as symbolizing an assault on
    black humans. D. W. Griffith's classic "The Birth of a
    Nation" continues to be shown, despite its biased depiction
    of Negroes, but Disney's classic will be seen no more. The
    movie was one of Disney's greatest moneymakers; the sound
    track alone has grossed more than $5,000,000, and "Zip-A-
    Dee-Doo-Dah" won the 1946 Academy Award as "Best Song."

15 LEARY, LEWIS, ed. Articles on American Literature 1950-1967.
    Assisted by Carolyn Bartholet and Catharine Roth. Durham,
    NC: Duke University Press, p. 234.
        Lists twenty articles on Harris. [For earlier edition
    see 1954.B9.]

16 MOONEY, JAMES. Myths of the Cherokee. New York: Johnson
    Reprint Corporation, pp. 233-34, 448, 450, 452.
    Reprint of 1900.B23.

17 MURRAY, ALBERT. The Omni-Americans: New Perspectives on
    Black Experience and American Culture. New York:
    Outerbridge & Dienstfrey, pp. 63, 130-32 passim.
        Refers to the worldly wit and wisdom of Uncle Remus.
    The Negroes were not as inattentive to Remus's style as the
    current civil rights spokesmen seem to have been. Compares
    Harris to Warren Miller: his Seige of Harlem (1964) is a
    minstrel show and the writer does a "saggy bottomed, tangle
    footed buck and wing in the guise of Joel Chandler Harris,
    which he ain't." Criticizes Miller's Negro stereotypes:
    "Harris was certainly no great shakes as a writer, but dog-
    gone my cats if his talking animals aren't infinitely more
    human than any character in either The Cool World or The
    Seige of Harlem."

18 REVELL, PETER. <u>James Whitcomb Riley</u>. New York: Twayne
    Publishers, pp. 21, 107-108, 110-11.
        Harris praised Riley's <u>The Old Swimmin' Hole and 'Leven</u>
    <u>More Poems</u> (1883) as catching "the true American spirit and
    flavor"; both writers worked with pastoral forms.

19 RUBIN, LOUIS D., JR. "Southern Local Color and The Black
    Man." <u>SoR</u>, NS 6 (October), 1014-15, 1016-22.
        Unlike Page's Negroes, Harris's do not exist "in order
    to chronicle the doings of white masters, and are not ulti-
    mately defined by a relationship with white men." Uncle
    Remus is to a considerable extent a stereotype, as Brown
    contends [<u>see</u> 1933.B1], but Remus is only the narrator of
    the stories he tells, not their hero. Darwin Turner [<u>see</u>
    1968.B15] also overlooks the significance of Brer Rabbit,
    who knows how to fend for himself in a world of more power-
    ful and predatory animals. Harris's animals are really
    people, and Brer Rabbit in many ways stands for the condi-
    tion of the black man in the South and exists in a "dynamic
    relationship" with Uncle Remus. Remus openly admires the
    rabbit for being everything that he is "careful not to ap-
    pear to be": young, self-serving, sexual. Harris was a
    segregationist who saw the black man as socially and bio-
    logically inferior, but as an artist who himself came from
    deprived and humble origins he sympathized with the under-
    dog and the outcast. Harris was not trying to deceive his
    public with the tales, but in his imagination he compre-
    hended "the situation of the black man in a society made up,
    so far as he was concerned, of foxes and wolves who pos-
    sessed all the money, the education, the power, the advan-
    tages."

20 SEARS, LORENZO. <u>American Literature in the Colonial and</u>
    <u>National Periods</u>. New York: Burt Franklin, p. 412.
        Reprint of 1902.B29.

21 WASHINGTON, BOOKER T. "The Economic Development of the Negro
    Race Since Its Emancipation," in <u>The Negro in the South:</u>
    <u>His Economic Progress in Relation to His Moral and Religious</u>
    <u>Development</u>, by Booker T. Washington and W. E. Burghardt
    DuBois. New York: Citadel Press, pp. 64-65.
        Reprint of 1907.B14.

22 WHITTEN, NORMAN E., JR. and JOHN F. SZWED, eds. "Introduction,"
    in their <u>Afro-American Anthropology: Contemporary</u>
    <u>Perspectives</u>. New York: Free Press; London: Collier-
    Macmillan, pp. 31, 32-33.
        <u>Uncle Remus</u> "opened the way for a string of literary
    treatments of Negro folklore and folk themes."

1971

1971 A BOOKS - NONE

1971 B SHORTER WRITINGS

1   ARMISTEAD, S. G. "Two Brer Rabbit Stories from the Eastern
     Shore of Maryland." JAF, 84 (October-December), 442-44.
          Transcribes "Mr. Rabbit Steals Mr. Fox's Butter" and
     "The Tar Pole," Maryland versions of two stories in Uncle
     Remus.

2   DORSON, RICHARD M. American Folklore and the Historian.
     Chicago and London: University of Chicago Press, pp. 193,
     et passim.
          Harris's stories are "vitally related" to oral Negro
     folklore and are cited by collectors. Longfellow and Harris
     treat their materials artistically, but Longfellow never
     lived among the Indians and The Song of Hiawatha possesses
     "no ethnographic value."

3   EICHELBERGER, CLAYTON L., comp. A Guide to Critical Reviews
     of United States Fiction, 1870-1910. [Vol. 1]. Metuchen,
     NJ: Scarecrow Press, pp. 149-51, 290.
          Lists seventy-four periodical reviews of twenty of Har-
     ris's books. Supplement: 1974.B5.

4   [ENGLISH, THOMAS H.]. "The Joel Chandler Harris Collection."
     Ex Libris: An Occasional Publication of Friends of the
     Emory University Library, no. 1 (February), pp. 6-8.
          During the past two years, more additions were made to
     the Harris Collection at Emory. It now contains almost all
     the editions of Harris's books and most of the works in
     which biographical and critical studies of Harris have ap-
     peared. Additional family letters and drawings by A. B.
     Frost have now been deposited.

5   _____ . "To Essie." Ex Libris: An Occasional Publication of
     Friends of the Emory University Library, no. 2 (May),
     pp. 5-6.
          Dated 6 April 1872, this courtship poem, "A Song in the
     Night: To Essie," was found in Esther LaRose Harris's album
     of girlhood keepsakes.

6   FLANAGAN, JOHN T. and ARTHUR PALMER HUDSON, eds. Folklore in
     American Literature. Westport, CN: Greenwood Press,
     pp. 406, 475, 489.
          Prints three tales and all seventy "Plantation Proverbs"
     from Uncle Remus, and one tale from Nights. Unlike Zora
     Neale Hurston, who transcribed the Negro stories she heard

1971

without imposing an artificial framework on them, Harris
uses Uncle Remus to give focus, unity, and artistic appeal
to his stories; it is "an interesting point whether the
character of Uncle Remus weakens or strengthens the stories
as folk tales." The moral of the Remus tales is "seldom
obtrusive," but there is "often the implication that the
rabbit represents the Negro and that the Negro can best advance his own aims by pitting cunning and strategy against
the superior strength of his antagonists." Remus's plantation maxims reveal a "close observation of Negro life and
a quiet and amusing skepticism."

7   FREDRICKSON, GEORGE M. The Black Image in the White Mind:
     The Debate on Afro-American Character and Destiny, 1817-
     1914. New York, Evanston, San Francisco, London: Harper &
     Row, pp. 205-206, 207, 208, 211, 213, 215, 260, 285, 301.
          Harris's editorials displayed the Atlanta Constitution's
     seemingly paternalistic and benevolent attitude toward the
     Negro; his Uncle Remus tales glorifying the old-time darky
     supplemented his essays on Negro progress and accomplish-
     ment. Like Grady, Harris was a "moderate white suprema-
     cist," and the figure of the Atlanta Uncle Remus really
     speaks for the whites when he argues against black permis-
     siveness and for moral improvement of the race. Harris
     identified with the New South cause and did not romanticize
     the Old South white planter.

8   GROSS, THEODORE L. The Heroic Ideal in American Literature.
     New York: The Free Press, pp. 112, 114-15, 138, et passim.
          Like other Southern writers of the postbellum period,
     Harris dealt in abstractions and polarities. He saw the
     "insurgent Negroes in absolute moral terms": as "egotis-
     tic" or "depraved." Tolliver is a conflict between past
     and present, the new and the old. Although not as defensive
     as Page, Harris succumbed to stereotypes in Tolliver as he
     "invoked a code of idealized behavior" for the prewar pa-
     ternalistic planters. Harris was, however, a "temperate
     raconteur" and he created the most realistic Negro charac-
     ters in nineteenth-century American fiction. Harris's sym-
     pathetic writing helped establish the Southern concept of
     Reconstruction in the national mind.

9   HAVLICE, PATRICIA PATE. Index to American Author
     Bibliographies. Metuchen, NJ: Scarecrow Press, p. 75.
     Indexes three primary and secondary bibliographies.
     Revision: 1975.B10.

1971

10   McDAVID, RAVEN I., JR. and VIRGINIA GLENN McDAVID. "The
     Relationship of the Speech of American Negroes to the
     Speech of Whites," in <u>Black-White Speech Relationships</u>.
     Edited by Walt Wolfram and Nona H. Clarke. Urban Language
     Series. Washington, D. C.: Center for Applied Linguistics,
     pp. 20, 32-33 n. 17.
     Reprint of 1951.B7.

11   PHILLIPS, ROBERT L., JR. "Joel Chandler Harris," in his "The
     Novel and the Romance in Middle Georgia Humor and Local
     Color: A Study of Narrative Method in the Works of Augustus
     Baldwin Longstreet, William Tappan Thompson, Richard
     Malcolm Johnston and Joel Chandler Harris." Ph.D.
     dissertation, University of North Carolina at Chapel Hill,
     pp. 313-459, et passim.
         Harris was more the romancer than the realistic novelist
     in his Uncle Remus books, local color tales, and novels.
     His narrators, which are analyzed in detail, saw Old South
     values as the ideal. Harris's works are compared most fre-
     quently to those of R. M. Johnston.

12   PIERSEN, WILLIAM D. "An African Background for American Negro
     Folktales?" <u>JAF</u>, 84 (April-June), 204-14 passim.
         The work of Dorson, Stith Thompson, and others has tended
     to stress the European rather than African origins of the
     American Negro folklore that Harris's work typifies, because
     European folklore has been more thoroughly studied and typed
     and because folklorists have overgeneralized. Harris, Elsie
     Clews Parsons, Herskovits, and others have argued for Afri-
     can sources. Piersen reviews the scholarship on the ques-
     tion and urges a more thorough study and classification of
     African folklore.

13   RUBIN, LOUIS D., JR. "The Literature of the New South," in
     <u>Fifteen American Authors Before 1900</u>. Edited by Robert A.
     Rees and Earl N. Harbert. Madison: University of
     Wisconsin Press, pp. 402-403.
         Includes four-item secondary bibliography and comments
     that no existing study of Harris "gets beneath the surface
     of his complex personality or his deceptive and often im-
     plicitly subversive art."

14   _____. "William Styron and Human Bondage," in <u>The Sounder
     Few: Essays from the</u> Hollins Critic. Edited by R. H. W.
     Dillard, George Garrett, and John Rees Moore. Athens, GA:
     University of Georgia Press, pp. 309, 310.
     Reprint, with Afterword, of 1967.B17.

1971

15 SCHEICK, WILLIAM J. "The Spunk of a Rabbit: An Allusion in
    The Adventures of Huckleberry Finn." MTJ, 15 (Summer),
    14-16.
        Twain was fond of Uncle Remus, and while he was working
    on a revision of Huckleberry Finn in 1879-1880 he may have
    been influenced by Brer Rabbit's posturing of helplessness
    and his knowledge of psychology in "How Mr. Rabbit Was Too
    Sharp for Mr. Fox," the conclusion of the tar-baby episode.
    Huck employs a similar ironic device to warn off two white
    men who think a Negro is aboard Huck's raft. In another
    possible reference to Harris's hero, Huck chastises himself
    for not having "'the spunk of a rabbit'" just prior to the
    raft episode. Negro folklore may have influenced Twain
    from another direction, for as a child he had heard stories
    about the rabbit from Uncle Dan'l, a slave on the Quarles's
    farm in Missouri.

16 STARKE, CATHERINE JUANITA. Black Portraiture in American
    Fiction: Stock Characters, Archetypes, and Individuals.
    New York: Basic Books, pp. 50-54, 96-97, 129-30.
        Discusses Harris's familiar sentimental free slave char-
    acters, Remus, Ananias, and Free Joe. Harris skillfully
    manipulates name and appearance to make Ananias seem "pa-
    thetically ludicrous" and, an apologist for slavery, shows
    Free Joe's difficulties and alienation outside the system.
    Cites "Where's Duncan?" as an excellent portrait of the
    tragic male mulatto that moves to its climax like a Greek
    drama of revenge. Mom Bi is an example of the archetypal
    Mammy pattern.

17 TURNER, DARWIN T. In a Minor Chord: Three Afro-American
    Writers and Their Search for Identity. Carbondale and
    Edwardsville: Southern Illinois University Press; London
    and Amsterdam: Feffer & Simons, pp. xv, 117.
        After the Civil War, collections of spirituals and Har-
    ris's folktales introduced some Americans to Afro-American
    talent for song and story. Unlike Harris and Chesnutt,
    Zora Neale Hurston did not try to transform the folktales
    she heard into art.

18 WOODWARD, C.[OMER] VANN. Origins of the New South: 1877-
    1913. Vol. 9 in A History of the South. Edited by Wendell
    Holmes Stephenson and E. Merton Coulter. Baton Rouge, LA:
    Louisiana State University Press, The Littlefield Fund for
    Southern History of the University of Texas, pp. 158, 166,
    168-69, 432-33.
        Reprint of 1951.B12, with expanded bibliography.

1972

1972 A BOOKS - NONE

1972 B SHORTER WRITINGS

1 BAKER, HOUSTON A., JR. Long Black Song: Essays in Black
   American Literature and Culture. Charlottesville, VA:
   University Press of Virginia, pp. 11-12, 21-24.
   Black folklore reflects the Negro's slavery: the cunning
   of Brer Rabbit, the woods as a refuge, and roots and herbs
   as magical powers over white masters. Its first heroes were
   animals. Brer Rabbit, as a trickster animal, differs sig-
   nificantly from animals of other lores; he projects the
   slave's strongest drives. Harris and Gonzales, in trying
   to identify the animal tales with Aesop and western tradition, miss the psychological aspects of these American
   tales. Brer Rabbit is one of the first black American
   figures "to repudiate the culture theorizing of whites."
   Harris's work does not truly represent black folk values;
   his is an antebellum perspective featuring the faithful
   black retainer. His animal tales show etiological beginnings giving way to fables with new meanings.

2 BROOKS, ROBERT PRESTON. History of Georgia. Spartanburg, SC:
   Reprint Co., pp. 372-73.
   Reprint of 1913.B4.

3 CANDLER, ALLEN D. and CLEMENT A. EVANS, eds. "Harris," in
   Cyclopedia of Georgia. Vol. 2: F-N. Spartanburg, SC:
   Reprint Co., pp. 217-28.
   Reprint of 1906.B4.

4 DILLARD, J.[OEY] L.[EE]. Black English: Its History and
   Usage in the United States. New York: Random House,
   pp. 121, 193, 291, et passim.
   Harris's "'Brer Rabbit says, sezee'" is probably based
   on a West African syntactic pattern. Harris and other outstanding writers of Black English learned it firsthand.
   Graduate schools rarely offer courses on Negro lore and
   traditions such as the trickster tales that were told so
   well by Harris.

5 DORSON, RICHARD M. African Folklore. Garden City, NY:
   Doubleday & Co., p. 389.
   Among Vai folktales of Liberia is a story about a land
   turtle who rides a leopard. In the Uncle Remus version of
   the tale, the rabbit rides the fox.

1972

6   HAWTHORNE, JULIAN; JOHN RUSSELL YOUNG; JOHN PORTER LAMBERTON;
    and OLIVER H. G. LEIGH, eds. The Masterpieces and the
    History of Literature: Analysis, Criticism, Character and
    Incident. Vol. 10. St. Clair Shores, MI: Scholarly
    Press, p. 332.
    Reprint of 1903.B7.

7   HUBBELL, JAY B. Who Are the Major American Writers? A Study
    of the Changing Literary Canon. Durham, NC: Duke
    University Press, pp. 141, 248–49, 289.
        Few contemporaries recognized Huckleberry Finn as a clas-
    sic, but Harris refers to Twain in 1908 as America's great-
    est humorist and fiction writer. Quotes Quinn [see
    1925.B8] that the Uncle Remus stories and "Free Joe" will
    be permanent contributions to literature. Hubbell believes
    that these old-fashioned local colorists are just an "eddy
    on the margin of the mainstream of American fiction."
    Cites results of a poll conducted by Lanier [see 1926.B6]:
    approximately 400 teachers of American fiction ranked Uncle
    Remus as fifth in American masterpieces of fiction.

8   JANETI, JOSEPH. "Folk Music's Affair with Popular Culture:
    A Redefinition of the 'Revival,'" in New Dimensions in
    Popular Culture. Edited by Russel B. Nye. Bowling Green,
    OH: Bowling Green University Popular Press, p. 225.
        Although America's academic concern with folklore might
    begin with Uncle Remus (1880), the credit should go to the
    founding of the American Folklore Society in 1888.

9   MUNRO, JOHN M. "The Arab Response to the Black Writers of
    America," in Asian Response to American Literature. Edited
    by C. D. Narasimhaiah. Delhi: Vikas Publications, p. 283.
        Harris's and Stowe's "uncles" conform to the white image
    of the Negro: childlike and loyal, speaking homespun
    wisdom.

10 RUBIN, LOUIS D., JR. The Writer in the South: Studies in a
    Literary Community. Mercer University Lamar Memorial
    Lectures, No. 15. Athens, GA: University of Georgia Press,
    pp. 10–12, 36–39, et passim.
        Harris occasionally protested some of the mediocre South-
    ern literature, yet he, Grady, and the Constitution were
    propagandists for everything Southern. His Library of
    Southern Literature is full of the "'Miss Sweetie Wildwood'"
    type of writing. The post–Civil War South, Harris included,
    believed in the inherent inferiority of the blacks. The
    Uncle Remus tales, as all Southern local color writing, pre-
    pared the North for the disfranchisement of the blacks by

1972

painting a rosy picture. Whether Harris meant it to or not,
"in the eyes of the nation the image of Uncle Remus re-
placed that of Uncle Tom." It is ironic that the War freed
the Southern writer from having to defend slavery, but instead he produced more and more effective propaganda. The
pastoral local color writers soon lapsed into relative
obscurity.

11   SKAGGS, MERRILL MAGUIRE. The Folk of Southern Fiction.
      Athens, GA: University of Georgia Press, pp. 32-33, 43-45,
      52-55, 62-64, 73-78, 94-97, 116-17, 120-24, 131-32, 134-35,
      151-52, 191-92, 210-14, et passim.
         Harris is virtually the only local colorist to portray
      the poor white. His belief in the Middle Georgia "demo-
      cratic spirit" and sense of pride and respect for the common
      people are evinced in most of his local color tales, al-
      though Harris was often gently satiric in his portraiture.
      His stories are carefully framed and tend to feature an om-
      niscient narrator who is humorous, aloof, amiable, and
      tolerant; besides Twain, Harris was the only Southern writer
      of his time who could make subtle social distinctions be-
      tween characters through dialect. Analyzes "At Teague Po-
      teet's," "Mingo" (which features Harris's most memorable
      poor white, Mrs. Bivins), "Ananias," "A Piece of Land," and
      several other stories.

12   SPILLER, ROBERT E., et al. Literary History of the United
      States: Bibliography Supplement II. New York: Macmillan,
      p. 176.
         Lists a new edited letter, a recent Bibliography of
      American Literature item, and six books and articles on Har-
      ris. Mistakenly includes an essay on George Washington
      Harris among the entries. Supplement to 1949.B12 and
      1959.B10.

1973 A BOOKS

1   LEA, JAMES W. "The Shadow at the Cabin Door: Implications of
      Reality in Joel Chandler Harris's Tales of Uncle Remus."
      Ph.D. dissertation, University of North Carolina at Chapel
      Hill, 135pp.
         Harris's critics have not properly measured his awareness
      of the social and ethical content of his stories, in terms
      of black experience in nineteenth-century Georgia. Harris
      was a psychologically complex figure who was sensitive to
      the black man; he was doubtless aware that the Negro folk-
      tales he retold disclosed a brutal, predatory world in which

the violent behavior of the animals is often symbolic of
black attitudes towards the white man. Themes of suffering,
slavery, black isolation, and loss appear more overtly in
Harris's other works of fiction and show the consistency of
his vision.

1973 B SHORTER WRITINGS

1   BITTICK, (MRS.) L. CARY, SR. "Typestand Used By Joel Chandler
    Harris." Monroe Advertiser (1 March), p. 1.
        Harris worked as a printer on the Monroe Advertiser,
    Forsyth, Georgia, from 1867 to 1870; his typestand has been
    preserved. J. T. Manry, Harris's helper, recalled that
    Harris often set his stories directly into type, without
    writing them out first. He also contributed a regular
    column to the Advertiser and printed short stories or
    sketches of fox-hunting for the paper.

2   BROOKS, CLEANTH; R. W. B. LEWIS; and ROBERT PENN WARREN, eds.
    American Literature. The Makers and the Making. Vol. 2.
    New York: St. Martin's Press, pp. 1255, 1709-15, 1724.
        The Uncle Remus stories have analogues all over the
    world: in the folklore told by the American Indian and the
    peasants of northern Europe and Asia, and by African peo-
    ples. In these tales of the Negro slave, the hero is not
  · the strongest animal, but the weaker rabbit, and occasion-
    ally even the less formidable Brer Tarrypin. Like Faulk-
    ner's Negroes, Brer Rabbit endures; he is always hopeful,
    resourceful and, at times, cruel. These stories speak for
    all humanity as did the tales of Aesop, a Phrygian slave.
    Harris worked and reworked the stories, shaping them loving-
    ly into artistic productions. Unlike many Southerners,
    Harris enjoyed firsthand experiences with the Negroes and
    was able to delve into the "archetypal patterns of behavior
    which transcend creed, class, and color." Uncle Remus is
    usually dismissed as a stereotype but his "attitude toward
    the white folks is more complicated than a careless reading
    would suggest." The Uncle Remus stories, along with the
    romances of Thomas Nelson Page and James Lane Allen, may
    well have changed the Northern view of the South and its
    abilities to deal with the Negro problem. Harris did re-
    veal the harsher side of the South, in such stories as
    "Where's Duncan?," but he is most successful with the comic
    or gently satiric modes. Anthologizes "Mr. Terrapin Shows
    His Strength" and "Brother Rabbit Has Fun at the Ferry."

1973

3   [CALLAWAY, H. L. and I. M. WALKER]. "Harris," in Cassell's
    Encyclopaedia of World Literature. Vol. 2. Edited by J.
    Buchanan-Brown. Revised edition. London: Cassell & Co.,
    p. 626.
    Minor revision of 1954.B2.

4   CALVERTON, V.[ICTOR] F.[RANCIS]. The Liberation of American
    Literature. New York: Octagon Books, pp. 146–47.
    Reprint of 1932.B4.

5   DAVIDSON, MARSHALL B., et al., eds. The American Heritage
    History of the Writers' America. New York: American
    Heritage Publishing Co., pp. 214, 215, 341.
        The Uncle Remus stories are among the greatest dealing
    with American Negro folklore; Harris used the material
    "with subtlety and appreciation" and created in Uncle Remus
    a "beloved, shrewd, and immortal figure" who could philos-
    ophically tell a white boy about the ability of the weak to
    overcome the strong. A. B. Frost's drawings "are insepa-
    rable from the text of the stories." The regionalism that
    flourished in the 1920's and 1930's "harks back" to the
    writings of Cable, Harris, and others.

6   DORSON, RICHARD M. America in Legend. New York: Pantheon
    Books, p. 126.
        The first field collection of American Negro oral litera-
    ture, made in 1867 by three Northerners, "discussed Negro
    folk music seriously, but its trove of spirituals and ring
    dances confirmed the stereotype of a gospeling, shuffling,
    ecstatically shouting black man giving vent to childlike
    emotions." Harris reinforced this stereotype in 1880, as
    did other collectors who followed in his wake. Only late
    in the twentieth century has new scholarship recognized
    "the covert protest against and deception of the white
    masters in slave spirituals edged with double meanings."
    In Northern urban Negro folk rhetoric, furthermore, the
    "cozening rabbit of the Southern briar patch" is portrayed
    as a hustler or "strutting badman," a "menacing, triumphant
    figure, modeled on the militant black culture heroes of a
    new day."

7   DUNDES, ALAN, ed. Mother Wit from the Laughing Barrel:
    Readings in the Interpretation of Afro-American Folklore.
    Englewood Cliffs, NJ: Prentice-Hall, pp. 524–25, 541, et
    passim.
        In his headnote to a reprinting of Wolfe's essay [see
    1949.B15 and 1973.B15], Dundes claims that the framework for
    the Uncle Remus tales "is offensive to contemporary American

1973

Negroes and some whites," because a grown Negro man depicted
as the playmate or nursemaid of a white boy is a "painful
reminder" of slavery times. "Because of this, the Joel
Chandler Harris collections of Negro tales are not used in
some racially mixed elementary schools"; thus, unfortunately, "black children may grow up deprived of a knowledge of
the marvelous rabbit trickster figure, a figure who ranks
with the finest inventions of the folk imagination ever
created." Of course, Harris was only retelling tales he
had heard, one of several examples of "white exploitations
of Negro folklore." Yet had Harris not been interested in
Negro folklore, "one of the great stimuli to collectors of
Negro folktales would have been absent, and many of the collections of tales inspired by Harris' efforts might never
have been made."

8   FLUSCHE, MICHAEL. "Joel Chandler Harris: Poor White Uncle
Remus," in his "The Private Plantation: Versions of the
Old South Myth, 1880-1914." Ph.D. dissertation, Johns
Hopkins, pp. 90-168; also, pp. 322-24, 327, 356-65.
Page, Harris, Dunbar, Chesnutt, and Cable discovered
that the stereotyped image of the Old Plantation that made
such popular magazine fare during the Gilded Age was con-
fining and inadequate in the light of post-Civil War social
and economic realities. Harris's pathological insecurity
and his discomfort among his peers contributed to his portraits of the often treacherous and violent animal and
human relationships in his Uncle Remus tales; to some extent, too, Harris must have sympathized with Brer Rabbit's
oddities as a trickster. Harris longed for a harmonious
society free from competition and strife. In his local
color stories his attempt to "blend realism with pathos was
the first step toward a conception of the tragic poor white
of Erskine Caldwell and William Faulkner." Beneath their
optimistic surface, <u>Plantation</u>, <u>Sister Jane</u>, and <u>Tolliver</u>
reveal Harris's loneliness, self-doubt, and anxiety and his
preoccupation with bizarre family relationships. Harris
sympathetically condescended to blacks in his stories and
his editorials, perhaps to bolster his own insecure self.
[Portions of this dissertation appear in 1975.B7 and
1975.B8, in revised form.]

9   HOLLIS, C. CARROLL. "Rural Humor of the Late Nineteenth
Century," in <u>The Comic Imagination in American Literature</u>.
Edited by Louis D. Rubin, Jr. New Brunswick, NJ: Rutgers
University Press, p. 175.
Relates Twain and Harris to rural humorists. <u>Uncle Remus</u>
is in a "different category," however, from the work of the
rural comedians.

1973

10   LYNN, KENNETH S. "Introduction," to The Octopus by Frank
     Norris, in his Visions of America: Eleven Literary
     Historical Essays. Contributions in American Studies,
     No. 6. Westport, CN: Greenwood Press, p. 118.
     Reprint of 1958.B15.

11   McGARRY, DANIEL D. and SARAH HARRIMAN WHITE, eds. World
     Historical Fiction Guide: An Annotated, Chronological,
     Geographical and Topical List of Selected Historical Novels.
     Second edition. Metuchen, NJ: Scarecrow Press, p. 405.
     Entry identical to 1963.B10.

12   OSTERWEIS, ROLLIN G. The Myth of the Lost Cause: 1865–1900.
     Hamden, CN: Shoe String Press, pp. 39, 45–46, 48, 52, 53,
     135, et passim.
           Mentions Harris's contributions to Scribner's and Century
     as typical of Northern magazine editors' interest in South-
     ern literature and "the Myth of the Lost Cause." "Free Joe"
     raises doubts about the black man's ability to survive with-
     out slavery.

13   TURNER, ARLIN. "Comedy and Reality in Local Color Fiction,
     1865–1900," in The Comic Imagination in American Literature.
     Edited by Louis D. Rubin, Jr. New Brunswick, NJ: Rutgers
     University Press, p. 163.
           Uncle Remus's speech may appear difficult, "but the sim-
     plicity of the tales and the recurrence of a relatively few
     expressions" make the dialect surprisingly easy.

14   VOSS, ARTHUR. The American Short Story. A Critical Survey.
     Norman, OK: University of Oklahoma Press, pp. 101–103,
     105.
           While Harris achieved fame from the Uncle Remus stories,
     his short stories in Mingo and other volumes "entitle him
     to a place in the first rank" of Southern local color fic-
     tion. "At Teague Poteet's" and "Trouble on Lost Mountain"
     compare with Murfree's best work in portraying the Southern
     mountaineer; his character descriptions are vivid, empha-
     sizing neither the crude nor the sentimental. Harris also
     avoided the overly sentimental in his "moving" depictions
     of slaves and former slaves in such stories as "Free Joe,"
     "Mingo," "Balaam and His Master," and "Ananias." "Azalia"
     is the best of the stories which describe the Middle Georgia
     people in the decade or so after the War. Although this
     story has a highly romantic ending, Harris ordinarily
     avoided contrived plots. "His stories have an air of au-
     thenticity and a naturalness of tone not often found in the
     same degree in the other Southern local colorists."

1974

15 WOLFE, BERNARD. "Uncle Remus and the Malevolent Rabbit,"
    in Mother Wit from the Laughing Barrel: Readings in the
    Interpretation of Afro-American Folklore. Edited by Alan
    Dundes. Englewood Cliffs, NJ: Prentice-Hall, pp. 524-40.
    Reprint of 1949.B15. [See also 1973.B7.]

1974 A BOOKS - NONE

1974 B SHORTER WRITINGS

1   ANDREWS, WILLIAM L. "The Significance of Charles W.
    Chesnutt's 'Conjure Stories.'" SLJ, 7 (Fall), 82-84, 85-98
    passim.
        Chesnutt acknowledged the superficial similarities be-
    tween Uncle Remus and Uncle Julius in The Conjure Woman yet
    insisted that he did not consider himself a writer of folk
    tales but rather a writer of the imagination. Furthermore,
    Chesnutt's stories do not yield the allegorical meanings
    that Harris's do. Uncle Julius is a "skillfully drawn suc-
    cessor to the prototypes created by Page and Harris." In
    The Conjure Woman Chesnutt did picture the black man as Har-
    ris had--as generous, loyal, "'childish,'" and "'ignorant.'"
    In other stories, however, he veered away from this stereo-
    type. His portraits of Southern middle and lower classes
    suggest Harris and Richard Malcolm Johnston.

2   BLOTNER, JOSEPH. Faulkner: A Biography. Vol. 1. New York:
    Random House, p. 93.
        Billy Falkner acquired books from his grandparents'
    library and from other family members as he grew up; among
    these volumes were Grimm's Fairy Tales, Uncle Remus, and
    Robinson Crusoe. "His friends remembered that Billy Falkner
    never forgot a word he read."

3   CRAWFORD, JOHN W. "Bred and Bawn in a Briar Patch--Deception
    in the Making." SCB, 34 (Winter), 149-50.
        Deception among heroes is a prominent theme in the
    Odyssey, in Gawain and the Green Knight and Chaucer's "The
    Pardoner's Tale," in Shakespeare's "Julius Caesar," and in
    Twain, Harris, and Faulkner. Flem Snopes, Brer Rabbit, Tom
    Sawyer, and Odysseus were all "bred and bawn in a briar
    patch."

4   DANIEL, PETE and RAYMOND SMOCK. A Talent for Detail: The
    Photographs of Miss Frances Benjamin Johnston. 1889-1910.
    New York: Crown Publishers, pp. 142-44.

1974

Frances Benjamin Johnston photographed Harris in Atlanta
in 1905; Harris was delighted with the photograph of himself, which revealed a "twinkle" in his eye. Johnston recalled Harris's "'comfortable rounded outlines,'" ruddy
face, black sombrero-shaped hat, and deep blue eyes. He
was shy and nervous at first, but she managed to take his
mind off posing. Her photograph was subsequently used on
the cover of Uncle Remus's Home Magazine and as the model
for the Harris commemorative three-cents stamp, issued in
1948. The photograph is reproduced on p. 142.

5   EICHELBERGER, CLAYTON L., comp. A Guide to Critical Reviews
    of United States Fiction, 1870-1910. Vol. 2. Metuchen,
    NJ: Scarecrow Press, pp. 126-27.
        Supplement to 1971.B3. Lists fifty-eight periodical re-
    views of twenty-one of Harris's books.

6   GODBOLD, E. STANLY, JR. "A Battleground Revisited:
    Reconstruction in Southern Fiction, 1895-1905." SAQ, 73
    (Winter), 100, 108-110, 111, 116.
        Among six novelists who treated Reconstruction [Cable,
    Page, Glasgow, Thomas Dixon, Jr., and John S. Wise are also
    discussed], Harris's was a voice crying in the wilderness
    "for faith in the innate goodness of man, white and black,
    Northerner and Southerner." Tolliver is an "extraordinary,"
    although unread, call for national and racial goodwill dur-
    ing those difficult times. While he managed to avoid facing
    many of the hard realities of the early twentieth century,
    Harris did blame these realities on the turbulent times
    rather than on malice or retribution by Yankees or Southern-
    ers, black or white. Harris was no revisionist; he sought
    to rationalize the actions of the people who lived through
    the era.

7   MacKETHAN, LUCINDA H. "Joel Chandler Harris: Speculating on
    the Past," in her "Pastoral Patterns in Post-Civil War
    Southern Literature." Ph.D. dissertation, University of
    North Carolina at Chapel Hill, pp. [151]-222; also [1]-4,
    5, 17-18, 30-31, 297-98.
        Treats Lanier, Page, Harris, Chesnutt, and Jean Toomer.
    Harris's reverence for the pastoral life and the plantation
    ideal appears as early as 1863 in an essay for Turner's
    The Countryman. Nostalgia for the country and the old plan-
    tation is a strong theme in the Uncle Remus volumes, but
    more so than Page and other pastoral writers Harris treated
    the less attractive features of slavery and sought to human-
    ize the Negro. Several Uncle Remuses appear in Harris's
    books and Harris himself held contradictory attitudes about

the race question and the South. Harris used the pastoral "trick" of implying a warm relationship between the races by having the "inferior" black defend the cause of his "superior," but the amoral Brer Rabbit, as Rubin points out [see 1970.B19], presents an ironic inversion of the plantation system and is "a rebuke to its inequities." Harris seems to have instinctively identified with the Negro and his hero.

8   McMICHAEL, GEORGE, ed. Realism to the Present. Vol. 2 of Anthology of American Literature. George McMichael, General Editor. New York: Macmillan, pp. 238-39.
    Harris's Uncle Remus tales, adapted from the folk myths of Europe and Africa, are memorable local color stories which depict a point in time yet have a lasting human appeal. Twain recalled that some of the happiest moments of his youth were spent listening to Uncle Remus tales. During Harris's time readers were fascinated by local color stories, and Uncle Remus had the same appeal as Twain's frontier yarns, Bret Harte's Sierra tales, and Kate Chopin's portrayals of the Louisiana Creoles. Harris's tales were also object lessons for the "downtrodden who used their wits to survive and to laugh at their oppressors." Anthologizes "How Mr. Rabbit Was Too Sharp For Mr. Fox" and "Free Joe."

9   PETTIT, ARTHUR G.[ORDON]. Mark Twain & the South. Lexington, KY: University Press of Kentucky, pp. 127, 131.
    Twain replaced his darky jokes in his lectures of the 1880's with carefully selected readings about blacks. He wrote Howells in 1881 that he had a "most rattling high time" reading Harris's "Tar-Baby" to a Hartford Congregational church. In 1889 he read "Tar-Baby" at the Brooklyn Academy of Music. In Life on the Mississippi Twain stated that Cable and Harris were the only Southern writers worth reading.

10   RENDER, SYLVIA LYONS, ed. "Introduction," in The Short Fiction of Charles W. Chesnutt. Washington, D.C.: Howard University Press, pp. 18, 23-24.
     Chesnutt followed but was not constrained by the literary dialect of Page and Harris. Although Uncle Julius in The Conjure Woman is clearly modeled on Uncle Remus, Julius is more organically part of the stories he recalls.

11   RUBIN, LOUIS D., JR. "Uncle Remus and the Ubiquitous Rabbit." SoR, NS 10 (October), 787-804.
     Harris was a complex figure, on the surface a journalist and optimist, but a "fiercely creative artist" and realist

1974

underneath who had doubts about the rising materialism in
the New South. Perhaps because of his illegitimate birth
and shyness, Harris was able to identify with the Negro's
real condition better than other local colorists and to portray the black man more sensitively in fiction. The rabbit
exemplifies the black man in his struggle "to survive and
flourish in a world in which society can be and often is
predatory." The Remus tales are not "parables of protest,"
however; they seek to depict "the actualities of the human
situation and by implication contrasting them with what we
hold to be ideal." Viewed not from the context of the
1960's and 1970's, as Darwin Turner views Harris [see
1968.B15], but from that of Harris's own times, his portraits of the blacks showed the misunderstanding and mis-
treatment of the day; Harris saw the black man as a human
being. Reprinted: 1975.B18.

12   SHANKMAN, ARNOLD. "Julian Harris and the Negro." Phylon, 35
(December), 442, 443.
       Harris's son Julian grew up in a South that romanticized
the antebellum days and believed the Negro to be the inferior race, but he came to be a courageous advocate of
civil rights. Joel Chandler Harris published a number of
stories that implied black inferiority, but "to his credit"
he was aware that the Negro question was also the white
man's question; Julian's father told Julian that hatred of
anybody or anything does not pay and sought to obliterate
racial prejudice in the South. In 1910, when he was still
of a conservative perspective, Julian wrote a play in which
Uncle Remus, one of the chief characters, typified "'the
dependence and almost helplessness of the Negro after
freedom.'"

13   SPILLER, ROBERT E., et al. Literary History of the United
States: History. Fourth edition, revised. New York:
Macmillan, London: Collier Macmillan, pp. 748, 851–54,
1505, et passim.
       Commentary identical to 1948.B17. Minor change in
bibliographical note, p. 1505.

14   WOODWARD, C. [OMER] VANN. The Strange Career of Jim Crow.
Third revised edition. New York: Oxford University
Press, p. 93.
       Revision of 1966.B11.

1975

1975 A BOOKS - NONE

1975 B SHORTER WRITINGS

1 BLAIR, WALTER. "Mark Twain's Other Masterpiece: 'Jim Baker's Blue-Jay Yarn.'" Studies in American Humor, 1 (January), 133, 139, 141-42.
   When he was a boy in Missouri, Twain heard Uncle Daniel tell tales that Harris was to immortalize. He later read Harris's Uncle Remus stories to audiences, included two of Harris's narratives in Mark Twain's Library of Humor (1888), corresponded with Harris, and tried to talk him into a lecture tour. He admired Harris's storytelling and framing techniques and may have been influenced by him in "Jim Baker's Blue-Jay Yarn." Both writers comically portrayed animal and human incongruities.

2 BONE, ROBERT. Down Home: A History of Afro-American Short Fiction from Its Beginnings to the End of the Harlem Renaissance. New York: G. P. Putnam's Sons, Capricorn Books, pp. 6-7, 11, 12, 13-17, 19-40, 79-81, 88.
   Harris was part of the plantation school of the 1880's and 1890's, although the plantation pastoral tradition in America dates from Kennedy's Swallow Barn in 1832 to Gone with the Wind in 1936; Harris was a major influence on Chesnutt. Uncle Remus was the "first literary statement of the New South," but like other plantation writers Harris masked over the brutal repression of the blacks to portray benevolent slave owners and a white supremacy perspective. Yet Harris was a schizoid and a neurotic, a Southern maverick who could not completely suppress the realities of the Negro's condition. He provided the missing link between the Afro-American folktale and the American short story; the frame for his stories was all white, but the tales of masking and countermasking were authentically black. The trickster-hero Brer Rabbit embodies the outlaw survival code of the black slave and the refusal to submit to the white world; he survives through deception and sheer endurance power. "Having been raised in a brier patch, he is one tough bunny."

3 BRESTENSKY, DENNIS F. "Uncle Remus: Mere Buffoon or Admirable Man of Stature?" West Virginia University Philological Papers, 22 (December), [51]-58.
   In Friends Uncle Remus sometimes plays the buffoon, but he attains real stature as a man of understanding and depth of character in Uncle Remus and Nights.

299

1975

4   DILLARD, J.[OEY] L.[EE]. All-American English. New York:
    Random House, p. 186.
    Some of Harris's characters speak a form of Plantation
    Creole.

5   DORSON, RICHARD M. "African and Afro-American Folklore: A
    Reply to Bascom and Other Misguided Critics." JAF, 88
    (April-June), 155, 156-57, 162.
    Disagrees with conclusions offered by Gerber [1893.B19],
    Ellis [1895.B17], Piersen [1971.B12], and others about the
    extent of African origins for the Uncle Remus stories and
    other Afro-American folk materials. Argues for a lesser
    influence than these folklorists suggest.

6   [ENGLISH, THOMAS H.]. "Fun in a Newspaper Office." Ex Libris:
    An Occasional Publication of Friends of the Emory University
    Library, no. 14 (June), pp. 8-10.
    Harris came to the Atlanta Constitution in 1876, already
    famous for his humorous paragraphs and red hair. Always
    fond of a well-executed practical joke, he no doubt enjoyed
    this broadside, done appropriately in red ink by someone on
    the staff, in the summer of 1878. Written in eight-lined
    stanzas, with a refrain, "'Thy Head is Embers,'" it wittily
    recounts the attempt on the part of the local fire brigade
    to quench Harris's "'flaming'" red hair. All attempts fail,
    whereupon the observation is made that Harris needs no
    chandelier to do his writing by, for his burning skull is
    sufficient light; in fact, he might charitably offer to be
    a lamp-post, to light the way of drunken men, or a light-
    house, to warn ships off dangerous reefs.

7   FLUSCHE, MICHAEL. "Joel Chandler Harris and the Folklore of
    Slavery." JAmS, 9 (December), 347-63.
    Sensitive and cautious study of the Uncle Remus animal
    fables, including structural and content analysis, suggests
    that the black slave saw his world as a hostile place of
    perpetual struggle; the trickster was the typical hero of
    the slave's imagination. Any social amenities among blacks
    and whites were only superficial. [Based upon 1973.B8.]

8   ____. "Underlying Despair in the Fiction of Joel Chandler
    Harris." MissQ, 29 (Winter), 91-103.
    Harris's pessimism "dominated his imagination even though
    his genteel conception of the role of literature led him to
    write optimistic and uplifting tales." Harris felt insecure
    and inadequate throughout his life, but compensated for
    these feelings by clowning, playing practical jokes, and
    telling stories that were light or humorous on the surface,

but hostile underneath. Harris could not portray normal
family relationships, but in Sister Jane, Plantation, Tolliver, and other works drew characters that were isolated,
maimed, or rootless. [Based upon 1973.B8.]

9 FORBES, W. STANTON. Lucy W. Stanton, Artist. Atlanta, GA:
    Special Collections Department, Robert W. Woodruff Library,
    Emory University, pp. 7, 38-40, 75, 77.
        Harris moved into a house across the street from the
    Stantons, in West End, Atlanta. As a girl, Lucy Stanton
    heard the Uncle Remus tales as they were being written. In
    1906 she did a full-size oil portrait of Harris from life,
    and then a miniature and an ivory. Her portraits show Har-
    ris's sensitivity and awareness of the tragedy that runs
    through life. The portraits are reproduced as plates.

10 HAVLICE, PATRICIA PATE. Index to Literary Biography. Vol. 1.
    Metuchen, NJ: Scarecrow Press, p. 522.
        Cites six sources of biographical information on Harris.
    Revision of 1971.B9.

11 KIRBY, DAVID K. American Fiction to 1900: A Guide to
    Information Sources. Detroit, MI: Gale Research Co.,
    pp. 119-21.
        Selected primary and secondary works are checklisted.
    The fifteen secondary items are briefly annotated.

12 LIGHT, KATHLEEN. "Uncle Remus and the Folklorists." SLJ, 7
    (Spring), 88-104.
        Harris read as much as he could about comparative folk-
    lore and ethnology after the first Uncle Remus tales were
    published. Articles in the Constitution and his lengthy
    survey of the field of folklore in the introduction to
    Nights indicate his attraction to theories of cultural evo-
    lution, but the sophisticated African Jack tales seemed to
    argue that the more "primitive" blacks were at the same
    time more culturally advanced than subsequent generations
    of Negroes. Harris was forced to "admit a level of black
    consciousness which threaten[ed] him as a white man"; "con-
    fused and troubled," he backed away from ethnology in later
    volumes and poked fun at the folklorists.

13 MUFFETT, D. J. M. "Uncle Remus was a Hausaman?" SFQ, 39
    (June), 151-66.
        Parallels in narrative rhythms, word forms, usage, idi-
    oms, and proverbs suggest that the Uncle Remus legends have
    their origin in the Hausa folklore of West Africa. "Uncle
    Remus" may even be a variant of the Hausan slave title,
    D'an Rimi.

1975

14 MUGLESTON, WILLIAM F. "Julian Harris, the Georgia Press, and
    the Ku Klux Klan." Georgia Historical Quarterly, 59 (Fall),
    284-85, 286.
    Harris's son Julian LaRose was "the earliest and most
    uncompromising anti-Klan voice in the Georgia press in the
    twenties," when Georgia was a major Klan bastion. Julian
    inherited his idealism and belief in human decency and non-
    violent settling of differences from his father. Both men
    believed that blacks and whites could live peacefully side
    by side in a segregated society. Julian followed his father
    in working as a reporter for the Atlanta Constitution and
    later as its managing editor; he also helped Joel Chandler
    found the Southern periodical, Uncle Remus's Magazine.

15 _____. "The Perils of Southern Publishing: A History of
    Uncle Remus's Magazine." JQ, 52 (Autumn), 515-21, 608.
    In 1907 Harris founded Uncle Remus's Magazine as a liter-
    ary journal with optimistic and socially ameliorative edi-
    torial content. Although it had solid financial backing,
    the magazine gradually lost income under Julian Harris's
    editorship primarily because Julian made it a quixotic and
    controversial journal of social and political commentary.

16 PEDEN, WILLIAM. The American Short Story: Continuity and
    Change 1940-1975. Boston: Houghton Mifflin, p. 147.
    One of the ironies of American literary history is that
    until relatively recently, with a few exceptions, "the most
    convincing and certainly the most sympathetic fictional por-
    trayals of American blacks have been created by Southern
    whites," from Harris to Faulkner, Eudora Welty, Flannery
    O'Connor, and others.

17 RUBIN, LOUIS D., JR. "Politics and the Novel: George W.
    Cable and the Genteel Tradition," in his William Elliott
    Shoots a Bear: Essays on the Southern Literary Imagination.
    Baton Rouge, LA: Louisiana State University Press, p. 77.
    Local color writers like Harris and Page were responsible
    for changing the nation's image of the black man from Uncle
    Tom to Uncle Remus. "The Negro seen as Uncle Tom carried
    the demand that he be saved from the southern white man's
    cruelty; seen as Uncle Remus, the implication was that he
    could best be left to the southern white man's understanding
    benevolence."

18 _____. "Uncle Remus and the Ubiquitous Rabbit," in his
    William Elliott Shoots a Bear: Essays on the Southern
    Literary Imagination. Baton Rouge, LA: Louisiana State
    University Press, pp. 82-106.
    Reprinting of 1974.B11.

1975

19 _____. "William Styron and Human Bondage," in his <u>William Elliott Shoots a Bear: Essays on the Southern Literary Imagination</u>. Baton Rouge, LA: Louisiana State University Press, p. 233.
Reprinting of 1967.B17, with an appended Afterword.

20 SHANKMAN, ARNOLD. "Julian Harris and the Ku Klux Klan." <u>MissQ</u>, 28 (Spring), 147, 167.
Harris's son Julian braved threats and menacing letters in his crusade against the Ku Klux Klan while he was editor of the Columbus, Georgia, <u>Enquirer-Sun</u>. Julian won a Pulitzer prize for his courageous journalism.

21 TAYLOR, RON. "Joel Harris Shy, Enigmatic." Atlanta <u>Journal and Constitution</u> (9 November), p. 14-B.
Harris had a humorous and a serious side. Although he was patronizing towards blacks, he was regarded as a liberal in his own day. Harris was "among the first to 'humanize' black characters in literature," and he is also regarded "as the first to depict poor whites as something more than 'white trash.'" How much Harris's illegitimate birth affected his personality is uncertain, but he was shy and stuttered all his life.

22 _____. "Uncle Remus Lives And Brer Rabbit Survives Thorny Issue." Atlanta <u>Journal and Constitution</u> (9 November), pp. 12-B, 13-B.
Informal essay reviews several popular and scholarly impressions of Harris's work. For many modern blacks Harris's portrait of Uncle Remus represents the "'Step-'n-Fetch-It'" stereotype, and during the civil rights movement Harris's books were taken off the shelves in Northern cities and a second release of Disney's "Song of the South" was protested in 1956. Resentment of Harris lingers in predominantly black West End, Atlanta, which was an affluent white neighborhood when Harris lived there. But the tide of opinion is still shifting; a third release of the movie in 1972 grossed almost twice as much as the first two releases combined, and a popular edition of the Remus tales regularly outsells <u>Gone With the Wind</u> in Atlanta's two largest department store chains. The black folklorist, Stella Brookes, praises Harris's achievement, and the black director of the Center for African and African-American Studies at Atlanta University, Richard A. Long, although viewing Harris as "an apologist for the Old South," is sympathetic to Harris's work in folklore and dialect. Thomas English of Emory University admires Harris's sense of humor and his creation of "a real language."

1976

23   TUMLIN, JOHN, ed. "Introduction," in Free Joe: Stories by
     Joel Chandler Harris. Savannah, GA: Beehive Press,
     pp. vii-xxi.
         Biographical sketch emphasizes Harris's reticent person-
     ality and his journalistic career. His Uncle Remus tales
     brought him international attention, but Harris began to
     turn to other Middle Georgia materials in writing Mingo and
     other collections of local color tales, which he considered
     to be more "serious" literature. He was an early advocate
     of "localism" in literature; he distrusted some of the New
     South values and often harked back to old plantation days.
     His local color tales contain vivid characters and dramatic
     power, and Aunt Minervy Ann, Blue Dave, and Free Joe are
     completely realized figures. Isolation is the theme of his
     best short stories, and "Where's Duncan?" presages the works
     of Faulkner. Reprints a score of Harris's tales.

1976 A BOOKS

1   GRISKA, JOSEPH MATTHEW, JR. "Selected Letters of Joel Chandler
     Harris, 1863-1885." Ph.D. dissertation, Texas A & M
     University, 195pp. & lxxxvi.
         Reproduces seventy-seven letters from 1863-1885 from the
     one hundred extant letters of the period. Headnotes and
     annotations to letters give circumstances of their writing
     and provide basic biographical and other primary data.
     Critical and biographical commentary is contained in the
     introduction. Textual apparatus and bibliography are in-
     cluded. Restrictions make the dissertation unavailable for
     library loan or microfilming.

2   STRICKLAND, WILLIAM BRADLEY. "Joel Chandler Harris: A
     Bibliographical Study." Ph.D. dissertation, University of
     Georgia, 297pp.
         Introductory chapter reviews the state of Harris bibliog-
     raphy. Chapter two lists and describes bibliographically
     Harris's books, itemizes their contents, and lists prior
     magazine publication where known. Chapter three lists and
     describes thirty original contributions to books; chapter
     four describes 181 contributions to periodicals (excluding
     newspapers); chapter six cites published letters; and chap-
     ters seven and eight give miscellaneous works and reprints.
     Appendix A lists Harris's contributions to Turner's The
     Countryman, 1862-1866; Appendix B checklists secondary
     scholarship in books and articles from 1869-1975; Appendix
     C indexes titles of Harris's works. [A portion of the dis-
     sertation appears in 1976.B5.]

1976 B SHORTER WRITINGS

1   COOK, SYLVIA JENKINS. From Tobacco Road to Route 66: The
    Southern Poor White in Fiction. Chapel Hill, NC:
    University of North Carolina Press, pp. 10-11, 20, 124.
    Harris created "several pitiable and near-tragic poor
    whites and greatly advanced the characterization of poor
    white women in the heroic figures of Mrs. Feratia Bivins
    and Emma Jane Stucky." Harris forces the "tragic" implica-
    tions of Feratia's experiences, but Emma Jane is more
    successful.

2   DAVID, BEVERLY R. "Visions of the South: Joel Chandler Harris
    and His Illustrators." ALR, 9 (Summer), 189-206.
    Recounts Harris's relationship with his early illustra-
    tors, Moser and Church, and Harris's and A. B. Frost's mu-
    tual discovery of each other's art in the mid-1880's; Frost
    became Harris's favorite illustrator. Includes letters and
    reproduced drawings.

3   [ENGLISH, THOMAS H.]. "First Meeting of Harris and Grady."
    Ex Libris: An Occasional Publication of Friends of the
    Emory University Library, nos. 16 and 17 (March), p. 5.
    Among the more amusing items in the Henry W. Grady col-
    lection at Emory is a cartoon, here reproduced, by Lewis
    Gregg, staff artist of the Atlanta Constitution, depicting
    Harris's first meeting with Grady in Rome, Georgia, in 1871.
    Grady loved carnivals and other public amusements, and when
    Harris met him he was riding happily upon a merry-go-round
    at a street carnival.

4   MATTHEWS, JOHN M. "Julian L. Harris: The Evolution of a
    Southern Liberal." SAQ, 75 (Autumn), 484-85, 486-87.
    Julian Harris, then editor of the Columbus, Georgia,
    Enquirer-Sun, won the Pulitzer Prize for Meritorious Public
    Service in 1926 for his crusading editorial attacks on
    lynching, the Ku Klux Klan, and political corruption.
    Julian, Harris's eldest son, acquired an interest in jour-
    nalism through his father and worked on the Atlanta Consti-
    tution in his early years; he inherited his father's "good
    will, his sympathy for beneficent causes, his red hair, and
    genial temperament." The older Harris was paternalistic to-
    wards the Negro and was never an active reformer, whereas
    Julian became an aggressive Southern liberal. When Julian
    inherited from his father the editorship of Uncle Remus's
    Magazine, he turned the journal into a controversial organ
    of social criticism of the South.

1976

5 STRICKLAND, WILLIAM BRADLEY. "A Check List of the Periodical
Contributions of Joel Chandler Harris (1848–1908)." <u>ALR</u>,
9 (Summer), [205]–29.
[Based upon portions of 1976.A2.] Under the headings
Fiction, Poetry, Essays, Articles, Editorials, Reviews, and
Letters and Miscellaneous Works, lists chronologically,
with annotations, Harris's periodical writings exclusive
of newspapers.

A Note about the Index

In addition to authors, titles of works by Harris and others, and the names of characters and people, this index incorporates significant commentaries or information on forty-two subjects and themes. In all cases, the subjects below are discussed with reference to Harris's life or works. When commentaries have been reprinted or republished in only slightly revised form, the first printing only is indexed; the entries themselves cite any later editions.

Index

The American Spirit in Letters,
  1926.B13
The American Spirit in Literature, 1921.B5
American Studies in Honor of
  William Kenneth Boyd,
  1940.B1, B7
The American Tradition in Liter-
  ature, 1956.B3
"American Writers in Europe,"
  1948.B14
American Writers on American
  Literature, 1931.B16-B17
America's Black Past: A Reader
  in Afro-American History,
  1970.B12
Ananias, 1891.B9, B19; 1892.B1;
  1916.B5; 1937.B3;
  1961.B4-B5; 1963.B7;
  1971.B16
"Ananias," 1891.B7; 1921.B6;
  1940.B11; 1972.B11; 1973.B14
"Anansi and Brer Rabbit,"
  1949.B3
Anansi tales, the, 1905.B12;
  1949.B3
And Horns on the Toads, 1959.B11
Andersen, Hans Christian,
  1893.B11; 1895.B8; 1934.B7
Anderson, Charles Roberts,
  1940.B1; 1945.B1-B3, B9-B10
Andrews, Alice E., 1929.B12
Andrews, William L., 1974.B1
The Angry Scar: The Story of
  Reconstruction, 1959.B2
"Animal Stories from the Indians
  of the Muskhogean Stock,"
  1913.B11
Annancy tales, the. See Anansi
  tales, the
Ante-Bellum Southern Literary
  Critics, 1962.B9
An Anthology of American Humor,
  1962.B11
Anthology of American Literature.
  See Vol. 2: Realism to the
  Present, 1974.B8
Anthology of American Negro
  Literature (Calverton)
  1929.B2; (Watkins) 1944.B3,
  B5

An Anthology of Famous American
  Stories, 1953.B5
Anthony, Edward, 1962.B2
"Apocryphal Biology: A Chapter
  in American Folklore,"
  1958.B6
Apologia (Newman), 1908.B26
Appleton, D. & Company, 1950.B2;
  1952.B8
Appleton's Cyclopaedia of American
  Biography, 1888.B25; 1900.B31
"The Arab Response to the Black
  Writers of America," 1972.B9
Arabian Nights, 1894.B1
"Archy and Uncle Remus: Don
  Marquis's Debt to Joel
  Chandler Harris," 1961.B9
Aristophanes, 1937.B9
Armes, Ethel, 1905.B14
Armistead, S. G., 1971.B1
Arnett, Alex Mathews, 1935.B10
Arnold, Gertrude Weld, 1909.B10;
  1912.B1
Arp, Bill. See Smith, Charles
  Henry
Artemus Ward: His Book (C. F.
  Browne), 1947.B17
Articles on American Literature
  1900-1950, 1954.B9
Articles on American Literature
  1950-1967, 1970.B15
"As a Little Child," 1910.B6
Asian Response to American
  Literature, 1972.B9
Aspects of Fiction (B. Matthews),
  1896.B27
Assessments, general, 1891.B18,
  B20; 1896.A1, B40; 1900.B9,
  B19; 1903.B7; 1904.B7;
  1905.B3, B5, B7; 1907.B7;
  1908.B17, B25, B29;
  1909.B12-B14; 1915.B1;
  1918.A1-A2, B9; 1920.B6;
  1923.B7; 1936.B1, B9;
  1938.B5; 1943.B10; 1948.B17;
  1951.B2; 1954.B4, B6;
  1956.B3; 1957.B9; 1960.B1;
  1965.B11; 1975.B22
Aswell, James R., 1947.B2
"At Snap Bean Farm" (Marquis)
  1909.B20; (Merriam) 1913.B9

Brown, Sterling A., 1933.B1;
1937.B3; 1939.B2; 1945.B5;
1950.B1; 1953.B3-B4;
1966.B2; 1970.B19
Brown, W. Norman, 1921.B1;
1922.B2, B10; 1929.B4;
1937.B4; 1938.B3; 1940.B9
Brown, Wenzell, 1949.B3
Browne, Charles Farrar, 1889.B8
Browning, D. C., 1958.B3
Bruce, Philip Alexander,
1905.B15
Brunvand, Jan Harold, 1968.B4
Bryant, William Cullen, 1948.B14
Bryson, Lyman, 1956.B16
Bu Allah. See Ben Ali
Buck, Paul H., 1937.B5
Builders and Books: The Romance
of American History and
Literature, 1931.B12
Bumppo, Natty, 1917.B7
Bunyan, Paul, 1935.B7
Burgum, Edwin Berry, 1944.B4;
1947.B4
Burke, Kenneth, 1946.B15
Burke, W. J., 1943.B2
Burrell, Angus, 1953.B5
Burrison, John A., 1968.A1
Burton, Richard, 1902.B20;
1903.B5; 1969.B3
Butcher, Margaret Just, 1956.B5
Butler, Ben, 1962.B4
"Butler the Beast," 1962.B4
Byrd, James W., 1967.B2
Byrd, Mabel, 1924.B3

C., J. N., 1892.B19
Cabell, James Branch, 1935.B9
Cable, George Washington,
1882.B2; 1883.B8; 1884.B6;
1885.B4; 1886.B6; 1893.B21;
1895.B23; 1898.B14, B20;
1900.B21; 1901.B15, B18;
1903.B9; 1909.B19; 1917.B2;
1925.B8; 1926.B8; 1928.B2,
B7; 1929.B6-B7; 1931.B15;
1932.B5; 1933.B3; 1936.B7;
1937.B3, B5; 1941.B3, B11;
1947.B15; 1949.B2; 1952.B3;
1957.B10; 1958.B4; 1959.B2;
1960.B9; 1963.B1; 1964.B8,

B12; 1966.A2; 1967.B13;
1968.B6; 1973.B5, B8;
1974.B6, B9
Cairns, Huntingdon, 1965.B11
Cairns, William B., 1912.B3;
1930.B2
Caldwell, Erskine, 1973.B8
Callaway, H. L., 1954.B2; 1973.B3
Calverton, Victor Francis,
1929.B2; 1932.B4; 1973.B4
Campbell, F. C., 1966.B3
Campbell, James Edwin, 1939.B11
The Cambridge History of American
Literature, 1918.B9;
1921.B7-B8; 1933.B8-B9
Camp, Mildred Harris, 1919.B5;
1933.B4; 1946.B1
Canby, Henry Seidel, 1922.B7;
1934.B3; 1948.B3; 1951.B1;
1965.B1
Candler, Allen D., 1906.B4;
1972.B3
Carnegie, Andrew, 1906.B1;
1907.B5-B6; 1908.B9;
1913.A1, B2; 1917.B10
Carpenter, Frank G., 1896.B43
Carroll, Lewis. See Dodgson,
Charles Lutwidge
Carter, Hodding, 1959.B2
"The Case of Mary Ellen,"
1899.B5; 1925.B5; 1926.B5;
1929.B8; 1948.B9
Cash, Wilbur F., 1941.B2
Cash, W. J., 1940.B2
Cassell's Encyclopaedia of World
Literature, 1954.B2; 1973.B3
"Catalogue of the chief novels
and short stories by American
authors dealing with the
Civil War and its effects,
1861-1899," 1940.B13-B14;
1941.B10
"The Catbird Seat" (Thurber),
1957.B11
Cather, Willa, 1969.B1
Catholicism, 1908.B26; 1937.B7;
1942.B5
"The Cause of the Difficulty,"
1964.B5
Caxton, William, 1956.B11
Centennial Edition of the Works

The Confident Years: 1885–1915,
1952.B2
The Conjure Woman (Chesnutt),
1928.B9; 1931.B4, B11;
1948.B9; 1974.B1, B10
Connelly, Marc, 1953.B4
Connor, Jane, 1928.B6
"A Conscript's Christmas,"
1891.B7; 1892.B1; 1964.B5
Constitution, Atlanta. See
Atlanta Constitution
"The Constitutional Staff,"
1879.B2
Contemporary American Novelists,
1900–1920, 1922.B16
"Contributions of the South to
the Republic of Letters,"
1911.B7; 1919.B6
Cook, Dorothy E., 1953.B6;
1956.B7
Cook, Sylvia Jenkins, 1976.B1
Cook, Will Marion, 1913.B5
The Cool World (W. Miller),
1970.B17
Coolidge, Archibald C., 1949.B13
Cooper, James Fenimore, 1901.B8;
1947.B9; 1963.B7
"The Cornfield Journalist,"
1932.B18; 1967.B18
Cosgrave, John O'Hara, 1968.B9
Cottrell, George W., Jr.,
1930.B5
Couch, William T., 1934.B4, B6,
B11
Coulter, Ellis Merton, 1933.B2;
1951.B12; 1954.B3; 1971.B18
The Count of Monte Cristo
(Dumas), 1888.B12; 1893.B22
The Countryman, 1862.B1; 1898.B23;
1918.A2; 1938.B8; 1939.B3,
B13; 1943.B7; 1949.B4;
1966.A1; 1968.A2. See also
Turner, Joseph Addison
"The Countryman: A Georgia
Journal," 1955.B6
"The 'Countryman': A Lone
Chapter in Plantation Pub-
lishing," 1945.B6–B7
Courses of Reading in American
Literature with Bibliog-
raphies, 1930.B17

Cousins, Paul Mercer, 1930.B6;
1966.A1; 1968.A2, B1, B14,
B18; 1969.B1
Cowie, Alexander, 1951.B2
Cracker, the. See Poor white, the
Crackerbox Philosophers in Ameri-
can Humor and Satire,
1964.B18
Craddock, Charles Egbert. See
Murfree, Mary Noailles
Craig, Newton, 1893.B18;
1894.B4
Crane, T. F., 1881.B14; 1891.B16;
1965.B4
Craven, Avery, 1950.B3
Crawford, John W., 1974.B3
"Creator of Uncle Remus Loved a
Good Joke--Even on Himself,"
1946.B11
Critical Guide: Prepared for the
Home Study Course in World
Literature, 1930.B5
Criticism and Fiction and Other
Essays, 1959.B6
Criticism in America, 1956.B15
Criticism Written 1960–1968,
1970.B9
Cross, Ethan Allen, 1914.B5
The Cruel Side of War (Wormeley),
1898.B18
Crum, Mason, 1940.B3
Crumbling Idols (Garland),
1894.B6
Crusoe, Robinson, 1935.B7
Cudjo, 1885.B3
Culture in the South, 1934.B4, B6,
B11
Cunliffe, Marcus, 1954.B4
Cunningham, Horace H., 1965.B3
Currell, W. S., 1899.B20;
1900.B1, B19
Current-Garcia, Eugene, 1952.B3;
1961.B7; 1964.B7
Curti, Merle, 1941.B12; 1943.B4;
1951.B3; 1954.B13; 1961.B11;
1964.B8
Curtis, Natalie, 1913.B5;
1920.B1
The Cycle of American Literature:
An Essay in Historical Criti-
cism, 1955.B4

Cyclopedia of Georgia, Vol. 2:
F-N, 1906.B4; 1972.B3
Cyclopedia of World Authors,
1958.B16

Dabbs, James McBride, 1958.B5;
1964.B9
Dabney, Virginius, 1932.B5;
1942.B3
Daddy Jack, 1883.B1-B2, B4;
1884.B4; 1908.B19; 1946.B15
Daddy Jake, 1889.B3; 1896.A1;
1897.B4; 1904.B7; 1926.B10
"Daddy Jake, The Runaway,"
1896.B22
Daddy Jake the Runaway and Short
Stories Told After Dark,
1889.B1-B7; 1890.B1;
1895.B18; 1896.B11, B14-B15,
B18, B21-B22, B25-B26,
B30-B31, B35-B36, B42;
1897.B4, B16; 1904.B7;
1906.B4; 1912.B6; 1913.B1;
1926.B7; 1962.B3; 1971.B11
"Daddy Joel Harris and His Old-
Time Darkies," 1968.B15
Daly, Charles A., 1943.B5
Dana, Charles A., 1884.B19
Dance, W. L., 1932.B6
"The Dance in Place Congo,"
1886.B6
Daniel, Frank, 1963.B4
Daniel, Pete, 1974.B4
Dante, 1965.B9
Dargan, Marion, 1952.B4
Dauner, Louise, 1948.B4
David, Beverly R., 1976.B2
Davidson, Donald, 1934.B4
Davidson, James Wood, 1869.B1;
1945.B2-B3; 1946.B4
Davidson, Marshall B., 1973.B5
Davis, Griff, 1945.B5
Davis, Henry C., 1914.B6
Davis, Rebecca Harding,
1893.B7-B8
Davis, Richard Beale, 1970.B3
Davis, Varina Jefferson,
1899.B21
Day, Arthur Grove, 1953.B7
Day, Martin S., 1970.B4
Dearmer, Mabel (Mrs. Percy),
1914.B1-B2; 1922.B5

"The Debt of Joel Chandler Harris
to Joseph Addison Turner,"
1930.B6
Deep Down in the Jungle...Negro
Narrative Folklore from the
Streets of Philadelphia,
1964.B1; 1970.B1
The Deep South in Transformation:
A Symposium, 1964.B16
Defoe, Daniel, 1911.B7
DeForest, J. W., 1961.B4-B5
DeLeon, T. C., 1962.B5
Dennis, Harvey, 1931.B9
Dent, Charles W., 1902.B21
Depew, Ollie, 1938.B1
Derby, George Horatio, 1881.B8;
1889.B8
Derby, James Cephas, 1884.B19
A Descriptiv [sic] List of Books
for the Young, 1895.B19
A Descriptive Guide to the Best
Fiction: British and Ameri-
can, 1903.B4
A Descriptive List of Novels and
Tales Dealing with History of
North America, 1895.B18
A Descriptive List of Romantic
Novels, 1890.B4
The Development of American
Thought, 1887.B6
The Development of the American
Short Story, 1923.B10
The Development of the Short Story
in the South, 1911.B1
Devine, Eric, 1932.B7
DeVoto, Bernard, 1933.B3;
1942.B4
Dialect. See Linguistics and
dialect
"Dialect Differentiation in the
Stories of Joel Chandler
Harris," 1955.B2
"Dialect in Literature," 1892.B25
Dibble, S. W., 1906.B5
Dickens, Charles, 1888.B20;
1911.B7; 1946.B7; 1947.B9
Dickey, Marcus, 1922.B3
Dickinson, Thomas H., 1932.B8;
1946.B6
A Dictionary of American Authors,
1901.B1

History of American Verse
    (1610-1897), 1901.B17
History of Atlanta, Georgia,
    1889.B10
History of Georgia (Brooks)
    1913.B4; 1972.B2; (Coulter)
    1954.B3
A History of Literature in
    America, 1907.B15
The History of North America,
    1905.B15
History of Southern Fiction,
    1909.B16
A History of Southern Literature,
    1906.B7
History of the Aesopic Fable,
    1889.B9
History of the Literary and
    Intellectual Life of the
    Southern States, 1909.B15
A History of the Old South,
    1949.B4
A History of the South (Simkins)
    1953.B12; 1963.B13. See also
    The South Old and New (A
    History: 1820-1947)
A History of the South
    (Stephenson) 1951.B12;
    1971.B18
The History of the State of
    Georgia From 1850 to 1881,
    1881.B13
Hoffman, Daniel G., 1951.B5;
    1961.B10
"Holiday Books for Young People,"
    1897.B40
Holliday, Carl, 1906.B7
Hollis, C. Carroll, 1973.B9
Hollis, Christopher, 1958.B10
Holman, C. Hugh, 1970.B3
Holmes, Oliver Wendell, 1896.B2;
    1909.B12
Homes of Famous Americans,
    1926.B12
Hopkins, J. G. E., 1953.B10
Hornady, John R., 1922.B6
Hornberger, Theodore, 1964.B3;
    1969.B2
Horowitz, Floyd R., 1963.B8
"The Horrible South," 1935.B9
Horton, Mrs. Thaddeus,
    1907.B5-B6

Houghton, Dr. ("The Little Church
    Around the Corner"),
    1899.B5
Houghton, Mifflin Company,
    1896.B32
An Hour of the American Novel,
    1929.B13
"How Literary Detectives Found
    Joel Chandler Harris' New
    Novel," 1946.B13
"How She Joined the Georgia
    Legislature," 1899.B5
"How Whalebone Caused a Wedding,"
    1898.B3
Howard, Robert West, 1959.B7, B9
Howe, Will David, 1929.B15;
    1943.B2
Howell, Clark, 1905.B3; 1948.B7
Howell, Evan, 1917.B9; 1943.B11
Howells, William Dean, 1888.B15,
    B20; 1889.B8; 1898.B20;
    1900.B21; 1901.B15; 1902.B25;
    1903.B6; 1908.B16; 1916.B2;
    1917.B2; 1920.B4; 1929.B6,
    B14; 1932.B10; 1946.B3, B13;
    1957.B4; 1959.B6; 1963.B7;
    1974.B9
Hoyt, Eleanor, 1903.B10
Hubbell, Jay Broadus, 1921.B4;
    1932.B12; 1934.B6; 1938.B4;
    1940.B7; 1954.B8; 1960.B5;
    1965.B9; 1972.B7
Huber, Miriam Blanton, 1935.B7
Hubner, Charles W., 1913.A1
Huckleberry Finn. See The Adven-
    tures of Huckleberry Finn
Hudson, Arthur Palmer, 1971.B6
Huff, Lawrence, 1962.B7; 1963.B9
Hughes, Langston, 1953.B4;
    1958.B11
Hugo, Victor, 1908.B15
Human Geography of the South,
    1935.B12
Humor, 1873.B1; 1881.B1, B7, B10,
    B13; 1883.B1-B2; 1884.B8;
    1886.B2, B4; 1893.B11;
    1895.B20-B21; 1896.B13;
    1899.B19; 1900.B7-B8;
    1901.B18; 1907.B13; 1908.B33;
    1922.B4; 1924.B9; 1928.B5;
    1930.B11; 1931.B8, B15;
    1934.B11; 1935.B3; 1936.B2;

1937.B1, B9; 1939.B5;
1940.B8; 1941.B3, B14;
1944.B6; 1945.B11; 1946.B8,
B15; 1947.B2; 1948.B1, B4,
B12, B17; 1949.B3-B4;
1954.B5, B8; 1958.B7, B18;
1959.B9; 1961.B9; 1962.B2,
B4, B11; 1964.B6, B10, B22;
1965.B9; 1966.A1; 1968.A2,
B2, B12; 1969.B2; 1973.B2,
B9
Humor of the Old Southwest,
1964.B6
"The Humor of the Southern
Yeoman," 1941.B3
Hurston, Zora Neale, 1935.B8;
1949.B1; 1953.B4; 1969.B6;
1971.B6, B17
Hutchison, Percy, 1931.B8
Hyman, Stanley Edgar, 1958.B12

I Hear America...Literature in
the United States since
1900, 1937.B10
"The Identification of Folklore
in American Literature,"
1957.B2
The Illusion of Life. American
Realism as a Literary Form,
1969.B7
Images of the Negro in American
Literature, 1966.B6-B7
"Immortal Uncle Remus," 1895.B21
In a Minor Chord: Three Afro-
American Writers and Their
Search for Identity,
1971.B17
In Dixie Land: Stories of the
Reconstruction Era by
Southern Writers, 1926.B11
"In Lighter Vein," 1903.B10
"In Memory of Uncle Remus,"
1940.B4
In Ole Virginia (Page), 1960.B5
"In the Matter of Belief,"
1908.B4
In the Tennessee Mountains
(Murfree), 1884.B15; 1887.B4;
1939.B10
"In Uncle Remus Land," 1967.B20
Index to American Author

Bibliographies, 1971.B9. See
also Index to Literary
Biography
Index to Literary Biography,
1975.B10. See also Index to
American Author Bibliographies
Index to Short Stories, 1923.B1
Index to Short Stories. Supple-
ment (First) 1929.B5;
(Second) 1936.B4
Indian, American. See Folklore,
American Indian
Indian Fairy Tales, 1892.B22
The Industrial Era, 1927.B1
Initial Studies in American
Letters, 1891.B14
"An Interesting Display of Uncle
Remus's Work," 1900.B24
"Introduction: Stereotype to
Archetype: The Negro in
American Literary Criticism,"
1966.B6
An Introduction to American
Literature, 1905.B20
An Introduction to American Prose,
1931.B14
Introduction to Georgia Writers,
1929.B9
Invisible Man (Ellison),
1958.B12; 1963.B8
The Invitation to Learning
Reader, 1956.B16
Irving, Washington, 1947.B17;
1957.B11
"Irwin Russell, First Dialect
Author," 1939.B9
"Irwin Russell's Christmas,"
1962.B10
Ivanhoe (Scott), 1901.B8
Ives, Sumner Albert, 1950.A2, B6;
1954.A1; 1955.B2

Jackson, Bruce, 1967.B11
Jackson, David Kelly, 1940.B1, B7
Jacobs, Joseph, 1888.B16;
1889.B9; 1892.B22; 1897.B15;
1919.B8; 1922.B2; 1929.B4;
1937.B4; 1970.B13
James, Henry, 1888.B17, B20;
1893.B21; 1908.B16; 1909.B11;
1932.B18; 1947.B10; 1963.B7

B8-B10; 1896.B4-B5, B10;
1935.B11
Muffett, D. J. M., 1975.B13
Mugleston, William F.,
1975.B14-B15
Mugridge, Donald H., 1960.B1
Mules and Men, 1935.B8; 1969.B6
Munro, John M., 1972.B9
Murfree, Mary Noailles, 1884.B11,
B14-B15; 1885.B4; 1887.B4;
1893.B21; 1900.B21; 1903.B5;
1918.B9; 1923.B10; 1932.B5;
1935.B12; 1937.B5; 1938.B8;
1939.B10; 1941.B3, B7, B11;
1947.B15-B16; 1949.B2;
1952.B3; 1957.B10; 1973.B14
Murray, Albert, 1970.B17
Mustanoja, Tauno F., 1960.B2
My Friendly Contemporaries: A
Literary Log, 1932.B10
My Novel, 1888.B12
My Souvenir of "The Wren's
Nest", 1929.A1
Myrick, Mary Robinson, 1950.B8
Myth. See Folklore
"Myth and Humor in the Uncle
Remus Fables," 1948.B4
The Myth of the Lost Cause:
1865-1900, 1973.B12
The Myth of the Negro Past,
1941.B6; 1958.B9
The Mythology of All Races,
1916.B1; 1925.B9; 1964.B2,
B21
"Myths of the Cherokees,"
1888.B19
Myths of the Cherokee, 1900.B23;
1970.B16

Narasimhaiah, C. D., 1972.B9
Nash, J. V., 1927.B8
National Cyclopaedia of American
Biography, 1898.B23
"The National Element in
Southern Literature,"
1903.B8
The National Temper: Readings
in American History, 1968.B20
"National Unity through American
Literature," 1943.B5

Native American Humor (Aswell)
1947.B2; (Blair) 1937.B1
Nature (Emerson), 1958.B13
NBC. A Listener's Aid to Pilgrimage of Poetry: Ted
Malone's Album of Poetic
Shrines, 1939.B7
Negro, the, 1880.B4; 1881.B8;
1883.B11; 1884.B19; 1892.B1,
B6, B18; 1895.B4, B16, B21;
1896.A1; 1898.B14, B17;
1899.B5, B25; 1900.B1, B20;
1902.B32; 1904.B7; 1906.B7;
1907.B1, B10, B14; 1909.B15,
B24; 1912.B4, B6; 1913.B1,
B3; 1916.B4-B5; 1917.B1;
1919.B1; 1921.B6; 1922.B9;
1923.B9-B10; 1924.B2;
1925.B2-B3; 1926.B4, B8, B10,
B13; 1927.B3, B5, B8-B9;
1928.B7; 1930.B2, B8;
1931.B6, B11, B17; 1932.B4,
B16; 1933.B1, B3; 1937.B2-B3,
B5; 1939.B6; 1942.B6;
1944.B4; 1945.B4; 1946.B6;
1947.B10-B11, B15; 1948.B9,
B17; 1953.B3-B4, B10;
1956.B5; 1957.B5; 1958.B5;
1960.B9; 1961.B4, B6, B12;
1964.B16, B19; 1966.B11;
1967.B17; 1968.B2, B15-B16;
1969.B5; 1970.B17, B19, B22;
1971.B8, B16; 1972.B9;
1973.B2, B6-B7; 1974.B1,
B11-B12; 1975.B2-B3, B12,
B16-B17, B21
"The Negro," 1959.B7
The Negro: A Selected List for
School Libraries, 1941.B1
The Negro and His Folklore in
Nineteenth-Century Periodi-
cals, 1967.B11
The Negro Author: His Development
in America to 1900, 1931.B11;
1964.B13
"Negro Character as Seen by White
Authors," 1933.B1
The Negro Character in American
Literature, 1926.B10
"Negro Dialect in American
Literature," 1924.B8

1968.A2, B19; 1970.B8;
1971.B7; 1975.B2, B23
"The New South" (Gaston)
1965.B6; (S. Lanier)
1880.B4; 1899.B24; 1945.B10
The New South Creed: A Study in
Southern Mythmaking,
1970.B8
New World Writing, 1952.B6
"New York as a Literary Centre,"
1903.B12; 1964.B14
Newcomer, Alphonso Gerald,
1901.B16; 1929.B12
"A Newly-Discovered Joel Chandler
Harris Letter," 1953.B11
Newman, Cardinal, 1908.B26;
1942.B5; 1947.B10
Nichols, Charles H., Jr.,
1949.B9
Nights with Uncle Remus: Myths
and Legends of the Old
Plantation, 1883.B1-B6;
1884.B1-B4; 1887.B5;
1888.B20, B25; 1889.B9;
1892.B11; 1893.B5, B17, B19;
1896.B45; 1902.B27; 1904.B8;
1905.B15; 1906.B4; 1908.B19,
B33; 1909.B10; 1912.B1;
1913.B1; 1917.B1; 1918.B9;
1919.B3; 1922.B4, B7;
1926.B1, B4; 1929.B3;
1931.B12, B14; 1932.B11, B14;
1935.B4, B11; 1938.B8;
1940.B11-B12; 1941.B1, B5,
B12; 1945.B8; 1946.A3, B15;
1947.B5; 1948.B3; 1956.B3,
B5; 1958.B8; 1960.B5;
1961.B7; 1968.A1; 1970.B4;
1971.B6; 1975.B3, B12
"Nine New 'Immortals,'" 1890.B3
"Nineteenth Century Fiction of
the Southern Appalachians,"
1942.B2; 1943.B3
Nixon, Raymond B., 1943.B11
"No Haid Pawn" (Page), 1893.B8
Noll, Arthur Howard, 1909.B15
Norris, Frank, 1903.B12;
1948.B14; 1958.B15; 1964.B14;
1969.B1; 1973.B10
North American [Mythology],
1916.B1; 1964.B2

North, East, South, West: A
Regional Anthology of American
Writing, 1945.B11
"Notes on Local Color and Its
Relation to Realism," 1952.B5
"Notes on Mexican Folk-Lore,"
1912.B2
"Notes on the Origin and History
of the Tar-Baby Story,"
1930.B7
Nott, G. William, 1939.B9
"The Novel and the Romance in
Middle Georgia Humor and
Local Color," 1971.B11
The Novel and the World's Dilemma,
1947.B4
"The Novel in America: Notes for
a Survey," 1936.B7
Nye, Russel B., 1972.B8

O., S. J., 1900.B24
O Rare Don Marquis. A Biography,
1962.B2
O'Brien, Edward J., 1923.B7;
1931.B13
O'Connor, Flannery, 1975.B16
The Octopus: A Story of
California (Norris), 1958.B15;
1973.B10
Oddities in Southern Life and
Character, 1883.B11
"Odds and Ends About Joel Chandler
Harris," 1948.B11
Odum, Howard W., 1925.B5;
1930.B12; 1947.B13; 1967.B9
Odysseus, 1974.B3
Oglethorpe, James, 1896.B16
O'Henry. See Porter, William
Sydney
Okerberg (artist), 1899.B2
"The Old Bascom Place," 1891.B4,
B7; 1908.B31
Old Si, 1886.B5
The Old Swimmin' Hole and 'Leven
More Poems (Riley), 1970.B18
"Old-Time Plantation Life,"
1892.B24
"Ole 'Stracted" (Page), 1916.B5
The Omni-Americans: New Perspec-
tives on Black Experience and
American Culture, 1970.B17

"Plantation Music," 1883.B7,
B9-B10; 1886.B6; 1928.B2,
B11; 1967.B11
Plantation Pageants, 1899.B6,
B13-B14, B16, B18, B26;
1900.B30; 1904.B7; 1915.B4
A Plantation Printer, 1892.B2-B4
"Plantation Proverbs of 'Uncle
Remus,'" 1924.B3
Plantation songs. See Songs,
plantation
Plantation tradition, the,
1881.B3, B8-B9, B13-B14;
1887.B3; 1892.B3, B6, B12;
1895.B13, B21; 1902.B29;
1904.B9; 1910.B8; 1911.B11;
1917.B1, B4; 1919.B1;
1921.B3; 1923.B9; 1924.B10;
1925.B3; 1926.B10; 1929.B9;
1930.B13; 1932.B5, B16;
1946.B15; 1947.B14; 1948.B2,
B6; 1949.B9; 1954.B10;
1965.B7; 1966.A1, B2;
1968.A2, B6, B15-B16;
1973.B8; 1974.B7; 1975.B2,
B23
Pochmann, Henry A., 1949.B10
Poe, Edgar Allan, 1906.B6;
1926.B6; 1927.B9; 1934.B8;
1951.B1; 1963.B4
Poems by Irwin Russell, 1962.B10
Poetry, 1869.B1; 1879.B1;
1881.B5; 1885.B5; 1896.B44;
1904.B6-B7; 1906.B8;
1918.B8-B9; 1931.B11, B16;
1957.B3; 1968.B11; 1971.B5
"Poetry after the Civil War,"
1931.B16
"Poetry South," 1922.B1
Poets of America, 1885.B5
Poets of the South, 1903.B13;
1968.B10
Political and Social Growth of
the American People 1865-
1940, 1941.B8
"Politics and the Novel: George
W. Cable and the Genteel
Tradition," 1975.B17
Pollock, Eileen, 1956.B13-B14
Poor Richard, 1917.B7; 1923.B6
Poor white, the, 1884.B6-B7, B9,
B11-B15, B18-B19; 1885.B2,

B4; 1887.B4-B5; 1888.B5,
B10-B11; 1896.B40; 1898.B20;
1899.B8; 1902.B30; 1903.B6;
1911.B1; 1915.B4; 1921.B6;
1923.B10; 1926.B13; 1929.B8;
1930.B8; 1932.B10; 1939.B8,
B10; 1940.B11; 1948.B10, B17;
1951.B8; 1954.B8; 1960.B5,
B8; 1964.B18; 1966.A1;
1968.A2, B1; 1972.B11;
1973.B8, B14; 1975.B23;
1976.B1
The Popular Book: A History of
America's Literary Taste,
1961.B6
Popular Culture and Industrialism
1865-1890, 1967.B19
Popularity, 1884.B5, B9; 1887.B5;
1890.B3; 1902.B21-B23, B26;
1905.B22; 1909.B12; 1911.B8;
1919.B6; 1923.B3, B6;
1925.B1, B8; 1926.B1, B6;
1947.B1, B12, B17; 1967.B4;
1970.B7; 1972.B7; 1974.B2,
B9-B10; 1975.B1
Porter, William Sydney, 1948.B14
The Portrait of a Lady (James),
1893.B22; 1909.B11
"The Possibilities of the South
in Literature," 1898.B22
"Post-Bellum--Pre-Harlem,"
1931.B4; 1937.B6
Pound, Ezra, 1970.B7
The Power of Blackness, 1958.B13
Prefaces to Contemporaries
(1882-1920), 1957.B4
Prejudices: Second Series,
1920.B6
Prescott, Frederick Clarke,
1931.B14
"President Gomper's Mascot,"
1912.B5
Pre-War America, 1930.B16
The Prince and the Pauper
(Clemens), 1953.A1; 1954.B7
Pritchard, John Paul, 1956.B15
"The Private Plantation: Versions
of the Old South Myth, 1880-
1914," 1973.B8
"The Problematic South," 1890.B2
Productions of Harris's works,
1895.B15; 1914.B1-B2;

1922.B5; 1933.B6;
1946.A1-A2, B10; 1963.B4;
1966.B3; 1970.B14; 1974.B12
"Professor Barrett Wendell's
Notions of American
Literature," 1901.B15
"Profits and Losses in the Life
of Joel Chandler Harris,"
1933.B10; 1938.B10
"The Provenience of Certain Negro
Folk-Tales. I. Playing Dead
Twice in the Road," 1917.B8
"The Provenience of Certain Negro
Folk Tales. III. Tar Baby,"
1919.B8
Proverbs. See Folklore
Provincial Types in American
Fiction, 1903.B6
Psychological criticism, 1881.B9;
1898.B17; 1900.B20; 1901.B13;
1902.B9; 1905.B9; 1924.B3;
1948.B4; 1949.B1, B5, B11,
B13, B15; 1951.B5; 1954.B8;
1956.B5, B8; 1960.B5;
1961.B3; 1966.B9; 1967.B14;
1968.B2; 1970.B19; 1972.B1;
1973.A1, B8; 1974.B11;
1975.B2, B8, B12
Publishers, Harris's relationship
to. See Editors and pub-
lishers, Harris's relationship to
"Publisher's Announcement,"
1908.B32

Qua, 1946.B3, B13
Qua: A Romance of the Revolu-
tion, 1929.B3; 1946.B3, B13;
1971.B11
Quarles, Benjamin, 1964.B15
"Queries," 1938.B2
The Quest for Nationality: An
American Literary Campaign,
1957.B10
"The Question Partially Solved,"
1866.B1
Quinn, Arthur Hobson, 1925.B8;
1929.B15; 1936.B9; 1951.B8;
1972.B7

Rabelais, 1873.B1; 1923.B4;
1940.B8; 1961.B13
Rabbit. See Brer Rabbit
"The Racial Bar Sinister in
American Romance," 1926.B5
"Ralph Ellison's Modern Version
of Brer Bear and Brer Rabbit
in Invisible Man," 1963.B8
Ramsey, Robert L., 1921.B6
Rankin, Thomas E., 1922.B12
Rapf, Maurice, 1946.A2
Ray, Charles Arthur, 1952.A1;
1969.B8
The Reader's Encyclopaedia of
American Literature, 1962.B6
The Reader's Encyclopedia: An
Encyclopedia of World
Literature and the Arts,
1948.B1
Reader's Guide to Prose Fiction,
1940.B10
"The Real 'Uncle Remus,'"
1900.B25
Realism, 1881.B3, B6, B9;
1892.B1, B17, B24; 1893.B16;
1896.B3, B40; 1898.B18;
1899.B14; 1900.B18;
1902.B9-B10; 1907.B9;
1908.B30; 1915.B4; 1923.B10;
1925.B3; 1930.B12, B14;
1931.B11; 1932.B5, B10;
1933.B11; 1934.B5; 1937.B3,
B5; 1939.B5; 1940.B1;
1947.B10; 1948.B4, B17;
1952.A1, B3, B5, B8; 1953.B9;
1954.B2; 1955.B5; 1956.B3;
1957.B10; 1963.B1; 1968.B11;
1969.B7; 1971.B8, B11;
1973.A1, B8
"Realism and Fantasy in Southern
Humor," 1958.B18
"Realism and Romanticism,"
1900.B18
Realism to the Present, 1974.B8
Reality and Myth: Essays in
American Literature in Memory
of Richmond Croom Beatty,
1964.B11
"The Reappearance of Uncle
Remus," 1918.B6
Reaver, J. Russell, 1968.B3

Sidney Lanier: Letters 1857–
1868, 1945.B2
Sidney Lanier: Letters 1869–
1873, 1945.B3
Sidney Lanier: Poems and Poem
Outlines, 1945.B1
Sidney Lanier: Tiger-Lilies
and Southern Prose,
1945.B9–B10
Sign of the Wren's Nest, the.
See Wren's Nest, the
"'The Sign of the Wren's Nest'"
(Avary), 1910.B5; (Myrick)
1950.B8; (Sherlock) 1926.B12
"The Significance of Charles W.
Chesnutt's 'Conjure Stories,'"
1974.B1
"Significant Dates in the Life
of Joel Chandler Harris,"
1940.B6
Silas Marner (G. Eliot), 1909.B1
Simkins, Francis Butler,
1947.B15; 1953.B12;
1963.B12–B13
Simms, William Gilmore, 1927.B9;
1940.B7; 1947.B16
Simon Legree, 1961.B6
Simpson, Claude M., 1941.B9;
1960.B8
Sims, J. Marion, 1885.B3
Sister Jane (character),
1896.B34, B37–B38, B49;
1897.B9, B11, B14, B41;
1900.B19; 1928.B5
"Sister Jane," 1897.B41
Sister Jane: Her Friends and
Acquaintances..., 1896.B1,
B3, B10, B12, B27, B29,
B33–B34, B37–B39, B49;
1897.B2, B5, B7–B11, B13–B14,
B38, B41–B42; 1898.B13;
1900.B9; 1902.B10; 1908.B26;
1926.B1; 1929.B8; 1936.B1;
1945.B12; 1963.B3; 1964.B4;
1965.B8; 1966.B12; 1971.B11;
1973.B8; 1975.B8
"The Sixth Sense" (Briscoe),
1899.B5
Skaggs, Merrill Maguire, 1972.B11
Sketches of 21 Magazines 1905–
1930, 1968.B9

"Skinflint, Obediah," 1937.B1
"Slave Narratives and the Planta-
tion Legend," 1949.B9
Slave Songs of the United States,
1959.B5
Small, Samuel W., 1879.B1–B2;
1886.B5; 1917.B9
The Small Town in American
Literature, 1939.B5
The Smiling Phoenix: Southern
Humor from 1865 to 1914,
1965.B7
Smith, Charles Alphonso, 1898.B22;
1907.B12; 1927.B9; 1956.B12
Smith, Charles Forster, 1885.B4;
1909.B9
Smith, Charles Henry, 1881.B13;
1937.B1; 1949.B10
Smith, Francis Hopkinson,
1925.B8; 1931.B17; 1961.B6
Smith, Guy E., 1957.B9
Smith, Henry Nash, 1961.B19
Smith, Herbert F., 1963.B14
Smith, Lillian H., 1940.B12
Smith, Rebecca Washington,
1932.B17; 1937.B11;
1940.B13–B14; 1941.B10
Smock, Raymond, 1974.B4
"Snap Bean Farm," 1953.B1
Snopes, Flem, 1974.B3
Snyder, Henry N., 1902.B30;
1907.B13
"Social Comment in the Writings
of Joel Chandler Harris,"
1966.A2
Social Historians, 1911.B11;
1969.B9
"Social Types in Southern Prose
Fiction," 1921.B3
Society and Thought in America,
1952.B8
Society and Thought in Modern
America, 1952.B8
Sociological criticism, 1881.B9;
1883.B2; 1884.B2, B15;
1891.B8; 1892.B20; 1893.B6;
1894.B6; 1896.B18, B27;
1897.B20; 1898.B2, B13, B16;
1899.B14, B19; 1902.B1, B8,
B10, B19; 1903.B8; 1909.B3;
1911.B5, B11; 1915.B3–B4;

Whitcomb, Selden L., 1894.B9
White, Elwyn B., 1941.B14
White, Katharine S., 1941.B14
White, Newman I., 1928.B10
White, Sarah Harriman, 1963.B10;
  1973.B11
White, William Allen, 1931.B17
The White Savage: Racial
  Fantasies in the Postbellum
  South, 1970.B6
Whitman, Walt, 1916.B2; 1925.B1;
  1929.B7; 1957.B10
Whitman to the Present, 1956.B3
Whitten, Norman E., Jr.,
  1970.B22
Whittier, John Greenleaf,
  1901.B8; 1909.B12; 1948.B14
Who Are the Major American
  Writers?, 1972.B7
Who Speaks for the South?,
  1964.B9
The Who's Who of Children's
  Literature, 1968.B5
"Why Is It?" 1864.B1
"Why the Confederacy Failed,"
  1900.B6, B24; 1902.B14;
  1931.B7; 1936.B3
Wiggins, Robert Lemuel, 1915.A1;
  1918.A2; 1921.B2
Wild Animals I Have Known
  (Seton-Thompson), 1901.B7
Wilkins, Mary. See Freeman,
  Mary Wilkins
William Elliott Shoots a Bear:
  Essays on the Southern
  Literary Imagination,
  1975.B17-B19
William Faulkner's Library--
  A Catalogue, 1964.B4
"William Orrie Tuggle and the
  Creek Indian Folk Tales,"
  1961.B7
"William Styron and Human
  Bondage: The Confessions
  of Nat Turner," 1967.B17;
  1971.B14; 1975.B19
Williams, Stanley Thomas,
  1926.B13; 1930.B17; 1937.B12
Wilson, Edmund, 1962.B12
Wilson, James Grant, 1888.B25;
  1900.B31

Wilson, Louis R., 1934.B12
"The Winning of 'The Wren's
  Nest,'" 1913.B2
Winterich, John T., 1930.B18;
  1947.B17
Wise, John S., 1905.B18;
  1974.B6
"Wise 'Uncle Remus' is Joel
  Chandler Harris," 1942.B5
Wish, Harvey, 1952.B8
With Aesop along the Black
  Border, 1924.B6
Witham, W. Tasker, 1947.B18
Wolfe, Bernard, 1949.B11, B15;
  1955.B5; 1956.B16; 1961.B12;
  1968.B20; 1973.B7, B15
Wolfram, Walt, 1971.B10
"The Wonderful Tar-Baby Story,"
  1883.B1, B8; 1888.B16;
  1889.B9; 1890.B5; 1892.B20,
  B22; 1895.B15, B17; 1897.B15;
  1899.B27; 1905.B7, B14;
  1909.B2; 1911.B6; 1914.B7;
  1916.B1; 1919.B8; 1921.B6;
  1922.B2, B4, B10; 1924.B5;
  1925.B10; 1929.B4, B14;
  1930.B4, B7; 1937.B4;
  1938.B3; 1940.B9; 1943.B9;
  1946.B5, B7; 1949.B3;
  1950.B2, B5; 1951.B8;
  1952.B8; 1953.B7-B8; 1957.B9;
  1959.B11; 1968.B4; 1970.B11,
  B14; 1971.B15; 1974.B9
Woodress, James, 1962.B13;
  1968.B21
Woods, George A., 1967.B20
Woodson, Carter G., 1936.B11
Woodward, Comer Vann, 1951.B12;
  1966.B11; 1971.B17; 1974.B14
Woolson, Constance Fenimore,
  1888.B17; 1932.B9, B15;
  1961.B4-B5
Wootten, Katharine Hinton,
  1907.B16; 1908.B7; 1909.B25;
  1917.B10-B11
"A Word List from East Alabama,"
  1935.B2
Wordsworth, William, 1958.B15;
  1959.B8
Work, Monroe N., 1928.B11